In Search of New England's Native Past

Gordon M. Day, ca. 1959. From the *Dartmouth Alumni Magazine* 52 (2), 1959. By permission of the Dartmouth College Archives, Hanover, N.H.

IN SEARCH OF NEW ENGLAND'S NATIVE PAST

Selected Essays by Gordon M. Day

Edited by Michael K. Foster and William Cowan

University of Massachusetts Press
AMHERST

A Volume in the Series

Native Americans of the Northeast:
Culture, History, and the Contemporary

Edited by

Colin G. Calloway and Barry O'Connell

Printed in the United States of America
LC 98-11154
ISBN 1-55849-150-3 (cloth); 151-1 (pbk.)
Set in Adobe Garamond with ITC Cheltenham display by Keystone Typesetting, Inc.
Printed and bound by BookCrafters, Inc.
Library of Congress Cataloging-in-Publication Data

Day, Gordon M.
In search of New England's native past : selected essays /
by Gordon M. Day ; edited by Michael K. Foster and William Cowan.
p.   cm. — (Native Americans of the Northeast)
Includes bibliographical references and index.
ISBN 1-55849-150-3 (cloth : alk. paper).
—ISBN 1-55849-151-1 (pbk. : alk. paper)
1. Abenaki Indians—History—Sources.   2. Abenaki Indians—Migrations.
3. Abenaki Indians—Social life and customs.
4. Ethnohistory—New England.   5. Ethnohistory—Québec (Province)
I. Foster, Michael K.   II. Cowan, William.   III. Title.   IV. Series.
E99.A13D39   1998
974'.004973—dc21   98-11154
                                                   CIP

British Library Cataloguing in Publication data are available.

Contents

Illustrations and Maps

Preface

In 1956, when Gordon M. Day (1911–1993) began researching the history, language, and traditional culture of the community of Odanak, in Quebec, Abenaki studies, which today is a flourishing subfield with practitioners from several disciplines, hardly existed. Other than the residents of the community and a handful of Quebec archivists, few knew that Odanak, or Saint Francis, had long served as a destination for refugees from locations all over New England, particularly after the dislocations caused by the plagues and warfare of the seventeenth and eighteenth centuries. These dislocations may explain why earlier writers tended to portray interior New England as virtually devoid of native inhabitants, save for the seasonal forays of roving bands of hunters permanently domiciled to the north and east. To Day belongs the credit for bringing about a revolution in the way we view the native history of Vermont, New Hampshire, and western Maine. Single-handedly, he established beyond all doubt the presence of Abenaki settlements on the eastern shore of Lake Champlain and along the middle and upper reaches of the Connecticut and Merrimack Rivers during the early historic period, a presence profoundly affected by the disruptions that followed European contact but by no means obliterated by them. Although he was not an archeologist, Day provided a framework by which others have been able to link the Western Abenaki people of today with prehistoric sites in Vermont and New Hampshire.

Day came to his interest in the ethnology, linguistics, and ethnohistory of the Abenaki and their neighbors from a background in forest ecology, which gave him unique insights into the culture of peoples attuned to life in the forest. He also amply demonstrated the value of approaching history and ethnography through the medium of the indigenous language: this enabled him to access the native world view and native interpretations of past events directly, rather than relying solely on nonnative accounts. He was an able practitioner of the approach William N. Fenton dubbed "upstreaming," by which one uses the results of ethnographic investigations to assess the documented past.

Day was an authority on the Western Abenaki language: his *Western Abenaki*

Dictionary is a monumental contribution to Algonquian linguistic studies, as will be his grammar of the language when it has been edited and prepared for publication. His monograph on the "Mots loups" manuscript of Jean-Claude Mathevet also adds significantly to our understanding of the poorly attested Algonquian languages of interior New England. For the Algonquian comparatist, these works provide a richness of data that will assist in the ongoing enterprise of reconstructing Proto-Algonquian, the theoretical parent of the Algonquian family of languages spoken some three millennia ago.

Day's publications total 75 items, of which around a third are reprinted in the present volume, either in whole or in part. We did not include any of the papers he wrote in his first career in forest ecology, and we did not include any book reviews. Our chief concern in selecting items was that the diverse approaches he took to historical reconstruction should be adequately represented. We chose the short paper "Dartmouth and Saint Francis," published in 1959, because it is a highly readable introduction to Day's research interests at a time when he had just begun working among the Abenaki and the problems he sought to resolve lay largely before him. In contrast, the excerpts from the *Mots loups* and Saint Francis *Identity* monographs show how far those interests and his understanding of the problems had advanced over the two decades that followed.

The analysis of native place-names occupies a central place in Day's work and is applied in one way or another in the majority of his papers. For around a third of the papers in the present volume, place-names are the focus of the discussion, a weighting that follows naturally from his interests. Not only did he clear away the confusion surrounding a number of New England place-names, but he established exacting standards for identifying the language of origin of the names and inferring their meanings and the geographic locations denoted by them. With Day's work, the era of speculative etymologizing, which had long plagued studies of place-names in New England, can fairly be said to have ended.

Several of the papers, especially "The Indian as an Ecological Factor in the Northeastern Forest" and "The Tree Nomenclature of the Saint Francis Indians," show that Day's background in forest ecology provided a valuable perspective for understanding cultures belonging to the Eastern Woodlands culture area. Three papers, "The Eastern Boundary of Iroquoia: Abenaki Evidence," "Oral Tradition as Complement," and "The Western Abenaki Transformer," illustrate one of Day's most fervently held and frequently voiced beliefs: that oral tradition, when approached with the same critical eye that the historian brings to written sources, can contribute importantly to our understanding of past events involving native groups. Because the different ways of remembering and recording history often reveal discrepancies between native and nonnative accounts, he argued that both are needed to gain the fullest possible picture of those events. Although few historians would dispute the point today, earlier writers tended to dismiss oral tradition as mere hearsay, thereby ignoring native populations' perceptions of events in which they often played major roles.

On the assumption that the *Handbook of North American Indians* is readily accessible, we did not include Day's coauthored chapters on the Nipissing and Algonquin in Volume 15, *Northeast*, but, given the focus of the present volume, it would have been irresponsible to omit his chapter on the Western Abenaki, which stands as a definitive summary by a leading authority on the subject. One paper, "The Penobscot War Bow," was included to illustrate Day's interest in material culture and museum collections. Although it might sound ingenuous in the postmodernist atmosphere of the late twentieth century, Day had an unswerving faith in the ultimate certainty and retrievability of "fact" in scientific endeavors, and he brought the same passion for separating the genuine from the spurious to evaluating museum specimens as he did to evaluating place-names, oral traditions, and historical documents.

We arranged the papers chronologically, with the goal of conveying the development of Day's ideas in his career in ethnology. Because he returned again and again to the question of the identity of the native groups of interior New England, a certain amount of thematic overlap in the papers is inevitable. The result is not mere repetition, however, but a gradually deepening and widening understanding of a set of complex and closely linked ideas. Aside from minor editorial corrections, we have let the papers stand as they are, avoiding the temptation to coordinate earlier and later work through editorial intervention, even where Day modified or reversed his position on the issues. The way his thinking evolved over time is of interest in itself. Practical considerations led us to omit the lengthy interim word list from the paper "A Saint Francis Abenaki Vocabulary"; we included the introductory sections, however, because they provide a context for Day's Western Abenaki linguistic work generally. So far as we can tell, all the words in the list appear in an updated orthography in his vastly more comprehensive *Western Abenaki Dictionary*.

In brief, we intend this selection of Day's papers to represent the essence of his contributions to the ethnology, linguistics, and ethnohistory of the Western Abenaki and their neighbors over the span of his career. We exercised our hand as editors by standardizing the styles of footnotes and source citations, both of which turn up in a variety of forms in the original papers. We have also added a headnote to each paper to place it in the broader context of Day's work. ("Oral Tradition as Complement" included an abstract, which we used instead of a headnote.) A list of sources that Day cites in the papers, including his own work, appears after the last paper, and a complete bibliography of Day's publications follows that.

A number of people assisted us in bringing this work to fruition. Barry O'Connell originally approached Day with the suggestion that he consider reprinting a selection of his papers for the present series, but that plan was suddenly and unhappily cut short by Day's death in 1993. O'Connell and Colin Calloway, coeditors of the series, encouraged us to pick up the project, and we thank them for their interest and support. At the University of Massachusetts Press we benefited from valuable editorial assistance, first from Janet Benton and later Clark Dougan and Pam Wilkinson. Deborah Klenotic ably copyedited the manuscript, and Doris E. Foster and Sarah M. Cowan kindly assisted with proofreading.

We are grateful to William A. Haviland and Neal Salisbury, who read the manuscript for the Press and offered useful commentary on the project as it evolved, and to James Axtell, Colin Calloway, Donal Day, Francis Jennings, Peter Thomas, and John Moody for commenting on a draft of the Introduction. Moody's response in particular helped us to better understand Day's work in relation to the contemporary Western Abenaki scene. Jeanne Brink, Brian Day, Donal Day, and Donald DeBlois provided valuable details on Day's life and career.

We are indebted to Geneviève Eustache and Christine Midwinter of the Library of the Canadian Museum of Civilization in Hull, Quebec, for furnishing information on the Gordon M. Day collection of papers archived at the museum, and to Debra Conner of the museum's library and Paul Filotas of the Carleton University Library for checking many details in Day's bibliography and the list of works cited by him in his papers. We would like particularly to thank the Trustees of the Vermont Historical Society in Montpelier, for providing a grant to defray some of the expenses incurred in preparing the volume, and Jan Westervelt and Alice Colwell of the society for making the grant arrangements.

Acknowledgments

Chapter 1 is reprinted from *Ecology* 34(2):329–346 (1953). By permission of the Publisher of the Ecological Society of America, Washington, D.C.

Chapter 2 is reprinted from *Dartmouth Alumni Magazine* 52(2):28–30 (1959). By permission of the managing editor of the *Dartmouth Alumni Magazine,* Hanover, N.H.

Chapter 3 is reprinted from *International Journal of American Linguistics* 27(1):80–85 (1961). By permission of the University of Chicago Press, Chicago, Ill.

Chapter 4 is reprinted from *International Journal of American Linguistics* 27(2):168–171 (1961). By permission of the University of Chicago Press, Chicago, Ill.

Chapter 5 is reprinted from *Ethnohistory* 9(1):24–40 (1962). Copyright American Society for Ethnohistory, 1962. By permission of Duke University Press, Durham, N.C.

Chapter 6 is reprinted from National Museum of Canada Bulletin 190, *Contributions to Anthropology, 1960,* part 2, pp. 37–48 (1963). By permission of the Canadian Museum of Civilization, Hull, Quebec.

Chapter 7 is excerpted from *International Journal of American Linguistics* 30(4):371–392 (1964). By permission of the University of Chicago Press, Chicago, Ill.

Chapter 8 is reprinted from *Ethnohistory* 12(3):237–249 (1965). Copyright American Society for Ethnohistory, 1965. By permission of Duke University Press, Durham, N.C.

Chapter 9 is reprinted from *International Journal of American Linguistics* 33(3):244–247 (1967). By permission of the University of Chicago Press, Chicago, Ill.

Chapter 10 is reprinted from National Museum of Canada Bulletin 214, Anthropological Series 78, *Contributions to Anthropology: Linguistics I (Algonquian),* pp. 107–112 (1967). By permission of the Canadian Museum of Civilization, Hull, Quebec.

Chapter 11 is reprinted from *Ethnohistory* 15(4):389–402 (1968). Copyright American Society for Ethnohistory, 1968. By permission of Duke University Press, Durham, N.C.

Chapter 12 is reprinted from *Man in the Northeast* 1(March):7–13 (1971). By permission of the editor of *Northeast Anthropology* (formerly *Man in the Northeast*), State University of New York at Albany, Albany, N.Y.

Chapter 13 is reprinted from *International Journal of American Linguistics* 38(4):226–228 (1972). By permission of the University of Chicago Press, Chicago, Ill.

Chapter 14 is reprinted from *Ethnohistory* 19(2):99–108 (1972). Copyright American Society for Ethnohistory, 1972. By permission of Duke University Press, Durham, N.C.

Chapter 15 is reprinted from *Studies in Linguistics* 23:31–37 (1973). By permission of Edith Trager Johnson and the family of George L. Trager, Santa Barbara, Calif.

Chapter 16 is reprinted from *Man in the Northeast* 6(fall):51–57 (1973). By permission of the editor of *Northeast Anthropology* (formerly *Man in the Northeast*), State University of New York at Albany, Albany, N.Y.

Chapter 17 is reprinted from *Contributions to Canadian Ethnology, 1975,* David Brez Carlisle, ed., National Museum of Man, Canadian Ethnology Service, Mercury Series Paper 31, pp. 1–15 (1975). By permission of the Canadian Museum of Civilization, Hull, Quebec.

Chapter 18 is excerpted from *The* Mots loups *of Father Mathevet.* National Museums of Canada, National Museum of Man Publications in Ethnology 8 (1975), pp. 44–64. By permission of the Canadian Museum of Civilization, Hull, Quebec.

Chapter 19 is reprinted from the *Journal of the Folklore Institute* 13(1):75–89 (1976). By permission of the Folklore Institute and the *Journal of Folklore Research* (formerly the *Journal of the Folklore Institute*), Indiana University, Bloomington, Ind.

Chapter 20 is reprinted from *Actes du huitième congrès des algonquinistes,* William Cowan, ed., Carleton University, pp. 26–31 (1977). By permission of the editor of the *Papers of the Algonquian Conference,* the University of Manitoba, Winnipeg, Manitoba.

Chapter 21 is reprinted from *Northeast,* Vol. 15, Bruce G. Trigger, ed., *Handbook of North American Indians,* William C. Sturtevant, gen. ed., pp. 148–159 (1978). By permission of the Smithsonian Institution, Washington, D.C.

Chapter 22 is reprinted from *Papers of the Tenth Algonquian Conference,* William Cowan, ed., Carleton University, pp. 10–15 (1979). By permission of the editor of the *Papers of the Algonquian Conference,* the University of Manitoba, Winnipeg, Manitoba.

Chapter 23 is reprinted from *International Journal of American Linguistics* 47(2):143–171 (1981). By permission of the University of Chicago Press, Chicago, Ill.

Chapter 24 is excerpted from *The Identity of the Saint Francis Indians.* National Museum of Man, Canadian Ethnology Service, Mercury Series Paper 71 (1981), pp. 1, 5–6, 107–117. By permission of the Canadian Museum of Civilization, Hull, Quebec.

In Search of
New England's
Native Past

Introduction

On an unspecified day in July, 1948, Gordon M. Day began his "Abenaki Journal" as follows:

> With the whole family I paid a brief visit to the St. Francis Abenakis. At the Pierreville corner I asked directions of the first Indian I met, who guided me all about the village. This was Edouard Hannis. I could buy no moccasins, but I was pleased to hear Indian spoken at the store. My guide spoke good English to me, Indian to a man in the store, and French to a girl in the Pierreville basket wholesaler's.[1]

This was Day's first visit to the village of Odanak on the Saint Francis River near where it empties into the Saint Lawrence, a location that in a few years would become the focus of his professional activities for the rest of his life. Saint Francis, as the village is also called, was founded as a Catholic mission in the 1660s. From the beginning, the majority of its inhabitants were Western Abenaki refugees, who arrived there from various locations in the New England interior during the colonial wars of the eighteenth century and well into the nineteenth century. These movements took place before the aboriginal culture, languages, and history of the area could be adequately documented in situ: only a thin trail of accounts of brief, often hostile, encounters with the newcomers has survived in the historical record, along with a scattering of tribal names and place-names. It seemed to Day that the twentieth-century descendants of the Saint Francis settlers, a number of whom in the 1950s still spoke their native language and carried an extensive oral tradition depicting their origins and postcontact history, might hold the keys to reconstructing the native past of interior New England.

Day found that the task of piecing together the postcontact history of the territory lying between western Maine and Lake Champlain and extending into northern Massachusetts could not be carried out effectively within the confines of

[1]This is the first entry on p. 1 of the "Abenaki Journal of Gordon M. Day: Work for [the] American Philosophical Society and Dartmouth College," the original of which is located in Special Collections at Baker Library at Dartmouth College, Hanover, N.H. A copy of the journal is in the archives of the Canadian Museum of Civilization in Hull, Quebec.

1

any one discipline, but required synthesizing the disparate and sometimes conflicting findings of ethnology, history, linguistics, and folklore. As a result, he developed skills in several fields and applied a distinctive holistic approach to solving problems. The approach can be characterized as both ethnolinguistic and ethnohistorical. Its success in shedding light on different facets of an area Day frequently referred to as *terra incognita* and a cultural "no man's land" was demonstrated again and again in his papers. This was no mean feat for one who had trained in forestry and microbiology and spent his early career as a forest ecologist.

From Forest Ecologist to Ethnologist

Gordon Malcolm Day was born on October 25, 1911, in Albany, Vermont, in the heart of Western Abenaki country. For the first eight years of his life, his world centered on a narrow strip of land lying between the Black River and the Lowell Mountains in northern Vermont, where, he once wrote, the seasonal round "set up a never-to-be-broken rhythm in my blood and brain."[2] He spent much time exploring this small world, mostly alone. One early playmate was part Abenaki, and another had a Penobscot father; such contacts, and others he made with Indians later, were not unusual in an area still being used by Abenakis for hunting and trapping. When Day was nearly six, he discovered in the tiny library of the one-room district school he attended a book that he later said gave direction to his whole life. This was Florence Holbrook's *The Hiawatha Primer,* in which vivid illustrations of shining waterways set against a backdrop of the gloomy northern forest animated Longfellow's celebrated poem.

When Day was eight, the family moved to the central Vermont city of Barre, where his curiosity about the state and its original inhabitants was further piqued by such works as *Vermont for Young Vermonters,* by Miriam Irene Kimball, which contained information on the Missisquois, the Cowasucks, and the Squakheags, groups whose histories he would later attempt to piece together from fragmentary sources and from his ethnographic investigations at Saint Francis. He read extensively on North American Indians, in time encountering such works as Walter Crockett's (1921) *Vermont: The Green Mountain State,*[3] which he later cited in some of his publications. In his teen years, Day immersed himself in Francis Parkman's (1909a) epic *France and England in North America,* through which, he said, he "discovered the Iroquois." Still, it was difficult to find hard information on the Indians of Vermont and New Hampshire, and he had to make do with collateral works such as Henry David Thoreau's (1950 [1864])

[2]This and other passages describing Day's early life are taken from an autobiographical sketch he prepared for his family. I am grateful to his son, Donal Day, for making this sketch available to me.
[3]Cited works by authors other than Day appear in the list of Works Cited in Day's Papers at the back of the book.

The Maine Woods, which mentions the Penobscots, close linguistic and cultural relatives of the Western Abenakis, and fictional accounts like Cooper's *The Last of the Mohicans.*

After graduating from high school in 1929, Day worked for a time for the Vermont Forest Service and spent a year at the New York State Ranger School. In 1934, he entered the New York State College of Forestry in Syracuse, New York, earning a bachelor of science degree in forestry in 1938. For his master's thesis, obtained from the same institution in 1939, he described variable rates of topsoil building from the annual litter fall of four commonly planted coniferous species, based on an analysis of different site samples; the issue was relevant to the development of reforestation policies. Day's first publication (Day 1940) was a condensed version of the thesis.[4] It shows the high respect for the interpretation of data that was the hallmark of his later ethnological and linguistic work. In pursuing his interest in forest ecology, he had yielded to what he later described as his "second love," for a time setting aside his "first love," his fascination with the native people of New England. Eventually, however, this love would come to dominate his professional interests.

In 1940–1941 Day continued his research on the ecology of selected tree species for the Northeastern Forest Experiment Station of the U.S. Forest Service, living in Bartlett, New Hampshire, and New Haven, Connecticut. It was in the latter city that he met Elsie A. Dornfeld, whom he married in November 1940. He joined the Forestry Department at Rutgers University as an instructor in 1941, teaching forest botany for two years. During the same period, he began doctoral studies at Rutgers in the Department of Microbiology. Under the influence of Selman A. Waksman, his interests turned to soil microbiology. But then World War II intervened, and in 1943 he enlisted in the U.S. Army. From 1944 to 1946 he served in France and Germany, conducting intelligence work at the European Theater Headquarters. While waiting for a troop ship home after his tour of duty, he read an Armed Services edition of Stewart Edward White's *The Forest* and received from it the inspiration, he later wrote, that would cause him ultimately to leave forestry and devote himself entirely "to saving Abenaki culture from oblivion." Although he would, within two years, make his first visit to Saint Francis and immerse himself more and more in the literature of the Northeast, it would be another decade before his plan became a practical reality.

Upon returning to America in 1946, Day rejoined the forestry department at Rutgers, in a short time becoming its chairman. He conducted research under the auspices of the New Jersey Agricultural Experiment Station, which was connected with the university. During this period he published six articles on a variety of topics in forest ecology and soil microbiology (Day 1949, 1950a,

[4]Cited works by Day appear in the Bibliography of Gordon M. Day at the back of the book.

1950b, 1950c, 1950d, 1951), and these publications, along with the 1940 paper, comprise his contribution to these fields. He simultaneously resumed his doctoral studies in the microbiology department. Under the direction of Waksman and Robert L. Starkey, he developed a topic around the influence of earthworms on forest soils.[5] Although a sizeable literature existed on the general effects of earthworms on soils, the specific effects were not well understood, and Day devised controlled experiments to measure the role of different sections of the digestive tract of worms on altering soil bacteria counts. For his dissertation "Studies on the Influence of Earthworms on the Microbial Population of Soil," he was awarded the Ph.D. in 1949. According to his son Donal, also a microbiologist, this work is still a classic in its field. Although the dissertation was not published, its principal points were summarized in an article (Day 1950a).

At Rutgers in the early 1950s, Day began to broaden his research interests to include the effects of human habitation on forest environments. The process continued after he took a post in 1952 as partner and research supervisor in the firm New England Forest Industries in Concord, New Hampshire, and moved with his family to the town of Contoocook in the state. The new outlook found expression in a paper published after the move: "The Indian as an Ecological Factor in the Northeastern Forest," which appeared in the journal *Ecology* (Day 1953). Although the paper reflects Day's continuing commitment to forest ecology, it represents a significant shift away from purely biological concerns to a perspective that may truly be called ethnological. He argues that although a number of sources, both popular and scholarly, gave an impression that before white contact the northeastern forests had been in a pristine state, there was much evidence, from both the ethnohistorical literature and ethnographic studies, that aboriginal subsistence activities and village life had fundamentally affected large sections of the eastern woodlands and that what the Europeans saw in many cases were second-growth—or even younger—stands, as well as numerous areas cleared for cultivation. Considering that the paper represents Day's first foray, at least in print, into the ethnohistory and ethnology of the Northeast, it shows a remarkable grasp of the extensive primary and secondary literature of the area. Its final sentence reveals as much about the direction of his interests at this point as it does about the issues at hand: "We must conclude that an area which was wooded when first seen by white men was not necessarily primeval; that an area for which there is no record of cutting is not necessarily virgin; and that a knowledge of local archeology and history should be part of the ecologist's

[5]A glance at Waksman's massive textbook *Principles of Soil Microbiology* (Baltimore: The Williams & Wilkins Company, 1932, second edition), with its lengthy discussions of autotrophic, heterotrophic, and aerobic bacteria; its treatment of soil algae, fungi, and protozoa; and its coverage of the many processes of soil transformation and decomposition, gives an idea of the complexity of the interrelations within soil populations and the science that has developed during the twentieth century to describe them.

equipment" (Day 1953:343). It is evident from his later work that Day followed his own advice and that he never looked back.

Consolidating a Research Program at Dartmouth

From the "Abenaki Journal," it appears that Day's second visit to Saint Francis took place in May 1956. In addition to making some new acquaintances, he took time to visit the seminary at Nicolet, Quebec. There he met Monseigneur Thomas-Marie Charland, with whom he carried on a correspondence over the years and whose *Histoire des Abénakis d'Odanak, 1675–1937* (Charland 1964) proved especially useful to Day's attempts to reconstruct postcontact Abenaki history. In the archives of the seminary, Day discovered a trove of manuscripts on Abenaki by the Jesuit Fathers Joseph Aubery, Jean Baptiste Nudénans, and others, which he later mined in his linguistic work. He also traveled to the archives of the Séminaire de Québec in Quebec City, where he found additional material. In October he again visited Saint Francis to tape-record some Abenaki songs and prayers. He had also located a few Abenakis who lived in Vermont and New Hampshire towns and was beginning to record their speech.

In August 1957, Day's long-awaited plan to devote himself entirely to Abenaki research at last became a reality when he was offered a position as a research associate in the Department of Anthropology at Dartmouth College, in Hanover, New Hampshire. It was an ideal opportunity, in that he could continue to live with his family in Contoocook, which would remain, as he put it, his research "headquarters," but commute to the college to teach occasional classes and offer lectures on Indian subjects. The department had something of a northern North American focus, and its aboriginal research program would now be expanded to include the area where the college was located (Day 1959c:30). Day's departmental responsibilities were light, freeing him to devote most of his time to his Abenaki work. A grant proposal dating from this period indicates just how central language was to the new enterprise:[6] the tasks he set for himself were to assemble a bibliography of all known published and unpublished materials on—and in—Western Abenaki; to make a phonological analysis of the language based on materials he had recorded himself; to compile a dictionary with separate Abenaki-English and English-Abenaki sections; and, finally, to produce a grammar of the language. All but the last goal were met over the next three decades, and extensive notes were made for a grammar that remains to be edited and published. From 1957 to 1960, Day's research was supported by grants from the

---

[6]The proposal does not carry a date, but internal evidence suggests that it may have been prepared as early as 1955. This was before Day went to Dartmouth, and the proposal was likely used to obtain support for the research he planned to conduct with the new appointment.

Spaulding-Potter Charitable Trusts of Manchester, New Hampshire, and from 1961 to 1964 it was supported by grants from the National Science Foundation.

From early on, Day believed in the advantages of an approach weighted toward language in dealing with ethnological and historical problems. The significance of such an approach to ethnology is summarized in the grant proposal:

> Language provides information on all phases of material and non-material culture—implements, customs, concepts of law, land tenure, and acculturation. Ethnologists, who study a group as a whole or a problem which cuts across groups, collect more or less linguistic information. It seems most likely, however, that the part which they do not collect, because it does not concern their plan, is also significant.

With regard to historical issues, from an intensive study of the dialects of Western Abenaki spoken at Saint Francis he hoped to reconstruct the linguistic map of northwestern New England, which, along with other data, would help to establish the identities and locations of groups known primarily from imperfectly recorded and analyzed place-names.

Day was methodical in pursuing his research aims. He arranged to have some 10,000 pages of manuscript materials and less accessible publications from various Quebec repositories microfilmed and deposited in the archives of Dartmouth's Baker Library.[7] By the fall of 1957, he was conducting intensive linguistic work on Western Abenaki with several native speakers. For his phonological analysis, he sought advice from Floyd G. Lounsbury at Yale University, whom he later credited with introducing him to the world of linguistics and converting him from a forest ecologist to a "practicing ethnolinguist" (Day 1994b:v). He taped his linguistic interviews on a Wollensak machine that took seven-inch reels (Figure 1).[8] He approached the question of Abenaki dialect variation by recording the Swadesh basic vocabulary list from his consultants. By comparing different pronunciations of terms on the list, he was eventually able to identify four "family" dialects of Saint Francis Abenaki (Day 1964:373, 1967b:111, 1981a: 116, 1985a, 1994b:ix).[9]

---

[7] "The Gordon M. Day Collection of Manuscripts on the Languages of the Indians of Canada," kept in Special Collections at Baker Library. A table of contents was prepared of this material, which provides for each source—when known—the original author's name and the date and title of the work, its location and a brief description of its contents. Although most of the material is Abenaki, some is from other Eastern Algonquian and Iroquoian languages.

[8] The whole collection, including material recorded after Day went to Ottawa, consists of some 68 reels, which have been deposited in the archives of the Canadian Museum of Civilization. Another, less complete set may be found in the Dartmouth College collection. The material has been indexed, with the name of the informant, the place and date, and the topic given in columns.

[9] Between 1956 and 1985, Day worked with more than three dozen Western Abenaki speakers on language and traditional texts. He collaborated especially closely with Edward Hannis and Ambroise Obomsawin (see figs. 1 and 2) and Théophile Panadis (Day 1964:374, n. 27; 1994b:v). He also drew on the published and unpublished work of the native Abenaki educator Pial Pol (Peter Paul) Wzôkhilain, who trained for the ministry at Dartmouth College between 1823 and 1829 (Day 1961a).

Fig. 1. Gordon M. Day working with Ambroise Obomsawin (*center*) and Edward Hannis in Ottawa, Ontario (undated). By permission of Donal F. Day.

Fig. 2. Edward Hannis (*left*) and Ambroise Obomsawin (*right*) in Ottawa, Ontario (undated). By permission of Donal F. Day.

Day's publications during this period reflect his commitment to the Dartmouth research program and the melding of old and new interests. In "Dartmouth and Saint Francis" (Day 1959c), he explains the origins of the Saint Francis mission and its role in influencing Eleazar Wheelock to relocate Moor's Indian Charity School from Lebanon, Connecticut, to Hanover, a move that also led to the founding of Dartmouth College. From the late eighteenth century until well into the nineteenth, the largest number of native students at Dartmouth were from Saint Francis. Another paper, published in the college's *Library Bulletin,* describes the salvage research program and what Day calls the "Dartmouth Algonkian Collection" (Day 1962b). In his first contribution to the *International Journal of American Linguistics,* he clarifies the etymology of the word *Abenaki* and deftly disposes of earlier speculation on this subject (Day 1959b). He made a similar study of the word *Contoocook,* the name of the town in which he was living. He concluded that it was an Abenaki word rather than a Massachusett one, implying that the central Merrimack Valley, which lay in a cultural and linguistic transition zone, must have looked more to the north than to the south (Day 1961b). These were the first of several papers in which he addresses the question of tribal names and place-names in New England. In his discussions and reviews of works on these subjects by others, he reveals himself to be something of a crusader in his efforts to weed out speculative etymologies and false tribal identifications and locations.

Day's Abenaki research was also beginning to pay off in more substantial papers on the speech and ethnohistory of Saint Francis. He was aware that although Algonquian was one of the earliest and best studied language families in North America, knowledge of the Eastern Algonquian languages, and of Abenaki in particular, was far from adequate. To draw scholarly attention to the language, he compiled an annotated bibliography of both major and minor works published in Saint Francis Abenaki (Day 1961a); this represents a significant updating of Pilling's (1891) *Bibliography of the Algonquian Languages* for this language. The 1960s were a period of ferment in comparative Algonquian studies: within a short time, Ives Goddard would establish Eastern Algonquian as a distinct subbranch of the family.[10] Day wanted to contribute to comparative Algonquian studies, but, realizing that it would be a number of years before his Abenaki-English dictionary was ready for publication,[11] he decided to follow Stanley

---

[10]This was accomplished in a series of papers by Goddard appearing between 1965 and 1974. For summaries, see Goddard, "Eastern Algonquian Languages" (pp. 70–77 in *Northeast,* Bruce G. Trigger, ed., Vol. 15 of *Handbook of North American Indians,* W. C. Sturtevant, gen. ed., Smithsonian Institution, Washington, D.C., 1978), and Goddard, "Comparative Algonquian" (pp. 70–132 in *The Languages of Native America: Historical and Comparative Assessment,* Lyle Campbell and Marianne Mithun, eds., University of Texas Press, Austin and London, 1979, esp. pp. 96–102).

[11]His two-volume, Abenaki-English and English-Abenaki dictionary appeared two decades later (Day 1994b, 1995).

Newman's (1952) advice and publish an interim vocabulary that combined several standard gloss lists—precisely the kind of data most often sought in comparative and lexicostatistical studies (Day 1964).[12] In a third paper, "The Tree Nomenclature of the Saint Francis Indians," he drew on his background and field experience in forestry to compile an exhaustive list of tree names in Western Abenaki (Day 1963a). Although the 64 species mentioned are listed under their Latin names, many of the entries contain detailed ethnobotanical information, from which it is possible to infer the basis for the native system of classifying trees. Day was intrigued by the differences between the scientific botanical system in which he had been trained and the native system, which used features of form rather than "reproductive structures" to group species (Day 1963a:48).

Perhaps the best overview of the challenges posed by the research program Day defined for himself during his Dartmouth years is provided in his paper "English-Indian Contacts in New England" (Day 1962a):

> the central problem of New England ethnohistory . . . [is] that of identifying the ethnic units within the region, establishing their affinities, locating them at the time of discovery, and following their movements, their partitions, regroupings, and mergers through the violent dislocations which followed European contact. (P. 26)

The "violent dislocations" were caused by disease and warfare. The plagues of 1616–1619 and 1633–1634 killed thousands of people in southern New England and countless more in the interior. But it was really the disastrous King Philip's War (1675–1676), named for the Wampanoag leader who rallied New England's Indians to take up arms against the English, that began the final dispersal of interior groups such as the Sokokis, Penacooks, Pocumtucks, Pigwackets, and others to the west and north, swelling the ranks of refugees at the village of Schaghticoke, a haven created for them on the Hudson River by New York governor Edmund Andros, and at the French missions, including Saint Francis, in Quebec. Well into the eighteenth century, Saint Francis received refugees from Maine; the upper Connecticut River valley; Schaghticoke; and especially Missisquoi, near present-day Swanton, Vermont. To complicate the historian's task further, there were reverse movements of people at different times from Saint Francis back to Schaghticoke and Missisquoi. Because most of interior New England underwent severe dislocations and depopulation before the groups involved were documented, locations that persisted throughout the period, such as Missisquoi, Schaghticoke, and Saint Francis, have assumed special importance for the historian and dialectologist.[13]

---

[12]One comparative study that drew on this paper was Frank Siebert's "The Original Home of the Proto-Algonquian People," pp. 13–47 in *Contributions to Anthropology: Linguistics I (Algonquian)*, Anthropological Series 78, National Museum of Canada Bulletin 214, Ottawa, 1967.

[13]In "The Indian Occupation of Vermont," Day (1965b) addresses the depopulation problem from a narrower

On the linguistic side, Day (1962a:31) expressed the hope that archives in Canada and the United States would "ultimately yield at least modest vocabularies for some of these peoples." As a particularly valuable find, he mentioned learning in 1959 about a substantial manuscript that might prove to be a record of an interior New England language. This was Jean-Claude Mathevet's "Mots loups," located in the Sulpician Archives in Montreal; because of its potentially great value, he would later prepare a facsimile edition of the manuscript and tentatively identify its provenience (Day 1975c). In the meantime, the modern speech of the Saint Francis Indians would have to serve as the main source for reconstructing the linguistic map of northwestern New England:

> This band is supposed to have received at one time or another increments from many parts of New England, including nearly all of the displaced Indians between the Kennebec River and Lake Champlain. The association of dialect isoglosses with specific families in the St. Francis band and the history of these families are now being studied with the hope of being able to ascertain the dialects of at least two groups—the Missisquoi and the Coosuck-Pequaket bands—in their pre-removal locations. (Day 1962a:31–32; cf. Day 1967b:111)

Aside from the scanty documentary records on the area, there was one other often neglected source that Day argued should be mined for historical information: the testimony of native oral tradition. In "Rogers' Raid in Indian Tradition" (1962c), he compares Major Robert Rogers's version of the raid on Saint Francis in 1759 with two oral accounts handed down at Saint Francis. He finds that the native accounts confirmed some details of Rogers's version as well as resolving important discrepancies between it and the official French report on the raid. Because so much of the colonial period involved conflict between Indians and whites, the historian should welcome native testimony in order to get the fullest possible picture of events. But such testimony was often ignored, simply because it was oral rather than written:

> It is unfortunate that historians, who have elaborate criteria for evaluating documents, have nothing of the sort for oral traditions. Some have solved the problem by rejecting all [oral] tradition as unworthy of serious consideration. To me this is unreal. A statement does not become true for being committed to paper. . . . Although we lack formal criteria for evaluation, we can recognize degrees of reliability within current St. Francis tradition. (Pp. 7–8)

Vermont perspective to dispel the notion presented in many standard histories that the state was devoid of aboriginal inhabitants before white contact. In their highly readable overview of 11,000 years of Vermont native history, *The Original Vermonters: Native Inhabitants Past and Present* (Hanover and London: University Press of New England, 1981), William Haviland and Marjory Power rely on this and other papers by Day to argue for the continuity of the state's native occupation over various archeological periods until the disruptions of the colonial period (reviewed by Day 1982). Continuing ethnohistorical research by John Moody and others, also drawing on Day's work as a point of departure, has strengthened the notion that the eastern shore of Lake Champlain in general, and Missisquoi in particular, had substantial Western Abenaki populations. During the colonial period, the Abenakis underwent cycles of dispersal and regrouping without ever entirely losing their foothold in the Missisquoi and Winooski areas (John Moody, personal communications, 1995–1996).

The idea that oral tradition can serve as a useful complement to written history recurs as a theme in Day's later work. The acceptance of this point by many historians of Indian-white relations today can in some measure be attributed to Day's efforts.

The Move to Ottawa: Expanded Responsibilities and Research Interests

In August 1964, Day attended a conference on Algonquian linguistics in Ottawa, Ontario, sponsored by the National Museum of Canada.[14] The conference was the first of what was to grow into the Algonquian Conference, a more or less annual event after 1968 (Day and Bishop 1986). In his contribution, a review of the source literature on the languages of New England, Day announced in a vivid metaphor what was by then a familiar theme for him: "In panorama, New England Algonkian is very reminiscent of a northern muskeg, with its islands of more or less firm ground rising out of a generally uncertain terrain" (Day 1967b:107).[15] The conference was organized by Karl Teeter, of the Harvard Linguistics Department, and A. Donald DeBlois, the chief ethnologist of the museum's Ethnology Division in the Human History Branch.[16] During the conference, DeBlois encouraged Day to apply for the newly created position of ethnohistorian in the Ethnology Division, and Day, whose National Science Foundation grants had run out and who was ready for a move, responded enthusiastically. The details were handled with unusual dispatch for a government agency.[17] The family moved from Contoocook to Ottawa that December, and Day took up his new duties in early January 1965.[18]

At first, Day was able to continue his Abenaki research program, the sponsorship of which, he later noted, was simply "taken over" by the museum (Day 1977b:2). Within a short time, however, his job title had changed to Eastern Canada Ethnologist, which meant he had responsibility for all of eastern Canada below the subarctic in the areas of divisional administration, collections building, and overseeing of Urgent Ethnology contracts for outside researchers. As if to keep pace with his expanded responsibilities, his research interests began to branch out to include other Algonquian groups in eastern Canada: the Nipis-

[14] Specifically, by the Ethnology Division of the Human History Branch of the museum. The Human History Branch was later renamed the National Museum of Man, by which it was known for many years, and today is called the Canadian Museum of Civilization.

[15] *Algonkian* is an alternate spelling of the more commonly written *Algonquian*. Both terms are used to designate the language family as a whole or, broadly, any group belonging to the family. They are distinguished from *Algonquin* (or *Algonkin*), the name of the Ottawa Valley tribe (cf. Day and Trigger 1978d).

[16] The papers were compiled by DeBlois and published as *Contributions to Anthropology: Linguistics I (Algonquian)*, Anthropological Series 78, National Museum of Canada Bulletin 214, Ottawa, 1967.

[17] A. Donald DeBlois, personal communication, September 11, 1995.

[18] When Day joined the staff, his office was located in the Victoria Memorial Building on Mcleod Street, which housed the Human History Branch's administrative offices, library, and exhibitions. To make more room for exhibitions in the later 1960s, the branch moved to Bells Corners in the west end of the city.

sing, the Montagnais, the Maliseet, the Ottawa, and the Algonquin, particularly the last, whose reserve at Golden Lake, Ontario, presented him with new opportunities for fieldwork. In staff reports from the early 1970s, he mentions collecting information on language, ethnobotany, medicine, mythology, history, world view, and material culture—topics he and his collaborators were asked to cover in encyclopedic articles on these groups (Day 1978c, Day and Trigger 1978d, Trigger and Day 1994a).[19] In addition, the broadening of interest gave him a new perspective from which to view the Western Abenaki of New England, whose culture in many ways seemed transitional between that of more northerly Algonquian hunter-gatherers and that of more southerly Algonquian and Iroquoian agriculturalists (Day 1978b). The position of Eastern Canada Ethnologist also carried with it administrative responsibility for the Iroquois of Quebec and Ontario, and Day took the opportunity to become actively acquainted with the Ahkwesahsne Mohawk Reserve at Cornwall, Ontario. This last involvement arose partly from an independent interest in the Iroquois that had developed during his teenage years and partly in response to requirements of the museum's exhibition programs.[20] Although Day occasionally groused about the amount of time he had to spend on exhibition planning, he delighted in selecting and arranging artifacts, no doubt because of his long-standing interest in natural materials (particularly wood) and native production techniques. In the area of material culture, as in all other areas of his scholarship, he was dedicated to separating the genuine from the spurious (Day 1975b).

Day was 53 years old when he went to Ottawa. The three decades in Ottawa were both demanding and productive. At the museum he was made head of the research section in the Ethnology Division,[21] and he was frequently called on to be acting chief of the division in the chief's absence. As noted earlier, he was occupied with the museum's exhibition programs for several years and bore a considerable load of administrative work as Eastern Canada Ethnologist. In the later 1960s, he was the prime mover in setting up the Algonquian Conference.[22]

[19] The last two articles are listed in the Bibliography as Day 1978d and Day 1994a. Day also published a brief popular article on the Ottawa (Day 1979b, 1979c).

[20] Altogether, between 1965 and 1972 Day was involved in the planning of three Iroquois exhibition halls at the Victoria Memorial Building. I assumed primary responsibility for the last of these, which opened in 1974, a little more than a year after coming on staff in 1970, but during the whole planning process Day gave generously of his time and knowledge, offering particularly useful advice on Iroquois material culture. I am further indebted to Day for establishing the practice of inviting knowledgeable native visitors into the museum's collections area to comment on the manufacture and uses of traditional artifacts. This afforded valuable opportunities to learn about traditional Iroquois culture and lifeways. The museum benefited from the expert advice of Frank Thomas, Corbett Sundown, and Jacob E. Thomas, among others. Day was responsible for introducing a new kind of conservation in the collections—beyond the physical requirements of storage and retrieval—when he initiated the practice of inviting Iroquois ceremonialists to the museum every few years to perform "feeding" ceremonies for the false face and husk face masks.

[21] Later, the Canadian Ethnology Service.

[22] Since 1961, Day had been attending the annual Conference on Iroquois Research, established by William N. Fenton in 1945, and he saw the need for a parallel conference for the Algonquianists (Day and Bishop 1986).

In the midst of these involvements he somehow found time to pursue an old interest in Irish Gaelic, sharing information and studying with Gordon W. MacLennan, a specialist in Gaelic who was a member of the museum's Canadian Centre for Folk Culture Studies. Day retired in 1979 but kept an office at the museum and continued his work, concentrating particularly on a two-volume Western Abenaki-English dictionary (Day 1994b, 1995) and a collection of Abenaki texts, which remains unpublished (Day, in preparation). He died of a heart attack at his home in Ottawa on August 11, 1993, at the age of 81.[23]

Synthesizing Years of Research

Day's publications during the Ottawa years are those of a mature scholar who, reaping the benefits of years of painstaking research, begins to synthesize his findings in hopes of providing the larger picture. His publications of this period may conveniently be grouped into two categories: a small set on Algonquian mythology and oral tradition that includes a contribution to Iroquoian studies and a considerably larger set that continues to probe the question of the linguistic and cultural identity of the native peoples of interior New England.

Day's interest in the Iroquois was inspired by his discovery of Francis Parkman's histories while he was still in school. He kept a hand in later by regularly attending the Conference on Iroquois Research and through his administrative responsibilities and exhibition work at the National Museum of Canada. During the period I knew him, I remember his having a detailed grasp of postcontact Iroquoian history. He was particularly fascinated by the structure and origins of the League. He published only one paper exclusively on an Iroquoian subject, although the Iroquois figure importantly in a number of his other papers, for the obvious reason that groups like the Western Abenakis and Mahicans were flanked by Iroquoian-speaking groups and frequently interacted with them— usually on opposite sides—during the Anglo-French colonial struggle.

In the one exclusively Iroquoian paper, he turned his skills as a student of Indian names to an old puzzle: the etymology of the word *Iroquois* itself (Day

---

After the Sixth Algonquian Conference in 1974, the conference proceedings were published by Carleton University annually under the editorship of William Cowan. With the Twenty-sixth Algonquian Conference (1994), the editorship was assumed by David H. Pentland at the University of Manitoba.

[23] Obituaries appeared in the *Newsletter* of the Society for the Study of the Indigenous Languages of the Americas, 10(4):3–4 (1994), and the *Anthropology Newsletter* of the American Anthropological Association, 35(2):43 (1994). Tributes were also paid to Day at the 1993 Algonquian Conference, held in Ottawa; the 1993 Conference on Iroquois Research, held in Rensselaerville, New York; and a memorial meeting of the Vermont Historical Society in Montpelier, Vermont, on November 21, 1993. During his life he was listed in *American Men and Women of Science* and *Who's Who in Science*. In 1960, the people of Saint Francis made him an honorary Abenaki chief. He belonged to a number of professional societies and in 1968 was elected president of the American Society for Ethnohistory.

1967c; cf. Day 1968a).[24] After disposing of some fanciful eighteenth- and nineteenth-century speculation, he brings to light an overlooked etymology from an obscure nineteenth-century source that suggests the word may have come into French by way of Montagnais. He shows, however, that the word cannot be analyzed within the morphological structure of Montagnais, so it is most likely a borrowing from still another source. He suggests that Portuguese, Breton, French, Basque, Beothuk, and Laurentian Iroquois should all be scrutinized as possible donors. This prescient conclusion was picked up some years later by Peter Bakker of the University of Amsterdam, who argued that the word was ultimately of Basque origin: it may have made its way into Montagnais through an eastern trade jargon.[25] Day's paper stands as a valuable contribution to the literature on the Iroquois.

Day's interest in the oral traditions of the so-called Wabanaki groups of eastern Canada and the United States (the Micmac, Maliseet, Passamaquoddy, Penobscot, and Saint Francis Abenaki) was undoubtedly linked to his linguistic work and the collection and analysis of texts as samples of the languages he studied, but he also viewed oral traditions as potential quarries to mine for information about New England's native past. In a coauthored overview of the native literatures of the Northeast written late in his life and published posthumously, he separates for the Eastern Algonquians what he calls "traditional histories" from fictional accounts, the latter comprising substantial creation legends and "shorter tales recited for amusement or to teach a moral lesson" (Day and Foster 1994c:74). Of course, it is traditional histories of the type exemplified by the native accounts of Rogers's raid on Saint Francis (Day 1962c) that speak most directly to real events in the past. Indeed, Day decided that the notion that oral tradition could serve as a complement to written history was sufficiently important to rework the earlier paper and present it as his presidential address to the American Society for Ethnohistory in 1968 (Day 1972b).

Even purely mythological accounts may contain clues useful to the historian. In a paper written to explain the differences between the more easterly Algonquian culture hero Gluskap and the Western Abenaki transformer culture heroes Odzihozo and Bedegwadzo (Day 1976), Day highlights the ending of the traditional origin story: after Odzihozo had created all the topographic features of the earth, including the Green Mountains and Lake Champlain, he transformed himself into Rock Dunder, which can be seen today as a small columnar island outcropping of slate and limestone lying half a mile off Shelburne Point opposite South Burlington. It appears that the Mohawks also had a name for this feature,

---

[24] Always willing to confront challenging problems of nomenclature, Day also devoted a paper to the name *Algonquin* (Day 1972a), in which he makes the case for its being of "Etchemin" (Maliseet) origin with the meaning 'they are our relatives, or allies'.

[25] Peter Bakker, "A Basque Etymology for the Word 'Iroquois'," *Man in the Northeast* 40:89–93 (1990).

known in English as *Rogeo,* whose variant spellings in the documentary record resolve into the form *rotsî:ʔyo,* analyzed as 'coward spirit' (Lounsbury 1960:60–62).
Day, however, makes a more convincing case that the Mohawk term is actually a
borrowing from the Western Abenaki word *odzíhozó,* the name of one of the two
primal transformers with the meaning 'he makes himself into something' (Day
1971a:11–12, 1976:81–82, 1981b:162–163). On the principle that a language
supplying a place-name implies earlier occupancy for its speakers than for the
speakers of the language borrowing the name, the linguistic evidence, when
added to the mythological, tends to support a prior Abenaki claim to the eastern
shore of Lake Champlain, a claim corroborated by other kinds of data considered
further below.[26] Although such conclusions are purely inferential, they under-
score the potential value of oral tradition for historical reconstruction.

Reconstructing the Tribal and Linguistic Map of Interior New England

The bulk of Day's publications during the Ottawa years carry forward his
efforts to reconstruct the tribal and linguistic map of interior New England. An
earlier statement defined the problem in geographic terms, specifically in terms
of river systems:

> Without underestimating the taxonomical problems of southern, and particularly
> of southwestern, New England, it appears that the region between the Kennebec
> River [to the east] and Lake Champlain [to the west] is the problem area. The
> Androscoggin, Saco, Merrimack, and upper Connecticut rivers, and the Vermont
> rivers which flow into Lake Champlain were areas of known Indian occupation,
> although historians have generally treated Vermont as an uninhabited area. Eth-
> nographically, it has been a virtual *terra incognita.* There does not seem to be,
> either in print or in manuscript, a single account of any group settled within the
> entire area prior to King Philip's War [1675–1676]. (Day 1962a:28)

Not only was there a tendency for Indian settlements to cluster along rivers and
the margins of lakes, but the region's tribal boundaries were generally defined on
the same basis. The waterways of interior New England thus assumed special
importance in Day's reconstructive efforts. Although he occasionally refers to the
rivers of south-central Maine (the Saco, the Androscoggin, the Kennebec, and
the still more easterly Penobscot), these are somewhat peripheral to the core area,
and it is the Connecticut River, the Merrimack River, and especially Lake Cham-

---

[26]In American Indian studies, it was Edward Sapir, in "Time Perspective in Aboriginal American Culture: A
Study in Method," who first enunciated the principle Day applies here. Sapir's paper appears in *Anthropological
Series 13, Memoirs of the Canadian Geological Survey* 90, Ottawa, 1916 (reprinted: pp. 389–462 in *Selected
Writings of Edward Sapir in Language, Culture, and Personality,* David G. Mandelbaum, ed., University of
California Press, Berkeley and Los Angeles, 1949; see esp. pp. 436, 445–447 in the reprinted version). Day
discusses the methodology of using place-names to delimit the homeland of a people in "Indian Place-Names
as Ethnohistoric Data" (Day 1977a; see esp. pp. 29–31, where he discusses Rock Dunder). Curiously, he here
entertains the possibility that the Abenaki may have borrowed their word for this feature from the Mohawks,
but he builds a far better case for the reverse direction of borrowing in the sources cited above.

plain that receive the most attention. The publications of the Ottawa period may accordingly be divided into three groups on the basis of the waterway that is the focus of a given inquiry, bearing in mind that his discussions often touch on the interaction of peoples from different locations within the whole region. His monograph *The Identity of the Saint Francis Indians* (Day 1981a, 1985b), represents a summing up and synthesis of all he had explored in shorter papers.[27]

Connecticut River Valley Focus

In the late 1960s, Day noted that "no dictionary or grammar, no trader's account, no missionary's working glossary nor even a casual word list has come to light for any dialect along the entire length of the Connecticut River" (1969a: 75), a difficult situation indeed for one hoping to reconstruct the linguistic map of New England. He proposed to attack the problem of determining the distribution of Western Abenaki dialects along the middle and upper Connecticut valley by continuing to comb the historical sources and by ransacking archives for overlooked, or at least insufficiently studied, manuscript materials documenting the Eastern Algonquian languages (Day 1967b, 1969a). His efforts paid off, in one case shedding light on the Connecticut valley origins of the earliest settlers of Saint Francis, and in another providing a linguistic analysis of two manuscripts—one brief and the other extensive—of Connecticut valley languages.

Saint Francis had begun as a mission village for New England refugees in the 1660s. Its later history was reasonably well documented, but its beginnings were shrouded in obscurity until the Dominican historian Thomas-Marie Charland, with whom Day corresponded over the years, established from church registers at Sorel, Quebec, that the first people to arrive at Saint Francis were from the group known in the French documents as the Sokokis (Charland 1942, 1964).[28] Well into the nineteenth century, the Sokokis maintained a separate identity from other residents of the village, who were simply termed Abenakis. Clearly, it was crucial to Day's enterprise to establish where the Sokokis came from.

Perhaps because of a vague similarity of names, the Sokokis were often equated in the historical literature with groups living on the Saco River in western Maine, though this inference had no direct support from early observer accounts. Another popular theory had Saint Francis being settled by Eastern Abenakis from the Androscoggin River valley east of the Saco, but, as Day (1979a) convincingly shows, this equation seems also to have arisen from a

---

[27]With one possible exception (Day 1984), he did not address the question of reconstructing the tribal-linguistic map of interior New England in any subsequent publication; he seems to have regarded the *Identity* monograph as his last say on the subject, at least with regard to contributing new information on it. His "Abenakis in the Lake Champlain Valley" (Day 1987), for example, is a popular summary of earlier work.

[28]Day began to note this fact in publications as early as 1959 (Day 1959c) and mentions it often in later work (e.g., Day 1961a:80–81, 1965c:241, 1972b:105, 1975c:38, 1978b:148, 1981a:12–16, 1987:283).

linguistic confusion, one that resulted from erroneously equating variant forms of the name *Androscoggin* (*Amascoggin, Amanoscoggin, Amarascoggin,* etc.) with variant forms of the name of the Saint Francis River (*Assagunticook, Arosagunticook,* etc.) (cf. Day 1969c). The impression that Saint Francis was settled by people from central and western Maine derived some of its impetus from the fact that in 1705–1706 the community had received refugees from the similarly named Saint-François-de-Sales mission on the Chaudière River, which empties into the Saint Lawrence about 75 miles below the mouth of the Saint Francis River. Many of the Chaudière people were originally attracted to that mission from the Kennebec and other rivers in Maine, some from as far east as the Penobscot area, and most of them spoke Eastern Abenaki dialects.

In a paper that shows his holistic approach to problems at its best, Day (1965c) straightens out the confusion surrounding the identity of the Sokokis and establishes their approximate original location as clearly as can be done from the available records. With regard to the confusion between the names *Saco* and *Sokoki,* he shows that the former derives from some variant of the Abenaki word usually written in the historical documents as *Sowacotuck* 'dead tree river', whereas the latter derives from some variant of the Abenaki *sohkwahkíak* 'the people who separated, broke apart'.[29] A crucial piece of the puzzle falls in place when he recalls that the Jesuit missionary Gabriel Druillettes had written during a trip to New England in 1650–1651 that a group he termed the *Sokokiois* inhabited the Connecticut River, which he wrote as *Kenetigouc.* Druillettes's term appeared only in the French literature, but it turns out that the English independently referred to the people of a village located at Northfield, Massachusetts, as *Squakheags*—sometimes as *Squakeys*—and this can be equated with the French term. In brief, the people who settled Saint Francis in the mid-seventeenth century could be placed with some confidence in the middle Connecticut River valley.

As noted, there are almost no preremoval documentary records of the aboriginal languages or the dialects comprising them for the entire length of the Connecticut valley. The only exception that can confidently be assigned a valley provenience is a word list of thirteen names for the months, which appears in an account book kept by the traders William Pynchon and his son John of Springfield, Massachusetts, during the mid-seventeenth century. Crude though the transcriptions of the names are, Day (1967a) was able to detect affinities for the language, which he tentatively identified as that of the Agawams, with both Saint Francis Abenaki and some of the better-documented languages of eastern Mas-

---

[29]Elsewhere, Day (1978b:159) renders the Abenaki word as *ozokwakiak* and translates it as 'the ones who broke up, broke away'.

sachusetts and Rhode Island, but identical to none of these. Whatever the specific identity of the group, the data best supported a location in the middle to lower part of the valley.[30]

A second apparent exception to the generalization that the Connecticut valley lacks in situ linguistic documentation is a far more substantial work located in the Sulpician archives in Montreal. This anonymous manuscript, titled simply "Mots loups," consists of 124 unnumbered pages in an Indian language and bound in the form of a field notebook. It carries no explicit date or indication of provenience, but it contains a number of clues that make a Connecticut valley location plausible if not fully demonstrable.[31]

Day quickly established that the language belonged to the Eastern branch of Algonquian, although it was not identical to any known language, including Saint Francis Abenaki.[32] From a handwriting analysis conducted by Thomas-Marie Charland, the manuscript was identified as the work of the eighteenth-century Sulpician Father Jean-Claude Mathevet, who served in Canada from 1740 to 1781. Although the early French writers and mapmakers applied the term *Loup* to various Algonquian-speaking groups, from western Maine to New York and as far south as Virginia, Day could eliminate most of the documented languages in this broad area as the language of the manuscript on the basis of features inconsistent with the phonologies and morphological structures of those languages and knowledge of the locations where Mathevet worked (Day 1967b: 110–111, 1969a:77, 1975c:35 ff.). This left the "no man's land" of interior New England as the most likely area in which to place it. This possibility, which must have come to Day as a kind of revelatory experience after years of struggling to find linguistic documentation for the area, may explain the particular care he took in preparing a facsimile edition and a detailed redaction of the manuscript, which he published as a monograph (Day 1975c).

---

[30]Apparently, the Pynchons had Indian contacts along the river from Wethersfield, Connecticut, to Northfield, Massachusetts. Day's inference that the month names were recorded in the language of the Agawams is based not only on the proximity of this group to Springfield, where the Pynchons lived, but also, and more ingeniously, on some internal evidence provided by the names themselves. Three of the names imply an early spring, and thus a "climatic and ecologic zone" that is more characteristic of Springfield than Northfield 50 miles to the north, and—although the evidence is negative—the lack of a name for a sugar-making month, as found, for example, in Saint Francis Abenaki, correlates with the lower frequency of the sugar maple in the Springfield area than in areas to the north. This is another instance where Day's background in forest ecology paid dividends in his ethnographic work.

[31]Day first learned of the manuscript in 1959 while he was at Dartmouth and had it microfilmed for the Algonkian Collection along with other materials (Day 1962a:31). He began intensive study and editing in 1963, and this would occupy him off and on for nearly a decade.

[32]Aside from the fact that the Loup forms are too divergent from comparable Saint Francis forms to be considered a sample of Abenaki, the manuscript contains a number of Loup-Abenaki comparisons, often arranged side by side to show contrasting elements (1981a:50–51). Since the Abenaki forms in the manuscript are nearly identical to corresponding Saint Francis forms of today, a contrast is implied between Loup and the language identified as Sokoki, as explained earlier (cf. Day 1967b:111). This would seem to eliminate the upper Connecticut valley as the source of the manuscript language.

In the end, Day made a reasonable case for the material's having been collected by Mathevet between 1749 and 1754 at the village of Missisquoi on Lake Champlain. By the mid-eighteenth century, the old village, which had long functioned as a traditional center for the Western Abenaki, was taking in increasing numbers of refugees from different locations in New England. Based on an analysis of the name the Loup speakers had for themselves, which can be interpreted as describing a distinctive topographic feature in northern Massachusetts, and the fact that the language is not identical to any of the languages originating farther upriver, Day tentatively identified the speakers as the Pocumtucks, whose earliest known village was located at the confluence of the Deerfield and Connecticut Rivers in northern Massachusetts (1975c:54–64). The case is circumstantial, but the historical and linguistic facts are weighed so carefully as to make the argument highly persuasive.[33]

Merrimack River Valley Focus

Although archeological surveys of the upper Merrimack River and Lake Winnipesaukee area show it to have been one of the most populous regions in aboriginal New England, as is the case for the Connecticut valley there are no known contemporary descriptions of the languages of the area (Day 1962a:29, 1967b:108). The term *Penacook* was applied in the historical records to both the people inhabiting the valley and their language. The Merrimack was of special interest to Day because it lay in the poorly understood border zone between the Eastern and Western Abenaki peoples, and between them and the coastal peoples of New Hampshire and Massachusetts, whose speech is usually identified as one or another dialect of Massachusett.[34]

In Day's view, even very limited data might provide clues as to the linguistic identity of the groups along the Merrimack, and very limited data were all there were, consisting of only a handful of place-names. Although he once described the inferences he drew from these names as grasping at straws (Day 1975a:385), he was able by careful analysis to extract some significant details from them. The approach involved two steps. First, he analyzed the names according to the phonology and word structure of the documented languages in the general vicinity to see which, if any, might accommodate them. Second, he attempted to match the names with particular features in the landscape, if, indeed, the meanings of the names could be determined. Day's background in forest ecology often proved useful in carrying out the second step.

As noted earlier, the name *Contoocook,* which once applied to a section of the

---

[33] Day's analysis of the Loup speakers' name for themselves—a crucial link in the argument for identifying them as the Pocumtucks—is nevertheless open to question, as William Cowan showed in his review of the *Mots loups* monograph in *International Journal of American Linguistics* 45(1):88–94 (1979).

[34] Goddard, "Eastern Algonquian Languages," op. cit., p. 72.

Merrimack River near Concord, New Hampshire, and today is the name of a lake, a town, and a river in the state, yielded to a Saint Francis Abenaki analysis but resisted a Massachusett one, from which Day concluded that the upper part of the river was Western Abenaki in speech (Day 1961b). He further argued that the name most likely derived from the Western Abenaki word *pagǫntékw* 'nut river', implying that this section of the river probably had "notable or abundant" nut trees (1961b:170). The question was, What tree did the name designate? Various species were ruled out as being rare in Southern New Hampshire, but the butternut was common there, particularly along the Contoocook River, which empties into the Merrimack a few miles north of Concord, and so he concluded that the name probably referred to that tree.

Day also worked on the name *Penacook* to try to determine which part of the river it denoted. He first showed that *Penacook* is a variant of the name *Openango,* which crops up sporadically in seventeenth-century French records (Day 1973a).[35] Later historians interpreted the name *Openango* as denoting, variously, the Hurons, the Passamaquoddies, the Delawares, speakers of Massachusett, the Mahicans, and the Abenakis (Day 1962a:29–30). Day ruled out all but the last of these groups on linguistic grounds. The prototype of the name, he suggested, was *penǫkók,* a word the Saint Francis Abenakis have for the historic village of Penacook on the Merrimack River near Concord. In Saint Francis, the word means 'at the falling bank', and this describes quite closely the known location of the village at the top of a hill close enough to the river to be subject to the effects of continuous erosion.

Altogether, analysis of the two names implied that the upper Merrimack fell within the Western Abenaki speech area. Additional support came from the fact that these names were among those appearing on a map of the river drawn by a surveyor named John Gardner around 1638 (Day 1975a; cf. 1961b:169). The map made it reasonable to posit a hypothetical border in the vicinity of Manchester, New Hampshire, between the Western Abenaki area lying to the north and the Massachusett area lying to the south (Day 1975a:384). At least some of the names north of this point were analyzable in Western Abenaki, whereas south of it none were (cf. Day 1978b:148–149).[36]

Champlain Valley Focus

In 1609 Samuel de Champlain traveled up the Richelieu River with a war party of Algonquians from the north and discovered for the French the lake that bears his name. When he asked his guides who occupied the mountainous region

---

[35] In another paper, he attempts to straighten out the confused later history of the Penacooks and their relations with the Iroquois (Day 1984).

[36] Of course, the argument would be strengthened if Day had been able to align the names below Manchester specifically with one or more of the documented Massachusett dialects; this he did not attempt to do.

to the east of the lake, he understood them to say the Iroquois. The observation is sometimes cited in the historical literature to argue that the Iroquois occupied the Green Mountains at this time. By the late seventeenth century, on the other hand, there is abundant documentary evidence that the region between Schaghticoke on the Hudson River and Missisquoi at Swanton, Vermont, was inhabited exclusively by Western Abenakis. The question Day set out to answer was where the eastern boundary of Iroquoia and the western boundary of Abenakia lay at the time of contact (Day 1971a). At the time, the archeology for the area was insufficient to shed much light on the problem, so he turned to oral tradition and place-name analysis as the best alternatives.

As noted earlier, Day used folkloric and linguistic evidence to infer a prior Abenaki claim to Rock Dunder off South Burlington, Vermont, for which both the Mohawks and the Abenakis had a name. In addition to this example, it turns out that there are around 30 "perfectly transparent" Abenaki place-names for points ranging from Whitehall, New York, to the Richelieu River, all but three relating to the eastern shore of the lake or to Isle La Motte and Grand Isle (Day 1971a, 1981b). A few locations have Iroquoian and Abenaki names (Whitehall, Ticonderoga, Rock Dunder, and the Richelieu River), but the names designating points on the western shoreline of the lake and points farther west are predominantly Iroquoian (Lounsbury 1960).[37] The data clearly point to Lake Champlain as being the boundary between the Iroquois and the Abenaki.[38]

Several other Abenaki names are of ethnographic or historical interest. One is the name for Lake Champlain itself: *bitawbágw,* which glosses as 'between-lake' or 'the lake between' (1971a:10, 1981b:para. 4.4). Abenaki speakers interpret this as meaning that the lake formed a boundary between the Iroquois and the Abenaki.[39] Variants of the early name for the Missisquoi River, and the bay at the northeast end of Lake Champlain into which it empties, resolve to *adáli masípsk-woóik* 'the place where it is flint, where it is flinty'; this refers to a chert quarry once used by the Abenakis, and so links the name to a specific locale and cultural activity (1977a:29–30, 1981b:para. 4.9). The Abenakis' name for Swanton, *dag-wáhôganék* 'at the mill', encapsulates a bit of later history. In the mid-eighteenth century, the French built a sawmill at this location that formed an important part of the local economy (1981b:para. 4.12) and, incidentally, gave Day some clues

[37] Day's paper "Abenaki Place-Names in the Champlain Valley" (Day 1981b) appeared in a special issue of *International Journal of American Linguistics* honoring Floyd G. Lounsbury (Vol. 47, No. 2) and was intended to complement Lounsbury's paper "Iroquois Place-Names in the Champlain Valley" (Lounsbury 1960). Lounsbury (1960:27–31) set forth in considerable detail the criteria that should be used in evaluating place-name etymologies, and Day applied them in his own work (1977a:26–27, 1981b:147).

[38] Day remained somewhat noncommittal as to how far south of Vergennes, Vermont, the Abenaki occupation might extend, noting that Mahican territory may have reached that far north (1965b:369–370, 1971a:7–8; cf. 1981b:144).

[39] Another possible meaning of *bitawbágw* discussed by Day is 'double lake', which can be interpreted as referring to the separation of Lake Champlain into two arms at Grand Isle (Day 1981b:153).

that helped him date the "Mots loups" manuscript (cf. 1975c:51, 58–59, 63).[40] The name for the Winooski River, *winóskitégw* 'onion land river', refers to sections of the river valley where wild leeks still grow in abundance (1977a:30, 1981b:para. 4.19).

The Identity of the Saint Francis Indians

Sometime in the mid-1970s, Day conceived of drawing together in a single comprehensive work the various lines of inquiry he had been pursuing during the previous two decades. "The resources for this holistic approach," he noted around 1976, "are now mostly at hand, and the work of the next year should produce a synthesis of history, oral tradition and cultural and linguistic evidence which will . . . explain the complex peopling of the village of Saint Francis . . ." (1977b:4). He dubbed the effort "The Abenaki Identity Project," and it resulted a few years later in the monograph, *The Identity of the Saint Francis Indians* (Day 1981a). He began by taking a backward glance at the problem to which he had devoted so much of his career:

> The problem of Odanak's linguistic and cultural identity was created as soon as the village acquired a mixed population. . . . It underlay my research from the beginning and rather early gave birth to the notion of reconstructing the origins of the new tribe at Odanak from a study of history, the integration of scattered documentary sources, oral tradition, family histories, family dialects, New England place names and other philological fragments. . . . I saw the problem this way,
> "The problem is not, then, that there is no St. Francis culture but that there are seemingly only one culture and one language in a village said to have been made up from ten or a dozen bands. Whose culture and language is it? Or if it is a composite, who contributed what?" My view at the time was, "I think that there is some reason to be optimistic that when an exhaustive and rigorous study has been made of the historical evidence for New England tribal movements, the peopling of Canadian missions, and the genealogies of the specific families at St. Francis, it will be possible to lay down the main boundaries of the language and dialects on a map of New England." (Day 1981a:10–11)

In this monograph Day gives the most exhaustive history of Saint Francis found in any of his work, and he adds to it the results of an extended genealogical inquiry into family names.

It must be said, however, that in the end the study falls somewhat short of the goals laid down so many years earlier. Although the historical record makes it possible to identify "the chief waves of immigration" from New England—and particularly Missisquoi—to Saint Francis, that record remains spotty in many crucial details (p. 62). Among other things, it is insufficient to produce anything like a complete "culture history" (p. 111). The genealogical inquiry also ran into

---

[40] He was also able to extract a number of details about life at the Indian village of Missisquoi near Swanton from the "Mots loups" manuscript (Day 1973b).

problems. The tribal composition of the community before 1768 could not be definitively determined, and even after that date, family lines had become confused because of the effects of "emigration and immigration, intermarriage and [the] lack of male issue" (p. 101). In effect, community members had such mixed ancestries that attempts to link their speech and cultural knowledge to specific founding groups remained elusive, and the genealogical inquiry eventually had to be abandoned (p. 112). For similar reasons, Day found it impossible to reconstruct the aboriginal language map of New England from the kinds of dialect variation he found among contemporary speakers at Saint Francis (pp. 113–116).[41] That he was able to discuss these shortcomings frankly in a work that represents the capstone of his career bears out the integrity of the man, and it is important not to be misled by this frankness into underestimating what he succeeded in accomplishing in the monograph and the work leading up to it.

In particular, he established, as far as the varied sources on which he drew allowed him, the fundamental role of groups in the middle and upper Connecticut River valley (the Sokokis, Penacooks, and Cowasucks), with some increments from the Eastern Abenaki area, in building the Saint Francis community in its early stages. Although it might no longer be possible to reconstruct the finer linguistic and cultural differences among the aboriginal groups of interior New England, whose names were tantalizingly scattered through the historical literature, a good deal of the cultural and linguistic picture could be recaptured if one assumed a fair degree of homogeneity for the area.[42]

Day's Career in Brief

We turn now to some general considerations regarding Day's career and what one might call his intellectual style—his orientation toward the phenomena he attempted to explain—with some final remarks on the man himself. To understand his career fully, one would need to review not only his published work, but his unpublished work and his correspondence as well. The latter materials would undoubtedly shed light on his shift in the 1950s from forestry and soil microbiology to ethnology and linguistics, but Day's published work is also revealing in this regard. Does the shift represent an abrupt departure from his earlier interests, or is it a more or less natural outgrowth from them?

At first glance, the shift would seem to involve a fundamental change in

[41]The details of the differences among Western Abenaki dialects are discussed elsewhere (Day 1985a, 1994b:ix). The differences were minor, and apparently by about 1800 the Saint Francis speech community had become relatively homogeneous.
[42]Day explicitly makes just such an assumption in an elegant summary of Western Abenaki culture that appears as his contribution to Volume 15 of the *Handbook of North American Indians;* the discussion covers in a short space traditional subsistence techniques, clothing and adornment, technology, life cycle, political and social organization, games, cosmogony, myth, and ceremonies (Day 1978b:153–158).

outlook: what could be further from the concerns of the behavioral sciences than a dissertation on the effects of the digestive tract of earthworms on bacteria in the soil? The contrast brings to mind a well-known conundrum involving a famous predecessor, Franz Boas, who changed fields from physics to geography and finally ethnology. Some have understood this as stemming from a profound shift in Boas's *Weltanschauung,* brought on by his trip to Baffinland in 1883, where, it is claimed, his prolonged contact with the Inuit resulted in a kind of conversion experience. However, just as George W. Stocking Jr. argued that this interpretation fails to take into account Boas's firmly grounded interest in geography—and in particular the relationship between humans and the environment[43]—it seems that Day's change of careers is better understood as an evolutionary process rather than a radical shift.

Day had developed a fascination with the native peoples of New England while still in his childhood. He always saw this interest as his "first love," whereas he regarded his commitment to forestry and ecology as his "second love." Throughout his early career he read widely in the ethnological and primary historical source literature of the Northeast. On the other hand, a number of his later papers, whose primary focus is some aspect of Abenaki language, or culture, reflect his interest and training in forest ecology—or, more broadly, his interest in the physical setting in which human cultures develop.[44] The sense of an evolving interest is nowhere more apparent than in his first venture into ethnology and ethnohistory, "The Indian as an Ecological Factor in the Northeastern Forest" (Day 1953). Here he recounts how Algonquians and Iroquoians cleared vast areas of the forest to prepare village sites and cultivable fields, how they were constantly in search of firewood, used fire for hunting, and even altered the vegetation cover by transplanting medicinal and edible plants to different sites. There has been a tendency, he concluded, to neglect the effects of these activities on the part of ecologists, who "may feel that procuring this information is properly an ethnologist's work, but the information is indispensable for understanding the ecological history of the Northeast" (p. 340). The key word is "indispensable." Once Day realized that the history and composition of the forests of the Northeast could not be understood without taking the human factor into account, his definition of forest ecology and its legitimate pursuits had changed forever, and he was on the road to his second career: all of his subsequent publications were ethnological, ethnohistoric, or linguistic in nature. Nevertheless, the other side of the equation—the physical setting in which the cultures

---

[43] George W. Stocking Jr., "From Physics to Ethnology," in his *Race, Culture, and Evolution: Essays in the History of Anthropology* (New York: The Free Press, 1968), pp. 133–160.

[44] This interest was also evident in Day's approach to organizing museum exhibitions after he went to Ottawa. He paid particular attention to the use of natural materials in the manufacture of tools and houses, native hunting and gathering techniques, medical practices, diet, the manufacture of clothing, and the like.

had developed—was never very far from the surface in his research and writing. He once wrote, "The Abenakis are a forest people. They may be studied in the library and in their homes, but they may be understood only in the forest."[45]

Day's study of the Penobscot war bow opens with a paean to the primacy of fact in scientific endeavors:

> A scientist's sole justification as a scientist is his search for fact and truth, and, though truth remain elusive, he must persist in his search for fact. He should insist that only fact is grist for his mill, and, to the extent that his "facts" are uncertain, to that extent, at least, must his hypotheses and general propositions remain doubtful. This is elementary, perhaps trite, yet it will bear restating, since in both anthropology and linguistics the descriptivist handed over authority to the theorist decades ago, and we have no reason to be complacent about the existing data on North American ethnology and linguistics. It cannot be doubted that decades hence North American studies will suffer from the data famine that has been and is being created by this attitude. (Day 1975b:3)

Day sought tirelessly to reduce the "data famine" of the fields in which he worked. At heart he was what he here calls a descriptivist, but one who had by no means relinquished his authority to the theorists. In fact, he tended to be bored by the arcane debates in historiography and linguistics, preferring instead to adopt only as much formal apparatus as would allow him to deal with the problem at hand.

To recall Boas again, Day's stance toward the phenomena he studied was more that of a "cosmographer" than that of a "physicist" or "naturalist." For Boas, the physicist-naturalist regards the phenomena he analyzes strictly in terms of the physical laws to which the phenomena are subject: once the laws have been discovered, the individual facts are no longer of special interest. The cosmographer, on the other hand, "holds to the phenomenon which is the object of his study, may it occupy a high or low rank in the system of physical sciences, and lovingly tries to penetrate into its secrets until every feature is plain and clear. This occupation with the object of his affection affords him a delight not inferior to that which the physicist enjoys in his systematical arrangement of the world."[46] This characterizes quite precisely, I believe, Day's scientific outlook, his attitude toward the problems he sought to penetrate, and the devotion he brought to his work.

Those who knew Day well will remember his quiet modesty, even in the areas in which he was a recognized authority, his intellectual honesty, his unfailing kindness and generosity of spirit, his sense of fairness and detachment in judging

---

[45] From a draft of the preface to the unpublished work *That's the Way It Was: The World of the Western Abenaki* (Day, in preparation).

[46] Franz Boas, "The Study of Geography," *Science* 9:137–141 (1887). The passage cited is from the reprinted version that appears in Boas's *Race, Language and Culture* (New York: The Free Press; London: Collier-MacMillan, 1940), p. 645.

people and situations. They will also remember his sense of humor, which was especially keen when he was assessing the scope and tenacity of human foolishness in institutional settings. Despite his years in Ottawa, he remained at heart a New Englander. He, as much as anyone, has helped us to find and honor New England's native past.

Michael K. Foster
Norwich, Vermont
February 1997

1

The Indian as an Ecological Factor in the Northeastern Forest

This article, published while Day was still a professional forester, reflects his growing interest in the early 1950s in the native peoples of the Northeast. Contrary to the impression left by some historians and popular writers that the Northeast was a vast unbroken tract of primeval forest until white contact, Day shows by a careful sifting of early observer accounts that the Indians' use of fire in their hunting practices and their preparation of village and agricultural sites, as well as their need for firewood and their many other uses of wood, all had a substantial impact on the northeastern forest cover, leaving large areas cleared and subject to later cycles of regrowth. The paper was originally published in *Ecology* 34(2):329–346 (1953).

There is a popular belief that the discoverers of eastern North America found everywhere an unbroken forest of giant trees. This belief has had much support from our popular literature. In the backdrop for *The Landing of the Pilgrim Fathers,* "The woods against a stormy sky their giant branches tossed" (Hemans 1826). America's fireside poet made us aware that, "This is the forest primeval" (Longfellow 1847). It has been said that a squirrel might have gone from Maine to Louisiana by leaping "from one giant tree to the next" (Bear 1951); might have traveled from bough to bough for a thousand miles without seeing a flicker of sunshine on the ground (Adams 1935); might indeed have traveled a squirrel's lifetime without coming down out of the white pines (Peattie 1950).

The vast, virgin forest recurs constantly in the works of Parkman (1909a, 1909b). He pictures for us "one vast, continuous forest . . . the depths of immemorial forests, dim and silent as a cavern." He paints Verrazzano off the New England coast surveying "the shadows and gloom of mighty forests." Between the French and English colonies lay "a broad tract of wilderness, shaggy with primeval woods." There was Maine, a "waste of savage vegetation"; the White Mountains "throned in savage solitude"; the Adirondacks, a "mountain wilderness"; Lake George lying in the "wild charm of untrodden mountains and

This paper is from the Journal Series, New Jersey Agricultural Experiment Station, Rutgers University—the State University of New Jersey, Department of Forestry.

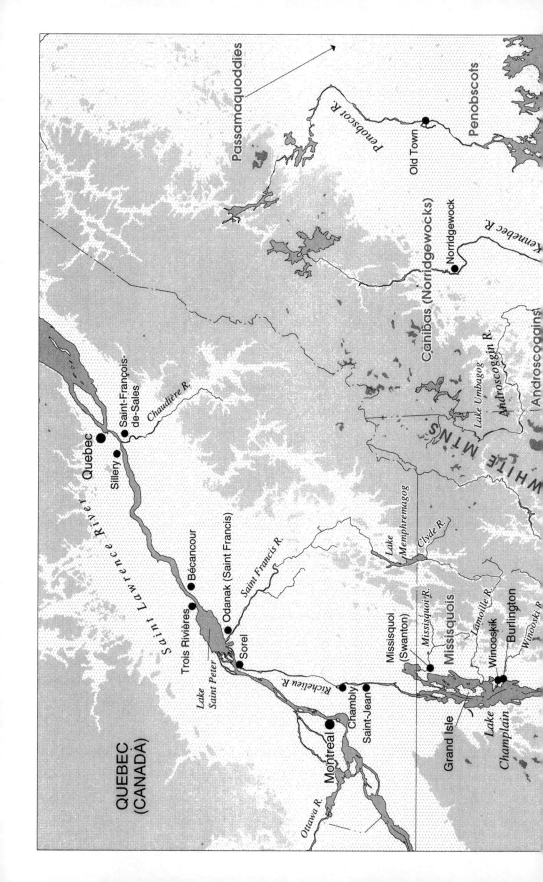

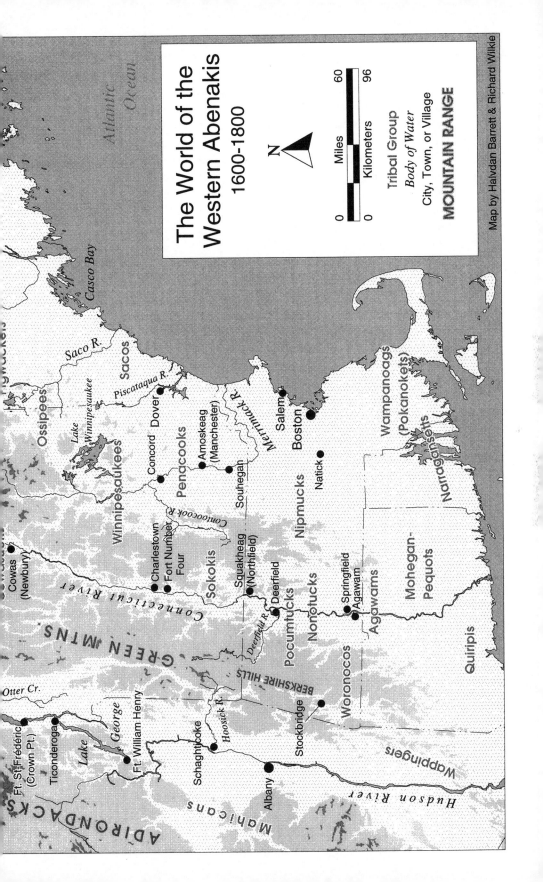

The World of the Western Abenakis
1600–1800

N

| Miles | 0 ___ 60 |
| Kilometers | 0 ___ 96 |

Tribal Group
Body of Water
City, Town, or Village
MOUNTAIN RANGE

Map by Halvdan Barrett & Richard Wilkie

Atlantic Ocean

Casco Bay

Saco R.

Sacos

Piscataqua R.

Ossipees

Lake Winnipesaukee

Winnipesaukees

Concord Dover

Pengcooks

Amoskeag (Manchester)

Souhegan

Merrimack R.

Salem

Boston

Contoocook R.

Natick

Nipmucks

Charlestown
Fort Number Four

Sokokis

Squakheag (Northfield)

Connecticut River

Cowas (Newbury)

Deerfield R.

Deerfield

Pocumtucks

Nonotucks

Springfield
Agawam

Agawams

Mohegan-Pequots

Wampanoags (Pokanokets)

Narragansetts

Quiripis

GREEN MTNS

Otter Cr.

BERKSHIRE HILLS

Woronocos

Woronocos

Wappingers

ADIRONDACKS

Ft. St-Frédéric (Crown Pt.)

Ticonderoga

Lake George

Ft. William Henry

Schaghticoke

Hoosick R.

Stockbridge

Albany

Mahicans

Hudson River

virgin forests." Frontenac's army approached Onondaga "among the dense columns of the primeval forest," and across Pennsylvania "a prodigious forest vegetation . . . wrapped the stern and awful waste in the shadow of the tomb . . . a realm of forests ancient as the world." The Saint Lawrence River rolled through the "vastness of lonely woodlands." Champlain ascended the River Wye in Ontario through "the primeval woods" and the Ottawa River through "ancient wilds, to whose ever verdant antiquity the pyramids are young and Nineveh a mushroom of yesterday."

Lillard (1947) thought the dominant feature of America at the time of discovery was the virgin woods.

Many botanists seem to share the popular belief in an unbroken virgin forest and to assume that human interference with natural succession commenced with white settlement. They appear to overlook or dismiss as unlikely the possibility of significant disturbance by the Indians. The claims of some foresters and ecologists, notably Maxwell (1910), Hawes (1923), Bromley (1935, 1945), and R. Gordon (1940), constitute a challenge to them and call attention to the fact that a fundamental question is still unsettled. Therefore, it seems desirable to examine the evidence further in order to improve our estimate of the Indian as an ecological factor. In this paper, attention will be largely confined to Indian activities in New England, New York, and New Jersey.

Village Clearing

Practically all of the northeastern Indians lived in villages which varied in size and permanence. Establishment of a village involved clearing for home sites and foraging within a considerable radius for the plants and animals necessary to the Indians' way of life—foods, fiber, medicines, wood and bark for utensils, weapons, canoes, and houses and particularly for fuelwood. In short, the woodland Indian drew upon the forest for a great variety of products (Densmore 1928; Speck 1938; Speck and Dexter 1951).

The temporary dwellings of a nomadic family band might be accommodated by a small partially cleared area, while semipermanent villages occupied clearings of considerable magnitude. In the Iroquois country, stockades sometimes enclosed as little as two acres and sometimes were 767 paces in circumference. Land outside the stockade was often cleared and occupied, the entire village site covering as much as 100 or 150 acres (Parker 1920).

Undoubtedly many village sites are still undiscovered, but archeologists have found hundreds in New England, New York, and New Jersey (Parker 1922; Willoughby 1935; Cross 1941–1956). Knowledge of the village sites in an area is clearly fundamental in studying disturbance of the forest.

Fuelwood Cutting

Beyond the village and fields, the Indian women carried on a never-ending search for fuelwood (Lafitau 1724). Although the small dead and down trees, sometimes referred to as "squaw wood," may have been picked up first, it is probable that live standing trees were systematically cut. This is probable because an Indian village used a large amount of firewood and exhaustion of the local supply meant moving the village (R. Williams 1643; C. Mather 1702; Lafitau 1724; Loskiel 1794). So important was firewood in Indian economy that the Narragansetts of Rhode Island thought the English had come to America because they lacked firewood at home (R. Williams 1643).

The prodigal use of firewood by the Iroquois and Delawares, which shocked Loskiel (1794), suggests that they had a more substantial supply than dead and down trees and makes it likely that they would make use of all the wood they could obtain nearby. Lafitau's statement that the longer an Indian village was occupied, the farther the forest receded from it clearly indicates that all trees were cut. Settlers found the site of Boston so clear that they had to go to the islands in the harbor for fuelwood (Bromley 1935).

The Indians knew how to fell trees with stone axes and fire (Sagard-Théodat 1939; Lafitau 1724; Kalm 1937; Waugh 1916). Some doubt may exist concerning the ability of Indian women to clear the primeval forest, but it appears that the men commonly cut the trees and left only the splitting and carrying to the women (Lafitau 1724; Parker 1910), although Indian women themselves were capable axe wielders (Eastman 1902).

Agricultural Clearing

Although considerable dependence was placed upon hunting, fishing, and collecting wild plant foods, the practice of agriculture was widely dispersed over the Northeast.

The northern Algonquians were hunters, but in the early seventeenth century, Champlain found the tribes along the Ottawa River and around Lake Nipissing growing a little maize, an art which they probably learned from the neighboring and friendly Hurons (Hunt 1940). The Montagnais-Naskapi, who even now live by the chase (Speck 1935a), also were growing maize in 1634 (Thwaites 1896–1901). By 1535, the Iroquois had pushed maize culture down the Saint Lawrence valley as far as Quebec (Anon. 1906a). In the next century, they had retreated from this region, and, according to De la Chesnaye's memoir of 1697, the nomadic Algonquians were pointing out to the French colonists young forests arising on former Iroquois village sites (Bailey 1933).

Waugh's (1916) supposition that agriculture was practiced in the Maritime Provinces rests on Verrazzano's rather vague statement that the savages towards "Penobscot Bay and Newfoundland" were "ruder and less agricultural" than those to the southward (Verarzanus 1850). Verrazzano, however, was not attracted by the northern coast of North America, and he does not appear to have examined it in detail. At the mouth of the Saint Lawrence River, Cartier (1906) saw no signs of agriculture and around Chaleur Bay only trees and "wilde corne," which was probably wild rice. Champlain (1922–1936) knew the Souriquois of Nova Scotia and the Etchemins of Sainte Croix and Penobscot Bay as nomadic hunters and fishermen. Eckstorm (1945) called the Etchemins "sea-faring, tide-dwelling Indians, expert canoe-men, hunting principally the porpoise and the larger fishes." Neither Champlain nor J. Smith (1836) found maize fields along the coast northeast of the mouth of the Saco River, nor did Waymouth see any along the lower Saint George River (Rosier 1906).

Champlain learned that maize was being grown in the interior in 1605 and had been grown at the mouth of the Kennebec River until enemy raids made it unprofitable. Its abandonment may have been recent, as Smith observed that along the Kennebec "where the Salvages dwelt there the ground is exceeding fat and fertill." Perhaps as a consequence of this move, the eastern Indians were raiding the coasts of Massachusetts for maize shortly after the arrival of the Pilgrims (Bradford 1908). There are other indications that the Saco River was not always the northeastern limit of agriculture on the coast. The vicinity of Mattawamkeag and Old Town, on the Penobscot River, was cultivated early (Eckstorm 1945), and in 1776, Pownall (1949) recorded that there were "old worn-out clear Fields," extending downriver four or five miles from Old Town.

In southern New Hampshire, the Penacooks apparently shared the semi-agricultural culture of the southern New England tribes (Speck 1928a). Explorers found agriculture generally practiced along the coast from the Saco River southward, and J. Smith (1836) noted enthusiastically that the coast of Massachusetts "shewes you all along large cornefields" and that there were "many Iles all planted with corne." Pring (1906) observed Indian "gardens" on Cape Cod, one an acre in extent.

The many fields, which the first settlers found after the plague had nearly exterminated the tribes around Massachusetts Bay, attested the extent of Indian agriculture in this region. *The Planters Plea* stated that the plague had left "in many places, much cleared ground for tillage" (White 1846). The Reverend Higgeson (1859), a resident of Salem, was more explicit: "I am told that about three miles from us a man may stand on a little hilly place and see divers thousands of acres of ground as good as need be, and not a tree in the same." Although this is hearsay, it is substantially confirmed by the appended letter of the engineer, Graves, who reported "open plains, in some places five hundred acres, some places more, some lesse, not much troublesome for to cleere for the plough to goe in."

In 1602, Edward Winslow and Stephen Hopkins found both sides of the Taunton River "for the most part cleared. Thousands of men have lived here which died in the great plague" (Willoughby 1935). These were the Pokanokets. The populous Narragansetts were also agricultural (R. Williams 1643), as were the Indians of Connecticut (B. Trumbull 1818). Southern Massachusetts was cultivated by the Nipmucks (Pynchon 1856; Speck 1928a) and the Connecticut River valley as far north as Vernon, Vermont, and Hinsdale and Winchester, New Hampshire, by the Pocumtucks (Hurd 1886; Sheldon 1895).

Northern New Hampshire and Vermont were more thinly settled, but some clearing for agriculture took place. The Coos Intervales in the upper Connecticut valley may be cited as an example. The first settlers found them nearly clear as the consequence of intermittent cultivation. Three or four separate clearings took place within historical times, namely, about 1628 by Mahicans from the Hudson valley, possibly again in midcentury by Penacooks, in 1704 by an unidentified band, and after 1725 by the Pequakets (Crockett 1921). The Indian name of the Intervales is striking testimony of its history—*koasuk* 'the place of *little* white pines' (Laurent 1884; Masta 1932).

The New England tribes in general "cultivated large quantities of maize, beans, pumpkins, and tobacco" (Mooney and Thomas 1907), and their clearings were probably responsible for the "many rich and fruitful spots of land . . . without trees or stones, near the banks of great rivers" in the New England which Hubbard (1815) knew.

The earliest observer of western Vermont and the Adirondacks was Champlain, who accompanied a war party down Lake Champlain in 1609. His Algonquian allies told him that the valleys on the Vermont side of Lake Champlain were cultivated by the Iroquois, but the war party did not actually encounter the Iroquois until it reached the vicinity of Ticonderoga. Champlain may have misunderstood his informants, who may have referred to a temporary cultivation by the Iroquois during their retreat from the Saint Lawrence sometime after 1541 (Fenton 1940).

Champlain also thought the Algonquians said that the Adirondack Mountains were thickly populated, but the paucity of archeological remains in this region suggests that the reference may have been to the protohistoric village sites in Jefferson and Fulton Counties. The Iroquois do not seem to have occupied the Adirondacks, although hunting and fishing camp sites are known (Parker 1922). Pownall (1949) could obtain no information about the region, but it is probable that the Indians were less ignorant than unwilling to give information about a favorite beaver-hunting ground.

Historians of New Netherland made frequent allusions to the agriculture of the Hudson River tribes. They mentioned large treeless flats "of seven or eight leagues and less" (Anon. 1909b) and "very fine flats and maize lands" which had "few or no trees" (Anon. 1909c). Henry Hudson bought maize from the Indians below the site of Poughkeepsie, New York (Juet 1909), and near Hudson, New York, he saw a bark storehouse containing "a great quantity of maize and beans" and drying beside the house "enough to load three ships, besides what was growing in the fields" (De Laet 1909). In 1636, the location of several maize fields along the river were noted by De Vries (1909). According to Jogues (1909), the first settlers around Albany used fields which had been cleared and abandoned by the Indians.

In 1626, Long Island, Staten Island, and the land between the Hudson and Hackensack Rivers were occupied by Indians who supported themselves by planting maize. Manhattan had good land on the north side, and on the east side there was a level field of 140 to 160 acres in such condition that it could "be ploughed without much clearing." The good land on the east side of the river above Manhattan "where formerly many people have dwelt" had been abandoned following war with the Wappingers (Rasieres 1909).

It is probable that the first white men on the scene here and elsewhere underestimated the amount of land which had been cleared by the Indians. This is suggested by Van der Donck's (1841) statement that, although there were large meadows in New Netherland, there would be "much more meadow ground" but for its quick reclamation by woods. More than once he was unable to recognize as former Indian cornfields land which had been out of cultivation only 20 years.

The Iroquoian tribes placed great dependence on agriculture (Parker 1910; Waugh 1916). At one time they grew maize, beans, squashes, sunflowers, artichokes, and tobacco, and soon after contact with the white men they were raising many European fruits and vegetables and even hogs. Early observers made numerous references to their large fields and caches of stored produce. In Ontario their fields were so extensive that when the missionary Sagard-Théodat (1939) traveled from village to village, he lost his way in the fields more often than in the woods. Champlain (1922–1936) traversed 60 to 90 miles of this region and called it "a well-cleared country." The peninsula between Lake Huron and Georgian Bay was mostly cleared.

Among the Mohawks of New York State, the unknown author of the journal of 1634 (Anon. 1909a) ate baked pumpkins and observed in some houses more than 300 bushels of stored maize. The military expedition of Prouville de Tracy and Rémy de Courcelle in 1666 destroyed "prodigious quantities of provisions." Cornfields extended for two miles on each side of an Onondaga village near Pompey, New York. In 1696, Frontenac's army spent three days cutting the corn in fields which stretched four to six miles from the Onondaga fort near Jamesville, New York (O'Callaghan 1849–1851).

In 1669, Galinée (1903) visited a Seneca village near Victor, New York, which stood in a clearing six miles in circumference. In 1687, Denonville's expedition destroyed a vast quantity of cached and standing corn at four Seneca villages. His estimate of 1,200,000 bushels may have been exaggerated, but 10 days were required for the work of destruction (O'Callaghan 1849–1851).

Sullivan's expedition into the Iroquois country in 1779 found an agriculture of surprising abundance. Every few miles his army stopped to destroy "a large quantity of corn" and "a great many fruit trees." After two days at Newtown, New York, the army moved on, because it would have taken too long to destroy all the crops there. The town of Genesee was "almost encircled with a clear flat, which extended for a number of miles, covered by the most extensive fields of corn, and every kind of vegetables that can be conceived." Among the Cayuga orchards, which were destroyed, was one of 1,500 fruit trees. Sullivan estimated that his force destroyed corn at 40 villages which "at a moderate computation, must amount to 160,000 bushels, with a vast quantity of vegetables." About the same time, Brodhead's troops were destroying more than 500 acres of cornfields along the Allegheny River and "a great quantity of corn in New Ground" along French Creek (Cook 1887).

After the Iroquois were dispersed, the first settlers and surveyors found in some places recent clearings (R. Brown 1943) and in other places pineries covering older clearings (R. Gordon 1940).

The early Dutch historians considered New Netherland to be all the country between the Delaware and the Connecticut Rivers, so their general statements about the Indians of New Netherland seem to apply to the Indians of New Jersey. They were said to live chiefly on maize, which they had in abundance (Wassenaer 1909; De Laet 1909; De Vries 1909). The Indians encountered near Sandy Hook had a "great store of Maiz" in 1609 (Juet 1909). Rasieres (1909) could learn little about the Indians between the Hackensack and the Delaware Rivers because of the enmity between the tribes, but we know now that the Indians of New Jersey were agricultural even into the eighteenth century (Loskiel 1794; Brinton 1885a).

Evelin's account of "New Albion" in 1648 stated that settlers might obtain from the New Jersey Indians 2,000 barrels of corn (S. Smith 1765). At a later date, settlers found considerable cultivated land along the Delaware River (Lindeström 1925), but it remains for archeology to locate many village sites in this imperfectly known area (Cross 1941–1956).

It appears probable that early writers saw only a small part of the agricultural clearing in the Northeast. Fields were abandoned as they wore out or as the white settlements came close. These abandoned fields grew up to forests. Occasionally expeditions striking at centers of Indian population saw Indian agriculture as it was, as when General Wayne reached the village of the Miamis and their allies in

1792 and found a continuous planting the whole length of the Maumee River from the present site of Fort Wayne to Lake Erie (Mooney and Thomas 1907).

Fire

The Indians of the United States commonly fired the forests and grasslands. Indeed, Hough (1926) regarded fire as a hunting aid used by primitive peoples generally. Information on Indian burning in the western part of the country has been summarized by Stewart (1951). He found numerous reasons for burning: driving game, improving visibility, facilitating travel, driving away reptiles and insects, increasing the supply of grass seeds and berries, and for offense and defense in war. Burning was commonly practiced in the central states (Loskiel 1794; Carver 1796; Michaux 1805; Ashe 1808; "New Yorker" 1835; Gray 1884; Shaler 1884; G. Marsh 1885; McClure 1899; Wislizenus 1912; Blane 1918; Shantz and Zon 1924; Bakeless 1950) and in the Southeast (Maxwell 1910; Swanton 1928).

The earliest travelers observed burning along the coast from Florida to New Hampshire. At Roanoke, Drake's chronicler noted that fires "are very ordinary all alongst this coast, even from the Cape of *Florida* hither" (Biggs 1893); Verrazzano saw "verie great fiers" along the Carolina coast in 1524 (Verarzanus 1850); and at Roanoke, White's (1906) expedition, following a smoke, found no sign of man. At another fire, they found only "grasse and sundry rotten trees burning." Percy (1906) saw fires set by Indians on the south side of Chesapeake Bay. This may well be the explanation of the forest of "trees without underwood, and not standing so close but they may anywhere be rode through" which "An American" (1939) observed in Virginia and Maryland. Fire-hunting was a trait shared by the Carolina, Virginia, and Potomac Indians (Flannery 1939), and J. Smith (1906) has left us a good account of its use by the Virginia Indians. Inland, fires were common east of the mountains, and more than 1,000 square miles of burned, treeless land in the Shenandoah valley stretched northward into Pennsylvania (Maxwell 1910; Bakeless 1950).

Hudson's crew saw "a great Fire" on the shore somewhere south of Sandy Hook (Juet 1909). In 1632, De Vries (1909) smelled smoke from fires, set by the New Jersey Indians to improve their autumn hunting, even before he could see land. S. Smith (1765) recorded the practice of fire-hunting in New Jersey, and Budd (1865) wrote of New Jersey: "The *Trees* grow but thin in most places, and very little Under-wood." Standing alone, this statement would permit only surmise as to the cause of these open woods, but Denton (1845) and Lindeström (1925) link them to the annual burnings by the Indians. Denton reported that between the Raritan and the Delaware Rivers, there were "but a few Indians," "stately Oaks" with "broad-branched-tops" and "grass as high as a mans middle, that serves for no other end except to maintain the Elk and Deer, . . . then to be burnt every spring to make way for new." Lindeström noted the abundance of thin, loosely-rooted high grass and the trees which "stand far apart, as if they were planted" and observed the firing of the dry grass to open the spring hunt. The Lenape Indians continued to burn the woods deliberately in the spring and fall and accidentally at other times after they had left New Jersey (Loskiel 1794). The New Jersey woods were still being burned in 1748, although Kalm's (1937) reference was probably to fires set by leaf-burning white settlers. Several observers have attributed the dominance of pines in southern New Jersey and the dwarfed growth of the "Plains" to these fires (Pinchot 1899; Stone 1911; Lutz 1934; Moore 1939).

The journals of early observers give us a rather clear picture of Indian burning along the coast of southern New England. In 1524, Verrazzano penetrated 15 to 18 miles inland from Narragansett Bay and observed "open plains twenty-five or thirty leagues in extent, entirely free from trees or other hindrances" and forests which "might all be traversed by an army ever so numerous" (Verarzanus 1850).

In 1602, Brereton (1906) remarked that the trees on Cuttyhunk drew "distinct and apart . . . upon greene grassie ground." The next year the Indians set fire to the woods on Cape Cod where Martin Pring (1906) was cutting a cargo of sassafras "which we did behold to burne for a mile space." In the early days of the Plymouth colony, two men, becoming lost, wandered onto a "place where the Savages had burnt the space of five miles in length" (Anon. 1906c).

Two early witnesses of burning in the Massachusetts Bay area wrote at some length:

> The Salvages are accustomed, to set fire of the Country in all places where they come; and to burne it, twize a yeare, vize at the Springe, and the fall of the leafe. The reason that mooves them to doe so, is because it would other wise be so overgrowne with underweedes, that it would be all a copice wood, and the people would not be able in any wise to passe through the Country out of a beaten path . . . for this custome hath bin continued from the beginninge. . . . For when the fire is once kindled, it dilates and spreads it selfe as well against, as with the winde; burning continually night and day, untill a shower of raine falls to quench it. And this custome of firing the Country is the meanes to make it passable, and by the meanes the trees growe here, and there as in our parks. (Morton 1838)

> And whereas it is generally conceived, that the woods grow so thicke, that there is no more cleare ground than is hewed out by labour of man; it is nothing so; in many places, divers Acres being cleare, so that one may ride a hunting in most places of the land, if he will venture himselfe for being lost: there is no underwood saving in swamps and low grounds that are wet . . . for it being the custom of the *Indians* to burne the wood in *November,* when the grasse is withered, and leaves dryed, it consumes all the underwood, and rubbish, which otherwise would over grow the Country, making it unpassable, and spoil their much affected hunting;

so that by this means in those places where the *Indians* inhabit, there is scarce a
bush or bramble, or any combersome underwood to bee seene in the more cham-
pion ground. . . . In some places where the *Indians* dyed of the Plague some foure-
teene yeares agoe, is much underwood, as in the mid way betwixt *Wessaguscus* and
Plimouth, because it hath not been burned. (Wood 1865)

In the spring of 1633, the Plymouth colony went to work clearing the woods
for cornfields, "the Lord having mitigated their labours by the Indians frequent
fiering of the woods, (that they may not be hindered in hunting Venson, and
Beares in the Winter season) which makes them thin of Timber in many places,
like our Parkes in England" (E. Johnson 1910).

We can obtain a glimpse of the Indians' attitude from Roger Williams's (1936)
theological arguments with his Narragansett friends:

When I have argued with them about their Fire-God: can it say they be but this
fire must be a God, or Divine Power, that out of a stone will arise in a Sparke . . . if
a spark fall into the drie wood, burns up the Country, (though this burning of the
Wood to them they count a benefit, both for destroying of vermin, and keeping
downe the Weeds and thickets?).

It is conjectural how far up the coast the practice of burning the woods
extended. The writer has found no early witnesses of actual fires north of Massachusetts Bay, but there are descriptions of the kind of forest which elsewhere
early writers attributed to fires. In 1607, Captain Gilbert described the trees at a
point on the Maine coast—probably Point Elizabeth south of Casco Bay. They
were "the most p^t of them ocke and wallnutt growinge a greatt space assoonder
on from the other as our parks in Ingland and no thickett growing under them"
(Anon. 1906b). Richmond Island nearby had "fine oaks and nut trees with
cleared land and abundance of vines which in their season bear fine grapes"
(Champlain 1922–1936). Along St. George's River, and inland from it, Waymouth found

good ground, pleasant and fertile, fit for pasture, for the space of some three miles,
having but little wood, and that Oke like stands left in our pastures in England. . . .
And surely it did all resemble a stately Park, wherein appeare some old trees with
high withered tops, and other flourishing with living greene boughs . . . the wood
in most places, especially on the East side, very thinne, chiefly oke and some small
young birch. (Rosier 1906)

It seems probable that the use of fire accompanied agriculture and fixed
habitations as far north as the mouth of the Saco River. If we assume that the fires
used to clear fields for planting occasionally escaped, we have to look for its
influence up the valleys of the principal Maine rivers and as far northeastward as
the Penobscot.

Historians and ecologists have assigned considerable importance to Indian
fires along the southern New England coast (B. Trumbull 1818; Burnaby 1904;

Dwight 1821; De Forest 1851; Hawes 1923; Bromley 1935, 1945; Walcott 1936; Colby 1941; Byers 1946). They are in general agreement that fires modified the species composition of upland forests and created extensive treeless or brush-free areas.

The outstanding dissent is that of Raup (1937). He believed that the early settlers, because of their European background, could not conceive of "open park-like woods growing naturally" and therefore assumed that the Indians had created them by fire. Actually, he pointed out, "Open, park-like woods have been, from time immemorial, characteristic of vast areas in North America. Almost anywhere one chooses to look on the periphery of the great arid plains of the interior of the continent he sees this savannah or park-land extensively developed." Raup cited no evidence for his assumption that the early settlers attributed the open woods to Indian fires because of an inability to imagine naturally open woods. Of the authorities cited in this paper, De Vries, Denton, Lindeström, Morton, Wood, Johnson, Williams, Van der Donck, and Kalm were in a position to see both the fires and their effect.

The existence of open woods on the periphery of the arid plains of the interior is not evidence for the existence of similar stands in the well-watered Northeast. There is, in fact, some question about how much of the open forest in central United States is natural and how much is the result of fire. There are many references to the creation first of open woods and finally of grassland by repeated fires and to thickets and woods which sprang up when burning was discontinued. A review of these references is beyond the scope of this paper, but attention may be called to Michaux (1805), who concluded that fire caused the "spacious meadows in Kentucky and Tennessea" and probably the plains of "Upper Louisiana and New Mexico"; to Shaler (1884), who believed that fire deforested the "prairie lands in Indiana and Illinois, and perhaps of more westerly regions"; and to Stewart (1951), who has suggested that even the tall-grass prairies may have been maintained by fires since early postglacial times.

Information about Indian burning and other Indian activities is harder to obtain for the interior of New England than for the coastal region because hostilities postponed settlement of the interior. Dwight (1821) asserted that the oak, chestnut, and pitch pine land in New England had probably been burned for over a thousand years, but his authority is not apparent. He may have been influenced by the oak openings which he had seen in western New York. Hawes (1923) thought that the effect of Indian fire was slight except in the coastal region. Bromley (1935), using the Indian population figures of Gookin (1792) quoted by Dwight, concluded that there were enough Indians in southern New England to burn over annually most of the country that was dry enough to burn. He thought this comprised "most of the southern New England region, except the Berkshire, Taconic and possibly the hilly region of North Central Massachusetts." Raup (1937) considered inconceivable a wholesale conflagration in Massachusetts, Rhode Island, Connecticut, and southern New York every year, reasoning that it would destroy the undergrowth, herbaceous species, and animal life if not the forest itself. He cited Whitney's history of Worcester County, Massachusetts, which "makes very few references to fire of any kind." Byers (1946) pointed out that Whitney's book was published 100 years after the country was settled and 50 years after the passing of a law forbidding burning. Worcester County, moreover, embraced the hilly region in which Bromley had doubted the influence of Indian fires. Other histories of interior Massachusetts towns mention Indian burning and the openness of the country. Temple's (Byers 1946) history of Brookfield stated that burning made travel by horseback feasible all through the district and that "From the top of Coy's hill cattle could be seen for a distance of three miles, and deer and wild turkeys a mile away." According to Judd (Byers 1946), the first settlers of Northampton, Hadley, and Hatfield found plenty of lowland ready for plowing and mowing and rather open home-sites on higher ground. "In Philip's war and in later years companies of horsemen and larger bodies of foot soldiers seem to have penetrated the woods without difficulty in every direction. . . . When some of the people of Northampton petitioned for a plantation at Squaheag (Northfield) in 1671, they stated that the Indians had deserted the place, and that for want of inhabitants to burn the meadows and woods, the underwood had increased." Annoyance with this situation may have given rise to the laws requiring "everyman to work one day a year clearing brush from the highway." It seems that there is no evidence in the early authorities for the wholesale annual conflagration of southern New England which Raup found unacceptable but only burning "in those places where the *Indians* inhabit" (Wood 1865) and outside of swamps. Frequently the fires appear to have resembled the light prescribed burns now used in some forest types (Little and Moore 1945, 1949), and there is no question about the ability of such fires to modify species composition and to create a parklike stand without destroying the herbaceous layer and the animal life. It was reported by De Vries (1909) that, in spite of burnings along the New Jersey coast, "the hills rise up full of pinetrees, which would serve as masts for ships."

In 1760, Burnaby (1904) was concerned about the protection of New Hampshire white pines from "that very destructive practice, taken from the Indians, of fire-hunting." Pierce's history of Winchester, New Hampshire (Hurd 1886), stated that prior to 1720 the Squakheags cleared land by repeated fires and "kept quite large areas treeless for the purposes of cultivation." Recently Bromley (1945) has pieced together the ecological history of the former Hatchet Lake Reservation in the towns of Southbridge, Massachusetts, and Woodstock, Connecticut, "the last stand of Indian influence that had once been felt throughout southern New England." Bradford family tradition supplied a description of the area as it was about 1831 when the reservation was abandoned: "the vegetation of this section was characterized by an open forest of oak, chestnut, and hickory on the slopes; white pine and hemlock in the swamps; and bushy plains and blueberry barrens on the overly drained acid-soil plateaus and hilltops." After Indian influence ceased, pine appeared on the upland.

The valleys of the Hudson River and upper Lake Champlain must be included in the area affected by Indian burnings. Van der Donck (1841) has left us a clear statement that the Indians of New Netherland regularly burned the woods in the fall and again in the spring to make hunting easier, to improve the growth of grass, and to surround game. He saw many such "bush burnings" scorch the bark of hardwoods without injuring them and go to the top of thick pine stands, especially in Rensselaerswyck about Fort Orange. Pownall's (1949) description of the pitch pine stand between Albany and Schenectady, which he saw between 1753 and 1759, strongly suggests a fire history. In 1749, Kalm attributed decrease in the extent of fir (spruce?) forests in the vicinity of Crown Point to "the numerous fires which happen every year in the woods, through the carelessness of the Indians, who frequently make great fires when they are hunting, which spread over the fir woods when everything is dry" (Kalm 1937).

Fire was used by the Iroquois of central New York for hunting (Morgan 1901), for improving the growth of grass (Loskiel 1794), and for clearing fields (Parker 1910; Waugh 1916). Although there appear to be few early accounts of burning by the Iroquois, it is hard to explain in any other way the grasslands and open oak forests reported by Galinée (1903). Between Lake Ontario and the Seneca village near Victor, New York, the country was "for the most part beautiful, broad meadows, on which the grass is as tall as myself. In the spots where there are woods, these are oak plains, so open that one could easily run through them on horseback." Galinée also was told that this sort of country extended eastward 300 miles and to the west and south an unknown distance, but it is very uncertain what his Iroquois informants meant to tell him. His Dutch interpreter knew Iroquois perfectly but French very little and later proved uncooperative. Brown (1943) believes that the Iroquois made large tracts of land treeless by their practice of firing the forest beyond their villages. This seems to be fully justified inasmuch as a number of travelers observed the "oak openings" of western New York about 25 years after the dispersal of the Iroquois. The appearance of openings near Batavia, New York, in 1805 was described by Bigelow (1876):

> Hundreds of acres may be seen together, on which there is scarce a single tree, there being at most but an oak or a poplar or two, scattered at great distances. The earth here is covered with small willow bushes, brakes, butterfly plant . . . wild grass and strawberry vines, with very young trees not more than knee-high. In many of these open grounds, a man may be seen at a distance of two miles. There are patches of trees interspersed among these open grounds. They are of the same

kind as are to be met with in the neighboring country, and are of various extent. . . . Various conjectures are indulged as to the scarcity of trees; but the most
probable is that it has been occasioned by the Indians repeatedly firing whatever
would burn here. . . . What serves to confirm this opinion is the frequent appearance of charcoal and burnt sticks, and the abundance of young trees which are
now shooting up. Wherever groves of trees are yet standing, it may be seen that
they were probably protected by the interposition of a stream of water, or by the
dampness of the soil where they grow.

Sutcliff (1812) saw these areas in 1804–1806 and thought that the Indians
might have taken advantage of blowdowns and kept them clear by burning.
Dwight (1821) saw them about the same time and agreed that fire was the
probable cause. The marks of fire could be seen on older trees, and young trees
were then springing up. At first, settlers thought the oak plains were inferior to
adjacent maple land, but when sowed to wheat they produced more. R. B.
Gordon (1940) has called attention to a modern example—a high terrace between Quaker Bridge and Onoville, New York, which according to the earliest
surveyor's report, bore a pure stand of white pine, probably growing on an
abandoned Indian cornfield. Repeated fires by reservation Indians have since
reduced it to a low growth of scrubby oaks and hickories.

Evidence for the deliberate use of fire by the Indians in northern New England
and the Adirondacks seems to be lacking. It is noteworthy that Perrot (1911)
described the use of fire for hunting buffalo on the prairies but does not mention
its use for hunting moose and caribou in the North. Flannery (1939) thought
fire-hunting was "not practical in inflammable forest country like the coniferous
North," although we have seen that it was practiced in other inflammable forest
regions. The usual incentives for burning, however, were lacking in northern
New England and the Adirondacks: agriculture was less practiced; summer travel
was by canoe rather than overland; winter travel by snowshoes or on the ice was
not hindered by underbrush; and deer hunting took the form of stalking or still-
hunting rather than driving (Speck 1940). Only a few weeks after Kalm (1937)
had described Indian burning at Crown Point, he noted that the Indians at the
northern end of Lake Champlain were careful in their use of fire:

> The natives usually make a fire during the night, both summer and winter,
> when they camp in the woods. One would think that as a result there would be
> many forest fires during the summer, but I was given to understand that although
> at times fires do start during the summer, it seldom happens, for the natives them-
> selves are very careful to put out the fires wherever they have made them, inasmuch
> as it serves their own interest. If a fire should break out and destroy the forest and
> the vegetation, the roe deer would flee from this region with the result that their
> hunting would be much less successful.

Early descriptions of this region placed more stress on the thickness of the
woods than on openings. For example, Josselyn (1672) called the country north

of the White Mountains "daunting terrible, being full of rocky hills, as thick as molehills in a meadow, and clothed with infinite thick woods." Irving (1934) recorded that, while returning from New York's Black River country, "We were a great part of the time passing through thick woods the underwood being so thick as to prevent our seeing to any extent." Still it is hardly to be doubted that even in northern New England and northern New York, the pyric factor was present in the form of an occasional escaped camp fire and of lightning.

Hunting Controls

The influence of the biotic factor on plants has been clearly stated (Daubenmire 1947). The existence, if not the details, of a dynamic plant-animal interrelationship is well known, but the influence which the Indians exerted indirectly upon forest composition through their hunting activities has gone largely unnoted. The writings of anthropologists (Speck 1914, 1931, 1938; Speck and Eiseley 1939; Cooper 1939, 1946; Hallowell 1949; Speck and Dexter 1951) give us considerable insight into the thoroughness of Indian control over animal population in portions of the northeastern woodland. Tribal land was divided into family hunting territories with definite boundaries. The proprietors of each territory knew intimately the plant and animal inventory therein, harvested the supply carefully with rituals of atonement and thanksgiving, and rotated their activities in such a way as to conserve the supply. We can hardly escape the conclusion that they maintained, as well as they were able, a balance favorable to their economy and that this was a different balance from that which would have obtained in an unpopulated country. No one seems to have attempted an evaluation of this factor on plant succession. In Bromley's (1945) observation that Indian burning in Massachusetts increased the food supply for heath hen, passenger pigeon, wild turkey and deer, the effect of animals is clearly secondary.

Favoring Food and Medicinal Plants

The Indian practice of favoring nut trees and other food plants was probably responsible for minor changes in the original forest. Bromley (1945) thought woods were burned partly for this purpose. Because nut tree stands on village sites are usually even aged, Baker (1950) advanced the theory that they originated when village establishment suddenly decimated the rodent population that planted the nuts. However, there appears to be an association of American chestnut, *Castanea dentata* (Marsh.) Borkh., groves and Indian village sites in lower Ontario, and W. Jury (personal communication, 1952) is inclined to the opinion that the trees were planted by the Indians. The Iroquois of New York planted the Canada plum, *Prunus nigra* Ait., and possibly Kentucky coffee tree,

Gymnocladus dioicus (L.) K. Koch, since it is most often found near village sites (Hedrick 1933).

Plants used by Indians for medicinal purposes may owe their existence in many localities to the transplanting hand of an Indian herbalist (Fenton 1942). Groundnut, *Apios tuberosa* Moench, and leek, *Allium tricoccum* Ait., were also cultivated (Hedrick 1933).

Evaluating the Influence of Indian Activities

We must conclude from the foregoing that the Indians of the Northeast cleared land for villages and fields, cut fuelwood and set fires beyond these clearings, exercised a wide indirect influence on vegetation through their hunting, and may have favored or even transplanted food and medicinal plants. These facts alone, however, are not very helpful in evaluating the extent and intensity of Indian influence in the Northeast or in reconstructing the history of a particular area. One needs rather full knowledge of four other factors which will be merely outlined in this paper—the duration of Indian occupation, the population density, population concentration and movements, and the local pattern of settlement or preferably the location of all village sites.

The peopling of North America began perhaps 25,000 years ago, but it did not take place uniformly and was not completed until rather late (Gladwin 1947). The age of archeological finds in the West has been placed at 6,000 to 10,000 years by radioactive carbon (Bell 1951). This kind of evidence does not seem to be available yet for the Northeast, but occupation of New England, New York, and New Jersey by a pre-Algonquian people began in very remote times (Parker 1922; Willoughby 1935). The entrance of the historic Algonquians and Iroquois into the Northeast has not been dated satisfactorily, but the Indians found in "Vinland" by the Norsemen about A.D. 1000 bore some resemblance to Algonquians (Haugen 1942). Indian traditions agree that the land had been occupied for generations before the arrival of the white men (Hale 1883; Brinton 1885a; Speck 1928a).

We shall never know the population of the northeastern tribes in the sixteenth century, because the white man's acquaintance with them was preceded by his diseases and his disruption of the primitive economic patterns (Ruttenber 1872; Ashburn 1947; Hunt 1940). Early statistics are fragmentary; they contain much hearsay evidence. It may be suspected that they were sometimes colored by the motives of their reporters (Gallatin 1836; Bancroft 1885). Often the observers suffered from language difficulties with their Indian informants and from confusion in tribal nomenclature. J. Smith (1836), for example, admitted that he wrote not fully but "as I gathered from the niggardly relations in a broken language to my understanding."

Indian populations were often reported only as numbers of fighting-men. As hostility was almost continuous along the border, this practice is understandable, but it is another source of error. The fighting-men were variously estimated as one-third, one-fourth, one-fifth, one-sixth, and one-ninth of the total popula-tion (Lahontan 1905; B. Trumbull 1818; Dwight 1821; Tyron in O'Callaghan 1849–1851; Beauchamp 1892; Thwaites 1896–1901 [*Relation of 1657–1658*]; Lloyd in Morgan 1901; Crockett 1921; R. Brown 1943). This is not the place to survey the rather extensive literature dealing with Indian numbers. The most complete enumeration is that of Mooney (1928), but it was frankly tentative and some errors are apparent. Ecologists may feel that procuring this information is properly an ethnologist's work, but the information is indispensable for under-standing the ecological history of the Northeast or specific portions thereof.

Although family groups sometimes lived apart, the northeastern Indian popu-lation characteristically congregated in villages which were moved seasonally or at intervals of several years. Even the nomads of Labrador gathered in villages in the summer (Speck 1935a). In northern New England, the Abenakis seem to have lived in villages part of the year (Speck 1940), while in southern New England, New York, and New Jersey a more agricultural population lived in villages of some permanence.

The villages of the Abenakis went through an annual cycle of migration—southward to seashore camps for the summer, northward to deep woods hunting camps in the fall and winter, returning to villages along the rivers for late fall feasting and spring fishing and planting. Apparently the seacoast and interior tribes of Connecticut made seasonal visits to each other's locations, even ex-changing residences altogether (De Forest 1851). The Lenape had a similar pat-tern of movement between seashore and interior in New Jersey (Philower n.d.).

Even the villages of agricultural tribes were moved at intervals as the soil declined in fertility; as the local supply of firewood became exhausted; or as weed infestation of fields, scarcity of game, or trash and vermin made the site unin-habitable (C. Mather 1702; Lafitau 1724; Loskiel 1794; Beauchamp 1892, 1905; Parkman 1909a; Ganong in Champlain 1922–1936; MacLeod 1936; Fenton 1940; R. Brown 1943). Other moves were dictated by military consider-ations (Champlain 1922–1936; Fenton 1940).

Lafitau (1724) reported the frequency of these moves vaguely as "after a certain number of years" and Loskiel (1794) as "frequently." Other estimates agree fairly well. Champlain (1922–1936) judged them to take place every 10, 20, or 30 years; Beauchamp (1905) every 10 or 15 years; and Fenton (1940) every 10 years and "about twice in a generation." These estimates are confirmed by the known locations in the village of Onondaga, which was near the present Syracuse, New York. As the federal capital of the Five Nations, who were feared and courted by both France and England for over a century, Onondaga was often visited by missionaries, travelers, hostile expeditions, and political emissaries. It appears from their accounts that Onondaga occupied at least nine different sites between 1610 and 1780 (Hewitt 1928).

The tendency of the Indian population to congregate in villages and to migrate had a direct bearing upon its effectiveness as a disturber of the primal scene. It is clear that the village habit localized and intensified disturbances, while seasonal migrations and periodic relocating of villages widened their influence. It should be recognized, however, that these movements were not random. Seasonal migrations followed much the same course each year, and there was a tendency for desirable village sites to be reoccupied by the same tribe or by their conquerors.

There is no substitute for a complete knowledge of the archeology of an area in determining where Indian influence may have been operative, but our tentative conclusions may be improved by knowing the historic locations of the Indian population and the kinds of sites which were usually chosen for villages and fields. It is natural to assume that most villages were located along streams and bodies of water because of the importance of fish food and the fertility of alluvial soil. Indeed, Marsh (1885) thought these were the only village sites. Islands and land partly enclosed by stream confluences and meanders were sometimes chosen for defensive reasons. Defensive needs, however, often dictated hilltop locations. This was characteristic of prehistoric and protohistoric Iroquois villages (Fenton 1940) and probably of others. Kellogg found that village sites in the Lake Champlain valley were often located "at a distance from any even moderately large body of water" (Crockett 1921).

While looking into the question of Indian disturbance, the writer has not emphasized the existence of large tracts of undisturbed forest. Their existence is generally accepted (Champlain 1922–1936; J. Smith 1836; Wood 1865; Josselyn 1672, 1833; Pownall 1949; Strachey 1849; Shaler 1884; Maxwell 1910; Hawes 1923; Willoughby 1935; Byers 1946; Bakeless 1950), although, as R. Gordon (1940) pointed out, it would be difficult to prove primeval status absolutely in any particular case. In fact, their existence and extent may have been accepted too readily. For example, when Hawes asserted that "while the Indian fires may have affected the forests near the coast, there were undoubtedly great stretches of virgin forests unbroken except by the occasional river meadows," this may have been true, but we should not assume that it was true for a particular locality without a careful study of local archeology and history.

A good case in point is Vermont, which is customarily treated as having had no Indian population worth mentioning. Champlain thought that the Vermont shore of Lake Champlain was inhabited in 1609, but subsequent events indicate that he was probably mistaken. His informants may have been referring to recent transient occupation by the Iroquois. During the French and Indian wars, Vermont's position made it a no man's land. Gallatin (1836) stated, "There do not appear to have been any tribes of any consequence in the northern part of New Hampshire, or in the State of Vermont." Ray (1843) asserted, "We know, indeed, that Vermont was wholly without aboriginal inhabitants." Gookin's (1792) editor commented that, "The Indians were never numerous in Vermont." Bancroft (1885) wrote, "Vermont and northwestern Massachusetts and much of New Hampshire were solitudes." Palfrey (1882) ignored Vermont in his enumeration of the New England Indians, apparently following Gallatin. Parkman (1909a) claimed that Vermont "had no human tenants but the roving hunter or prowling warrior." Willoughby (1935) agreed: "There seem to have been but few Indians in Vermont" at about the beginning of the seventeenth century. In Van de Water's (1941) appraisal, there was an unbroken forest, virginal and empty, between Lake Champlain and the Connecticut River.

It would seem that here if anywhere the original forest should be free of anthropic influence. An ecologist in a hurry might so assume and in so doing would make a serious mistake. Crockett (1921) brought to light the little-known fact that Indians from southern New England and from Maine occupied parts of Vermont following their defeats in 1676 and 1680. The French maintained missions among them on Otter Creek and on the Winooski and Missisquoi Rivers until about 1760. There were permanent Squakheag and Missiassik settlements in the extreme southeastern and northwestern corners of the state, respectively, and there were intermittent settlements along the upper Connecticut River. The Mahicans repaired annually to the Walloomsac and Battenkill valleys. The Caughnawagas, after locating on the Saint Lawrence River, hunted and trapped for decades west of the Green Mountains. After listing evidence of occupation in 29 Vermont townships, Crockett concluded that such evidence had doubtless been found in every township in Vermont. This should make the ecologist wary of supposedly uninhabited regions.

Summary

The northeastern United States was occupied from remote times by an Indian population whose size has not been—and perhaps can never be—determined accurately. Most of this population lived in villages. These Indians created sizeable clearings for their villages and fields and probably expanded the clearings as they foraged incessantly for firewood and other necessary materials. Over much of the region, they set fire to the woods to improve traveling and visibility; to drive or enclose game; and to destroy "vermin." They probably exercised some influence on the forest through their control over the animals they hunted and through planting food and medicinal plants. It is certain that their activities destroyed the forest in some places, and it is hardly doubted that they modified it over much larger areas. Seasonal migrations and the periodic relocating of villages widened the range of Indian influence, which extended into unexpected localities and supposedly uninhabited regions.

We must conclude that an area which was wooded when first seen by white men was not necessarily primeval; that an area for which there is no record of cutting is not necessarily virgin; and that a knowledge of local archeology and history should be part of the ecologist's equipment.

2

Dartmouth and Saint Francis

Beginning with the first arrivals in 1774, Saint Francis Indians from Quebec made up the majority of the native people attending Dartmouth College for the next 80 years. In this paper written for a popular audience, Day outlines a problem that was to occupy him for the rest of his career. Saint Francis had been the home of refugees fleeing from settlements in interior New England after the devastating colonial wars and epidemics of the seventeenth and eighteenth centuries, and it was to their twentieth-century descendants that Day turned in his efforts to reconstruct the cultural and political history of native New England. The paper was originally published in *Dartmouth Alumni Magazine* 52(November):28–30 (1959).

Pleasantly situated on the high east bank of the Saint Francis River in Quebec, about six miles from the point where it mingles its waters with the broader waters of Lake Saint Peter, is an Indian village whose history has been more than ordinarily intertwined with that of Dartmouth College. This is the village of Saint Francis, known to its inhabitants, and for the past 43 years to the Bureau de Poste, as *Odanak* 'at the village'. This is the home of the famous—or infamous, depending upon the point of view—Saint Francis Indians who figured so importantly in New England history.

Here live the descendants of the original inhabitants of the northern and central New England States—a region in which the Indian population today is so negligible that a "real Indian" is a curiosity. Here live the descendants of many tribes whose supposed complete disappearance from the face of the earth was chronicled with a romantic sigh by local historians in the last century, Indians whose family names are written large in frontier history—Taxus, Wawa, Gill, Wazomimet, Capino, and others.

From this village came the war parties which raided the New England frontier and warriors who ambushed Braddock; from it came Hannah Dustin's captors and the attackers of Fort Number Four, now Charlestown, New Hampshire. This is the village where John Stark was captive and which was burned by Rogers's Rangers. And oddly enough, this is the village which provided one of Eleazar Wheelock's strongest motives for locating his Indian school at Hanover.

In 1768, Wheelock was looking for a new location. His agents, the Reverend Ebenezer Cleaveland and John Wright, reported that Haverhill and Orford, New Hampshire, were closer to the Six Nations than was the old location at Lebanon,

Connecticut, and were about 60 miles from the Saint Francis Indians on the Saint Lawrence River. About this time, Wheelock lost both his Six Nations pupils and the assistance of Sir William Johnson, Superintendent of Indian Affairs with the Six Nations. Although he tried until 1772 to regain this field, it can hardly be doubted that the Canadian Indians took on increased importance in his plan after this event. This supposition is confirmed by the fact that the parties which he sent out in 1772 and 1773 to recruit students went directly to the Canadian villages. They surely discovered the hard fact that Saint Francis was some 225 miles by canoe route from Hanover and even farther by the pioneer roads across Vermont to Montreal and thence down the Saint Lawrence, but the discovery came too late to influence the location of the college. Such a recruiting expedition by Wheelock himself and by Levi Frisbie in 1773 was the beginning of relations between Dartmouth and Saint Francis.

One might well wonder why Saint Francis figured so importantly in Wheelock's plans—why indeed he thought he could obtain candidates for the Congregational ministry from that tribe. Saint Francis was the Catholic mission of Saint-François-de-Sales. In 1705 it had become the new home of the Abenakis of the Kennebec, who had been converted by Father Druillettes and gone voluntarily to settle in missions at Sillery and on the Chaudière. These were the Abenakis whom the Jesuits extolled for their native mildness, their exemplary piety, and whom Canadian historians lauded for their loyalty and military qualities in the service of New France. These were the model converts whose conversion consoled the Fathers for the destruction of the Huron Nation by the Iroquois and the debauching of the Algonquins of Three Rivers by the fur traders. Their spiritual needs were being attended in 1773 by two Jesuits, Fathers Germain and Maquet, and the destruction of their village by New Hampshire men only 14 years before must have been fresh in their memories. It is not readily apparent why Wheelock chose it for his chief mission field. Did he think the village still contained some pagans, or did he plan to win converts away from the Jesuits?

Actually, the situation at Saint Francis was favorable to Wheelock, but it is not clear whether he or his informants had intelligence of this or were merely fortunate. For one thing, the head chief was Joseph-Louis Gill, a son of English captives, whose American sympathies are a matter of record; and the four little boys who returned with Wheelock were all named Gill. For another thing, the Saint Francis Indians were a tribe of mixed origins, but how this fact operated in Wheelock's favor cannot be so quickly told.

Saint Francis had received practically the whole Caniba (Norridgewock), Arosagunticook, Pigwacket, Cowasuck, Pocumtuck, Schaghticoke, and Missisquoi tribes, as well as individuals and fragments of bands broken by the wars in southern New England. Parish records show there were Indians at Saint Francis as early as 1676, and fresh increments were still coming in after 1780. Inasmuch as the group is always referred to by the name of *Abenaki,* the usual suppositions are that either the Abenakis greatly outnumbered the other constituents and absorbed them or that most of the constituents, whatever their local names, were Abenaki by race and culture. Upon closer examination, however, we find that there were two important groups, the Abenakis and the Sokokis; that the Sokokis settled at Saint Francis before the Abenakis; and that within the memory of men living in 1865 the village had been divided into two moieties, Abenaki and Sokoki, for councils, ceremonies, and games.

Today the name *Sokoki* is almost forgotten among the Indians, but early French writers applied it to the Indians from the Saco River to Lake Champlain, including those known to New Hampshire historians as Penacooks. The Jesuits had missions among these Indians too—at Pigwacket, Cowas, Otter Creek, Winooski, and Missisquoi, but so little information has come to light about these missions that they may have been short-lived affairs. The significance of the Sokoki moiety for Wheelock's Indian school may have rested in one particular group, namely, that part of the Penacooks who fled to the Hudson in 1676 after Richard Walderne's seizure of 200 Indians at Dover.

This group, which is known in history as the Schaghticoke Indians from their new place of residence near Albany, numbered about 1,000 persons in 1702, and by 1754 they had all gone to Canada. It is not likely that before this time they had been much influenced by the French, but they were in direct contact with the English and Dutch, with the Mahicans to whom Jonathan Edwards ministered, and with the Mohawks who had driven out the Catholic converts of their own nation. Whether the Schaghticokes remained pagan or became Protestants, as a few had done before leaving the Merrimack, they probably represented a sizeable group not persuaded to Catholicism when they migrated north between 1702 and 1754. In particular, the 12 families who arrived in Saint Francis in 1754 were probably not assimilated when Wheelock was considering school locations 14 years later. Perhaps the later arrivals from Schaghticoke and the Missisquois, who probably arrived about 1780, were especially important in making up the present-day composition of the band, because the original band, whatever its composition, was decimated by smallpox in 1730 and suffered losses during the wars until 1783.

Much of the above is conjecture, but it may explain why Wheelock obtained students on his first trip to Saint Francis and why for the next 80 years boys from Saint Francis made up over half of all the Indians attending Dartmouth and preparatory schools with Dartmouth funds. It is clear that, although Wheelock may have been deceived regarding the distance between his new school and Saint Francis, he was not deceived regarding the opportunity there.

Much might be said about the subsequent influence of Dartmouth on the

Saint Francis tribe, especially during the Revolution, but the next chapter in the story I wish to tell concerns Peter Paul Osunkhirhine, better known at Dartmouth by his stepfather's name of Masta. Peter walked all the way from his home village to attend the college and was in attendance between 1823 and 1829. He returned to Saint Francis to found a church and a school, marry the daughter of head chief Simon Obomsawin, and become influential in the affairs of the tribe. Of him Leon B. Richardson wrote in this magazine (June 1930), "He became, perhaps, the one Indian in whom the purposes of the school were most fully realized. He passed his life in laborious service as schoolmaster and minister of his tribe." In the course of his work, he published three little books in his native language. One of them, a book of sermons based on the Ten Commandments, which this writer is now translating, gives considerable insight into Masta's religious thought.

If, as we surmise, the Sokoki part of the village supplied Wheelock with his students, Dartmouth now reciprocated through Masta in supplying institutions within which distinctive traits of the Sokoki enclave might survive within the Abenaki village. Linguists know that children tend to talk like their companions rather than like their parents, and therefore two dialects in a community tend to become alike. Had not something been interposed, it is highly probable that the Sokokis and Abenakis would have blended into a group in which distinctive traits would have been lost. The church and the school founded by Masta seem to have provided the kind of force which favors segregation; religious differences between the groups discouraged intermarriage, and separate schools provided a measure of insulation for distinctive linguistic traits and traditions. It may also have contributed to the dilution of the Indian blood, as with two groups in so small a village, each turned at times to white neighbors of appropriate faith for marriage partners. The Catholic Abenakis today have considerable French blood, and prominent family names in the Protestant group can be traced to Huguenot, English captive, and Hessian origins. And it is probably significant that all the family names found in the rolls of Dartmouth students—Masta, Gill, Annance, Tahamont, Benedict—are found today in the Protestant part of the village. Masta's church was eventually succeeded by a mission of the Church of England attended by the same families, but his school, later taught by Simon Annance (who had been to Dartmouth), by Henry Masta (descended from Peter's stepfather), and by Andrew Emet, existed until about 20 years ago.

At the present time [1959] about 130 Indians live at Saint Francis, but the band numbers over 500 registered members. There is in addition a sizeable number of persons of Saint Francis descent who have given up formal connections with the band and live in other parts of Quebec, in Ontario, and in the northeastern states, often not known as Indians by their neighbors. In all this number there remain only about 50 persons who can speak the native language fluently. The native speakers are mostly over 65 years of age, and with few exceptions the children are not learning the language. The language, like the people, is called *Abenaki,* but this name may prove to be more convenient than accurate. It may prove to be essentially the speech of the Sokokis, or it may be an Abenaki dialect from the Androscoggin from which comparative, family-oriented studies may be able to identify Sokoki or Penacook traits.

The village itself has a modern look, and the Indians' conventional attire will disappoint the one who expects to find Wannalancet in full regalia. The number who earn their living by traditional Indian pursuits such as guiding are becoming fewer each year. Nevertheless, the lover of the primitive will find much of interest in the native dances, the language, and the native lore which lingers. The village is still a treasure-trove of tradition, folklore, and folkways which can be rescued by prompt and sympathetic research.

And this closes the circle. Since 1957 Dartmouth's program of anthropological research, already focused upon the native peoples of the North, has been expanded to include this current rescue operation, thanks to a generous grant from the Spaulding-Potter Trusts. Notebook, tape recorder, and camera are capturing the spoken language, the traditional history, the folklore, native arts and crafts, the ancient manuscripts, and the physical likenesses of this interesting people. Eventually, Baker Library will house a collection of Abenakiana of incalculable value for the student of anthropology, linguistics, and early New England history.

Thus Dartmouth pays its debt to Saint Francis for its present salubrious location above the Connecticut River, celebrates the memory of an outstanding Indian student, and saves from oblivion a heritage which his labors helped to preserve for this generation.

3

A Bibliography of the Saint Francis Dialect

Given the composite nature of the Saint Francis community, Day hoped to uncover dialect variation within the community that could be traced to earlier political and linguistic divisions in interior New England. To that end, he assembled an annotated listing of major and minor published works both in and on the speech of Saint Francis by native and nonnative writers. The listing is useful for its detailed description of each source. The paper was originally published in *International Journal of American Linguistics* 27(1):80–85 (1961).

This is an attempt to list all the original linguistic material which has been published in the speech of the Saint Francis Indians. The term "Saint Francis Indians" is used here to designate the residents of the Indian village which was established on the Saint Francis River in Quebec sometime in the seventeenth century.[1] Published histories do not record the origin of the village. Charland (1942:16) cited baptismal records at Sorel as evidence that Indians were at Saint Francis in 1676. J. Maurault (1866:276) recorded a tradition that the Indians were living near their present location prior to the settlement of the Seigneur, Jean Crevier, which according to Sulte (1918:82; 1929:90) took place in 1671. The Indians still have a tradition that there were 20 families living at Saint Francis in 1660,[2] and the probability of this is increased by the record of a Sokoki baptism in Three Rivers in 1658 (Sulte 1929:94). The village on the Saint Francis River has been confused with Saint-François-de-Beauce, which had an Indian population for a period during the eighteenth century (Provost 1948:13–27), and with the Mission of Saint-François-de-Sales, which was located at the falls of the Chaudière River ca. 1683–1706.[3]

The Saint Francis Indians, thus defined for a bibliographical effort, need not be regarded as an ethnic or linguistic unit. Although at present the Indians admit

Much of the data have been gathered in the course of research made possible by grants from the Spaulding-Potter Charitable Trusts of Manchester, New Hampshire.

[1] This village has long been known to the Indians, and since 1916 to the Bureau de Poste, as *Odanak* 'at the village'. It is located in Yamaska County, Quebec, on the eastern bank of the Saint Francis River, about six miles from its confluence with the Saint Lawrence River and adjacent to the Canadian village of Pierreville.

[2] Obtained from descendants of Louis-Napoleon Obomsawin.

[3] This confusion has been assisted by the fact that the Mission of Saint-François-de-Sales was removed from the Chaudière River about 1705–1706 (Charland 1942:74) to the Saint Francis River, where it is at the present time.

of only one dialect in the village, history shows that the band was formed by increments from several linguistic areas, and it would not be surprising if the works herein listed reflect that fact. Titles which deal with known or supposed constituent groups before their arrival at Saint Francis are not given, but those containing data obtained from former residents of the village are arbitrarily included without establishing their antecedents and length of family residence at Saint Francis.

No attempt has been made to list any but first editions. Reprints, citations, and extracts which are known to be copies are omitted. In order to present all the Saint Francis material in one list, it has been necessary to repeat a few titles found in other bibliographies. All but two of these, however, appear for the first time with correct annotations. Major works are listed chronologically by publication date. Minor works are listed alphabetically by author. The writings of native authors are indicated by an asterisk. The names of informants or other sources of the data are given, when known, to assist students in assessing the value of the data and in identifying subdialects. While the writer's intention has been to produce a complete bibliography, he would be mildly astonished to find that he had succeeded, and additional items falling within the scope of this bibliography will be welcomed.

It may be noted here that manuscripts pertaining to this dialect amount to six or seven times the volume of the published materials, and most of them were written in the eighteenth century, while publication did not commence until 1809. Microfilms of these manuscripts are being assembled in the Abenaki Collection of Baker Library, Dartmouth College, and a listing of them is intended.

The abbreviations used are familiar to readers of the International Journal of American Linguistics excepting perhaps the following:

AA   American Anthropologist.
AAA-M   American Anthropological Association, Memoirs.
AJP   American Journal of Philology.
APS-P   American Philosophical Society, Proceedings.
BAE-AR   Bureau of American Ethnology, Annual Reports.
BRH   Bulletin des Recherches Historiques.
ICA-P   International Congress of Americanists, Proceedings.
JAF   Journal of American Folk-Lore.
MHS-C   Massachusetts Historical Society, Collections.

Major Works

*Wzôkhilain, P. P. 1830. Wôbanaki kimzowi awighigan, P. P. Wzôkhilain kizitokw. Boston. 90 pp. [A primer which Pilling (1891:539) erroneously called

Penobscot. Prince (1910:202) and Hallowell (1928:102, n. 20) corrected this error, but it was subsequently copied by Eckstorm (1941:248) and the Newberry Library (1941). The author was "a native Abnaki, educated in Moor's Indian school, Hanover, N.H., who maintained a mission-school at St. Francis from 1830 to 1858. Ozunkherhine spoke and wrote English with ease and accuracy,[4] and—living among and writing for his own people—his authority is of the highest, on all that concerns the western Abnaki dialect" (J. Trumbull 1872:137).]

*Wzôkhilain, P. P. 1830. Wawasi lagidamwoganek mdala chowagidamwoganal tabtagil, onkawodokodozwal wji pôbatami kidwôgan. Boston. 35 pp. [Selected Scriptural texts and short sermons based on the Ten Commandments. This work was also mistaken by Pilling for Penobscot. The orthography used in Wzôkhilain's writings was based on that proposed by John Pickering (1837 32:268) as a uniform method for writing Indian languages.]

(Desfossés, Basilide.) 1832. Kagakimzouiasis ueji Uo'banakiak adali kimo'gik aliuitzo'ki Za Plasua. Quebec. 44 pp. [A Catholic catechism which was attributed to Wzôkhilain by Pilling on the authority of Trumbull. The orthography, however, is totally different from that used in works known to be Wzôkhilain's, and it is highly probable that this is the catechism which Father Bellenger caused to be prepared by Basilide Desfossés and published at Quebec in 1832 (Charland 1942:235). Desfossés was schoolmaster at Saint Francis.]

*(Wzôkhilain, P. P. 1845.) St. Mark. (Montreal) 58 pp. [The Gospel of St. Mark in the Saint Francis dialect. Pilling attributed this work to Wzôkhilain, but apparently he had not seen Laurie's (1885:229) statement that "the Gospel of Mark was translated by Peter Osunkerhine, a missionary of the Board, into Abenaquis, his native tongue, and printed at Montreal in 1845."]

*Masta, Henry Lorne. 1883. P8batammi linto8ganal ta sall8mno8ganal wji kw8ih8mgi Kchi Niwaskw. Montreal. 19 pp. [A Protestant hymnal. The contents are practically identical with the Tahamont manuscript and with proof sheets in Baker Library Archives,[5] which are marked "Masta" and there assumed to be the work of Wzôkhilain (also called Peter Masta). Only one copy of this work is known to the writer.]

*Laurent, Joseph. 1884. New familiar Abenakis and English dialogues. Quebec. 230 pp. [Lexical and grammatical material, conversational phrases, and place-name etymologies by a former chief and schoolmaster whom this generation remembers as an authority on the language. The most widely available book in this dialect. The Laurent family at Odanak possesses a copy corrected by the author for a revised edition which was not printed.]

[4]Both *Wzôkhilain* and *Osunkherhine* were written by the author himself.
[5]The Tahamont manuscript is in the Bureau of American Ethnology Archives, Washington, D.C.

Prince, J. Dyneley. 1901. The modern dialect of the Canadian Abenakis. Miscellanea Linguistica in Onore di Graziado Ascoli, 343–362. Torino. [A grammatical sketch treating phonetics and noun and verb morphology and presenting a table of the verb *to see* with incorporated pronominal elements. Prince commenced the study of Abenaki before 1888 and carried it on for several years in Canada and northern New York (Prince 1902:18). Later he wrote, "Personally I could talk Abenaki nearly as fast as English once, but have lost my conversational fluency of late years" (McAleer 1906:38). His New York informant was probably Mitchell Sabattis, but his Canadian informants are nowhere identified.]

Hallowell, A. Irving. 1928. Recent changes in the kinship terminology of the St. Francis Abenaki. ICA-P 22.ii.97–145. [Kinship terms recorded from Henry Masta and other aged informants. Hallowell was the first to call attention to non-Abenaki components in the lexicon of this dialect.]

*Masta, Henry Lorne. 1932. Abenaki Indian legends, grammar, and place names. Victoriaville, P.Q. 110 pp. [A valuable little book written by a man who was for 20 years chief and for 31 years schoolmaster at Saint Francis. Of him Hallowell (1928:103) wrote, "He is recognized as a master of Abenaki as a medium of expression and at the same time possesses a philological detachment from it unequalled by any other member of the community."]

Minor Works

Alger, Abby Langdon. 1885. A collection of words and phrases taken from the Passamaquoddy tongue. APS-P 22.240–255. [Includes Saint Francis words, poorly transcribed, possibly from Joseph Capino (Leland 1884:220).]

Crockett, Walter Hill. 1921. Vermont: The Green Mountain State. 4 vols. New York. [Vermont place-names from Rowland Robinson's collection, some of them not found in Robinson's published works.][6]

Day, Gordon M. 1959. Note on St. Francis nomenclature. IJAL 25(4).272–273. [Words from Ambroise Obomsawin.]

Deming, Mrs. E. W. 1902. Abenaki witchcraft story. JAF 15.62–63. [One word from Margaret Camp.]

Eckstorm, Fannie Hardy. 1941. Indian place-names of the Penobscot Valley and the Maine Coast. University of Maine Studies, Ser. 2, No. 55. [Words from the manuscript dictionaries of J. B. Nudénans and Father Joseph Aubery.]

Emmons, Ebenezer. 1841. Fifth annual report of Ebenezer Emmons, M. D. of the survey of the Second Geological District. Geological Survey of the State of New York, 1840–41. Albany. [Adirondack place-names poorly transcribed

---

[6]These are described below.

from Elijah Benedict. Meanings given are sometimes descriptions rather than translations.]

Gill, Charles. 1886. Notes sur de vieux manuscrits Abénakis. Montreal. [Notes on some of the manuscripts then at the Saint Francis Mission and words from Aubery's dictionary.]

Girouard, D. 1905. L'etymologie du mot Missisquoi. BRH 11.270–277. [A place-name from Father Joseph DeGonzague.] 1906. Origine du mot Missisquoi. BRH 12.33–37. [Etymologies of Missisquoi suggested by Joseph Laurent.]

Holden, A. W. 1874. A history of the Town of Queensbury, in the State of New York. Albany. [Adirondack place-names from "Sabele" (Sabael Benedict) and "Sabattis" (Mitchell Sabattis) obtained "years ago." The transcription is poor, and the meanings given are often descriptions rather than translations.]

Hubbard, Lucius L. 1884. Woods and lakes of Maine . . . to which are added some Indian place-names and their meanings now first published. Boston. [Largely Penobscot, but some Saint Francis names from Louis Annance and perhaps from Silas Wzôkhilain.]

Kendall, Edward Augustus. 1809. Travels through the northern part of the United States in the years 1807 and 1808. 3 vols. New York. [New England place-names from "the Indians at St. Français" with translations.]

Leland, Charles Godfrey, and J. Dyneley Prince. 1902. Kulóskap the Master, and other Algonkin poems. New York. [Words and sentences.]

McAleer, George. 1906. A study in the etymology of the Indian place-name Missisquoi. Worcester, Mass. [Place names from Joseph Laurent and words supplied by Prince.]

Maurault, Rev. J. A. 1866. Histoire des Abenakis, depuis 1605 jusqu'à nos jours. Sorel, P. Q. [Words and brief rules for pronunciation. Maurault was preaching in Abenaki in 1842, only one year after undertaking its study (Charland 1942:298–299). His name etymologies, however, are frequently conjectural.]

Michelson, Truman. 1912. Preliminary report on the linguistic classification of Algonquian tribes. BAE-AR 28.221–290. [Words and a table of verb terminations from Sapir's notes in BAE Archives, portfolio 2806, pp. 7–12. Michelson came to an incorrect conclusion about loss of initial n (p. 287) because Sapir's exposure to the dialect was too brief or his informant too poor to discover the initial voiceless nasals.]

Pickering, John, ed. 1823. Doctor Edwards' observations on the Mohegan language. MHS-C Ser 2, 10.81–160. [Vocabulary obtained by Dr. Abiel Holmes and Rev. Thomas Noyes from two girls in Needham, poorly transcribed but interesting as an early example of an l-dialect at Saint Francis.]

Prince, J. Dyneley. 1888. Notes on the language of the eastern Algonkin tribes. AJP 9.310–316. [Words "from the mouths of the Indians in . . . Canada."] 1900. Forgotten Indian place-names in the Adirondacks. JAF 13.123–128. [Place-names from Mitchell Sabattis.] 1900a. Some Passamaquoddy witch-craft tales. APS-P 38.181–189. [Words from "a colloquial knowledge of the kindred Abnaki language of Canada."] 1901. Notes on the modern Minsi Delaware dialect. AJP 21.295–302. [The glossary contains Abenaki words and the Lord's prayer.] 1902. A modern Delaware tale. APS-P 41.20–34. [Abenaki words "from a dictionary of the modern dialect now in course of preparation by myself."] 1902a. The differentiation between the Penobscot and the Canadian Abenaki dialects. AA 4.17–32. [A text, words, sentences, and commentary on phonetics and a grammar.] 1903. The name Chahnameed. JAF 16.17. [Words.] 1905. A tale in the Hudson River Indian language. AA 7.74–84. [Words.] 1906. A Micmac manuscript. ICA-P 15.i.87–124. [Words.] 1907. Last living echoes of the Natick. AA 9.493–498. [Words.] 1909. A Passamaquoddy aviator. AA 11.628–650. [Words "from my own manuscript dictionary of the Abenaki, as still spoken at Pierreville, Quebec."] 1910. The Penobscot language of Maine. AA 12.183–208. [Words.] 1912. An ancient New Jersey Indian jargon. AA 14.508–524. [Words.] 1914. The morphology of the Passamaquoddy language of Maine. APS-P 53.92–117. [Words. The manuscript dictionary mentioned above has disappeared and was probably lost in the fire which destroyed Prince's library about 1910 or 1911.[7] Nevertheless, a sizeable lexicon could be extracted from the glossaries of the papers cited.]

Prince, J. Dyneley, and Frank G. Speck. 1903. The modern Pequots and their language. AA 5.193–212. [Words and sentences.] 1903a. Dying American speech-echoes from Connecticut. APS-P 42.346–352. [Words.] 1904. Glossary of the Mohegan-Pequot language. AA 6.18–45. [Words and a sentence.]

Robinson, Rowland E. (1860).[8] A sketch of the early history of Ferrisburgh. The Vermont Historical Magazine 1.31–34. [Vermont place-names and a tribal name.] 1892. Vermont: A study of independence. Boston. [Words and Vermont place-names.] 1892a. What's in a name? The Atlantic Monthly 70.576.[9] [Vermont place-names.] 1894. Along three rivers. The Vergennes Vermonter. [Vermont place-names.] 1901. A hero of Ticonderoga. Burlington, Vt. [Words.] 1901a. Sam Lovel's boy. Boston and New York. [Words.] 1905. Out of bondage and other stories. Boston and New York. [Words, Vermont place-names, personal and tribal names. Most of Robinson's data may be ascribed to John Watso and dated ca. 1859. The transcription is erratic and often poor, but without his record we should know little about the Abenakis of Otter Creek.]

---

[7] Charles A. Philower, personal communication, 1959.
[8] Although this is found in Volume I of Hemenway (1868–1891), it appears from the editor's preface and from Edward D. Collins's foreword to Volume 4 of the centennial edition of Robinson's works (Rutland, Vermont, 1934) that it was first published in 1860.
[9] An unsigned essay generally known to be Robinson's work.

(Roubaud, Rev. P. A.)[10] 1900. Letter from Father ***, missionary to the Abnakis, Saint François, October 21, 1757, *in* Jesuit Relations and Allied Documents, Thwaites ed. (Cleveland, 1896–1901) 60.90–203. [Words.]

Rousseau, Jacques. 1947. Ethnobotanique Abénakise. Archives de Folklore (Montreal) 2.145–182. [Names of plants from Robert Paquette. The transcription "basée sur la valeur française des lettres" appears to suffer in places from the informant's enunciation but is generally good.]

Siebert, Frank T., Jr. 1941. Certain Proto-Algonquian consonant clusters. Language 17.298–303. [Words from Eli Wawanolet.]

Speck, Frank G. 1918. Kinship terms and the family band among the Northeastern Algonkian. AA 20.143–161. [Kinship terms from Maude Benedict.] 1919. The functions of wampum among the Eastern Algonkian. AAA-M 6.1–71. [A text and words from Maude Benedict.] 1919a. Penobscot shamanism. AAA-M 6.239–288. [A text and words from Maude Benedict.] 1921. Bird lore of the Northern Indians. University of Pennsylvania Lectures 7.349–380. [Bird names.] 1923. Reptile lore of the Northern Indians. JAF 36.273–280. [Words.] 1926. Native tribes and dialects of Connecticut. BAE-AR 43.199–287. [Words.] 1945. Abnaki text. IJAL 11.45–46. [A text from Eli Wawanolet. Speck's transcription was phonetic.]

Thoreau, Henry David. 1858. Chesuncook. The Atlantic Monthly 2.305–317. [Maine place-names from Tahmunt Swasen.]

Vassal, H. 1885. List of names of certain places in the Abenakis language. Canadian Department of Indian Affairs, Annual Report for 1884, Pt. 1, 26–31. [Quebec and Vermont place-names from Joseph Laurent, Lazarre Wasanminett, and Henry Masta. Poorly transcribed but a useful record.][11]

---

[10]The writer of the letter was identified by Thwaites and can be identified from internal evidence as Roubaud, the assistant and later the successor of Father Aubery.

[11]The Abenaki words which appeared in the works of Robert G. Latham between 1846 and 1862 are of uncertain origin. Gatschet (1886:426) thought they had been collected by W. E. Cormack or his attendents. This would date them before 1829. Use of the name "Benekee" suggests the Saint Francis band, but the usage may be Gatschet's rather than Latham's. Cf. Hodge (1907–1910 1:5).

4

The Name *Contoocook*

This paper is the first of a series Day wrote on Abenaki and other Algonquian place-names in New England. In it he argues that *Contoocook* derives from a Western Abenaki word meaning 'at nut river'. The word is most likely a reference to the butternut tree which is abundant in southern New Hampshire, where *Contoocook* is today the name of a lake, a river, and a village. Day became an authority on the native place-names of New England, synthesizing his skills in forestry with his knowledge of Algonquian languages and northeastern ethnohistory to develop exacting standards in a field that had been rife with speculation. This paper was originally published in *International Journal of American Linguistics* 27(2):168–171 (1961).

The name *Contoocook* is now borne by a lake, a river, and a village in southern New Hampshire. From 1733 to 1760 it was the name of the New Hampshire township which on the latter date was incorporated under the name of Boscawen (Price 1823:47), but prior to 1733 only the river was known as Contoocook to the English colonists.

A number of attempts to analyze this name have been made during the last hundred years, but without disparagement these must be considered guesswork in view of the fact that none of the authors had seen the full Indian name. In 1852, Judge Chandler E. Potter assumed the editorship of *The Farmer's Monthly Visitor* (National Cyclopedia of American Biography 1897 7:538) and for two years wrote prolifically in its pages about the New Hampshire Indians. He reworked part of this material for Schoolcraft's magnum opus (Schoolcraft 1851–1857 5:217–237), and the numerous place-name etymologies in it have influenced almost every writer on the subject since that time. By the repeated use of a few words and parts of words from Williams (1827) and Cotton (1830) and of others whose origins have defied research, he analyzed New Hampshire Indian place-names with great assurance (Potter 1856b). Of Contoocook he wrote, "Auke, a place . . . Kongkaunt, The crow . . . Contoocook, Kongkaunt, auke" (Potter 1853:323). Ballard (1866:449) followed Potter without acknowledging the source and wrote, "The Contoocook was the 'Place of the Crow'." True acknowledged a debt to Ballard and wrote, "Contoocook, from Konkontoo,—a

The data for this paper were gathered in the course of research made possible by grants from the Spaulding-Potter Charitable Trusts of Manchester, New Hampshire.

crow," but he queried this meaning and seemed to prefer "Contecook—Stream-place, or up-stream place" from "Conte—up stream," a form I have found nowhere else.[1] Douglas-Lithgow (1909:70, 393) repeated "Crow place or river." It appears that the crow theory originated with Cotton's 'kongkont' or Williams's 'Kaukont' and that both Potter and True exercised some freedom in spelling it.

A break with this tradition, as well as considerable ingenuity, appears with Coffin's suggestion that 'Contook-' might be an onomatopoeic rendering of the call of the bittern, a bird which is still found on the lower reaches of the Contoocook River.[2] Masta suggested *Nik8ntekwok* 'the branch ahead',[3] no doubt as the result of his familiarity with a branch of the Saint Francis River which is known by this name to the Indians.[4] As a native speaker of the Saint Francis dialect he might have used, but did not, two homophonous stems which earlier writers probably did not know: *kǫt* 'hidden' and *kǫt* 'leg'. "Hidden River" would be appropriate if the mouth of the river were hidden, which it is not; "Leg River" seems to have no justification. Smith merely suggested that the final *-ook* of the name might mean 'at', although his work shows Potter's influence elsewhere (R. V. Smith 1952:33).

Against the background of these efforts, it is gratifying to discover on John Gardner's plan of the Merrimack River a form which is longer by one syllable.[5] Gardner's plan is undated, but a number of facts point to ca. 1673 as the date of its drafting, and the data it presents have been variously attributed to the Wood-man survey of 1638 and to the Willard-Johnson survey of 1652 (Kimball 1878). On this plan, between "Peny Cook" (Concord, New Hampshire) and the forks of the Merrimack, a river which can only be the Contoocook is shown entering the Merrimack from the west. Written parallel to the course of this river is a name which is perfectly clear on the Kimball facsimile except for two characters. It may be rendered tentatively "Pacuntehu." The 't' is only slightly smudged and only slightly in doubt. The 'e' could easily be interpreted as any other rounded lowercase letter, as a fold in the original map seems to have passed through this character, rendering it quite undecipherable in the photograph. In the photograph of the Putnam copy, there is likewise a smudge for these characters, suggesting that even Putnam with the original in front of him could not decipher

[1] Cf. True (1868:147). It is possible that True deduced this form from Vetromile's (1866:54) statement regarding the St. Croix River: "Its real Indian name is *Peskadamiukkanti* 'it goes up into the open fields'.
[2] F. Parkman Coffin, personal communication, 1955.
[3] Masta (1932:83) used the symbol "8" to represent a back nasal vowel, not to represent the sequence "ou" as did the early French writers.
[4] "The Chenal Tardif."
[5] Unfortunately, the original map, which was formerly in the files of the Court of General Sessions of the County of Sussex, Massachusetts, has disappeared. An exact copy to scale drawn by Charles A. Putnam in 1877, which was formerly in the New Hampshire Historical Society Library, has also disappeared, but a photograph of it is in Baker Library, Dartmouth College. A photographic facsimile of the original, bound with Kimball (1878), is the best copy presently available. The Berlund sketch bound in Browne (1906:facing page 140) is crude and incomplete.

them with certainty. The Berlund copy has only a scribble at this point, perhaps a deliberate one. Browne presented it as "Pacuneshu," which it plainly is not.

There are reasons for believing that "Pacunteku" was intended by the original surveyor: (1) The name is clearly the name of a river and might reasonably contain either the free or bound form for 'river', e.g., Abenaki *sip8* or *-teg8* (Râle 1833:523), Massachusett *sepu* or *-tukq* (J. Trumbull 1903:166, 315); (2) all the subsequent spellings of the name used by the English resembled the present spelling—Contoocook—and thus strongly suggest that "Pacun-" was followed by some variety of the bound *-teg8, tukq,* etc., plus locative *-k.* It is possible that Gardner produced "Pacuntehu" from "Pacunteku" merely by failing to close a lowercase 'k', but this theory receives only slight encouragement from the plan itself, on which 13 'k's are perfectly plain and only one—the final character of Uncanoonuk, thereon spelled "occonunech"—appears to be 'h'. It is more likely that Gardner made an error in copying the field notes or sketch of the original surveyor.

Massachusett vocabularies are no help in explaining "Pacun-," but Abenaki provides us with *pagan* 'noix' (Râle 1833:386). When the word "Pacunteku" has been offered to Saint Francis speakers they have invariably responded with *pagǫntékw* 'nut river', implying a river where nut-trees are notable or abundant (Day 1956–1979). In the next appearance of the name after Gardner (Jeffrey 1720) and in all subsequent appearances, the vernacular name of the river ends in *-k.* This could represent Massachusett *ohke* 'land' (J. Trumbull 1903:102), a device much favored by the naive etymologists of the last century because it permitted explanation of many place-names by the use of the Massachusett vocabularies available to them. It was also used by the scholarly Trumbull (1870), whose orientation was Massachusett. The *-k* could be interpreted more simply as an Abenaki- or Mahican-type locative suffix. This would harmonize with an Abenaki explanation of "Pacun-" and would premise *pagǫntegók* 'at nut river' as the form which became shortened to *Contoocook.* It is irrelevant that the name on Gardner's plan does not contain a locative, since it is simply the name of the river.

The species of nut referred to was probably *Juglans cinerea* L., butternut, which is fairly abundant throughout southern New Hampshire. *Juglans nigra* L., black walnut, is not native even as far north as the mouth of the Merrimack River (Sargent 1885:124–134; Munns 1938). The hickories *Carya* spp., are relatively rare in the region[6] and are named differently in Saint Francis, as are the oaks and chestnut.[7] The case for butternut is strengthened by the facts (1) that it is present

---

[6]There is a stand of shagbark hickory *Carya ovata* (Mill.) K. Koch, on the southern edge of Turtle Pond in East Concord, about two miles from the site of the old Indian village of Penacook and five miles from the mouth of the Contoocook River. It may be the successor to an older stand.

[7]The Saint Francis terminology is *pagǫ́n* 'butternut', *pagǫ́nezí* 'butternut tree', *pagimén* 'hickory nut', *pagi-*

today in stands along the Contoocook River and at the mouth and (2) that, according to Coffin's testimony, the intervale at the mouth—a favorite camping ground of the Indians—was originally covered with a heavy growth of butternut, basswood, elm, and maple (Coffin 1878:6–7).

That the original name was *pagǫntékw* 'nut river' or *pagǫntegók* 'at nut river' and that the nuts to which the name referred were butternuts is therefore about as plausible as it can be without the direct testimony of a contemporary writer, a luxury place-name etymologists must usually do without. Considering the uncertain and disputed place of the Merrimack valley dialects, it is interesting to find this name yielding to an Abenaki analysis and resisting a Massachusett analysis. Not that the problem of the Merrimack valley dialects will be solved by any analysis of this name, however intensive, but the result may call attention to the Gardner map as a primary document in New England dialect study.

---

ménakwám 'hickory tree', *watsíl* 'white oak acorn', *watsílmezí* 'white oak tree', *anáskimén* 'red or black oak acorn', and *anáskimezí* 'red or black oak tree'. The introduced black walnut is known to this generation and is called *págimizí*. Chestnut is not forgotten, but was formerly called *wǫbimizí* (Wzôkhilain 1830b:62).

5

English-Indian Contacts in New England

Conflict and disease caused major disruptions and movements among the native peoples of interior New England during the colonial period, and these disruptions plus a lack of more than a few firsthand observer accounts, make the area virtually terra incognita—a term that recurs regularly in Day's work. To establish the ethnic units of the region, Day proposes drawing on all the evidence available to the modern scholar: contemporary oral tradition as well as written histories, native place-names, and dialect differences among Western Abenaki speakers at Saint Francis. Only such a comprehensive approach can shed light on the original identities and locations of the refugee groups in New England that founded Saint Francis in the seventeenth century. This paper was originally published in *Ethnohistory* 9(1):24–40 (1962).

In approaching the history of English-Indian contacts in New England, we are faced with the fact that contact commenced long before significant records were made. For the casual reader, the history of New England began in 1620 with the landing of the Pilgrims on Plymouth Rock, yet he is confronted with the anomaly of Samoset's greeting, "Welcome, Englishmen." We may search hopefully in the relations of the voyage of 1602 (Archer 1843; Brereton 1843), but our quest for the precontact Indian is hardly satisfied by the Indians who met Captain Gosnold then at Cape Neddick, clad in European clothes and rowing "in a Baskeshallop," or by the Cuttyhunk natives who tossed off in English such phrases as "How now are you so saucie with my Tabacco?"

During the century which preceded Gosnold's voyage, an unknown number of vessels had coasted or touched upon the New England shore (Harrisse 1892; Winsor 1884–1889), but they seem to have left us only two accounts of encounters between Europeans and Indians, the accounts of Giovanni da Verrazzano (Verarzanus 1850) and André Thevet (1575). These accounts were not written with ethnographers in mind, moreover, and the tiny light they shed into a dark century is tantalizing. We sense in them a pattern of contact which became explicit in the more abundant narratives of the seventeenth century—an initial friendly reception by the Indians followed by brisk trading and terminated by hostilities. Sometimes the hostilities appear to have been precipitated by misun-

This paper was presented in the symposium entitled "Indian-White Contacts in Eastern North America" at the ninth annual meeting of the American Indian Ethnohistoric Conference held at the John Carter Brown Library, Brown University, October 20–21, 1961.

derstandings, the result of unsatisfactory communication. Sometimes they were the clear result of the European practice of kidnapping Indians for exhibition at court, for slaves, or for interpreters. This practice commenced as early as 1501 with the kidnapping of Newfoundland Indians by the Portuguese (Harrisse 1892:63), and when we read that even these Indians possessed silver discs and a sword, both of Italian origin (Harrisse 1892:73), our hope of finding northeastern Indians who were completely unaffected by European trade goods diminishes. A probable source for these items was the second expedition of John Cabot, that of 1498, but we have no information whatever about any Indians seen by this expedition.

This is not to say that a hundred years of sporadic trading and skirmishing transformed the New England Indian into a European. We may doubt that it had more than a superficial effect on any particular tribe, but an awareness of the sixteenth century prevents us from assuming that a particular cultural trait was a native trait merely because it was observed by an explorer in the early seventeenth century. Yet if we approach the seventeenth century accounts in a critical fashion, we can probably construct a fairly accurate, if limited, picture of the precontact Indian of those tribes with which the English became well acquainted, that is to say, the coastal tribes between the Merrimack River and Narragansett Bay. For early information on Indians east of the Merrimack River we are, in the main, dependent on French accounts, and for Indians west of Narragansett Bay, on the Dutch. Thorough historical ethnographies, such as Bernard Hoffman (1955b) has prepared for the Micmac, are high-priority desiderata for the tribes which the English knew. The mere thought of historical ethnographies, however, brings up a problem which is perhaps the central problem of New England ethnohistory, namely, that of identifying the ethnic units within the region; establishing their affinities; locating them at the time of discovery; and following their movements, their partitions, regroupings, and mergers through the violent dislocations which followed European contact.

For example, we may not assume a one-to-one identity between the Etchemin Indians of the French and the Maliseet-Passamaquoddy of the English, between the Obenaquiouoit of Champlain (Laverdière 1870 2:1180) and the various groups known as Abenaki to the English, between Asokwekois and the Sokoki of the Saco River, between the French Loups and the English Mahicans, or between the Almouchiquois and any tribe at all. Early French writers were inclined to lump the southern New England tribes as "Almouchiquois" and later "Loups," while the English had an early tendency to lump the northern New England tribes as "Tarrantines" or "Eastern Indians." The English also exhibited a tendency to create a distinct band for each river, village, or fishing camp as their acquaintance with the country grew. Perhaps we should, pending the unraveling of the nomenclature by a concordance of historical and linguistic data, place more trust in the entities recognized by the French among their northern New England allies and in those recognized by the English among the southern New England coastal tribes, who were, if not allies, at least close neighbors, good customers, and sometimes converts. If ethnographers are still uncertain and poorly informed about the interior tribes—and they are—it is probably because the missionaries, men like John Eliot and Roger Williams, confined their activities largely to the coastal tribes and because the soldiers and traders who penetrated the interior were less inclined to study the Indian, less literate, or less fortunate in the treatment which time has accorded to their documents.

Should we once resolve the identities of the ethnic units for which the data of the early explorers apply, we then must be prepared for population shifts following the plagues which ravaged the coast. There was one in 1617 which killed thousands of Indians between Cape Cod and the Saco River (Bradford 1908: 118). There was one in 1631 south of the Merrimack River which, as Increase Mather (1864:110) tells us, swept away whole towns. It had a successor on the lower Connecticut River in 1634 from which, according to William Bradford (1908:313), "very few escaped." Less has been written about plagues in the interior of New England, but there is a strong possibility that the European diseases, which were highly virulent to the Indians, followed contact everywhere. For example, in 1648 some Abenakis appeared at Quebec with the intelligence that some malady had "destroyed a good part of their nation" (Thwaites 1896–1901 28:203–205). This possibility and its potential for population changes and movements may provide the explanation for incongruities between earlier and later data.

The period between the plagues and the outbreak of King Philip's War in 1675 must have been one of very active acculturation for the populations which survived in southern New England. Although European contacts with the tribes of northern New England were less intensive, we may recall that the Etchemins had met the French at Tadoussac in 1603 (Laverdière 1870 1:76). The French had reached the Abenakis in the interior of Maine by 1628 (Laverdière 1870 2:1180) and established a mission on the Kennebec River by 1646 (Thwaites 1896–1901 28:225). They had a mission on Lake Champlain before 1682 (Thwaites 1896–1901 62:161). The English trading posts were near the coast at first, but there was one on the upper Merrimack River by 1668 (New Hampshire Historical Society 1832:214). It may be suspected that the Indians of northern New England, sandwiched between two European cultures, each with its own reasons for making their acquaintance, did not long remain entirely unaffected by these cultures.

Of course, King Philip's War (1675–1676), that cataclysm in New England history, changed everything. When the smoke had cleared away, southern New England contained only what might be called reservation Indians, who had made some kind of peace with the English, and northern New England would contain southern New England refugees for the next 125 years.

Without underestimating the taxonomical problems of southern, and particularly of southwestern, New England, it appears that the region between the Kennebec River and Lake Champlain is the problem area. The Androscoggin, Saco, Merrimack, and upper Connecticut Rivers, and the Vermont rivers which flow into Lake Champlain, were areas of known Indian occupation, although historians have generally treated Vermont as an uninhabited area (Day 1953: 342). Ethnographically, it has been a virtual *terra incognita*. There does not seem to be, either in print or in manuscript, a single account of any group settled within the entire area prior to King Philip's War. Scattered items there are in Canadian, New York, and New England colonial documents, whose synthesis will give us a useful, even if incomplete, chronological framework of villages, sagamores, band names, populations, and political alliances. We are permitted to hope, and have some reason to expect, that, as work with manuscript collections continues, a substantial account from this region will turn up.

Extensive and unambiguous linguistic data, which would be most helpful in ordering ethnic relationships, are wholly lacking. In their absence, all linguistic classifications which have been made for the area must be considered tentative. The classification of Penacook, as the speech of the Merrimack valley tribes has usually been called, may be used to illustrate the situation.

The Merrimack is the central valley of the region in question. Daniel Gookin (1792:149) estimated the early population at 3,000 warriors. History points to half a dozen centers of population on the river, and archeological reconnaissance indicates that the Lake Winnipesaukee region at the source of the river may have been one of the most populous centers in New England (Moorehead 1931:51). The Merrimack empties into the ocean not far from Salem, the first capital of the Massachusetts Bay Colony. Traders were on the river by 1630 (Boynton 1898 iv), and it had been explored to the source by 1652 (Massachusetts 1853–1854, 3:288). Eliot preached to the Indians at Haverhill, Lowell, and Souhegan (Whitfield 1651:19). Throughout most of the seventeenth century the Merrimack River Indians were friendly to the English, and a few still lingered at Concord, New Hampshire, when it was settled in 1726 (Bouton 1856:48). It is somewhat disconcerting to find that, in spite of these apparently favorable circumstances, we do not have a single dictionary, trader's glossary, or casual word list which was taken from or known to be applicable to the Indians of the Merrimack valley.

This did not seriously hamper two writers of the last century, who wrote at length on the Penacook language (Potter 1853; Crawford 1898). They borrowed their data *in toto* from the Abenaki "Dialogues" of Joseph Laurent (1884) and the Massachusett vocabulary of Josiah Cotton (1830), not only without justifying the extrapolation but without even a line acknowledging the fact. We might be merely amused by this were it not for the curious vitality which error exhibits and for the fact that these fictitious linguistic accounts have found their way into standard reference works.

The opinions of serious students on the affiliation of Penacook, based of necessity on other than linguistic considerations, have exhausted all the possibilities, namely, that (1) it was related to the Abenaki dialects on the east (Michelson 1912:290; Swanton 1952:17), (2) it was related to the Massachusett dialects on the south (Mooney and Thomas 1910:225), (3) it was related to the Mahican dialects on the west (Voegelin and Voegelin 1944; F. Johnson 1940:9), and (4) it was distinct from all three (Driver et al. 1953; Trager and Harben 1958). A supposed Abenaki affiliation was based on geography and the fact that, when uprooted, some of the Penacooks joined the "Eastern Indians." A supposed Massachusett affiliation was based probably on early statements that the tribes between the Piscataqua and Connecticut Rivers could communicate with each other (Gallatin 1836:33) and the fact that John Eliot, after studying Massachusett, was able to preach to the Indians assembled at Lowell Falls for the fishing. A Mahican relationship has been postulated apparently on the basis of Penacook cooperation with the Mahicans against the Mohawks and the fact that some Penacooks joined the refugee village at Schaghticoke on the Hudson River (Mooney and Thomas 1910:225). The Algonquins of the Saint Lawrence valley have seemed too remote for consideration, so those writers who have rejected the adequacy of the foregoing reasons have had to regard Penacook as a distinct language, and there the question rests for the present.

Adjoining our problem region are several concentrations of linguistic information. We have Sebastian Rasles's (1833) Abenaki dictionary from the Kennebec River and the abundant documentation of Massachusett in the works of Eliot, Cotton, and Rev. Experience Mayhew,[1] although early distinctions between the speech of the Bay and that of the Cape, or of the Wampanoags and of Martha's Vineyard, are not clear. There is substantial lexical material for Narragansett and Quiripi in the works of R. Williams (1643) and Abraham Pierson (1658). Anthropologist Frank G. Speck (1903, 1904, 1928a) salvaged a sample of Mohegan-Pequot in this century. Except for some late Stockbridge material (Edwards 1788; Holmes 1804; Quinney 1795), the rest of New England is represented only by fragments or by deep silence. The tribes known to us as the Missisquoi, Cowasuck, Squakheag, Penacook, Pigwacket, Sokoki, and Arosagunticook—to mention only the larger groups to the northwest—cannot be classified by direct linguistic evidence. The Nipmucks have been classified usually on the strength of one ambiguous sentence in Eliot's (1832:4) grammar, and the Pocumtuck, by historical extrapolations.

---

[1] For references to these works, see Pilling (1891) under the authors' names.

Although the tone of the preceding sketch has been negative, we do not need to assume that the status quo is fixed. There is reason to hope that the archives will ultimately yield at least modest vocabularies for some of these peoples. For example, a vocabulary was compiled about 1740 for the Ossipee and Pigwacket bands by Ammi Cutter, who ran a truck house on the Saco River (Sullivan 1795:265). It was still in existence in 1795, but recent searches have failed to discover its whereabouts. Seventy-five years ago, Father Jean-André Cuoq, the learned Sulpician at the Oka Mission near Montreal, reported that an ancient "Loup" dictionary from the hand of Father Jean-Claude Mathevet had been destroyed by fire in 1877 (Cuoq 1886:198). This manuscript, however, or one similar to it, perhaps the original for Mathevet's copy, was discovered only during the summer of 1959 and has been microfilmed for the Dartmouth Algonquian collection. Of course, we must determine what Mathevet meant by that much overworked name "Loup." One possible lead to the identity of the Loups of Oka is found in the fact that Missisquoi at the northern end of Lake Champlain is known to have been a mixed Loup-Abenaki mission in Mathevet's time and was probably the nearest Loup location to Montreal (Montgomery 1950:6).

Another promising source of information about the speech of the tribes of our no man's land, only recently approached, is the modern speech of the Saint Francis Indians. This band is supposed to have received at one time or another increments from many parts of New England, including all or nearly all of the displaced Indians between the Kennebec River and Lake Champlain. The association of dialect isoglosses with specific families in the Saint Francis band and the history of these families are now being studied with the hope of being able to ascertain the dialects of at least two groups—the Missisquoi and the Cowasuck-Pigwacket bands—in their preremoval locations.

The burden of the foregoing is that we cannot profitably study the effect of European contact on New England Indian cultures unless we know what the pre-contact cultures were and unless we can identify the several entities with which they were associated. When we can surely identify our ethnic units, we shall have a framework on which to hang the data of ethnographic studies. When tribal nomenclature has been cleared up, a new population study of aboriginal New England can be attempted with hope of improved results. There is a growing interest in attempting to correlate Indian populations with climate, soil, plant cover, and game animal herds. This must wait on adequate basic data. It is no criticism of the pioneers in this field—the anthropologists James Mooney (1928) and Alfred L. Kroeber (1939)—to anticipate that the higher power magnification which will be possible through concentration on local problems should achieve a definition which their general surveys could not. We have not yet begun to extract full value from the data of Indian place-names and personal names. These data should be studied, with the utmost respect for the complexities inherent in them, by linguists acquainted with the appropriate Indian languages.

These problems appear to be basic to a study of English-Indian contacts in New England. There are problems of another order which are common to the study of ethnohistory in all regions, namely, that of making the stores of critical data in manuscript collections more easily and more widely accessible. Of course, the search for new material and the finding of an occasional gem among the dusty files does add to the excitement of the chase, but the sheer volume of pertinent manuscripts is so large that, with their help, the next generation will probably rework our best estimates and conclusions.

One final word may be appropriate, not about a problem but a matter of emphasis. Archives will endure, but the other source of ethnohistorical data, the well-informed native informant, is rapidly diminishing. Anthropologists know how incomplete supposedly complete field notes become when it is time to write them up far from the field station. It seems to be only common prudence to exploit vigorously the shrinking opportunities for field ethnography in the Northeast in order to reduce to the minimum now possible the next generation's legacy of frustration.

6

The Tree Nomenclature of the
Saint Francis Indians

Before he turned his attention to linguistics and ethnology, Day was a professional forester. His interest in trees and his interest in the Abenaki language and culture come together in this exercise in ethnobotany. Sixty-four tree species indigenous to northern New England and Quebec are listed by their Latin botanical names, their common English and French names, and their Abenaki names. Something of an Abenaki taxonomy of trees emerges, and, not surprisingly, it is based on classificatory criteria different from the standard botanical ones. This paper was originally published as pp. 37–48 in *Contributions to Anthropology, 1960*, Part II, National Museum of Canada Bulletin 190, Ottawa (1963).

In the latter half of the seventeenth century, an Indian village sprang up on the east bank of the Saint Francis River a few miles above its junction with the Saint Lawrence. The subsequent history of this village, although known only imperfectly, shows complex population changes, characterized by immigration of many increments from tribes in Maine, New Hampshire, Vermont, and Massachusetts; attribution by war and disease; and emigration and reimmigration (J. Maurault 1866; Charland 1942; Provost 1948; Vassal 1811–1889). The inhabitants of this village are known in history as the Saint Francis Indians. Also known in English as Abenakis and in French as Abénaquis, they call themselves *wòbànâkìák,* a matter of some interest when one considers the mixed origins of the band.

In the years immediately following World War I, the population of the village was reduced by emigration to Canadian and American cities to about one-third. The remaining population has intermarried to some extent with whites and with the Hurons of Lorette. At present the band numbers over 500 persons, of whom about 130 reside in the home village, known to the Indians, and since 1916 to the Bureau de Poste, as Odanak. Descendants of Indians who left the village during the past 150 years and do not maintain any formal connection with the band probably number several hundred.

As might be expected of so small a group surrounded by white neighbors and influences, the Saint Francis Indians are strongly acculturated. The native language is an Algonquian dialect whose nearest living relative is Penobscot. A five-year search has discovered only about 80 persons who can be called speakers of this dialect and only 40 who are fluent and speak it by preference.

Inasmuch as this band represents the last source of new data about its homeland in northwestern New England—a virtual *terra incognita* ethnologically—and about a moribund culture, Dartmouth College in 1957 initiated a study of the band, supported by grants from the Spaulding-Potter Trusts of Manchester, New Hampshire. Building on this research, the writer, in August and September 1960, undertook a study of Saint Francis plant nomenclature with the assistance of the National Museum of Canada. A part of the data obtained by the study, that part pertaining to trees, is presented here.

There is very little published information concerning the ethnobotany of the northeastern tribes. For the Saint Francis Indians, the names of a few plants may be extracted from the works of three native authors: P. P. Wzôkhilain (1830b), Joseph Laurent (1884), and H. L. Masta (1932). Rousseau (1947) has given us a sketch of the subject which contains a rather full treatment of splint basketry, though limited in other directions by the amount of time he was able to spend in the field. It was a source of satisfaction to the writer to find that practically complete nomenclatural data could be obtained for the tree species and that a very considerable corpus can still be collected for the rest of the plant kingdom. The few lacunae remaining in the tree data presented here do not represent a lack of information on the part of the informants but rather a lack of opportunity on the part of the writer to check all species in the field.

Fieldwork was conducted on the reservation in Quebec and at several localities in Vermont and New Hampshire. Five informants were consulted: Messrs. Théophile Panadis, Siegfroid Robert Obomsawin, Louis Portneuf, Edward Hannis, and Ambroise Obomsawin. These are probably the best informed persons in the band on forest lore. The first four are retired woodsmen and guides, and the fifth is the son of a renowned herbalist.

The data are presented according to one of the conventional phylogenetic arrangements. Family and genus sequence follows Dalla Torre and Harms (1900–1907), and, within genera, species are arranged alphabetically by their Latin names. English nomenclature follows Elbert Little (1953), and French nomenclature is largely that of Marie-Victorin (1935) supplemented by Dominion Forest Service Bulletin No. 61 (Canada, Dominion Forest Service 1949). All native names from the literature are listed chronologically after the author, abbreviated thus: (W) Wzôkhilain, (L) Laurent, (M) Masta, (R) Rousseau. Names obtained from informants are given in allophonic notation in unpossessed singular and plural forms.[1] Those names which have meaning for present-day speakers are translated, and morphemes are identified when possible.

A certain few morphemes which occur repeatedly in this list are (1) *-bakw* 'leaf'; (2) *-ozi, -mozi, -mezi, -mizi* 'woody plant, tree, or shrub'; (3) *-ask* 'medicinal root';[2] (4) *-akw* 'woody stem'; (5) *-akws* 'little woody stem'; and (6) *-akwam* 'woody plant, stick' (*-akwam* is found only as a suffix to the name of a fruit, e.g., species Nos. 20, 21, 35, 37, 38, 39, 40, 41, 42, 43, 44, 45, 46, 49, 50, and 64).

Saint Francis Tree Nomenclature

1. **Pinus banksiana** Lamb., jack pine, pin de Banks, pin gris, cyprès.

pílòwì pâsàákw, pílòwì pâsàakók. From *pilowi-* 'strange, different', and *pâsàákw*, the name of *Pinus resinosa.* This species is uncommon in New England and unknown on the Saint Francis Reservation. It was encountered by the Indians in their hunting and guiding north of the Saint Lawrence River[3] and reminded them of the other hard pine of their acquaintance, *Pinus resinosa.*

2. **Pinus resinosa** Ait., red pine, pin résineux, pin rouge. (W) *pasaakw* 'red pine'; (L) *pasaakw* 'red pine'.

pâsàákw, pâsàakók.

3. **Pinus strobus** L., eastern white pine, pin strobus, pin blanc. (W) *kowa* 'pine tree'; (L) *koa* 'pine tree'; (M) *koa* 'pine'; (R) *kohah'sis, Pinus strobus.*

kôá, kôàák. kôá is used also for "log," because white pine furnished most of the logs for

---

[1] Space does not permit a complete description here of the phonemes of the Saint Francis dialect. Their publication is planned for the near future. The sounds of the modal allophones, however, are given with approximate imitation labels in order to give some idea of the pronunciation. [p] unaspirated as in *spin;* [b] as in *bow;* [t] unaspirated as in *steel;* [d] as in *ado;* [k] unaspirated as in *skin;* [g] as in *ago;* [s] as in *sister;* [z] as in *zoo;* [h] similar to *h* in *high,* strong aspiration except in intervocalic position; [l] clear *l* as in French *pâle;* [m] as in *mama,* but voiceless initially before a voiceless consonant; [i] articulated between the *i* of *machine* and the *i* of *sit;* [e] somewhat like the *e* in *label;* [a] as in *psalm;* [o] as in *so,* but after very weak [i] more like the vowel in *you;* [ǫ] nasal vowel as French *on;* [w] voiceless finally after [k] and between [k] and another voiceless consonant, otherwise voiced as *u* in *guano;* [´] strong accent; [^] medium accent; [`] weak accent; very weak accent, no diacritic. Accent is composed of stress and pitch proportionally combined. Syllable length is determined by the accent, which is written over the vowel or other syllabic. Syllable lengthening is realized on the last segment of the syllable. Syllable boundaries for the forms given may be determined by three rules: (1) a consonant after a very weak vowel is ambisyllabic; (2) the first consonant of a two-consonant intervocalic cluster ends a syllable, and the second consonant commences a syllable; (3) a weak, medium, or strong vowel ends a syllable except before a consonant cluster. An aurally detectable pause is indicated by a space between segments. Utterance-final vowels are shorter, and utterance-final consonants are longer than elsewhere. The forms in this paper are given in a normal citational intonation, which is chiefly characterized by a rapidly falling pitch over the last part of the last voiced segment in the utterance and a relaxation of force over the last part of the last segment, whether voiced or voiceless. The analysis is based on the speech of a single informant, inasmuch as each idiolect remaining in the band is being considered separately in a dialect study. [Wzôkhilain's ǫ, Laurent's ô, and Masta's 8 represent the nasal mid-low back vowel. See Item 9.—Eds.]

[2] This identification is mine, not the informants'.

[3] The family hunting grounds of the Saint Francis Indians were in the watersheds of the Saint Maurice, Mattawin, and Vermillion Rivers, a territory which the tradition states they obtained by treaty from the Algonquins.

the lumber industry on the Saint Francis River and for the log drives on the Ottawa and Saint Lawrence Rivers in which the Indians participated. Rousseau's form is the diminutive *kôàsís*.

4. **Larix laricina** (DuRoi) K. Koch, tamarack, mélèze laricin, épinette rouge. (L) *pôbnôdageso* 'tamarac'; (R) *oblanda'gasouk* 'Larix laricina'.

pòbenôdàgezó, pòbenôdàgezòák. From *pen-* 'falling' (reduplicated); *pòben-* 'continually or strongly falling'; *-ọdag-,* possibly a reshaping of *-ọtkw-* 'branch'; and *-ezo,* an unidentified morpheme which resembles the third singular passive verb suffix. This name is puzzling, because it seems to refer to the relatively minor feature of drooping branchlets, whereas the most conspicuous feature of the species, unique among conifers in the region, is the deciduous leaves. One informant translated the name "leaves fall every year," and the others agreed on "branches droop." Rousseau's informant seems to have been especially obscure in this instance.

5. **Picea glauca** var. **glauca,** white spruce (typical), épicéa glauque, épinette blanche. (W) *msazesso* 'white spruce'; (L) *msazesso* 'white spruce'; (M) *mzazesso* 'white spruce'; (R) *skaské* 'Picea glauca'.

mesâzessó, mesâzessòák. All the better informants agreed on this name. Rousseau's form may be explained by the fact that those present-day Indians who are not well versed in woods lore retain the name for red and black spruce (see Nos. 6 and 7) as a kind of generic name for the spruces.

6. **Picea mariana** (Mill.) B.S.P., black spruce, épicéa marial, épinette noire.

7. **Picea rubens** Sarg., red spruce, épinette rouge. (W) *mskask* 'spruce'; (L) *mskak* 'black spruce'; (M) *mskask* 'spruce'.

mskásk, mskâskák. These two species, which are dubiously distinguished by taxonomists, have the same Saint Francis name. The Indians, however, do recognize the difference between *Picea rubens* on the reservation and *Picea mariana* north of the Saint Lawrence River, where it is characterized by bog habitat, drooping branches, and a coating of caribou moss. Laurent's form is probably a misprint.

8. **Tsuga canadensis** (L.) Carr., eastern hemlock, Tsuga du Canada, pruche. (W) *setti* 'hemlock'; (L) *alnisedi* 'hemlock'; (M) *sedi* 'hemlock'; (R) *al'nézité* 'Tsuga canadensis'.

âlnìzedí, àlnîzedìák. From *alni-* 'common, ordinary' and *sedí* 'branch of an evergreen or conifer'.

9. **Abies balsamea** var. **balsamea,** balsam fir (typical), sapin baumier, sapin. (W) *kokokhọakw* 'fir'; (L) *kokokhôakw* 'fir-tree'; (M) *kokokh8akw* 'fir tree'; (R) *kokôk-wank* 'Abies balsamea'.

kòkôkhàọkw, kòkôkhàôkọk. Wzôkhilain's ọ, Laurent's ô, and Masta's 8 represent the nasal mid-low back vowel and permit identification of the morpheme *-akw* 'woody stem', which vowel metathesis has since concealed.

10. **Thuja occidentalis** L., northern white-cedar, thuja occidental, cèdre, balai. (W) *molodakw* 'cedar'; (L) *môlôdagw* 'cedar'; (M) *m8l8dakw* 'cedar' (R) *malan-dak* '*Thuja occidentalis*'.

mòlòdáku, mòlòdàkók. molod- is meaningless now, although it resembles *molod-* 'deep'; *-akw* is 'woody stem'. The wood of white-cedar is *kóksk* 'brittle wood', and this name is commonly transferred to the tree. It is also called *sèdi* 'evergreen branch' or *sèdiák* (plural), because it often furnishes the branches which are used for the celebration of Palm Sunday. \

11. **Juniperus virginiana** L., eastern red cedar, genévrier de Virginie, cèdre rouge.

mkwísàgezó, mkwísàgezòák. From *mkwi-* 'red'; *-sakw-* 'inside'; and *-ezo,* unidentified morpheme (see No. 4). This species does not occur either on the reservation or in the northern hunting grounds, but it was known to one informant whose family formerly lived on Lake Champlain.

12. **Populus balsamifera** var. **balsamifera,** balsam poplar (typical), peuplier tacamahaca, peuplier baumier, peuplier, tremble noir.

mkázàwì ôssâgáku, mkázàwì ossâgâkók. From *mkázàwì* 'black' and *ôssâgáku* 'poplar'. The Indians call all native poplars *ôssâgáku.* They recognize species, however, and note for this one the gummy buds and exudations and brown-streaked wood which leaves an ash, when burned, resembling that of hardwoods more than that of other poplars. They will, when pressed, produce the name above, which may be in analogy to French peuplier noir.

13. **Populus deltoides** Bartr., eastern cottonwood, peuplier à feuilles deltoïdes, peuplier du Canada.

14. **Populus grandidentata** Michx., bigtooth aspen, peuplier à grandes dents.

15. **Populus tremuloides** Michx., quaking aspen, peuplier faux-tremble, tremble. (W) *wessagakw* 'poplar'; (R) *os'sagakwé* '*Populus tremuloides*'.

ôssâgáku, òssâgàkók. From *ossag-* 'bitter' and *-akw* 'woody stem', referring to the taste of a medicine made from the bark.

16. **Populus nigra** var. **italica,** Lombardy poplar, peuplier noir, peuplier d'Italie, peuplier de Lombardie. (L) *wawabibakw* 'poplar'.

wàwâbìbáku, wàwâbìbàkók. From *wawabi-* 'up high' and *-bakw* 'leaf', referring to the conspicuous height of this slender species. Laurent's term belongs here, although he was not specific, and this caused Rousseau to assume that it referred to "le peuplier, sans distinction d'espèces."

17. **Salix** L., willow, saule, chat. (L) *kanozas* 'willow'; (R) *kano'zass* Salix . . . "les espèces arbustives."

kànòzás, kànôzàsák. This is the name for all willows, both shrubby and arborescent. When it is desired to specify a shrubby willow, the diminutive is used, *kànôzaàsís, kànòzâsìzák.*

18. **Juglans cinerea** L., butternut, noyer cendré, arbre à noix longues. (W) *pagonozi* 'butternut tree'; (L) *pagônozi* 'walnut-tree'; (M) *pag8nozi* 'butternut tree'.

pàgônòzí pàgônozíák. From *pàgón* 'nut' and *-ozi* 'woody plant, tree, or shrub'. Butternut, which is the only walnut native to northern New England, appears to be the original object of the name. *pàgônòzí* is now used both for butternut and as a general term for nut-bearing trees, including even the oaks.

19. **Juglans nigra** L., black walnut, noyer noir. (W) *pagimizi* 'walnut'; (M) *pagimizi* 'walnut tree'.

pâgìmìzí, pàgìmîzìák. From *pagi-* 'hit with an instrument' and *-mizi* 'woody plant'. The morpheme *pagi-*, which occurs in the names of all walnuts and hickories, refers to the nuts which require hitting with an instrument to open them. While the Indians today are acquainted with *Juglans nigra* as an introduced ornamental, the early date of Wzôkhilain's writing suggests the possibility that late-arriving increments of Hudson valley emigrants may have brought knowledge of this species into the band.[4]

20. **Carya cordiformis** (Wangenh.) K. Koch, bitternut hickory, caryer cordiforme, noyer amer.

21. **Carya ovata** (Mill.) K. Koch, shagbark hickory, caryer ovale, arbre à noix piquées, noyer tendre.

pàgîmenàkwám, pàgìmênàkwàmák. From *pagi-* 'hit with an instrument'; *-men* 'fruit'; *-akwam* 'woody plant'. This name was verified in the field as correct for *Carya ovata,* and it appears likely, from conversations with informants, that it is used for all species of hickory known to them.

22. **Betula alleghaniensis** Britton, yellow birch, bouleau jaune, merisier.

23. **Betula lenta** var. **lenta,** sweet birch (typical), bouleau flexible, merisier rouge. (W) *wins* 'black birch'; (L) *wins* 'black birch'.

wíns, wînsák.

24. **Betula papyrifera** var. **papyrifera,** paper birch (typical), bouleau à papier, bouleau blanc, bouleau à canot.

25. **Betula populifolia** Marsh., gray birch, bouleau à feuilles de peuplier, bouleau rouge, bouleau gris. (W) *maskwamozi* 'white birch'; (L) *maskwamozi* 'birch'; (R) *maskwàmosé* '*Betula papyrifera*'.

---

[4]The Saint Francis band is said to have received the entire population of the village of Schaghticoke on the Hudson between 1702 and 1754 (Hodge 1907–1910 2:486).

màskwâmòzí, màskwâmòzìák. From *màskwá* 'thin, peelable bark' and *-mozi* 'woody plant'. *Betula papyrifera* and *Betula populifolia* are grouped under one name, although their differences are clearly recognized. When my informants wished to be specific, they said *wǫbìgít màskwâmòzi* and *wíbegwìgít màskwâmòzí*, white and grey *màskwâmozí* respectively, perhaps in analogy to English usage. Three types of bark from *Betula papyrifera* are named: *pîtòskwá*, a thin smooth bark suitable for writing and drawing material; *màzôzìgwá*, a thick leathery bark used for canoes; and *òskânàskwá*, a hard brittle bark of little utility. These names are transferred to the trees which produce the particular types of bark.

26. **Alnus** B. Ehrh., alder, aulne, aune, aunage, verge, verne. (W) *wdopi* 'alder'; (L) *wdopi* 'alder tree'; (M) *wdopi* 'alder'; (R) *otópé* '*Alnus rugosa* var. *americana*'. *odôpì, odôpìák.*

27. **Fagus grandifolia** Ehrh., American beech, hêtre à grandes feuilles. (W) *wajwimizi* 'beech'; (L) *wajoimizi* 'beech'; (M) *wajwimizi* 'beech tree'.

wâdzòimìzí, wâdzòimìzìák. From *wâdzó* 'mountain'; *-i-* possessive *-mizi* 'woody plant'. This name is not meant to indicate a high mountain species. Rather it is recognition by the Indian that, in the spruce-fir-northern hardwoods region, beech grows above the spruce flat cover type. This usage must have developed in northern New England rather than in the Saint Lawrence valley.

28. **Quercus alba** L., white oak, chêne blanc. (W) *wachilmezi* 'white oak'; (M) *wachilmezi* 'white oak'.

wàtsílmezí, wàtsílmezìák. From *wâtsíl*, an edible acorn of the white oak group, and *-mezi* 'woody plant'.

29. **Quercus rubra** L., northern red oak, chêne boréal, chêne rouge.

30. **Quercus velutina** Lam., black oak, chêne de teinturiers. (L) *anaskemezi* 'oak'.

ànâskemèzí, ànâskemèzìák. From *anaski-*, unidentified morpheme (s), and *-mezi* 'woody plant'. The name of the red oak acorn is *ànâskìmén; -men* is 'fruit', and *anaski-* may possibly be from *wanask-* and may refer to the fact that two seasons are required to mature this acorn.

31. **Ulmus americana** var. **americana,** American elm (typical), orme d'Amérique, orme blanc. (W) *anibi* 'elm'; (L) *anibi* 'elm'; (M) *anibi* 'elm'.
ànìbí, ànìbìák.

32. **Ulmus rubra** Mühl., slippery elm, orme roux, orme rouge, orme gras.

pèzâkhòlìgán, pèzâkhòlìgànák. Properly, *pèzâkhòlìgán* is the soft inner bark of any tree, but the name is often transferred to *Ulmus rubra* as a species name because its mucilaginous inner bark is conspicuous among northeastern trees. Otherwise, this species is named with *Ulmus americana*.

33. **Sassafras albidum** (Nutt.) Nees, sassafras.

sàzôgebàmáku, sàzôgebàmàgók. This species, which is not native in Quebec, is remembered by a single family from Lake Champlain.

34. **Platanus occidentalis** L., American sycamore, platane d'Occident.

pàbàláku, pàbàlákók. From *pabal-* 'smooth' and *-akw* 'woody stem'.

35. **Malus** Mill., apple, crab apple, pommier, pommetier. (W) *aplesakwam* 'apple tree'; (L) *aplesakuam* 'apple-tree'.

âplesàkwám, âplesàkwàmák. From *âples* 'apple' and *-akwam* 'woody plant'. *áples* is a loan word from English. English words were frequently borrowed in the plural form. A crab apple is given the diminutive form *âplesís, âplesízák,* and the crab apple tree is *âplesìzàkwám, àplesîzàkwàmák.*

36. **Sorbus americana** Marsh., American mountain-ash, sorbier d'Amérique, cormier, maska, maskouabina. (W) *mozmezi* 'moose stick'.

môzmezí, môzmèzìák. From *móz* 'moose' and *-mezi* 'woody plant'. In northern Vermont this Indian name has been anglicized to "moose-missey."

37. **Amelanchier laevis** Wieg., Allegheny serviceberry, amélanchier glabre, petites poires. (R) *mohéménak'wam* 'Amelanchier sp.'.

òmwàímenàkwám, òmwàímenàkwàmák. From *òmwa-* 'wax'; *-i-* possessive; *-men* 'fruit'; and *-akwam* 'woody plant'; a reference to the texture of the epidermis of the ripe fruit.

39. **Crataegus** L., hawthorn, aubépine, cenellier. (W) *Chignaz* 'thorn plum'; (L) *chignazakuam* 'thorn tree'; (R) *ti'ginasak* 'Crataegus sp.'.

tsìgenâzàkwám, tsìgenâzàkwàmák. From *tsîgenáz* 'the haw fruit or thorn apple' and *-akwam* 'woody plant'.

40. **Prunus avium** (L.) L., mazzard.

41. **Prunus cerasus** L., sour cherry.

ktsí àdebîmenàkwám, ktsí àdebîmenàkwàmák. From *ktsí-* 'large', *àdebîmén* 'cherry', and *-akwam* 'woody plant'. The name for these introduced species is adapted from that of the native species (see Nos. 45 and 46).

42. **Prunus nigra** Ait., Canada plum, prunier noir, prunier sauvage. (L) *azawanimenakuam* 'plum tree'.

àzàwánimènàkwám, àzàwánimènàkwàmák. From *azawan-* 'choking, catching the breath'; *-i-* possessive; *-men* 'fruit'; and *-akwam* 'woody plant'.

43. **Prunus pensylvanica** L.f., pin cherry, cerisier de Pennsylvanie, petit merisier, arbre à petite merises. (L) *maskwazimenakuam* 'wild-cherry tree'.

màskwâzimènàkwám, màskwâzimènàkwàmàk. From *màskwá* 'thin peelable bark' (see

Nos. 24 and 25); *-z-* diminutive, perhaps pejorative here, indicating that this bark is not useful like the *màskwá* of *Betula papyrifera; -i-* possessive; *-men* 'fruit'; and *-akwam* 'woody plant'. Rousseau's suggestion that this name may belong to *Prunus virginiana* is incorrect.

44. **Prunus persica** Batsch, peach, pêche. (L) *piches* 'peach'.

pîtsesàkwám, pîtsesàkwàmák. From *pítses* 'a peach' and *-akwam* 'woody plant'. *pítses* is a loan word from English.

45. **Prunus serotina** var. **serotina,** black cherry (typical), cerisier tardif, cerisier d'automne.

46. **Prunus virginiana** L., common chokecherry, cerisier de Virginie, cerisier à grappes. (L) *adbimenakuam* 'cherry-tree'.

àdebîmenàkwám, àdebîmenàkwàmák. From *adeb-* 'dry mouth'; *-i-* possessive; *-men* 'fruit'; and *-akwam* 'woody plant'.

47. **Pyrus communis** L., pear, poire.

kwàgwŷnagwèzít àplés, kwàgwŷnagwèzìdzík âplesák. From *kwVn-* 'long' (reduplicated) and *kwagwŷn-, -agwezit*, singular animate third singular passive suffix "it is made. . . ." The compound means "elongated apple."

48. **Zanthoxylum americanum** Mill., common prickly-ash; clavalier d'Améri-que, frêne épineux. (W) *kagọwakw* 'prickly ash'; (M) *kag8wakw* 'prickly ash'.

kàgǫ̀wákw, kàgǫ̂wàkók. From *kagọwi-* 'angry' and *-akw* 'woody stem', a reference to the impression made by this plant on the Indians who collected its bark for medicine.

49. **Rhus typhina** L., staghorn sumac, sumac vinaigrier, vinaigrier. (W) *salọn* 'sumach'.

sàlộnàkwám, sàlộnàkwàmák. From *sàlộn* 'the sumac fruit' and *-akwam* 'woody plant'. *sàlộn* refers to the acidulous taste of the fruit. No smaller form could be clearly identified, but it may be that *sal-* is acidulous, and *-ǫn* is a seed or nutlet.

50. **Ilex verticillata** (L.) A. Gray, common winterberry, houx verticillé.

tsìgwálimènàkwám, tsìgwâliménàkwàmák. From *tsìgwál* 'frog'; *-i-* possessive; *-men* 'fruit'; and *-akwam*. The significance of this name could not be obtained. It may be either a reference to the wet habitat of the species or an opinion on the fruit as a comestible.

51. **Acer negundo** L., boxelder, érable négondo, érable à Giguère, plaine Giguère, plaine du lac.

pîlkìmìzí, pílkìmîzìák. From *pil-* 'new', *ki* 'land', and *-mizi* 'woody plant'; probably a reference to its common establishment on alluvial and cleared sites.

52. **Acer nigrum** Michx. f., black maple, érable noir.

53. **Acer saccharum** Marsh., sugar maple, érable à sucre, érable franc, érable franche. (W) *senomozi* 'maple'; (L) *senomozi* 'maple'.

senòmòzí, sènòmôzìák. From *sén* 'stone'; *-o-* unidentified morpheme; and *-mozi* 'woody plant'. Wzôkhilain's name shows that *-o-* was formerly *-ǫ-*. This appears to be confirmed by Rasles's word *ssenañ8*.

54. **Acer pensylvanicum** L., striped maple, érable de Pennsylvanie, bois d'orignal, bois barré. (R) *onsé'gak* ᵘᵏ '*Acer pensylvanicum*'.

ôsàgákw, ǫsàgàkók. From *ǫsag-*, unidentified morpheme; possibly *ǫshagi* 'queer' and *-akw* 'woody stem'. Rousseau's form is the plural.

55. **Acer rubrum** var. **rubrum,** red maple (typical), érable rouge, plaine rouge.

56. **Acer saccharinum** L., silver maple, érable argenté, plaine blanche, plaine de France, érable du Canada. (R) *skôba'gish* '*Acer rubrum*'.

meskwèbáges, meskwèbâgezák.

57. **Acer spicatum** Lam., mountain maple, érable à épis, plaine bâtarde.

wǫbâkwsék, wǫbâkwsegíl. From *wǫb-* 'white'; *-akw* 'woody stem'; *-s* diminutive; *-ek* singular animate verbal suffix translatable by 'that which is', freely, 'little white stems'.

58. **Tilia americana** L., American basswood, tilleul glabre, bois blanc. (W) *wigbimizi* 'basswood'; (L) *wigbimizi* 'bass-wood'; (M) *wigbimizi* 'basswood'.

wîgebìmîzí, wîgebìmîzìák. From *wígebì* 'fibrous bark' and *-mizi* 'woody plant'. In the last century, *wígebì* has acquired the added meaning of 'basket splint'. A few speakers have even forgotten the older meaning and translate *wîgebìmîzí* as 'splint tree' and identify it with ash.

59. **Cornus stolonifera** Michx., red osier dogwood, cornouiller stolonifère, hart rouge. (R) *mamkawa'kousek* '*Cornus stolonifera*'.

màmkwâkwsék, màmkwâkwsegíl. From *mkwi-* 'red'; reduplicated *mamkwi-* 'very red'; *-akw* 'woody stem'; *-s-* diminutive; *-ek* verbal suffix (see No. 57), freely, "bright red little stems."

60. **Fraxinus americana** L., white ash, frêne d'Amérique, frêne blanc, franc-frêne. (W) *ogmakw* 'black ash'; (M) *8gmakw* 'white ash'.

ôgemákw, ôgemàkók. From *ôgém* 'snowshoe' and *-akw* 'woody stem'. Considering the complete agreement of modern informants and of Masta that *ôgemákw* is white ash, as well as the technical properties of the wood and its actual uses, we may assume that Wzôkhilain was mistaken, perhaps not in his identification but in his understanding of the English name and its application.

61. **Fraxinus nigra** Marsh., black ash, frêne noir, frêne gras.

62. **Fraxinus pennsylvanica** Marsh., green ash, frêne de Pennsylvanie, frêne rouge. (W) *mahlakws* 'ash'; (L) *mahlakws* 'ash'; (M) *mahlakws* 'black ash'.

mâhàlákws, mâhàlâkwsák. This is a generic term embracing all varieties of these two species, including those formerly described under the name *Fraxinus pennsylvanica lanceolata.* Four other names for ecological and taxonomic varieties were obtained but not verified in the field. They are here assigned tentatively on the basis of the informants' descriptions: (1) *mkázàwì mâhàlákws* or *mkâzàwìgít mâhàlákws* 'black *mâhàlákws*', so named from the darker bark. This appears to be the swamp-grown variety of *Fraxinus nigra,* which is characterized by slower growth and hence by thinner and more brittle basket splints. (2) *wìzǫ̀wì mâhàlákws* 'yellow *mâhàlákws*', a variety growing by streams and on moist but fairly well-drained soil, with yellowish inner bark, thicker and stronger splints. This seems to be an ecological grouping from both species. (3) *wâdzòìmâhàlákws* 'mountain *mâhàlákws*'. This name was obtained from only one informant. It does not suit the characteristic habitat of either species and may be an alternate name for *Fraxinus americana* (see No. 60). (4) *pskwâsàwǫni mâhàlákws* 'flower *mâhàlákws*'. Rousseau's information indicates that this is *Fraxinus nigra,* the 'frêne à bouquet' of his informant. Inasmuch as my informant stated that this is the best variety for baskets, it is probably not the swamp form but the *wìzǫ̀wì mâhàlákws.* The name probably derives from the clusters of staminate and polygamous flowers which, appearing before the leaves, are more conspicuous than those of other ashes.

63. **Sambucus canadensis** L., American elder, sureau du Canada, sureau blanc. (L) *saskib* 'elder'.

sâskíp, sâskìbál.

64. **Viburnum cassinoides** L., witherod viburnum, wild raisin, viorne cassinoïde, alisier, bourdaine, bleuets sains. (L) *adotomenal* 'beam-tree berries'; (R) *ada'tominan* '*Viburnum cassinoides*'.

àdàtômènàkwám, àdàtômènàkwàmák. Also *àdàtômenizí, àdàtòméniziàk.* From *adato-* an unidentifiable morpheme; *-men* 'fruit'; and *-akwam* 'woody plant', or *izi* 'woody plant'.

Conclusions

Only one tree species, which was adequately examined, seems to be unknown, namely, *Pinus rigida* Mill., pitch pine, pin dur. This species was seen by two informants in the vicinity of Concord, New Hampshire, but not recognized. It is possible that this species was the original *pílòwì pâsàákw* and that the name was transferred to *Pinus banksiana* when the Indians removed from New England to the Saint Lawrence valley.

There was no opportunity to check several species in the field, namely, *Carpinus caroliniana* Walt., American hornbeam; *Ostrya virginiana* (Mill.) K. Koch, eastern hophornbeam; *Castanea dentata* (Marsh.) Borkh., American chestnut; *Hamamelis virginiana* L., witch-hazel; *Rhamnus cathartica* L., European buckthorn; *Cornus alternifolia* L.f., alternate-leaf dogwood; *Nyssa sylvatica* var. *sylvatica,* black tupelo (typical). It is probable that some, perhaps all, of these species will be named as soon as they and good informants can be brought together in the field, as several Indian names were obtained for trees which were not seen in the field.

The present data, however, furnish us another example of the variety of man's approaches to classifying and naming natural phenomena. There can be little doubt that, until they ceased in the last generation to live largely in and from the forest, the Saint Francis Indians knew the flora of their habitat intimately. They are still perfectly familiar with most of it. They named those kinds which were important in their way of life as well as a few of the unimportant ones which were especially striking in some way. Grouping of kinds into something comparable to the botanist's genera is apparent in the application of some names; e.g., *kànòzás* is equivalent to *Salix, òssàgákw* is nearly equivalent to *Populus,* but, as might be expected, the Indian's genus does not always coincide with the botanist's. While the latter bases his classification on the similarities of reproductive structures, which are ephemeral and often inconspicuous, the Indian, in general, bases his classification on morphological features that are striking or significant in his economy and usually quite stable. Under these principles, an entire genus, though well known, may remain unnamed or receive one name for all its species, while in another genus even ecological varieties and forms (ecotypes and eco-phenes) may receive separate names. Historically, the procedure may have been to name important and well-known species and to later include superficially similar species under the same name, with a qualifying adjective when desired, e.g., *wîbegwìgít màskwâmòzí* 'grey *maskwa*-tree'. This procedure was utilitarian, locally oriented, and resembled the white man's plant lore on the folk level rather than his scientific taxonomy. I was unable to discover whether phylogenetic concepts are held or not.

It appears from the data obtained on trees and other plants that those men who in their youth lived the old hunting and fishing life and maintained lifelong contact with the woods as guides have preserved a very full corpus of plant lore in spite of the acculturated condition of the band. Whatever additional knowledge of medicinal and other plants which may be the possession of the elder women of the band has not been investigated.

7

From "A Saint Francis Abenaki Vocabulary"

In this first modern linguistic description of Western Abenaki, Day remarks on the state of research for the Eastern Algonquian languages at the time of writing and provides a detailed phonological sketch of Western Abenaki in the tradition of Leonard Bloomfield. The actual vocabulary of some 900 items indexed alphabetically by English glosses is not included here. Most, if not all, of the forms may be found in Day's *Western Abenaki Dictionary* (Day 1994b, 1995) in the revised orthography he used in later work. This paper was originally published in *International Journal of American Linguistics* 30(4):371–392 (1964).

Eastern Algonquian

Although the Algonquian family was one of the families recognized in Gallatin's (1836) pioneering classification, and although it is one of the few Indian language families which have received considerable comparative study (e.g., Michelson 1912, 1935; Bloomfield 1925, 1946; Siebert 1941b; Geary 1941; Hockett 1957; Haas 1958a, 1958b; Voegelin 1941a), knowledge of its eastern members is still very inadequate.[1] Bloomfield (1946:85–86) reconstructed a protolanguage from four geographically central languages—Fox, Menominee, Ojibwa, and Cree—and, after taking into consideration the studies of Michelson and Siebert on some western and eastern languages, viewed it as Proto-Algonquian. Voegelin and Voegelin (1946) agreed in an opinion published the same year. Hockett (1948:130) queried the validity of the reconstruction for the entire family, however, remarking, "The course of wisdom for the reader of Bloomfield's Sketch is to replace 'PA' everywhere with 'PCA', standing for 'Proto-*Central*-Algonquian', and to withhold judgment on the status of the eastern and Plains languages until a good deal more of descriptive and comparative work has been done." Haas (1958a:162, 170) distinguished PCA from PCEA (Proto-Central-Eastern Algonquian) and pointed out that no reconstruction has taken eastern accentual systems into account. Although these different views apparently per-

This paper is based on research carried out in 1957–1963 and made possible by grants from the Spaulding-Potter Charitable Trusts of Manchester, New Hampshire, and from the National Science Foundation.

[1] It is instructive to compare the names and groupings of the eastern Algonquian languages in the following works: Michelson (1912), Bloomfield (1946), Voegelin (1941b), Voegelin and Voegelin (1944, 1946), Driver et al. (1953), Vinay (1953), and Trager and Harben (1958). It is apparent that considerable differences exist both in the entities recognized and in the relationships postulated.

sist, data for studying the question are scarcely more plentiful than they were in 1946 when Bloomfield called the grouping of Algonquian languages uncertain, "since most of them are scantily or poorly recorded" (1946:85). The only published description of a geographically eastern Algonquian language in modern terms was then and is now Voegelin's (1939, 1945, 1946) study of Delaware.

Data from the other living eastern languages are clearly desiderata. It may be noted here that the term "eastern" is misleading, inasmuch as the Montagnais-Naskapi dialects of Cree extend about as far eastward as Micmac, but "eastern Algonquian" has usually referred to languages south of the Saint Lawrence River and is so used here for want of a more accurate, simple alternative. Besides Delaware, the living languages in the region are Micmac, Maliseet-Passamaquoddy, Penobscot, and Saint Francis Abenaki[2]—the languages which Michelson (1912), using limited criteria, assigned to his Eastern Subtype. Linguists are now studying Micmac, Maliseet-Passamaquoddy, and Penobscot, and this paper presents data from Saint Francis Abenaki.

The Saint Francis Abenaki Dialect

The home village of the Saint Francis Abenakis is Odanak, Quebec, on the Saint Francis River, but about three-quarters of the band must now be sought in scattered locations in the eastern provinces and states. About 100 persons may be called speakers of Abenaki, having learned it as their first language, but probably less than 30 now speak it by preference. There are no monolingual speakers. Even those persons who were reared and still live in Abenaki-speaking homes speak either French or English as a second language, and the majority speak both. The children are not learning the native language, and the indications are that it will die with the older generation, although fragmentary knowledge will persist for some time to delight the tourist and confound the naïve. All informants agree that the nearest living relative to their dialect is Penobscot, excepting one informant who found Passamaquoddy more intelligible. Another close relative was briefly documented by Speck (1928b) just before it died out on the nearby Bécancour Reserve a few decades ago. Informant testimony further indicates that Abenaki speakers understand enough of Maliseet-Passamaquoddy to allow essential communication but understand practically nothing of Micmac, Montagnais, Tête-de-Boule, Algonquin, Saulteaux, and the dialects of Ojibwa.

The Saint Francis village has a history of complex population changes which have never been worked out in detail. It was formed about 300 years ago by refugees from New England,[3] and until sometime in the nineteenth century it received repeated increments of immigrants from New England and the upper

---

[2] In addition, a small vocabulary has been obtained recently from the last speaker of Wampanoag.
[3] The founding of the village was treated briefly in Day (1961).

Hudson River valley. The dialect is invariably called Abenaki, and large numbers of Abenakis did settle in the village in the early eighteenth century, arriving from central Maine both directly and via the missions of Sillery and the Chaudière (Bacqueville de la Potherie 1753 1:309; Charland 1942). This has tended to obscure the fact that the first settlers of the village were Sokokis,[4] and that in subsequent years large but unknown numbers of immigrants came from the region west of the Abenaki proper[5] and from tribes which, whatever the justification, are known by different names to both historians and linguists.[6] While the English usually referred to this band simply as "the Saint Francis Indians," French writers until a century ago recognized two groups within the village—the Abenakis and the Sokokis (J. Maurault 1866:572–573). They call themselves *wɜbanáhkiák* 'dawn land people', and this practice goes back at least 130 years,[7] but prior to this the more recent increments at least were known by names indicative of their places of origin (Kendall 1809). These distinctive names may have been of purely local rather than of gentilic significance, and without more information we may only speculate on the reason for the ascendency of the name Abenaki over the other names.

Neither is it clear yet whether a mixture of dialects or the predominance of one dialect accounts for the differences—first remarked by Maurault (1866:37, n. 2)—between the r-dialect recorded in seventeenth- and eighteenth-century manuscripts and the l-dialect of his time and of the present. Hallowell (1928) has discussed some of the implications of the mixture of immigrants and has called attention to non-Abenaki items in the kinship terminology. Traces of three dialects appear in the writer's recent data. It does not lie within the scope of this paper to seek out the antecedents of the current Saint Francis dialect. It will be called Abenaki here in conformity with general usage, but, considering its uncertain phylogeny, this arbitrary usage should not lead anyone to assume that the present-day speech is simply a descendent of the Abenaki recorded by Aubery[8] at Saint Francis or by Rasles (1833) at Sillery and perhaps elsewhere.

Purpose and Method

The full lexicon and grammar of Saint Francis Abenaki are not ready for publication, and the writer has been influenced by the thinking of Newman

[4] Charland (1942:16). His forthcoming history of Odanak will contain clearer evidence for the priority of the Sokokis in the village.

[5] That is, of those who bore the name in the earliest period, the Abenaki of Champlain, Druillettes, Bigot, and Rasles.

[6] The literature peoples the country between the Kennebec River and Lake Champlain with such tribes as the Arosagunticooks, Sokokis, Pigwackets, Ossipees, Penacooks, Cowasucks, Missiassiks, Pocumtucks, Squakheags, Nipmucs, and Mahicans. The original inhabitants of this territory largely found their way into the Saint Francis band.

[7] As shown by the title and text of Pial Wzôkhilain's (1830b) *Wôbanaki Kimzowi Awighigan*.

[8] For the writings of Father Joseph Aubery, see Pilling (1891:18–19).

(1952) and his discussants to offer a selected vocabulary as an interim paper. The purpose of this paper is to provide a vocabulary which will serve as a tool for both comparative studies and lexicostatistic investigations and which therefore should be comparable to existing Algonquian data at as many points as is permitted by the size of the vocabulary. The method chosen for approaching this perhaps unattainable goal has been to combine the English glosses found in several standard lists—those of Gallatin (1836), Gibbs (1867) and Swadesh (1955); glosses of forms cited in the comparative studies of Bloomfield, Voegelin, Geary, Siebert, Hockett, and Haas; additional items suggested by Karl V. Teeter; a full schedule of body parts; and the names of a few natural objects whose occurrence throughout the Algonquian-speaking areas seemed probable. These glosses have been alphabetized and provided with the best Abenaki equivalents known to the writer. Most of the Abenaki forms given here have been heard many times, and all have been verified anew by two or more of the best informants during the preparation of this paper.[9] When translation of a gloss taken from one of the above comparative studies does not yield an Abenaki cognate for a published PCA reconstruction, another Abenaki form containing a cognate or a possible cognate is given if one is known, but the noncognate form is allowed to stand as evidence of lexical variation. Where no Abenaki cognate appears, none could be found. In such instances, we are not entitled to conclude that a cognate does not occur in Abenaki, but its occurrence must be considered unlikely considering the extent of the search. PCA forms are cited without reference to their sources. Cross-references lead to additional examples and to possible cognates. The third-person singular animate is translated by 'he, him, his' except in a few instances which demand a feminine pronoun.

Orthography

Inasmuch as this vocabulary precedes publication of Saint Francis Abenaki phonology, a brief explanation of the orthography used is in order. The Abenaki forms represent the dialect spoken by the majority of the band. They are the most explicit forms heard for each word, excepting only the overexplicit, syllable-by-syllable examples furnished occasionally by informants to help the writer through his more obtuse moments. Spaces between words represent open juncture in the form of a brief, soundless hiatus before word-initial /p t k s/ and other points of potential open juncture before other word-initial phonemes.

The vowel phonemes are short oral /e/, which is usually [ə]; normal oral /i a o/; and normal nasalized /ɔ̃/. A smooth onset is usual for initial vowels and does not contrast with occasional [ʔV] initial sequences. Vowel sequences are numerous

---

[9] In all, 36 informants have been consulted, but 3 have been particularly helpful in verifying this vocabulary: Ambroise Obomsawin, Théophile Panadis, and Edward Hannis.

and include two consecutive enunciations of the same vowel which are distinguished by distinct chest pulses even when stress is uniform for the sequence. The consonant phonemes are long, fortis stops /p t k/; short, lenis stops /b d g/; long, fortis sibilant /s/; short, lenis sibilant /z/; spirants /w h/; lateral /l/; and nasal continuants /m n/. /p t k s/ are always voiceless. /b d g z/ are voiceless in word-final position and in word-initial position when preceded by open juncture—either preutterance silence or the optional interword juncture—or by /p t k s/ in the preceding word. They are voiced in word-medial position and in word-initial position when preceded by a vowel or by /w l m n/ in the preceding word without an intervening juncture. /w/ is voiced except between consonants and in word-final position after /k/. /l/ is voiced except after /h/, where it is voiceless, and after /nh/, where it is voiceless and spirantized. /h/ is always a voiceless spirant, except when it follows a vowel and precedes /p/, /t/, /k/, or /s/, where its more usual allophone is a brief soundless hiatus. /m n/ are voiced except in utterance-initial position before /p/, /t/, /k/, /s/, or /h/, where voiceless allophones are more usual.

Stresses are strong /ˊ/ and normal (unmarked). Normal stress appears as weak stress [ˇ] on /e/ and as medium stress [ˋ] on /i a o ɔ/ and on syllabic /m n/. All nonfinal syllabics except /e/ are lengthened by strong stress, except when the syllabic is followed by a long consonant or /h/. A strong stress on a word-final syllable lengthens /b d g z/ and usually lengthens /m n l/. A strongly stressed final vowel is lengthened but devoiced over the last part of its duration, giving the impression of a short vowel.

No exposition of intonation patterns will be given here. Rather, for the sake of uniformity, all forms are given in the citation intonation. This is one of the simplest intonations and the only one in which all utterances, even interrogatives, may be heard. Its pitch patterns are nearly identical with its stress patterns, that is, pitch rises as stress increases, with an additional half-tone rise in pitch on the last strongly stressed syllable in the utterance. The relationships of stress, pitch, and segment length may be illustrated by the words /menónigén/ 'it is smooth', /bɔ̃gwigíd/ 'pure animate one', and /mátkadá/ 'it is all burned up'. Phonetically these are respectively

$$
\begin{array}{cccc}
1 & 3 & 2 & 4 \\
\end{array}
$$
[m ɔ̌ n ó· n ì g ɔ́ n:],
$$
\begin{array}{ccc}
2 & & 2 \quad 4 \\
\end{array}
$$
[p ɔ̌ ŋ g w ì g í ṭ:],
$$
\begin{array}{ccc}
3 & & 2 \quad 4 \\
\end{array}
$$
[m á ṭ: ḳ· à d ḁ́ą],

where [ˌ] indicates a fortis stop or sibilant and [ₒ] indicates a voiceless coda of a vowel.[10]

[10][The vocabulary that concluded this paper has been omitted.—Eds.]

8

The Identity of the Sokokis

Specifying who the Sokokis were and where they were located in early colonial times is important for Western Abenaki history, because they were the principal founding group at Saint Francis and have remained a significant presence there. Past historians often assumed that the Sokokis migrated to Quebec from the Saco River in western Maine, in part because of the vague similarity between the names. However, examination of seventeenth-century French and English documents reveals variants of the name such as *Sokokiois, Suckquakege,* and *Squakey* that appear to equate with *Squakheag,* the name of a village and a tribe in Northfield, Massachusetts. If the equation is valid, this places the Sokokis in the middle Connecticut River valley rather than western Maine. This paper, which demonstrates the value of place-name analysis for piecing together the history of a poorly documented region, was originally published in *Ethnohistory* 12(3):237–249 (1965).

It is now orthodox ethnography to place a tribe named Sokoki on the Saco River in western Maine in the early seventeenth century, the period of discovery and exploration in that region (Hodge 1907–1910 2:613; Swanton 1952:14; Speck 1928b:173). The purpose of this paper is to query this generally accepted tenet. There were, to be sure, Indians living on the Saco River, and there was a tribe named *Sokoki.* It is only the equivalence of the two which will be questioned.

Doubt enters when we realize that none of the contemporary writers called the Saco River Indians "Sokokis." The Indian village at the mouth of the river was first visited by Samuel de Champlain (1922–1936 1:323) in 1605, and he called the Indians *Almouchiquois.* This name, which was probably learned from the Micmacs among whom the French were then settled at Port Royal, was also used by Marc Lescarbot and Father Pierre Biard (Thwaites 1896–1901 1:6, 2:229, 3:209). The English also learned of the Saco River in 1605 from the Indians whom George Waymouth took captive to England, but they recorded no name for the tribe (Purchas 1905–1907 4:1873–1875). Captain John Smith visited the mouth of the Saco with one of Waymouth's Indians in 1614, but neither he nor Ferdinando Gorges's men who wintered there in 1616 left us any tribal name (J. Smith 1836 2:27, 42; Gorges 1837 5:57). The Indians at the head of the river were known as Pigwackets from the time they were visited by Gorges and Richard Vines in 1642 (Winthrop 1853 2:89). Throughout the seventeenth

This paper was presented at the Twelfth Annual Meeting of the American Indian Ethnohistoric Conference held at the American Philosophical Society, Philadelphia, November 6–7, 1964.

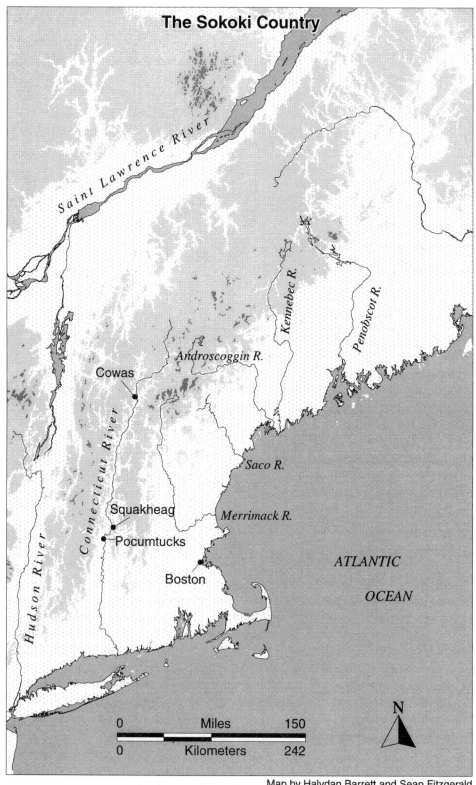

The Sokoki Country

Saint Lawrence River

Kennebec R.

Penobscot R.

Androscoggin R.

Cowas

Connecticut River

Saco R.

Squakheag

Merrimack R.

Hudson River

Pocumtucks

Boston

ATLANTIC

OCEAN

0   Miles   150

0   Kilometers   242

N

Map by Halvdan Barrett and Sean Fitzgerald

century, the English referred to the Indians on the lower river simply as Saco Indians, and they were still called "the Saco tribe" in the 1726 census when there were only four men left (Wendall 1866).

The tribal name *Sokoki* appeared first in the *Jesuit Relations* for the year 1643 (Thwaites 1896–1901 24:183, 193). The occasion was the appearance of a Sokoki captive brought to Three Rivers by the Algonquins and ransomed by the French as a peace gesture toward the Iroquois, whose allies the Sokokis were at that time. In return, the Sokokis made an unsuccessful attempt to ransom Father Isaac Jogues from the Mohawks. For the next 20 years or so the Sokokis reappear in the French documents in a series of minor incidents, and then they begin to appear as new and not yet stable residents along the Saint Lawrence River. In all the French record, excepting only one statement which we shall examine later, we can deduce only that the Sokokis were on the border of Acadia and New England and between the Abenakis and the Iroquois.

The first writer to place the Sokokis on the Saco River seems to have been William Williamson, whose history of Maine was published in 1832 (Williamson 1832 1:28, 458, 465). Williamson was obviously a century too late to have known the Saco Indians himself, and, although he made good use of his materials, definitive information on the Sokokis was even less available to him than to us. He cited only Baron Louis Armand Lahontan as saying that Acadia included the Saco and that the Sokokis were one of the tribes of Acadia. Actually, Lahontan bounded Acadia at the Kennebec River, and, although he included Sokokis in his table of Acadian tribes, in his text he included them in "some other erratick Nations, who go and come from *Acadia,* to *New-England*" (Lahontan 1905 1:90, 327, 339). But to do Williamson justice, his proposal was frankly tentative. He said merely, "The *Sokokis* are supposed to have been the natives, who dwelt about the river Saco in Maine" (Williamson 1832 1:458). He seems to have been helped toward this conclusion by the resemblance of the names, because he later remarks, a bit ambiguously, "The tribe must have inhabited the banks of Saco River, for there is none other of that name upon the Atlantic Coast" (Williamson 1832 1:465). I take this to mean that there is no other river but the Saco whose name resembles Sokoki. And indeed, the resemblance of the names may have had more than a little to do with stabilizing the assumed association of the tribe and the river. It completes the alliterative array of tribes and habitats in Maine— the Passamaquoddies on Passamaquoddy Bay, the Penobscots on the Penobscot River, the Canibas on the Kennebec, the Arosagunticooks on the Androscoggin, and so, naturally, the Sokokis on the Saco.

But when we examine the origins of these names, we find that they come from two quite different words. It is important to straighten out this linguistic snarl, because the superficial similarity of the names is seductive, and Williamson is not the only one who has been led astray.

The Saco River. Place-name students have made heavy weather of this name for a century, but the early forms show a surprising uniformity. The earliest recorders all wrote something like "Sowacotuck," Champlain's variant "Chauocoet" being probably the pronunciation of his Micmac interpreter.[1] It seems to be an Abenaki word, because the English learned it from the Indians of the middle Maine coast. We find the Abenaki Chief Atiwaneto using it in 1752 (O'Callaghan 1853–1887 10:252), and it is still a good Abenaki word, recognized at once by native speakers. The correct form is *msoákw̥-htə́kw̥.* The initial *m* and the *w*'s are voiceless, and saying this word over almost convinces one that this is the word which John Smith and the others heard. It means 'dead tree river' and can refer to trees killed by fire, beaver flooding, or girdling for land clearing. When the English learned that the last syllable, their *-tuck* or *-tock,* meant 'river', they may well have decided that it was easier to say "Sowaco River" than "Sowaco-tuck." From "Sowaco" to modern "Saco" is but a step, and we note Christopher Levett's short form "Sawco" as early as 1623 (Baxter 1893:93).

The Sokoki Tribe. The conventional form of this name is much the same as the earliest form used by the French writers and the one used most commonly by them ever since,[2] although almost every possible combination of *k, c,* and *q* have been used for representing the two *k* sounds. But we may observe the early and occasional occurrence of a *w* vowel sequence after the first *k,* that is, *sokwe-* or *sokwa-* instead of *soko-.* Which form was closer to the Indian word which the French heard? One way to get at this is to decide what language the name came from. The French may have heard it from the Sokoki captives and visitors, but they more probably heard it from the Algonquins, their neighbors, converts, and allies. If this be true, we should notice particularly Father Jérôme Lalemant's statement that the Algonquins called this tribe "Assokwekik" (Thwaites 1896–1901 28:275).

We need not infer that this is an Algonquin word. It is more probably the Algonquin form of the Sokokis' name for themselves.[3] No Sokoki vocabulary has come down to us, but the only identifiable Sokokis are to be found in the Saint Francis Abenaki band. Father Thomas Charland has shown recently that the Saint Francis band was founded by the Sokokis (Charland 1942:17, 1964:17). Father Joseph Maurault described the functioning of the Sokoki and Abenaki moieties in the band in the early nineteenth century, and official records until about 1850 referred to the Abenakis and Sokokis of Saint Francis.[4] From this band we have three more witnesses for the *kw* form. Augustin Gill, a native

---

[1] The Micmac initial sibilant was formerly *š* (Pacifique 1939:11).
[2] These are, namely, Vimont's "Socoquiois" and Jogues's "Sokokiois" (Thwaites 1896–1901 24:183, 295).
[3] This seems likely inasmuch as the English obtained a similar name for the tribe in its premoval location.
[4] See for example "Rapport des Commissaires spéciaux, nommés le 8 septembre, 1856, pour s'enquérir des affaires des Sauvages en Canada," in Bergeron (1960:19).

Indian Agent, gave us "Ozoquackki" (Vassal 1811–1889 File 16, 6[7], 28 June 1816); Maurault, the Saint Francis missionary a century ago, wrote "Sokwakiak" (J. Maurault 1866:5); and Rowland Robinson, whose ear for dialect was uncommonly good, got "Zooquagese" from his Indian informant at Lake Champlain (Robinson 1892a:34).

I am happy that it turns out this way, because *soko-* is quite untranslatable, but *sokw-* was a morpheme in good standing in the dialect of the Abenakis who came from Maine to the Canadian missions. J. B. Nudénans's (1760:161) dictionary of Abenaki roots and Latin equivalents gives "s8k8i. *dissolutio, diviso, in partes.*" Father Joseph Aubery's Abenaki-French dictionary gives a number of forms with the root "s8hk8" and such meanings as 'dissoudre, mettre en pieces, démonter' (Aubery 1715a:688). *Sohkw-* is still a morpheme in good standing at Saint Francis, and with the same range of meanings. There we have words like *sohkwá* 'break thou it open'; *sóhkwihlá* 'it breaks apart'; *nzóhkwigí* 'I am weakening, falling apart'; and *sóhkwiná kwíazón* 'open thy bundle'. And most important of all, they have the word *sohkwahkíak* 'the people who separated, broke apart'.

This furnishes us with a fairly good hypothesis that the Sokokis should be the Sokwakis and that the name meant 'the people who separated or broke apart'. Confirmation for our hypothesis, for both the form and the meaning applied to the Sokokis of Saint Francis, is tucked away in Rowland Robinson's history of Vermont. It derives from Robinson's long acquaintance with the Saint Francis Indians, who could be found on the eastern shore of Lake Champlain until about five years ago. He quoted his friend, John Watso, as saying, "they gave themselves the name of 'Zooquagese,' the people who withdrew from the others" (Robinson 1892a:34).

We have digressed, but what I think we have achieved is demonstrating that, while the modern conventional names "Saco" and "Sokoki" resemble each other, the original names, "Sowaco" and "Sokwaki," did not. Therefore Williamson's proposal was not soundly based, but that it was false remains to be shown.

The existence of a single piece of French testimony regarding the homeland of the Sokokis was mentioned earlier. The writer was Jesuit Father Gabriel Druillettes, who visited New England in 1650 and 1651 on political missions for the Council of Quebec. His purpose was to enlist the support of the English and of the New England Indians against the Iroquois in return for free trade with Quebec, which the Massachusetts Bay Colony desired. Druillettes's report on the first mission contained an unequivocal statement about the location of the Sokokis in the seventeenth century. He wrote plainly, "Kenetigouc est la rivière des Sokokiois" (Ferland 1882 1:393).

Since so much turns on this statement, let us scrutinize Druillettes's credentials. First, he was a contemporary. His New England trips took place only seven and eight years after the Sokokis appeared in Canadian history and before they began to move to the Saint Lawrence. Second, he had considerable opportunity to learn of their whereabouts from people who probably knew. He had made the acquaintance of the Abenakis on the Kennebec and of John Winslow, the Puritan agent at Augusta, six years before. He spoke with governors, magistrates, commissioners, the Reverend John Eliot, and others on his New England trips, and these officials were in communication with the Pynchons who were settled at Springfield among the River Indians and knew them well. Third, and most important, he had considerable personal contact with the Sokokis themselves. At his request, four tribes—the Penacooks, Sokokis, Pocumtucks, and Mahicans—held councils during the winter of 1650 and 1651 to debate the question of taking up arms against the Iroquois, and in April 1651, it was the Sokokis who brought him word of their decision to do so. Perhaps most significantly, a Sokoki accompanied Druillettes on his return trip from Quebec in the summer of 1651. In all this we should bear in mind that part of his mission was to learn about and report on the New England Indians. It is hard to doubt that Druillettes knew where the Sokokis lived, and he stated that they lived on the Connecticut.[5]

This leads us to inquire why, if the Sokokis, who were so prominent in the French documents, were natives of the Connecticut valley, the English records did not mention them. I think the answer to this is that they did. Let us recall that Sokoki is a French version of the tribal name and that the English heard, not that, but rather the native name, which was probably *Sohkwahki*, plural *Sohkwahkiák*. When we allow Druillettes to direct our attention away from the Saco and toward the Connecticut, and when we look on the Connecticut—not for Sokokis but for Sokwakis—our eye is at once caught by the name of the village which existed at Northfield, Massachusetts, until 1669—Squakheag. Perhaps Squakheag does not sound convincingly like Sokwaki, but this is only one of many early forms of the name, the one which has become usual since J. H. Temple and George Sheldon (1875) wrote their history of Northfield. Magistrate Daniel Gookin (1792:160), who was there in 1669, as well as the Connecticut Council, and others, wrote "Suckquakege" and "Soquogkeeke," while naming the Indians "Squakeys."

New England historians have treated the Squakheags as merely another Connecticut River band, and most of what we know about them in place was collected by Temple and Sheldon. But the Massachusetts people seem not to have gotten as well acquainted with them as with the tribes farther down river. We are not obliged to interpret Druillettes's succinct statement to mean that all the Connecticut River tribes were Sokokis. Their distinctiveness from the Pocumtucks, their neighbors on the south, is indicated by Druillettes's naming the Sokokis and Pocumtucks as independent tribes (Thwaites 1896–1901 36: 101);

---

[5] The documents pertaining to Druillettes's missions were collected in Druillettes (1857).

by John Pynchon's distinguishing the Sowquackicks or North Indians from the Pocumtucks and other River Indians whom he knew well; and finally by the protestations of the Pocumtucks themselves in 1663 that "they deplore it exceedingly, repudiate the deed and swear at the Sowquackick, because they have killed the Maquaas and they will have nothing to do with them." They also protested that "they were at too great a distance to prevent the proceedings of the Sowquackick [who] live at the head of the river of Caneticut" (O'Callaghan 1853–1887 13:308–309). The next year the Pocumtucks told the Dutch commissioners from Albany that "we have not troubled ourselves about our neighbors, the Soquackicks, when the Maquaes were at war with them last year" (O'Callaghan 1853–1887 13:380).

It appears highly probable that Gookin's name "Squakeys" was *Sohkwahki* with English plural -*s* and that his "Suckquakege" was the same name with the locative suffix -*k*. Thus the English and Dutch testimony is seen to confirm the Saint Francis testimony for the *sohkwa-* form and Druillettes's testimony that the Sokokis belonged on the Connecticut River.[6]

At present it is not clear—at least not to the writer—just how far up the Connecticut River the Sokoki territory extended. Late deeds by them state their claims on both sides of the river upstream into Vermont and New Hampshire (Wright 1905:125–128). These deeds were obtained for the purpose of clearing title to Fort Dummer and its environs 50 years after the Indians had left the Connecticut, but by the time settlements were made farther upstream the Sokokis were in Canada as either the belligerent or defeated allies of the French, and no deeds from them were thought necessary. Pynchon understood that they lived at the head of the Connecticut River, and while this may not have been exact, it does imply an occupation farther north than Northfield (O'Callaghan 1853–1887 13:308). The name of the Mascoma River suggests a Sokoki family hunting territory half way to the source.[7] It is entirely possible that the Cowas settlement of this period at Newbury, Vermont, was a Sokoki village. If we assume this, it makes it easier to understand how the Sokoki hunters could get involved with Algonquins from the Saint Lawrence River in 1643.

The foregoing now seems to be fairly straightforward, and in retrospect we may wonder how Williamson's association of Sokoki and Saco became established in the literature. Some of the routes by which it spread can still be traced. Only four years after Williamson's work, Albert Gallatin (1836:32) came to the

---

[6]The early English literature contains two other tribal names which should be noticed in passing. Gorges (1837:90) mentioned a tribe called the "Sockhigones," which was probably the Sokokis. The form of the name is unique, but after our experience with Sokoki and Sokwaki, my guess is that the original was *sohkwi-hkōn-i* 'the separated camp person' plus the English plural -*s*. Rasles (1833:522) mentioned a tribe which he called "les Sañ8anakets." The name is Abenaki and means 'southerners', but we are left to speculate which of the tribes south of the Abenakis was intended.

[7]As the family hunting territory of one "Mascommah." See Wright (1905:123, 128, 133).

same conclusion in his *Synopsis of the Indian Tribes,* which became a standard reference. He did not mention Williamson and may not have seen his work, but he was surely influenced by the apparent similarity of the names "Saco" and "Sokoki." Trying to fix the boundary between the Abenakis and the southern New England Indians, he said, "Governor Sullivan placed it at the River Saco; and this is corroborated by the mention made by the French writers of a tribe called Sokokies." Williamson was copied directly in Lorenzo Sabine's (1857:27) *Indian Tribes of New England* in 1857, but the same year dissents and partial dissents commenced to appear. In the next 15 years there were five of them. In 1857 John G. Shea brought out his edition of Druillettes's writings, and his footnote on the Sokokis gave both Williamson's and Druillettes's statements without comment (Druillettes 1857:317). In 1866, his six-volume translation of Father P. F. X. de Charlevoix's history of New France began to appear, and Shea again paraphrased Druillettes in a footnote without expressing his own opinion (Charlevoix 1866–1872 2:155, n. 1). The same year, J. Maurault (1866:5), who knew the writings of both Druillettes and Williamson, tried to reconcile their statements by extending the Sokokis from the Connecticut to the Saco. To accomplish this, he had to include the Penacooks on the Merrimack River. While these two tribes appear to have been friendly and were possibly related, they were distinguished in contemporary documents, and Maurault's solution was sheer expediency. The same year, Father Eugene Vetromile (1866:21, 27) equated the Sokokis with the Massachusetts and Narragansetts, because on François Du Creux's map the name Soquoquioii was spread across southern New England. But Du Creux worked in France and never visited Canada, and we do not know his sources for New England (Du Creux 1951–1952 1:xii). It appears that they were limited and that he tried to cover the map with them as well as he could. In 1872, Edward Ruttenber also objected that the Sokokis could not have been Saco Indians, because Count Frontenac had placed them "toward Lake Champlain."[8] Frontenac's statement, however, was made 13 years after the Indians had left the Connecticut valley following King Philip's War.

It seems likely that whatever influence these scattered objections might have had was lost when the editors of two important collections of early documents adopted Williamson's solution. Both Edmund O'Callaghan, who edited the New York colonial documents, and Reuben Gold Thwaites, who edited the *Jesuit Relations,* followed Williamson in their notes, and these opinions seem to have been decisive in the scholarly world.[9] In any event, when the *Handbook of American Indians* appeared about 60 years ago, it stated that the Sokokis oc-

---

[8]Although for some reason he chose to call them by the old name of the Saco River "Sowacotucks," probably by way of trying to bestow a more ancient name on the tribe, having already assumed the Saco as their location.
[9]O'Callaghan (1853–1887 9:5, n. 1) wrote, "Or Saco Indians; they were an Abenaqui tribe. *Williamson* [1832] I. 465." Thwaites wrote (1896–1901 24:311, n. 15), "An Abenaki tribe settled along the Saco River."

cupied the banks of the Saco River, almost Williamson's own words (Hodge 1907–1910 2:613), and I think there has not been a contrary voice raised from that day to this.

Summary. "Sokoki" was a French convention. The native name was probably "Sokwaki." No early writer placed either Sokokis or Sokwakis on the Saco River, but our best contemporary witness, Druillettes, placed them on the Connecticut River. Both English and Dutch writers knew Soquackicks or Squakheags on the Connecticut River north of the Pocumtucks. The idea that the Sokokis belonged on the Saco was proposed tentatively by two writers who were a hundred years too late to know the Saco Indians and two or three decades too early to see the crucial documents in print. It seems probable that they were led astray by the superficial similarity of the names Saco and Sokoki and that the true identity of the Sokokis was obscured by the superficial dissimilarity of Sokoki and Squakheag. Somehow, this erroneous opinion became established in our reference literature with two curious results: New England historians have known a Squakheag tribe, which, like many others, simply fled to Canada and disappeared, and Canadian historians have been at a loss to identify the Sokokis who were prominent in their early history.

9

An Agawam Fragment

Determining the distribution of the original languages and dialects of the middle and upper Connecticut River valley has been stymied for lack of all but a few scraps of data. One such fragment is a list of 13 month names recorded during the mid-seventeenth century by the trader William Pynchon and his son of Springfield, Massachusetts. The language, tentatively identified as that of the Agawams, is of a New England type, with affinities to Massachusett, Narragansett, and Western Abenaki. Some interesting ethnographic details can be gleaned from an analysis of the names, which describe phases in the seasons of the year. This paper was originally published in *International Journal of American Linguistics* 33(3):244–247 (1967).

Linguistic data from interior New England have always been scarce, and linguistic classifications in this region have been tentative as a consequence (Voegelin and Voegelin 1946; Day 1962b). The only data for any dialect of the Connecticut River valley are 13 names of months, if we disregard the place-names and personal names which come to us without translations. These names of months are found in an account book of William Pynchon of Springfield, Massachusetts, which is now among the Judd papers in the Forbes Library at Northampton, Massachusetts.[1] Inasmuch as these names may well be the only specimens of this dialect which we shall ever have, they deserve careful scrutiny. They have already appeared in print at least twice, having been copied by S. J. of N. (probably Sarah Jacobs of Natick [Jacobs 1856]) and by Harry Andrew Wright (1949 1:253). These students agreed that the list is in the handwriting of William Pynchon's son, John. Their readings of this handwriting differ in places, and neither attempted any analysis, being content to reproduce Pynchon's definitions.

The following is based on the writer's examination of the Pynchon account book in 1962. From their position in the book, we may suppose that the names of the months were written in late 1645. Apparently a first draft attempting to equate the Indian and the English months once occupied the top of the page which has been torn off leaving only:

The data for this note were gathered under National Science Foundation Grant No. G-17946.
[1] The Forbes Library catalog provides some pertinent bibliographical data: "Pynchon, William, 1590–1662. Record of accounts with early settlers and Indians. Carried forward from previous book around Sept. 1645 and to a new book around Mar. 1650. In handwriting of John Pynchon, his son, 137 l., 34 cm. Binder's title: Judd Manuscript: Accounts, Springfield, Mass." The names of the months occupy the reverse of leaf iii.

-arr—November
-kesos—December
-pquaho—January

A later version, which remains on the lower part of the page, is transcribed below. For those names which are followed by both a meaning and an identification, the meaning was written first and on the line in the original, and the identifications in terms of English months were inserted above and indicated by a caret. These insertions are placed within parentheses in the transcription.

"Papsapquoho, &, Lowatanassick they say are both one: : And then if they be reckned both for one: they recken but <u>12</u> months <u>to</u> ye yeare as we doe And the [sic] make ye yeare to begine in Squannikesos (as far as I yet can <u>understand</u> <u>ym</u> so call ye first month

1. Squannikesos—When they set Indian corne (pt of Aprill & pt of May)
2. moonesquan nimockkesos—when women weed theire corne (pt of May & pt of June)
3. Towwakesos—when they hill Ind corne (pt of June & pt of July)
4. matterl lawawkesos—when squashes are ripe & Ind beans begin to be eatable micheeneekesos—when Ind corne is eatable
6. pah[?]quitaqunkkesos—ye middle between harvest & eating Ind corne
7. pepewarr—bec: of white frost on ye grass & grain
8. qunnikesos
9. papsapquoho, about ye 6.th day of January or, Lowatannassick: So caled bec: they account it ye middle of winter.
10. Squo chee kesos—bec ye sun hath strength to thaw
11. Wapicummilcom—bec ye ice in ye river is all gone (pt of February & pt of March)
12. Namassack kesos—because of catching fish (pt of March & pt of Aprill)."

For the analysis of these names, available vocabularies for other southern New England languages were consulted and proved useful in a few instances. Most progress, however, was made through the Saint Francis Abenaki dialect,[2] which, being a living language, offered the practical advantages of resources which could be explored with informants. This procedure had some theoretical justification, inasmuch as most of the River Indians eventually found their way into the Saint Francis band.

"Squannikesos": Abenaki *sigwani gizos* 'spring's moon'.

"moonesquan nimockkesos": Narragansett *monaskúnnemun* 'to weed' (R. Williams 1866:124) provides the most similar stem, but an Abenaki type animate and intransitive infinitive *-mek* is indicated. Abenaki *mezaskenimek* 'keeping weeds out' is inappropriate for the first weeding implied, and *mazastaimek* 'cleaning weeds out' lacks phonetic similarity.

---

[2] For orthographical values see Day (1964). Stress is unmarked in the present note, because many of the words were obtained from informants speaking different subdialects not yet described.

"Towwakesos": Abenaki *ɔ̃towahkahigamek gizos* 'hilling corn moon'.

"matterl lawawkesos": Abenaki *matahtawal gizos* 'mature flowers moon'.

"micheeneekesos": Abenaki *mitsini gizos* 'eating's moon'.

"pahquitaqunkkesos": Abenaki *pohkwidagwɔ̃goo gizos* 'it is early fall moon'.

"pepewarr": This word bears some resemblance to forms for 'winter', Abenaki *pebon,* Massachusett *pópon* (J. Trumbull 1903:131), but this month is too early for winter, and 'winter' is not close to Pynchon's explanation. More likely are Massachusett *toohpuwudt* 'when there is frost' (J. Trumbull 1903:166) and Abenaki *tohpoihla* 'there is white frost', even though they require that Pynchon have misheard *t* as *p*.

"qunnikesos": This name, the only one for which Pynchon did not give a definition, is transparently 'long moon', in Abenaki *kwenigizos.*

"papsapquoho": Abenaki *babassɔ̃pkwao* 'he [winter] half passes'.

"Lowatanassick": Abenaki *nɔ̃wihponassik* 'where it is middle winter'. It becomes obvious now why the Indians said these two names were for the same moon and why Pynchon got only one meaning for the pair, but one name may have been for the date of midwinter and the other for the month which followed.

"Squo chee kisos": Abenaki *tokskwatsit gizos* 'ice honey-combs moon'.

"Wapicummilcom": The best Abenaki fit for this name is *ohpihkamalkin* 'stepping on it' with the established connotation 'ice solid enough to walk on' as distinct from ice which can be crossed only by crawling. This is exactly contrary to Pynchon's understanding of the word, but possibly he was given a negative, something like *mat ohpihkamalkino* 'not stepping on it', and failed to hear it all.

"Namassack kesos": Abenaki *namassak gizos* 'fishes moon'. It should be noted that both S. J. and Wright read Pynchon's word as "namossack," which is a little closer to Natick *namohsog* but still differs in the plural suffix.

Pynchon did not specify the band from which he obtained this list of names. His records show trading contacts with Indians from Wethersfield, Connecticut, on the south to Northfield, Massachusetts, on the north, so any of the tribes within these limits may be considered as possible sources. The natural assumption, however, is that he would obtain them from the neighboring Agawams or from the related, perhaps identical, Woronocos with whom he was in frequent contact. The earliness of the spring, as indicated by months 1, 11, and 12, suggests the vicinity of Springfield rather than that of Northfield, which is in a different climatic and ecological zone in spite of a mere 50 miles of separation (Westveld et al. 1956).

It is natural to examine this unique specimen for clues to the nature of the dialect, but it would be easy to make too great demands on so slender a bit of data. Not only is the sample small, but we cannot expect certainty in John Pynchon's record of a language which he admits he had not learned. Certain tentative observations may nevertheless be advanced. The most obvious characteristic is the persistence of Proto-Algonquian *l*. It was this, apparently, together with Eliot's much-quoted statement regarding Massachusett *n* and Nipmuck *l* (Eliot 1832; R. Williams 1866:129), which prompted S. J. to call the dialect Nipmuck, but this is not justified until Nipmuck is better defined, as PA *l* seems to have persisted in Penacook, Pocumtuck, and Squakheag also. The nasalized vowel observed in Mohegan-Pequot, Narragansett, Massachusett, and Kennebec Abenaki seems to occur in Pynchon's sixth month (Goddard 1965). Matching both the sound and sense of Pynchon's forms requires one Massachusett-Narragansett stem which Abenaki lacks, namely, *monaskúnne-* 'weed', and four Abenaki roots which Massachusett-Narragansett lacks, namely, *gizos* 'month', *-ahtawa-* 'blossom', *babass-* 'half', and *ɔpkwa-* 'pass'. Four Abenaki affixes lacking in Massachusett-Narragansett are required, namely, animate and intransitive infinitive *-mek;* inanimate plural *-l, -Vl;* animate *-k, -Vk;* and generalized locative *-assik.* Months 1, 5, 7, 8, and 12 can be explained by Massachusett-Narragansett vocabularies, and months 3, 10, and 11 might possibly have been explained if the full resources of the living language could have been tapped. Mohegan-Pequot sources and the Mahican sources available to the writer offer little help with these names. The important Moravian manuscripts were not seen, however.

A few details of Agawam culture may be gleaned from these names for the ethnologist, but there is little that is new. Subsistence appears to have been primarily agricultural, considering that the annual cycle commenced with spring planting, and six months took their names from corn, beans, and squash culture. The name of one month points plainly to utilization of the spring runs of fish in the Connecticut River. The lack of a maple sugar making month, found among the Abenakis, is no more than suggestive, as the Penobscots, who made maple sugar, nevertheless did not name a month for it (Speck 1940). If, as we suppose, the names originated in the Springfield region, the lack becomes significant, as the sugar maple is not a common component of the forest there as it is farther up the river (Bromley 1935). Although no month was named for hunting, there is no reason to doubt that hunting was practiced. The 1636 deed to Agawam reserved the Indians' right to take deer (Wright 1905:12), and a single year of trading by the Pynchons yielded 2,000 skins of beaver alone (Wright 1949 1:41). Any significance which may repose in the number of months recognized, in the spring new year, or in the midwinter date must be extracted from a comparative study beyond the scope of this note.

10

Historical Notes on
New England Languages

A survey of sources on Algonquian languages spoken now and formerly in New England reveals a hiatus for the interior—particularly the western part of that region—leaving today's Saint Francis Abenaki as the principal source for the area. Day mentions his hope that the "Mots loups" manuscript, which he had discovered several years earlier and was in the process of preparing as a scholar's edition (Day 1975c), would provide substantial documentation of at least one language in the poorly attested area, and he voices optimism that a careful collation of data from all the available sources should make it possible to reconstruct the aboriginal linguistic map of New England, at least in its main outlines. This paper was originally published as pp. 107–112 in *Contributions to Anthropology: Linguistics I (Algonquian),* Anthropological Series 78, National Museum of Canada Bulletin 214, Ottawa (1967).

In panorama, New England Algonquian is very reminiscent of a northern muskeg, with its islands of more or less firm ground rising out of a generally uncertain terrain. The firmest ground is formed by the two dialects still spoken in the region—Penobscot and Maliseet-Passamaquoddy—living languages offering no particular obstacles to the techniques of descriptive and historical linguistics, and it is gratifying that Frank Siebert's extensive study of Penobscot continues and that Karl Teeter has commenced the study of Maliseet-Passamaquoddy. No other Algonquian dialects are still spoken in New England, although two or three persons possess a limited knowledge of Wampanoag which may be vernacular. The Saint Francis Abenaki dialect, having western New England origins, is still spoken at Odanak, Quebec, and by members of the band elsewhere.

For two extinct dialects, there is abundant documentation from the seventeenth and eighteenth centuries. The speech of the Abenakis, who came from the Kennebec River to the Sillery and Chaudière missions, is represented by Rasles's celebrated dictionary.[1] In fact, this dialect is one of the best documented of Algonquian languages. Besides Rasles, both Crespieul and Bigot wrote in it at Sillery, and to this dialect belongs also the two-volume dictionary of Aubery, although it was signed and dated at Saint Francis. The large dictionary of

Most of the data in this paper were obtained in the course of research under grants from the Spaulding-Potter Charitable Trusts of Manchester, New Hampshire, and from the National Science Foundation.

[1] See Pilling (1891) for all Algonquian works not cited in a reference.

LeSueur, if it is ever found, will probably prove to be in the same dialect, judging from the fragment in the archives of the Séminaire de Québec. Lesser works by Virot and Roubaud and Nudénans's dictionary of roots are in this dialect also. The mouth of the Kennebec, the Pemaquid region, is witnessed only by the short but significant vocabulary collected by the Waymouth expedition in 1605.

The other large linguistic monument in New England is formed by Eliot's Massachusett Bible, grammar, and religious tracts. These are supplemented by Cotton's vocabulary and a psalter and some notes by Experience Mayhew in the Martha's Vineyard dialect. Other southern New England dialects are represented by printed monuments ranging in volume and worth from Roger Williams's Narragansett "Key" through Pierson's Quiripi catechism and the late Mohegan-Pequot material salvaged in this century by Prince and Speck.[2] Some kind of all-time low in dialect documentation was reached for Schaghticoke, the refugee village on the Housatonic. From this almost completely acculturated group, Speck rescued three sentences and 23 words in 1903 (Prince and Speck 1903).

The Stockbridge band west of the Berkshires has provided us with several minor works—the vocabularies of Edwards and Jenks and the prayer books of the Sergeants and of Quinney and Aupaumut. These works and the vocabularies collected from Stockbridge descendants in Wisconsin by half a dozen students are generally counted as Mahican, but the dialectologist should consider the number of refugees who reached Stockbridge from the Wappinger country in Connecticut. Some future student of Mahican should examine all these documents and compare them with the Moravian manuscripts which represent the dialect of the Mahicans who migrated to the Susquehanna and later to the Ohio country.

It may be noted that all these data originated east of the Androscoggin River in Maine, on the southeastern coast, and west of the Berkshires. Perhaps the most conspicuous feature of Algonquian New England is the linguistic and ethnographic no man's land which occupies the heart of it—western Maine, New Hampshire, Vermont, most of Massachusetts, and northern Connecticut. There is not a single account or even an extended set of remarks about any group residing between the Kennebec River and Lake Champlain prior to the disruption of the early pattern by the plagues and by the wars which were almost continuous after 1675. Nor does there seem to be any linguistic data from this region—definite, dated, and derived from a specific tribe in its original location. The only data existing are place-names and personal names which are linguistic data of a sort but which are seldom unambiguous.[3] In the absence of data, all linguistic classifications for the region must be regarded as provisional.

[2] Speck (1928a) is the most substantial publication of this material and contains a bibliography of the other Mohegan-Pequot material in footnote 1, p. 206.
[3] There is one fragment from the periphery of the problem area. The account book of William Pynchon of Springfield, Massachusetts, contains the names of 13 months and three fur-bearing animals in the dialect of

This absence of data, however, has opened the door to invention. The Penacooks, who occupied the valley of the Merrimack River, may be taken as an
example. Both archeological reconnaissance and early documents indicate that
they were an important group. They were in generally friendly contact with the
English for about a century, but no one was thoughtful enough to leave a
Penacook vocabulary. Local enthusiasm could not tolerate this vacuum, and in
1853 Judge Chandler E. Potter wrote an article entitled "The Language and
Religion of the Pennacooks," actually an essay on local place-names, explaining
them all by the use of Cotton's Massachusett vocabulary. In 1898 John G.
Crawford wrote an article entitled "Indians of New Hampshire: Etymology of
their Language," in which he rebuked Potter for using Massachusett and then
produced an alleged Penacook vocabulary which had obviously been cribbed
from Laurent's *New Abenakis and English Dialogues* that had appeared a few years
before. Potter was a sober historian when he was not writing about the Penacooks, but his imaginative essays on them have taken the place of history in the
popular mind and even in the schoolroom. His writings were also reprinted in
Schoolcraft (1851–1857 5:217–237), and from there they found their way into
the *Handbook of American Indians* (Hodge 1907–1910). Serious students likewise have had their troubles trying to classify the Penacooks and have associated
them at times with the Abenakis, with the Massachusetts, and with the Mahicans, as well as at times according them separate status.[4]

It is much the same story for other tribes in the problem area, groups of dubious
affiliation which are mere names on the linguist's map when they appear at all—
the Missisquois, Cowasucks, Squakheags, Pocumtucks, Nonotucks, Agawams,
Woronocos, Nipmucs, Pigwackets, and others. Lacking linguistic data from them
in place, one must attempt to follow their migrations through the French and
English documents with the hope of catching up either with their modern
descendants or with a linguistic work which, although made at another station,
may be traced back to a particular band's place of origin in western New England.

Practically all the tribes in this problem area settled, after one to several
removals, at two mission villages on the Saint Lawrence River—the so-called
Abenaki villages of Saint Francis and Bécancour—but there is the additional
complication that these villages also received the more eastern Abenakis from the
Chaudière mission in 1705–1706 (Charland 1942:74), and Penobscot and Maliseet families at a later date. Bécancour now contains only three families and
practically no linguistic recollections. The descendants of those Bécancour families that migrated to Lake Saint John are now Montagnais in culture. Speck
(1928b) caught the last gasp of native language at Bécancour in 1912, but his

some Indians who traded with him about 1650. The original is in the Sylvester Judd papers, Forbes Library,
Northampton, Massachusetts.
[4]These efforts are summarized in Day (1962b).

naming it 'Wawenock' should be queried pending a thorough study of the history of the band.

This leaves Saint Francis as the only living linguistic and ethnographic source for western New England. The Saint Francis band, with its long existence as a small native enclave in rural French Canada, its 250 years of Christianity, its intermarriage with New England captives, and its Dartmouth-educated boys, has often been regarded as too civilized and has been largely by-passed by students in favor of what appeared to be more primitive groups. The band still contains a handful of elderly conservatives, however, and among them they have preserved a surprising amount of old lore. The language is still perfectly vigorous among the elderly and middle-aged. The problem is not, then, that there is no Saint Francis culture but that there are seemingly only one culture and one language in a village said to have been made up from ten or a dozen bands. Whose culture and language is it? Or if it is a composite, who contributed what? I have made a study of the family dialects within the band, of the genealogies of and dominant speech influences on each speaker, and finally of the historical movements of the various components of the band. Historical conclusions are not yet clear, but four family dialects have been distinguished, and the first data on the principal dialect, whatever its provenience, have just been published (Day 1964).

The other possibility for identifying dialects—that of finding a manuscript grammar, dictionary, or other linguistic record from some specific Western New England group en route to Canada—did not seem at all bright until 1960. Repeated attempts to find the LeSueur dictionary and the Cutter manuscript had failed.[5] But in that year, two breaks occurred. First, a map was found in the collection of the New Hampshire Historical Society (1795–1810), which showed that the language of the Indians on the upper Connecticut and Androscoggin rivers in the late eighteenth century was essentially the modern Saint Francis dialect. Second, and much more important, the archives of the Order of Saint Sulpice in Montreal became accessible to students for the first time in many years. These archives contain the manuscript dictionaries, grammars, and devotional texts produced by the Sulpician Fathers at their several Iroquoian and Algonquian missions. Eventually these missions were all united at Lake of Two Mountains, and there in the last century the manuscripts were seen by two investigators from the Bureau of American Ethnology, Erminnie A. Smith and James C. Pilling. Unfortunately, the Smith and Pilling lists do not entirely agree and together do not name all the manuscripts in the collection, which is a veritable treasure-trove of high interest to Algonquianists and Iroquoianists.[6]

---

[5]A vocabulary from the Indians who visited Cutter's truck house on the lower Saco River between 1742 and 1746. See Sullivan (1795:265).

[6]Many of the manuscripts are described in Pilling (1888, 1891) under the separate Sulpician authors. All of them may now be seen on microfilm at the American Philosophical Library in Philadelphia.

According to the Sulpician philologist, Jean-André Cuoq, there were formerly among the Sulpician documents two manuscripts which might have come from Western New England. In his Algonquin dictionary, in a footnote to the word "Maingan, *loup,*" he wrote, "Maingan is still the name of an extinct nation of Loups. Their language, judging by two notebooks in the hand of M. Mathevet, appears to me to hold a middle place between Algonquin and Abenaki, with a mixture of Iroquois. These two notebooks unfortunately perished in the fire of 1877" (Cuoq 1886:198). Again in his historical sketch of the Sulpician missions, he remarked, regarding Father Mathevet, "There remains to us still from this missionary other proofs of his zeal and of his ability, namely a vocabulary in the language of some Loups, a language which he would have wished to learn in order to instruct the poor infidels of that tribe, who would come to settle at the Lake" (Cuoq 1894:173). At one time or another, the French included under the name "Loup" all the tribes between Massachusetts and Virginia and even the Pawnee of the Great Plains. Of what possible significance, then, would Mathevet's lost notebooks be for New England studies? It seems to have escaped general attention that early maps placed the Loups on the lower Connecticut River, at Cowas on the upper Connecticut, at Penacook on the Merrimack, and even in western Maine.[7] It is true that a few Pawnees were known in the Montreal missions before Mathevet's time, and during the early years of his residence in Canada, Delawares from the Ohio country were well known to the French. Nevertheless, the Loups nearest Montreal and most likely to have been encountered by a Sulpician were those of western New England and the fugitive Schaghticokes on the Hudson. This made the loss of Mathevet's notebooks especially regrettable, but prior to 1960 there was no reason to suspect the existence of other Loup documents.

A search of the archives in 1960, nevertheless, turned up a Loup manuscript.[8] It was anonymous, approximately octavo, of about 120 pages, and was entitled simply "Mots loups." It was obvious from quick inspection that it was Algonquian and therefore not Pawnee. It was in an *l*-dialect and therefore not Wappinger or Mahican. Lexically, it was not Delaware. This seemed to leave only some tribe from the western New England region as the source. A study of the handwriting has since shown that the author was Father Jean-Claude Mathevet,[9] and circumstances point toward the period after 1740 and perhaps before 1760 as the time of its composition. Nowhere is the tribe that spoke this dialect clearly identified. Their own name for themselves is given, but it is a new name in the

[7] Especially the anonymous (1680) *Carte d'une Grande Partie du Canada* and Father Joseph Aubery's (1715c) *Carte pour les hauteurs de terre . . . .*

[8] I am grateful to J. Raymond Denault, director of the Canadian Microfilming Company, for discovering this manuscript and calling it to my attention.

[9] I am indebted to Father Thomas-Marie Charland, O.P., on whose paleographic authority this identification rests.

literature. Eventually it may prove informative. Internal evidence suggests that the manuscript may have been made at Missisquoi or from Indians who had migrated from Missisquoi. Inasmuch as Missisquoi may have been a refugee village at the time, this information permits only speculation that the dialect may have been Penacook or Schaghticoke, the Schaghticokes themselves being a refugee band of southern New England origins. In its present state, the manuscript is in two parts, which may represent two fascicles sewn together. The first 39 pages and a foreleaf appear to be a field notebook in which Mathevet recorded his first impressions of this dialect, judging from the crossed-out words and interlined corrections. The remainder of the manuscript is a revision which incorporates, in no particular order, new words and phrases and the writer's second thoughts on some, but not all, of the first part. It may well be that these are the same notebooks which Cuoq saw and thought had been lost.

This manuscript might have been mined immediately for linguistic and ethnographic data, but it appeared to be a reference point for Algonquian linguistics in New England on a par with Rasles's dictionary, Eliot's works, and Roger Williams's "Key," and, as such, deserving of publication. The redaction was accordingly commenced last year and is now well advanced. Pending the publication of the complete work and commentary, a few sidelights may be mentioned.

The words and phrases are arranged to form a Loup-French word and phrase book, but there is no alphabetical order. The order is either random or by groups of related ideas or objects, such as commonly occur in eliciting vocabulary. Verbs are frequently expanded. Loup words often have Algonquin or Iroquoian equivalents, and there are several inserted paragraphs in some Iroquoian language. These indications that the writer knew both Algonquin and Iroquoian were not very helpful even at the beginning of the study, because several of the Sulpicians learned both languages. Since it has been determined that the writer was Mathevet, whose knowledge of both languages is well exemplified in other manuscripts, these entries serve only to expand the semantic referents of the Loup words.

The most significant of the non-Loup insertions are some three pages of Loup-Abenaki comparisons and some miscellaneous Abenaki entries. The interesting thing about these Abenaki data is that they are unlike all the other Abenaki writings of the eighteenth century but practically identical with the modern speech at Saint Francis. They also shed new light on the century-old controversy about the apparent change from an *r*-dialect to an *l*-dialect among the Canadian Abenakis. Missionaries were still writing an *r* in 1760,[10] and educated Indians sometimes wrote *r* in their signatures until about 1850, at which time the spoken

[10]For example, Nudénans's (1760) dictionary and Father Pierre Roubaud's letter to the Abenakis in the Haldimand Papers, M.G. 2, Vol. B-26, Public Archives of Canada.

language most probably employed *l*.[11] It is very noticeable, but not particularly diagnostic, that most of the loan words in this dialect were drawn from English.

Scattered clues to the culture of these Loups will probably be of more value for characterizing the culture of the group when it has been identified than for identifying it.

In résumé, western and central New England have always been unknown territory linguistically, and no particular hope has been held out for new information on it. Four dialects from this region, however, still survive at Saint Francis, probably modified by contact with each other, and Mathevet's "Mots loups" probably represents another and much more divergent dialect from the region. I think that there is some reason to be optimistic that when an exhaustive and rigorous study has been made of the historical evidence for New England tribal movements, the peopling of Canadian missions, and the genealogies of specific families at Saint Francis, it will be possible to lay down the main boundaries of the languages and dialects on a map of New England.

[11]For example, Peter Paul Wzôkhilain signed his name Osunkhirhine, although he wrote four books in Abenaki employing "*l*" throughout.

11

Iroquois: An Etymology

A review of etymologies for the word *Iroquois* from eighteenth- and nineteenth-century sources underscores their inadequacies, but one, suggested by a nineteenth-century Oblate missionary based on a term borrowed from Montagnais into French, appears plausible. Because the word does not yield a satisfactory morphological analysis in Montagnais, however, it probably represents a borrowing into Montagnais from still another language. In an insightful observation, Day lists some European contact languages in addition to two Indian ones as possible donors. Subsequent research suggests that the word most likely originated in Basque, a possibility considered by Day, whence it was borrowed by way of a trade jargon into Montagnais and finally into French and English. This paper was originally published in *Ethnohistory* 15(4):389–402 (1968).

As William N. Fenton (1940:160) has remarked, "Perhaps no other people in the Americas has had more ink spilled over them than the Iroquois," but the meaning of their name has remained a mystery. They had been known to Europeans for nearly a century and a half when the explanation of Father P. F. X. de Charlevoix (1866–1872 2:189) was printed in 1744. He wrote:

> The name Iroquois is purely French, and is formed from the term *Hiro* or *Hero,* which means *I have said*—with which these Indians close all their addresses, as the Latins did of old with their *dixi*—and of *Koué,* which is a cry sometimes of sadness, when it is prolonged, and sometimes of joy, when it is pronounced shorter.

As late as 1867 Charlevoix's statement was being quoted without any strenuous objections (Parkman 1899:xlvii–xlviii, n. 1), and Abbé André Cuoq's (1870:103–104) etymology three years later was little more than a restatement of Charlevoix.[1] Nearly 150 years were required for a written dissent to appear, when Horatio Hale (1883:171) disposed of it with the comment, "It might be enough to say of this derivation that no other nation or tribe of which we have any knowledge has ever borne a name composed in this whimsical fashion." Hale himself thought that *Iroquois* came from the Huron language, inasmuch as Champlain learned the name before he had ever seen an Iroquois. He proposed no solution from Huron, however, falling back on Five Nations dialects and suggesting Mohawk *ierokwa* 'they who smoke' and Cayuga *iakwai* 'a bear'. J. N. B.

[1] Cuoq proposed Mohawk *iro* 'espece de terme sacramental employé dans les harangues' or '*il est arrivé*' and *kwe* 'hail'.

Hewitt (1888:188–189) denied the existence of *iakwai* in Huron and doubted the existence of *ierokwa* in any Iroquoian language. Hale (1888:290–291) replied to Hewitt's criticism, and Hewitt (1891:217–220) responded with a detailed rebuttal. Other explanations derived from Five Nations dialects followed— David Boyle's *karakwa* 'the sun' (Beauchamp 1905:166) and J. O. Brant-Sero's (1901:166) *I-ih rongwe* 'I am the Real Man'—but such contrivings seemed rather pointless after Hewitt (1888:189) had pointed out that the French had probably heard a Montagnais word rather than an Iroquois or Huron word. His counterproposal was Montagnais *irin* 'true' or 'real', *ako* 'snake', plus the French termination *-ois*. William M. Beauchamp (1905:165–166) agreed that *Iroquois* must have had its origin in the Algonquian languages, but of Hewitt's solution he commented, "This is much better, if not quite satisfactory. . . . The latest Algonquin dictionaries of the eastern nations do not contain Mr. Hewitt's words. The nearest approach to *ako* is *achgook*." Nevertheless, Hewitt reiterated his proposal in the *Handbook of American Indians,* revising the spelling to *Iri^{n}akhoiw* plus *-ois* and changing the source from Montagnais to Algonquin (Hodge 1907–1910 1:617). This time W. R. Gerard (n.d.) called the etymology impossible and denied the existence of an Algonquian word *akhoiw* 'snake', but neither he nor anyone else came forward with a Montagnais etymology.

The purpose of this paper is to call attention to a Montagnais etymology which was in print in an obscure journal even before Hale started the controversy, although it was apparently unknown to those who wrote on the subject about the turn of the century and, insofar as mention in the literature may be a criterion, appears to be still unknown. In 1880, Father Charles Arnaud, an Oblate missionary to the Montagnais, wrote a letter reporting on the Mission at Lake Saint John, and to this letter he appended explanations from Montagnais of some place and tribal names, including *Iroquois*. This letter and its appendix were printed in the *Annales de la propagation de la foi pour la province de Québec* for June 1880. A few extracts from the letter, including his explanation of *Iroquois,* were reprinted in the Annual Report of the Canada Department of Indian Affairs for 1884 (Vassal 1885). Then it dropped from the literature and from the consideration of students. Arnaud (1880:153) had written:

> Champlain qui a entendu ces noms pour la première fois de la bouche des montagnais, ses alliés, comme il les appela, et avec lesquels il voyageait dans ses découvertes, les a appliqués aux nations dont on lui parlait et a francisé ces noms: Iroquois, irnokué en montagnais, homme redoutable, homme à craindre. Je vous ai déjà fait observer que les lettres *l r n* se confondent et qu'on peut très bien dire irokue: pour homme terrible, redoutable. Cette nation était redoutable en effet à toutes les autres.

Arnaud heard *l*-dialects of Montagnais at his missions, so when he cites *irnokué* we may wonder what he was citing. A clue to the identity of this dialect and to the source of Arnaud's knowledge of it is found in his reference to "l'ancien montagnais que parlent encore certains de nos naskapis et dont la pronunciation est presque celle d'ottaouais" (Arnaud 1880:149). It is known that he was acquainted with Naskapis, both strays at the coastal missions and bands in the interior as far north as Fort Chimo and Baie des Esquimaux (Carrière 1958:86ff., 102, 104, 111, 112, 114, 116, 119, 120), and it was presumably from one of these groups that he became acquainted with what he called "l'ancien montagnais."

This is an attractive etymology. It has the desired Montagnais origin, and considerable confidence may be placed in Arnaud's authority. At the time of writing the above statement he had lived 30 years with the Montagnais, even being mistaken for an Indian, and the Indians acknowledged his excellent command of the language (Carrière 1958:33–34, 63, 64, 66, 72, 75). His *irnokué* is close to "Irocois," which Champlain probably pronounced [irokwɛ]. And it is superfluous to document the statement that the Iroquois were terrible to their enemies. Although Hunt (1940:23–32) pointed out that the invincibility of the Iroquois has been a bit overdone by some writers, the impression they made upon the very Montagnais of Champlain's acquaintance is found in his statement that "the mode of warfare which they [the Montagnais] practice is altogether by surprises; for otherwise they would be afraid, and too much in dread of the said Iroquois" (Champlain 1922–1936 1:103). In short, this etymology is so plausible that, had it appeared in a well-known journal, it would probably have become the accepted explanation of the name, and the 30-year controversy would not have taken place.

Arnaud's form will inevitably arouse the curiosity of Algonquianists, and satisfying this curiosity will not be easy. To really verify the form we need to know from what dialect of Montagnais it came and to have a full lexicon of that dialect. We neither know the one nor have the other. There are several dialects of Montagnais (Michelson 1939), and it is a fair assumption that there were several dialects in 1603. The earliest documentation—about 1625 to 1637—testify to three different dialects in the Quebec-Saguenay region. There is evidence (Cooper 1945:40–43) of two subsequent dialect changes in the mission populations—one after 1676 and one between 1782 and 1844.[2] The dialects recorded by

---

[2] A brief survey of the Montagnais dialects is in order. Since Truman Michelson's 1912 statement, the several dialects of Cree on one hand and those of the Montagnais and Naskapi bands on the other have been regarded as one language. A thorough survey of these dialects has never been made. Michelson published a preliminary survey in 1939, utilizing an initial breakdown into *l, r, n, y,* and *th* dialects, so named for their reflexes of Proto-Algonquian **l,* but he was aware of grammatical and lexical isoglosses cutting across these boundaries. Our knowledge of the varieties of speech north of the Saint Lawrence River at the time of European contact is even more limited. It is historically witnessed only by a few pages of prayers, words, and phrases by Gabriel Sagard-Théodat and Fathers Massé and Le Jeune (Massé 1870; Sagard-Théodat 1866, 1939; Thwaites 1896–1901 5–7). About 1670 there began at the missions a fairly steady production of vocabularies, prayers, catechisms, and grammars which has continued to the present day (Pilling 1891). Of these, two, namely Crespieul's prayers and

Fathers Enemond Massé and Paul Le Jeune disappeared, possibly in the epidemic of 1669–1670 (Thwaites 1896–1901 53:59–61, 77, 123). Early mortality from European diseases was high, and it would not be unreasonable to suppose that losses in mission populations were replaced from healthier bands from the interior or from down river. Thus, while any interpretation must be speculative, it is not unlikely that the later missionary records represent additional dialects which were contemporary with those caught in the early missionaries' small sample.

There will be discontent among Algonquianists with Arnaud's form. He proposed *irnokué* 'terrible man'. This can be resolved into *irno* 'man' and *kué* 'terrible'. It is not difficult to assume a form *irno* in some old Montagnais dialect between the attested *iriniou* of Le Jeune (Thwaites 1896–1901 7:23, 153) or *irini8* of Father Bonaventure Fabvre (1970:76) and the *ilnu* of the modern Lake Saint John dialect (Lemoine 1901:146). Arnaud's suggestion that *r* might be further substituted for *n* to give *irro* appears unlikely, because *r* is substituted for *l* or for *n* when *n* is a reflex of Proto-Algonquian **l*, but the *n* of *irno* comes from Proto-Algonquian **n*, which is considered invariable (Bloomfield 1925:146).[3] This is not a serious objection. We can get along with *irno*. The difficulty is with *-kué*, which by elimination must be 'terrible' and, as it stands, must be either a suffix or a word.

-kue appears to be related to the root which C. W. Hockett (1957:265) has reconstructed as "**koq *fear:* only with following **-t* or **-θ*, joined without connective. P[otawatomi] suggests **-wa-* or **-we-* instead of **-o-*; so do the few S[hawnee] cognates." And so, we might add, do the cognates from Micmac, Abenaki, and the oldest Montagnais. A form as short as *-kwe* finds no support in

---

Silvy's instructions, appear to belong to the same dialect as the writings of Massé and Le Jeune—an *r*-dialect about midway between Cree and what we now think of as Montagnais. That is to say, it showed Cree *k* before *i* and *e* (in contrast to Montagnais *č*), Montagnais locating *-ts* (in contrast to Cree *-k, -ki*), and animate plurals in both Montagnais *-et, -ets* and Cree *-khi*. Sagard-Théodat's material attests a true Montagnais dialect with *č* before *i* and *e* ("du pain . . . Pacouechigan"). Sagard-Théodat's distinction between "Canadiens" and "Montagnets" is further evidence that the French came in contact with at least two dialects. Missionary documents beginning in 1678 retained no trace of the Cree-like phonology, and by 1844 works produced in the eighteenth century were no longer usable at Montagnais missions. Mission Montagnais had become a group of *l*-dialects with other points of divergence from the eighteenth-century writings. We might regard these changes as evolution of dialects with time, but it would probably be at least as realistic to regard them simply as evidence of shifting populations at the mission centers, with accompanying replacement of moribund dialects by others of different provenience. We have no way of knowing the number and nature of Montagnais-Naskapi dialects in the Labrador Peninsula in 1600 nor how many of them were represented in Anadabijou's war party. We know nothing about the Naskapi of Arnaud except that it was an *r*-dialect and was thought by him to be "ancien," which probably means only that it was like some older missionary work with which he was acquainted. Eighteenth-century works existed at Lake Saint John when Father Flavien Durocher went there in 1844 and were probably still there when Arnaud arrived a few years later. It is entirely possible that all the recorded varieties of Montagnais and Naskapi existed simultaneously in 1600.

[3] Yet *irro* from PA **ileniwa* would not be more aberrant than Moose Cree *ililiw* (Ellis 1962:1, 3–21, 24).

the other Algonquian languages. The root alone should be *kwet-*. Adjectival effects in Algonquian are achieved by prefixed uninflected particles or by verbal forms. Arnaud's *-kué* is not prefixed, and, being even shorter than the root, does not contain any verbal endings. At this stage we are faced with a choice of two solutions, neither of them entirely satisfactory: either (1) some Naskapis of Arnaud's acquaintance preserved until 1880 an *r*-dialect extant in 1603 and containing the phonologically and grammatically unique form *-kwe;* or (2) Arnaud, needing an *r*-form for "Iroquois" and knowing that eighteenth-century Montagnais writings showed *r,* and knowing also of the root *kwet-* 'fear', constructed *irnokwé* to fit his need.

Early names for the Iroquois in the lower Saint Lawrence region provide partial confirmation for Arnaud's name. In 1634 Le Jeune recorded *kouetakiou* 'Hiroquois' at Three Rivers (Thwaites 1896–1901 8:23). Fabvre (1970:126) recorded at Tadoussac "*k8etatchi8in* (perhaps [kwedačiwin]) . . . de natn [nation] Huron, Iroquois." Father Pacifique's (1939:106) modern Micmac grammar gives "*Goeṭaṭjigoei . . . avoir l'air terrible; goetètjg, les Iroquois.*" Translating Pacifique's orthography into more usual phonetic symbols, *goéṭètjg* is [kwedɛčk]. The final *-k* is probably the animate plural.[4] The morpheme *-ɛč* has the same shape as the diminutive but here is probably an animate nominalizing suffix cognate with Abenaki *-ɔs,* hence *kwedeč* 'terrible animate one'. Fabvre's word is nearly identical to the Micmac word, the terminating *-i8in* being the connective *-i-* and the noun-final *-win* 'person'. Fabvre's extension of the Montagnais name to the Hurons and the likelihood that the Micmac name was applied to the Laurentian Iroquois (Hoffman 1955a:77–79) are fairly good indications that the name was an ancient one for Iroquoian peoples generally. We could bring Arnaud's form into harmony with other Algonquian data by constructing *irno kwedač* and assuming that Champlain's interpreter pronounced this but that Champlain heard only *irno kwe,* a simple communication failure, especially if the strongest stress fell on *kwe;* thus *irno kwédač.* If we assume this, however, we must also assume that Arnaud knew *irno kwedač* was the correct form, and we need to explain why he cited only part of it. I can only guess that, if our assumption is true, he did it in order not to weaken his explanation in the mind of his lay readers.[5]

Our construct has an incongruity which at first repels, then attracts. The incongruity is this: *kwedač* is already a complete form meaning 'an Iroquois'. *irno* means 'man' in the sense of 'human being, *homo*'. *irno kwedač* does not mean an Iroquois male. We have met the explicit form for this in Fabvre's *kwedačiwin.* Rather *irno* and *kwedač* are independent names and must stand in apposition to

[4] Pacifique (1939:36). Analagous to *oénetj* 'français', plural *oénetjg.*
[5] He would have known that his French-speaking readers would pronounce it *irnokwedáč* and may have left out the last syllable to avoid this. He was not, after all, writing for a scholarly journal.

each other, as though one were to say 'a man, an Iroquois'.[6] Champlain's interpreter may have said this once under certain conceivable circumstances, but it is not an expression one would expect to find in frequent usage. It could not have been the ordinary Montagnais nomenclature for the Iroquois, but this apparent disadvantage turns out to be an argument in its favor when the history of the name is reviewed.

The first appearance of the name in history is in Samuel de Champlain's (1922–1936 1:96ff.) account of his first visit to Tadoussac in 1603. Here he found about a thousand Indians—"Estechemins, Algoumequins, & Montagnes"— gathered to celebrate a victory over "les Irocois." It is noteworthy that, although the Hurons became Champlain's allies some years later, there was no mention of them at the 1603 gathering at Tadoussac, nor was there mention of any Iroquois prisoners who might have spoken their own name in Champlain's hearing, but only of Iroquois scalps. Champlain's contacts were a continuation of those made by French traders at Tadoussac. His companion was François Gravé, Sieur du Pont, who had voyaged to Canada before 1600 and had, in 1600, established a trading post at Tadoussac. These contacts were presumably with the Montagnais, who were the native people of the Tadoussac region. Champlain's communication was probably carried on through Indians who had been taken to France and returned with the voyage of 1603 as interpreters and who were also presumably Montagnais because of their origin. Conversation seems to have been chiefly with the Chief Anadabijou. He was probably a Montagnais, firstly, because he was host to the Tadoussac gathering; secondly, because the Algonquin chief was named as Besouat; and thirdly, because there is some indication that Anadabijou was not an Etchemin. Champlain did not name the Etchemin chief, but the Etchemins whom George Waymouth encountered two years later on the coast of Maine knew an "Anadabis or Anadgijon" who lived far to the north of their own country, and was therefore presumably not an Etchemin (Purchas 1905–1907 4:1874). Therefore, if *Iroquois* came into French through Champlain, it does appear most likely that it came from Montagnais speakers.

It is a curious fact, however, that, from the date of Champlain's record, *Iroquois* was common usage only in the French language. Hewitt (1888:188) pointed out that the Iroquois tribes never adopted it, and we must differ here with Beauchamp (1905:165), who thought that Champlain found the name in constant use among the tribes of the lower Saint Lawrence River. Other contemporary names for the Iroquois were used by the Montagnais and Micmacs, as we have seen. It is particularly significant that Le Jeune used 'Hiroquois' as the French translation of the Montagnais name "*kouetakiou*" (Thwaites 1896–1901 8:23).

---

[6]There is some doubt whether *irno* would be applied to an Iroquois. Indians generally were not very ready to grant full human status to unfamiliar or unfriendly tribes. Words like *irno* 'human being', 'man', were usually reserved by Algonquians for speakers of their particular language, with other epithets being used for foreigners.

Perhaps five possibilities remain: (1) When Champlain wrote "les Irocois," he was not hearing the name for the first time. This suggests that several languages might be scrutinized for a reasonable etymology. At least Portuguese, Breton, French, Basque, Beothuk, and Laurentian Iroquois are eligible by virtue of availability and phonetic inventories.[7] (2) If *Iroquois* came from contact, made before Champlain's time between traders and Montagnais speaking some unrecorded dialect, we can only contrive reasonable explanations from other dialects, but the real solution may be permanently lost. (3) If the name originated with Champlain, we have an argument for our incongruous construct *irno kwedač,* the sort of thing which might be uttered once by a struggling interpreter and, once recorded, never heard again by the French. (4) Arnaud's *irnokué* may have been an aberrant but genuine form in an undocumented Montagnais or Naskapi dialect.

There is one more possibility (5) which is at least equally probable. During the long years of contact between the Algonquian and Iroquoian speakers on the Saint Lawrence before 1570, it would have been easy for some Montagnais group to have adopted, with appropriate phonetic changes, a name heard from Iroquoian speakers. Such a name need not have replaced any native Montagnais name but could have remained in circulation along with it. It would resist our attempts to analyze it with Montagnais morphemes—as *Iroquois* does—but it might acquire a folk etymology among the Montagnais. For example, Brant-Sero's (1901) Mohawk *I-ih rongwe,* passed through Montagnais, would probably come out [i:rohkwe]. To Montagnais folk-etymologizers, this would suggest their words *irno* and *kwedač,* the latter their own name for the people in question, and Arnaud's Naskapis may have fed him this very solution. This would eliminate the need to explain Arnaud's abbreviating *irno kwedač* to *irnokué.* It is a bit awkward, as folk etymologies often are.

There seems to be no reason why it could not have happened in this way and no evidence at all that it did. But it is perhaps the best accounting for all the evidence that we have at present.

---

[7] And contrary to our assumption, Champlain might have heard it from "Estechemin" or "Algoumequin."

12

The Eastern Boundary of Iroquoia: Abenaki Evidence

Champlain's assertion in 1609 that western Vermont was inhabited by Iroquois probably arose from a misunderstanding between him and his guides. When the data from the historical record, Abenaki oral tradition, and especially the distribution and analysis of Abenaki and Iroquois place-names are all taken into account, the evidence overwhelmingly points to Lake Champlain as the boundary between the two groups—at least north of Vergennes, Vermont. This paper, a fine example of Day's interdisciplinary approach to solving historical problems, was originally published in *Man in the Northeast* 1(March):7–13 (1971).

This topic is hardly the subject of current controversy. It is a rather quiet little problem which has attracted little attention since, half a century ago, it became apparent that the available evidence was inconclusive, and that further speculation was unprofitable. I revive the subject now because a little new information has turned up and because I hope it will remind others of pertinent information which they will share.

This problem is part of a larger phenomenon, namely, a general deficit of ethnographic information for all northwestern New England (Day 1962b). To be sure, maps of tribes, languages, and culture areas show firm black lines through and around this region, but all of these must be extrapolations inward geographically from a better documented periphery or backward in time from a better documented later historical period.

I am not aware of any archeological data for the eastern shore of Lake Champlain which can be applied with confidence to the period of contact, and with the exception of a single statement, history commences for this region only in 1680, a date four years after the Indian populations of southern New England had been completely disarranged by King Philip's War, permitting one who is so inclined to take the position that this 1680 reference, and all subsequent references to Indians on Lake Champlain, refer to new arrivals, not to old inhabitants.

An early version of this paper was read at the Algonquian-Iroquoian Conference held at Trent University, Peterborough, Ontario, August 29, 1970.

Of the existing information, the data of toponymy is the most conspicuous (Beauchamp 1907; Huden 1957; Lounsbury 1960). We find both Iroquois and Abenaki names for the Lake itself, predominantly Iroquois names for places on the western shore, and predominantly Abenaki names for places on the eastern shore. The few Abenaki names for places in the Adirondack Mountains can be traced to three well-known Abenaki guides of the nineteenth century (Emmons 1841; Prince 1900). On the eastern shore of the lake there is only one well-attested Iroquois name, to which we shall return later. The impression gained from any casual scrutiny is that Lake Champlain was a boundary between Iroquois and Algonquians. The Algonquian names south of Otter Creek might be profitably studied with Mahican in mind. But at Otter Creek and northward, the eastern shore of the lake is abundantly supplied with place-names in Abenaki, forming the western edge of a region of Abenaki place-names, which extends eastward to the Atlantic Ocean. Those on the lake are all in the dialect now spoken at Saint Francis and are perfectly transparent. With one possible exception they have no mysteries, contain no incongruities, and give no indication of being loan words from any other language. They are surely evidence of an Abenaki occupation of this region—but not necessarily an old occupation. The few Iroquois names around the lake are no more numerous than one would expect to develop from the knowledge the Iroquois had of this much traveled waterway.

History gives us one early testimony, that of Champlain recording the moment of discovery in July 1609, as he accompanied a war party of northern Indians up the Richelieu River and into the northern end of the lake. Since his statement is the beginning of the historical record, we study it eagerly, hoping for something which will clear up the matter. Champlain had been told earlier that, prior to the wars between the Iroquois and the northern Indians which had begun about 1570, the shores of the Richelieu River and the islands of Lake Champlain had been inhabited. When he spied the Green Mountains on the east side of the lake, he enquired about the country and was told that beautiful valleys and rich corn fields were to be found there and that they were inhabited. He understood the Indians to say they were inhabited by the Iroquois (Champlain 1922–1936 2:92–93). It is almost certainly this statement of Champlain's which caused the legend "Irocoisia" to be spread across Vermont in the Dutch map of 1614 (Viereck 1967:facing p. 162) and the idea to get abroad that Vermont was originally Iroquois country. There is no other record of Iroquois occupation of the eastern shore of the lake. Were there Iroquois there in 1609 who later left? If there were, why did not Champlain's war party, which was in search of the Iroquois, merely turn eastward to the Vermont shore instead of continuing on what would have been a journey of many days to the Mohawk Valley had they not by chance encountered an Iroquois war party near Ticonderoga? What kind of Iroquois could have been on the eastern shore in 1609? All indications are that the Mohawks were even then on the Mohawk River west of Scoharie Creek. It is rather unlikely that they were Saint Lawrence Iroquois in the process of withdrawing after 35 or 40 years of war. The northeastern shore of Lake Champlain would have been about as vulnerable to attack by the victorious Algonquians as the islands which had been abandoned. My reading of Champlain's statement is that the Vermont shore was indeed occupied, since his Indian companions went on to describe valleys and fields, but that the occupants were not Iroquois since this is incongruous. It is likely that Champlain was having a spot of interpreter trouble, and this assumption has some support since he was surely having interpreter trouble a few lines below when he stated that the Adirondack Mountains were thickly populated. In any event, Champlain's statement, though early, does not really clear the air.

All during the years of the Iroquois-Mahican wars, the Iroquois attacks on New France for which Lake Champlain was one of the highways, the narratives of French captives taken this way to the Iroquois country, and the establishment and occupation of Fort Sainte-Anne on Isle La Motte, there is not a single reference that I have been able to find to any inhabitants on the eastern shore of the lake. Does this mean that there were none? It is possible that, being tucked away behind the islands and out of the way of the west shore route they escaped the notice of most travelers, and it is likely that any inhabitants of this region would have withdrawn to safer places in wartime just as the Missisquoi Indians are known to have done several times in the eighteenth century.

Commencing in 1680, there is a steady stream of evidence for occupation of several parts of the Vermont shore between Otter Creek and the Missisquoi River by Abenakis. During King George's War and the War of the Conquest, they withdrew from the line of fire. They repeated this maneuver during the American Revolution, but the new international boundary line separated them from their brethren at Saint Francis, so they gradually abandoned the Champlain shore and settled in Canada. A numerous party returned in 1825 to collect the rents from their lands at Missisquoi, but they never returned in force to reoccupy them (Barney 1882:998–1000). Groups of families did return steadily to various points on Lake Champlain, and the Abenaki occupation cannot be said truly to have ended until the death of the last two residents on Thompsons Point in 1959.

There is one very significant bit of evidence regarding Iroquois occupation of the Champlain region buried in Sir William Johnson's delineation of English territories in North America in 1763 (O'Callaghan 1853–1887 7:573). In doing this, he was asserting English rights to the maximum empire that the Six Nations had achieved by conquest, and it is noteworthy that the northeastern corner of the Iroquois territory was Rock Rogeo near Burlington. And this represented the maximum claim made by the Iroquois at the peak of their conquests.

When we turn to oral traditions, we encounter an apparent shortage of Iroquois traditions pertaining to the occupation of the Lake Champlain region. This shortage may be more apparent than real, since no one seems to have made a determined attempt to recover such traditions from the most likely sources, namely, Caughnawaga, Oka, and Saint Regis. I am aware of only three Iroquois traditions which apply—a puzzling statement in Radisson (1967:45ff.) about a transient Huron visit from the north, an equally puzzling account in Lafitau about migrations under a female leader (Lafitau 1724 1:101–102), and the still green Caughnawaga tradition which manifests itself periodically as a land claim against the State of Vermont for the northwestern quarter of the state.

Abenaki traditions are more in evidence, and a few words about the Saint Francis Abenakis are in order. Saint Francis is known as a mission village which, between about 1660 and 1800, received increments from all the Abenaki groups between the Penobscot River in Maine and Lake Champlain and the entire contents of another refugee village at Schaghticoke, New York, which had earlier received all the Indians from central Massachusetts. Saint Francis has been regarded as a melting pot, but the significant fact about it is that, despite its speckled history, it is now essentially composed of descendents of families from Lake Champlain. The Missisquoi band was the last sizeable band to settle at Saint Francis, and it came into a village considerably attenuated by wars and epidemics. As a result, about 85% of the family names in the band over the last 150 years had their origins in the Lake Champlain region. Under these circumstances, it is not astonishing that their recollections most often focus on this region.

Two traditions have appeared in print. In 1766 an Abenaki spokesman asserted that the Abenakis had occupied Missisquoi "Time unknown to any of us here present" (Public Archives of Canada n.d. a:328). This probably meant that their tradition contained no knowledge of a different homeland, but the wording of the translation is ambiguous and permits other readings. Charland (1961: 319–324) interprets it as meaning no more than a settlement of Abenakis from Saint Francis and Bécancour becoming established at Missisquoi sometime before 1733. The Abenaki name for Lake Champlain is *bitawbákw* 'the lake between', and native testimony about 1830 interpreted this as meaning 'the Lake between the Abenakis and the Iroquois' (Robinson 1892a:6; Eckstorm 1941:67; Douglas-Lithgow 1909:92). The name itself means simply 'the lake between' and is usually applied to a lake between two other points on a water route. Applied to Lake Champlain it could refer to a position between Abenakis on the east and Iroquois on the west, but it could just as properly refer to a position between Abenakis at the lower end of the lake and Iroquois beyond the upper end or to its obvious position between the Richelieu-Saint Lawrence Rivers and the Hudson.

An Abenaki tradition still current identifies the northern part of the boundary between these two peoples specifically as the east bank of the Richelieu River (Day 1962c). I give this particular tradition a high rating for reliability, since it is an Abenaki tradition which favors the Iroquois, conceding to them fishing rights around the islands and restricting Abenaki fishing to the eastern shore. These traditions surely testify to an Abenaki occupation of Lake Champlain, but just as surely they are no guarantees of an early contact period occupation, although the 1766 statement strongly suggests it. The last tradition may be only preserving the terms of an adjustment arrived at by the Caughnawagas and the Saint Francis Abenakis after both had taken up their mission stations on the Saint Lawrence River in the seventeenth century.

The new information mentioned at the outset comes from the unlikely field of mythology. It may come as a surprise that the Saint Francis Abenaki still have a mythology, since Speck concluded in 1918 that the transformer tales had all been forgotten (Speck 1918:188, n. 1), and since no transformer tales have ever appeared in print. It is probably too late to recover a cycle such as Mechling (1914) obtained from the Maliseets in 1910–1912. The Abenaki tales which persist are episodic, but of this sort I have been able to collect more than 20 trickster and transformer tales alone. Both have as their setting the long-ago time when the world and its inhabitants were young and plastic. The trickster tales have little to say about our present problem, since they are meant to be entertaining and instructive and are usually told either with no locale specified or in locales changed to suit the pleasure of the story teller. Our clue comes from the transformer tales. Transformers bear different names and show different characters in different parts of the Algonquian area. But under whatever name, a transformer is that personage who was instrumental in shaping the face of the earth, modifying the elements, and altering the biological species, usually from giant protospecies to their present size and form. Many transformer tales have specific locales, as indeed those which treat the shaping of specific landscape features must have. It is especially significant that, with most of New England to choose from, the transformer tales of the Saint Francis Abenaki focus on the eastern shore of Lake Champlain.

These tales relate the origins of places like Split Rock and the lower falls of Otter Creek; they contain incidental episodes, for example, the adventures of the underwater creatures called Manógemasák, which took place on the Missisquoi River; there are episodes which are central to Wabanaki cosmology, as the conquering of the Thunders, which took place between an island in Lake Champlain and the western shore. Publication of the full collection of Western Abenaki texts is planned.

The most significant story of all is the account of the general transformation of the earth's surface by the major transformer. This hitherto undescribed Western Abenaki transformer is not the Gluskap of the Micmacs, Maliseets, Passamaquoddies, and Penobscots as some have assumed he would be. Rather he is reminiscent of the Kitpusiagana of the Micmacs, the Mikumwes of the Maliseets, the Shikabish of the Montagnais and Eastern Crees, and a grotesque transformer of the Bécancour Abenakis to whom the name Gluskap was applied by one narrator but who is very unlike the Gluskap of other tales. He is named Odzihozo.

It was Odzihozo who laid out the river channels and lake basins and shaped the hills and mountains. Just how long he took is a subject which Abenakis, only recently deceased, used to discuss over their campfires. At last he was finished, and like Jehovah in Genesis, he surveyed his handiwork and found it was good. The last work he made was Lake Champlain and this he found especially good. It was his masterpiece. He liked it so much that he climbed onto a rock in Burlington Bay and changed himself into stone so that he could better sit there and enjoy the spectacle through the ages. He still likes it, because he is still there and used to be given offerings of tobacco as long as Abenakis went this way by canoe, a practice which continued until about 1940. The rock is also called Odzihozo, since it is the transformer himself. It is the one called Rock Dunder on modern maps.

The similarity of the Mohawk and Abenaki names for Rock Dunder is obvious—Mohawk Rotsio (Lounsbury 1960:60–62), Abenaki Odzihozo. I suggest that the difficulty in analyzing the Mohawk name could be resolved by regarding it as a loan from Abenaki, and that the contradictory Mohawk traditions about the rock could be resolved as folk etymologizings of the Mohawk form confused with the historical drowning of Arent Van Curler near the rock in 1667. This seems warranted by the fact that the rock holds a central place in Abenaki traditions and apparently a peripheral one in Mohawk traditions.

What bearing does all this have on the question of who occupied the eastern shore of the lake? Simply this: by placing their transformer and other cosmological tales in this region, the Saint Francis Abenakis show that they regard it as their original homeland. In particular, by making the formation of Lake Champlain the climax of the transformer's activities and by identifying Rock Dunder as the transformer himself, they give the occupation some antiquity. How much is an open question. It impresses me as being evidence for occupation of considerably greater age than the historically documented date 1680. As argument, I have only that I find it incongruous that a people who can clearly recall historical events which took place in the seventeenth century would, in the same century, create in a new locale, or move from one locale to another, the principal event of the first age of the earth and invent or move to this new locale the physical manifestation of the transformer.

To sum up: Until archeology focuses on the region and produces protohistoric and contact data, we must rely on the data of history, toponymy, and oral tradition. At the time of discovery, Champlain thought he was told by his Indians that the eastern shore was then occupied by some variety of Iroquois. This statement stands in isolation, is at least questionable, and is hard to reconcile with what is known about Iroquois on the Saint Lawrence earlier and on the Mohawk River at the same time. Apart from Champlain's statement, history tells us of Abenakis on the lake, but only after 1679. Toponymy affirms an Abenaki occupation but is unable to prove that this occupation was early. Oral tradition at Saint Francis knows of no earlier home than Lake Champlain, and, while I take this as a good indication that their occupation was one of long standing, a skeptic on the reliability of all oral traditions could reject this conclusion. It is a little surprising that, after the conventional disciplines of history and prehistory have failed to provide more than inconclusive hints, the most convincing evidence should come from a mythology whose existence was unexpected. This evidence agrees with the most probable interpretation of the Abenaki testimony of 1766 and with one of the interpretations which Champlain's statements permit.

13

The Name *Algonquin*

The word *Algonquin* derives from seventeenth-century French sources and today is the name of a people in the Ottawa River valley who speak a dialect of Ojibwa. It is also the basis for the extended form *Algonquian,* which designates the language family as a whole, as well as any group speaking an Algonquian language. Day argues that the source of the name may have been Etchemin, an extinct and extremely sparsely documented Algonquian language. This paper was originally published in *International Journal of American Linguistics* 38(4):226–228 (1972).

Few explanations for the name "Algonquin" have ever been attempted, although it is one of the earliest recorded tribal names and the one which gave its name to the Algonquian linguistic family. I know of no explanation from the early writers. In 1870, Cuoq (p. 104) took a guess at it, suggested Huron *iako-ken?* 'have they arrived?', and extended his guess to the possibility that the Hurons said this while waiting for their allies, the Algonquins, to show up at a rendezvous. Surely this is an odd name for a tribe; there is no evidence to support it, and one feels that the speculation was unworthy of Cuoq. The first volume of the *Handbook of American Indians* carried an explanation provided by the Bureau's Iroquoianist, J. N. B. Hewitt.[1] He suggested that "Algonquin" was probably derived from Micmac *algoomaking,* which he translated as 'at the place of spearing fish and eels [from the bow of a canoe]'. The root of this word can be found in Rand's Micmac dictionaries, namely, *algoome* 'hunting for something in the water' (Rand 1888:111, 1902:13). Hewitt's form appears to end in a locative, thus agreeing with his translation, but a locative is not appropriate after a verb root, and if *-ing* is a locative, it is not a Micmac type locative. It is not clear where the *-k-* comes from. It may be observed, moreover, that although a people may derive its name from the name of a place, a place-name is not the name of a people.

Any inquiry into a name should start with examination of its early history for the shape of the earliest forms and for clues to help in identifying the donor language and possible meanings. The first appearance of the name "Algonquin" in history is probably Champlain's recording of it in 1603 (Champlain 1922–

---

[1] Quoted by Mooney and Thomas (1907:38).

1936 1:96ff.). The occasion was his arrival at Tadoussac on his first trip to Canada. It is in the account of this occasion that we must seek the original form, the identity of the donor language, and the signification of the name.

Champlain found at Tadoussac a thousand Indians of three tribes, Montagnais, Etchemin, and Algonquin, gathered to celebrate a recent victory over the Iroquois. This seems to limit our search for the name to these three languages and thereby to eliminate Cuoq's Huron-derived suggestion and Hewitt's Micmacderived suggestion, since neither Huron speakers nor Micmac speakers were present on the occasion. Champlain wrote not "Algonquin," but "Algoumequin," and this becomes our basic datum. Considering the spelling freedom which prevailed at the time, the final syllable may have been intended for [-kwin] or [-kãe] or even [-kaen]. Champlain did not leave us any hint as to the meaning of the name, but it is fairly clear from his account that the Algoumequins at the Tadoussac meeting may be identified as Algonquins from the Ottawa valley, since their chief "Bessouat" was most probably the Ottawa valley chief, Tessouat, who later became well known to the French (Jury 1967). It may be noted that Hewitt took Champlain's spelling into account while Cuoq had ignored it.

There is a little-known Montagnais etymology which deserves attention. It was proposed by Father Charles Arnaud in 1880 (p. 153) and appeared in an obscure journal. Working from the *l*-dialects of Montagnais which he knew at Lake Saint John and Betsiamites and following Champlain's spelling, he proposed *algoumekuots* 'those who paint themselves red' ("Algoumekuins—les montagnais disent: Algoumekuots, ceux qui se vermillonnent, se peignent en rouge"). This is an intriguing solution bringing to mind the Beothuks and even the Red Paint People, but it raises the further question why this name should be applied to the Algonquins.

The principal difficulty in accepting this as the original of Champlain's name comes when accounting for the *l*. Champlain wrote *l*, but the Montagnais encountered by the French on the Saint Lawrence in the early part of the seventeenth century appear to have spoken an *r*-dialect or dialects (Cooper 1945:40–43). We could assume that this was a weak untrilled *r* or an intermediate phone like Japanese *r* which Champlain heard as *l*, but there is no evidence, and the same difficulty is encountered when we consider Algonquin itself as a possible donor language, since the earliest specimens of Algonquin are all in an *r*-dialect (Vimont 1898 24:39–43; Anonymous 1661; André 1688–1715; Crespieul 1676; Anonymous 1662). One must note Lahontan's (1905) nominally Algonquin vocabulary, which shows *l*, but there is some question whether this is really a specimen of Algonquin proper. The extent of Lahontan's travels makes it quite possible that he obtained the vocabulary from a more western people, possibly the Ottawas. André had written, "Les algonquins n'ont pas d'l, et les outaouois n'ont pas d'r," and an anonymous writer of the same period wrote that in Ottawa "faut prononcer l ou n pour r algonquine." If Champlain correctly recorded *l*, and if both the Montagnais and Algonquins who frequented Tadoussac in Champlain's time lacked *l*, our attention is necessarily directed to the only other group represented at that Tadoussac gathering, namely, the Etchemins. If we then equate Etchemin with Maliseet, which is usual practice, we have a possible source language which contains *l*. To accept Maliseet as the source language, we must, however, discount the set of nominally Etchemin numerals recorded by Lescarbot in 1606 or 1607, which contains *r*-forms (Lescarbot 1907–1914 3:665–668). This does not appear to be a serious obstacle, since in his time the name Etchemin embraced Maine tribes speaking Abenaki *r*-dialects. Although every objection cannot be disposed of with complete certainty, Maliseet does seem to be the most likely source language.

There are at least two words in Maliseet which deserve mention as possible sources of "Algoumequin." One is [ɛlagánkwin] 'they are dancing hard, they are really dancing'. This word can claim consideration, since Champlain's account tells how, at the victory celebration, the Algonquin chief sat in front of the women and between the scalp poles while the men danced. It is therefore possible that Champlain asked the name of the people who were dancing, and, as a result of imperfect communication, received instead the answer to the question "What are they doing?" While no one knows just what took place at that encounter, I am inclined to believe that, after several years of trading at Tadoussac, either the Indian interpreters would have understood French "Qui?" or the French interpreter would have understood Etchemin "Wen?", either of which, accompanied by pointing, would have elicited an identification of the Algonquins rather than a comment on their actions. Moreover, [ɛlagánkwin] resembles the conventional French and English corruptions of the name rather than Champlain's original.

The other Maliseet word which deserves consideration is [ɛlægómogwik] 'they are our (incl.) relatives, they are related to us (incl.)'. This term is extended, even in modern Maliseet usage, to mean 'they are our (incl.) allies'. This appears to be a plausible solution. Although this was hardly the proper Etchemin name for the Algonquins, it would have been very appropriate on that occasion for the Etchemins to refer to them as 'our allies'.

There are two objections to be disposed of before accepting [ɛlægómogwik] as the source of "Algoumequin." First, the Maliseet word ends in -*k* rather than in -*n*. This is not a serious objection, since it is unreasonable to expect perfect transcriptions under the circumstances. A more important objection is that the form is a first-person plural inclusive form, that is, the Etchemin would have been saying that the Algonquins were not only his, but also Champlain's, relatives or allies. If the word were understood in the sense of 'relatives', it would have to be rationalized as a grammatical lapse, but in the sense of 'our allies' the word would be correct as it stands, that is, the Algonquins would be designated as an ally of all the other Indians and the French against the common foe, the Iroquois.

It is, of course, possible that the Etchemin informant used the first-person plural exclusive form [ɛlægomógik] and that Champlain misheard not one, but two segments in the final syllable. Although one cannot feel comfortable speculating about the intentions of recorders of uncertain literacy in the days before standardized spellings, I personally find it more satisfying to equate "Algoumequin" and [ɛlægómogwik], thereby making Champlain's *-quin* stand for something more than could have been represented in the French of the time merely by *-kin,* and to assume that 'our (incl.) allies' was meant.[2]

To sum up, the earliest form of "Algonquin" was "Algoumequin." It was probably heard first from an Algonquin, a Montagnais, or an Etchemin at Tadoussac in 1603. Since it is doubtful that the Algonquin and Montagnais dialects encountered on the Saint Lawrence River at that time contained *l* and it is probable that Etchemin did, Etchemin (Maliseet) is the probable source language. Maliseet [ɛlægómogwik] 'they are our (incl.) relatives or allies' is suggested as the most probable origin of the name.

[2] I am indebted to Ambroise Obomsawin of Odanak, Quebec, and to Peter Paul of Woodstock, New Brunswick, for their enterprise and patient assistance with this little problem.

14

Oral Tradition as Complement

[Day's abstract] American Indian historical traditions are commonly discounted as historical evidence. Some groups, however, transmitted traditions with great care, and these should be taken into account in our reconstruction of the past, since our documents are usually partial and always ethnocentric. The Abenaki traditions of Rogers's Raid are used as an example of a case where history and tradition taken together form a more believable whole. The paper was originally published in *Ethnohistory* 19(2):99–108 (1972).

My general topic is North American Indian oral traditions and their possible contribution to our reconstruction of the past. My specific topic is the phenomenon of complementation which occurs repeatedly in Abenaki traditions.

Since Indian traditions about historical events had their origins with different witnesses than did our written records, they are at least potential sources of new information. This is important, since our written record is ethnocentric and since the white observers seldom knew what went on in the Indian camp. All through the period of discovery, exploration, and colonization they caught only glimpses of the Indian's attitudes, motivations, and understanding of the situation, and they were obviously not in a position to observe many events which were witnessed by Indian observers. When Indian traditions are evaluated with the same degree of care which would be used for a document and the dubious ones set aside, the remainder may be genuine and valuable contributions to our knowledge of the past. Since I have only stated the obvious, let me demonstrate.

I commenced fieldwork with the Saint Francis Abenaki band in 1956. Superficially this band appeared to be almost totally acculturated. Their houses and clothes were Euro-Canadian. They had had the attention of Christian missionaries for 300 years; they had commenced sending boys to Dartmouth College in 1773. They had not hunted and trapped for a living since about 1922; and the only reminder of their woodland economy was a handful of men who reported seasonally to guide sportsmen in the Laurentian Mountain clubs. Aside from the persistence of an Indian physical type, the one native trait which was apparent was the language, which was then spoken as the language of choice by about 60

Presidential address delivered at the annual meeting of the American Society for Ethnohistory at San Diego, California, October 10–12, 1968.

of the elder generation. (Today I can count only 22.) I commenced with the study of the language and have tried to approach the ethnography through the language as far as possible. Considering these circumstances, it was very gratifying to discover that the memories of the older people contained a considerable body of culture, including both mythology and historical traditions.

It was even more gratifying to find that certain of the old people remembered traditions which, as children, they had heard from grandparents who were born in the early nineteenth century. These traditions often touch the historical record at certain points. At these points, they usually coincide with the historical record or are at least compatible with it, and of course go on to present new statements about the event, which, if true, enlarge our knowledge of it. This congruity with history must increase our confidence in the traditions where it is not the result of acquaintance with history, a thing to be watched for in a literate community. That is, the validity of the oral tradition is enhanced by its goodness of fit with the historical data. But the phenomenon which struck me was the frequency with which the traditional statements solved puzzles created by the partial coverage of the documents and the frequency with which the data of history and the data of tradition taken together form a congruous and more believable whole. This phenomenon I have chosen to call *oral tradition as complement.*

I want to demonstrate how this can work, using as an instance an event of the last French and Indian War. This event was the destruction of the Abenaki village of Saint Francis by Major Robert Rogers and his Rangers. The year was 1759, probably the decisive year of the war. The previous year had seen the fall of the French forts guarding the extremities of their defense line, Fort Duquesne in the west and Louisbourg in the east. General Amherst's 1759 campaign was directed against the Lake Champlain-Richelieu River waterway which was held by French forts—Carillon at Ticonderoga, Saint-Frédéric at Crown Point, and Isle-aux-Noix at the outlet of the lake. By early August, both Carillon and Saint-Frédéric had fallen, with Fort Niagara for good measure. On September 13, Wolfe defeated Montcalm on the Plains of Abraham, and Quebec came also into English hands. The day before this, Amherst sent Major Rogers and the Rangers to attack Saint Francis on the south side of the Saint Lawrence River, the home of the most active and troublesome of New France's Indian allies.

This raid has become a rather celebrated event in colonial history. Rogers told the story in his journal, which was published in England not long afterwards, and it has since been retold many times by historians and romancers alike—by Francis Parkman and by writers of boys' stories, in *American Heritage* and in *Cavalier Magazine.* The versions most familiar to the general public are surely those found in Kenneth Roberts's novel *Northwest Passage* and the movie made from it. You may recall the outline: the Rangers set out from Crown Point and descended Lake Champlain in whaleboats to Missisquoi Bay at the northern end. They then set out on foot across swampy country, and after a nine-day march struck the Saint Francis River, which flows northwestward into the Saint Lawrence. They crossed it about 15 miles above the Indian village and marched down the far side. Rogers and two officers reconnoitered the village during the evening, attacked it just before dawn, destroyed it, and set out on their return journey up the Saint Francis River on foot, only a few hours ahead of French and Indian parties which pursued them. After eight days they broke up into small parties, two of which were killed or captured by their pursuers. A number died of starvation, and the remainder found their way back to Crown Point or to Fort Number Four, now Charlestown, New Hampshire.

In order to have an event covered both by the documents and by Indian tradition, we must focus on the attack itself, that is, the period of about 12 hours from the time when Rogers first sighted the Saint Francis village in the evening until he departed in the morning. For what happened during this period, English historians have been almost completely dependent on Rogers's own account, although bits and pieces of recollections were collected from other members of the expedition years later and are to be found in the histories of northern New England towns. The French historians could add only the testimony of the parties which found Rogers's boats on Missisquoi Bay, those who waited for him in vain on the Yamaska River, and those who arrived at the village a few hours after the attack. Rogers's account, then, is the only primary document in English and, as the framework of our demonstration, is worth reading in full. He wrote in his journal (Rogers 1765:107–109):

> The twenty-second day after my departure from Crown Point, I came in sight of the Indian town St. Francis in the evening, which I discovered from a tree that I climbed at about three miles distance. Here I halted my party which now consisted of 142 men, officers included, being reduced to that number by the unhappy accident which befell Capt. Williams and several since tiring, whom I was obliged to send back. At eight o'clock this evening I left the detachment, and took with me Lieut. Turner and Ensign Avery, and went to reconnoitre the town which I did to my satisfaction, and found the Indians in a high frolic or dance. I returned to my party at two o'clock, and at three marched it to within five hundred yards of the town, where I lightened the men of their packs and formed them for the attack. At half hour before sunrise I surprised the town when they were all fast asleep, on the right, left, and center, which was done with so much alacrity by both the officers and men that the enemy had not time to recover themselves, or take arms for their own defense, till they were chiefly destroyed except some few of them who took to the water. About forty of my people pursued them, who destroyed such as attempted to make their escape that way, and sunk both them and their boats. A little after sunrise I set fire to all their houses except three in which there was corn that I reserved for the use of the party.
> The fire consumed many of the Indians who had concealed themselves in the cellars and lofts of their houses.

About seven o'clock in the morning the affair was completely over, in which time we had killed at least two hundred Indians, and taken twenty of their women and children prisoners, fifteen of whom I let go their own way and five I brought with me, viz. two Indian boys and three Indian girls. I likewise retook five English captives which I also took under my care.

When I had paraded my detachment, I found I had Capt. Ogden badly wounded in his body, but not so as to hinder him from doing his duty. I had also six men slightly wounded and one Stockbridge Indian killed.

This seems to be an unemotional, factual report of what happened at Saint Francis on the morning of October 4, 1759, and we might assume that, even if they were still available, Indian accounts could do little more than embellish it or add personal anecdotes. It contains one curious discrepancy with the French accounts, however. Rogers reported that the Rangers had killed "at least two hundred Indians." This was the gauge of the effectiveness of the expedition and must have been the item of most significance to General Amherst. The French documents consistently reported only 30 Indians dead, 20 of these being women and children. These documents include a report to Colonel Bourlamaque written two days after the raid; the statement of Father Roubaud, the missionary, who arrived on the scene only about six hours after the attack; and the report of Archibishop Pontbriand to the King. A note in Marshall Levis's journal is in the same vein (Charland 1964:117–118). The French observers should have had much better information than Rogers, and they would hardly be falsifying the figures in their internal correspondence.

How should we resolve this inconsistency? Was Rogers exaggerating the damage he did to offset criticism for his own considerable losses on the expedition? Was he reporting honestly, but mistakenly, a much too large Indian casualty figure? If so, how had he made such an error, having reconnoitered the village the evening before the attack and having been right on the spot during and after it? It is precisely at this point that Abenaki traditions make their contribution.

During my first years at Saint Francis I had heard some traditions about this raid, but they were either unreliable or irrelevant to the narrow period we are considering here. At the time I stumbled onto the first substantial tradition in January 1959, there were no Abenaki traditions about the raid in print excepting a curiously garbled account of the Rangers' retreat from Saint Francis (C. M. Day 1869:137–143). In May 1961, I acquired another somewhat shorter tradition. Both of these were recorded on tape in Abenaki, and then in May 1963, I learned of a manuscript in private hands containing observations made at Saint Francis in 1869, which included some family traditions of the raid (E. Harrington 1869:14, 19–20). These make up all the Indian traditions obtained so far.

The first tradition was obtained from an elderly lady, Olivine Obomsawin, who had heard it as a little girl from an elderly aunt who brought her up. The aunt had in turn heard it as a little girl from her grandmother, who was a little girl at the time of Rogers's coming. You have probably seen, as I have, the value of oral traditions discounted because of the supposition that they must be retold every generation, say every 30 years, with the consequent increased chance for errors of transmission. Abenaki traditions, however—and I suspect eastern Algonquian traditions in general—seemed to have been passed on by an aged person carefully and deliberately training young children until some of them knew the old stories verbatim, as an American child of my generation might know *The Night Before Christmas*. In any event, this procedure has brought us the story of an eye-witness to a 1759 event in only two steps (Day 1962a:3–17). It is interesting to have a witness from the other side, since we can set the details over against Rogers's account, but I think that, in addition, this tradition is worth presenting so that it may make its own impression:

> Elvine is speaking. When we lived with Aunt Mali, she told us the way of living at Odanak. Her grandmother at that time was little. And the Indians at that time in the fall were dancing. Already the harvest was all gathered. . . . And they danced and sometimes celebrated late, dancing and sometimes going out because it was a nice cool night. They rested, some went to smoke and rest. And one, a young girl, a young woman, she did not immediately go in when the others went in. When they went into the council house to dance again that one, the young girl, the young woman, did not go in because it was cool and she stayed outside. She remained longer outside, and it was dark, and when she was ready to go in at the start of the dancing inside the house, when she was ready to go in, then someone stopped her. He said, "Don't be afraid." In Indian, you understand, he said, "Friend. I am your friend, and those enemies, those strange Iroquois, they are there in the little woods [planning] that when all [the Abenakis] leave for home they would kill them all, their husbands, and burn your village, and I come to warn you." And surely the young woman went into the council house, the dancing place, and she warned the other Indians what he told. She warned what she had been warned. And some did not believe her, because she was so young, because she was a child. Some of them stopped and went home to see about their children and get ready to run away. And some of them did not listen to that young girl, the young woman. Now my aunt, the one who raised us, . . . she was the one that tells us about her grandmother at the time of that fight. My aunt was about 60 years old [at the time of telling the story]. Her grandmother was young at the time of the fight. And some Indians at once hurried home. They stopped dancing and went home, and they went to see about their people, their children, in order to run away as soon as possible, so they could hide. And my aunt was the one who told us, who passed it on to us from her grandmother. Our aunt's great-father gathered everyone—it was dark, of course—in the dark no one kindled a light. They gathered their children in the dark, you can be sure. And they left to hide somewhere where they could not find them. Of course it was night at that time and they hid—in a big ravine where they could not find them. And that man, the old man, they counted their children to see if they were all there—there where it

was deep. And one had been left! My aunt's grandmother was the one who was missing! And she did not know that she was alone in the house, but already she was awake, and she was sitting at the foot of the bed and she was looking out of the window leaning on the window sill. She was singing, she was calmly singing [to herself]. She did not even know that the others were gone. Suddenly then her father quickly entered in the dark, entering quickly, and he took her—he found her singing, this one.

Right away he took her and left as quickly as he possibly could to the ravine—the big ravine that is where Eli Nolet's house [now] is, that's where the ravine is, At the Pines, that's what they call it at Odanak, At the Pines. And there they hid, the Indians, the Abenakis. And *my* grandfather, the Great Obomsawin, the Great Simon, he crossed the river, just as the sun was rising. Just as the sun is seen first. He didn't arrive soon enough, and just at that time he is almost across the river when the sun showed. And his hat—something shone on his hat, something [bright] that he wore. And there he was shot down on the other side—he was the only one [to get across]. All that were with the houses—well, that was when they burned the village—the others, surely many were killed of the others, all that were with the houses.

Some of the elements of this tradition must come as a surprise to those who are familiar with the existing secondary accounts of the raid; for example, the dance in a house rather than on a hard-packed dance ground around a drum as in Kenneth Roberts's story and the existence of frame houses with window sills on which the little girl could rest her elbows. The latter is attested by the reports of travelers and captives, and the dance house stood until about 1912. When it was demolished, the frames on one side of the door and windows were found to be filled with musket balls aimed at its defenders. The one totally unsupported element is the warning of the Abenakis by a strange Indian, and this is the one element that could explain the curious discrepancy in the casualty statistics. In the statement that the Indians were warned, that some hid and some, disbelieving, did not, lies the best explanation we have for harmonizing Rogers's belief that he had killed at least 200 Indians when the French apparently knew that he had killed only 30, and for explaining how Rogers could believe that he had surprised the village if he had not; namely, that those who remained in the houses *were* surprised. Rogers did not count the dead; he could not, because some perished in the burning houses. He probably estimated the population of the village on his evening reconnaissance, subtracted the 20 captives, and assumed the rest to be dead. But the idea of one of Rogers's Stockbridge Indians warning the Abenakis appears, on the face of it, unlikely. The Stockbridges had suffered at the hands of the French and were fierce partisans of the English throughout the war. Five of them had been captured by the Abenakis a short time before.

If, however, we take into account the so-called Mahican village of Schaghticoke located on the Hudson River above Albany, everything falls into place. This may have been a Mahican village at one time, but after 1676 it became a village of New England refugees from King Philip's War, mostly Connecticut River Indians. Some of them were Sokokis, and we should note that other Sokokis had already fled to Saint Francis where they were among the founders of the village and always made up one of the moieties of the so-called Saint Francis Abenakis. About 1700, groups began to drift northward from Schaghticoke, settling on Lake Champlain and mingling with Abenakis at Missisquoi. Finally, in 1754, just before the outbreak of war, the remainder suddenly abandoned Schaghticoke in the night, even leaving behind a few families which were out hunting (Charland 1964:81). With war imminent and unable to make a safe getaway, these families most probably had to join the neighboring Stockbridges. If they did this, they must of necessity have joined them in war, and if some of them were with Rogers's Stockbridge companies, one might well have taken an opportunity to warn the village where his friends and relatives were. If he took the long chance of warning the Abenakis at the very time when Rogers had the village under surveillance, it is small wonder that he refused to come out of the dark shadows when talking with the young woman, as my informant told me after the recorder had been switched off.

The second tradition was obtained from an elderly man, Théophile Panadis, who had it from his grandmother, who was born in 1830 and had known persons who were alive at the time of the raid. This contains elements which greatly increase the likelihood that there was a warning and that the warner was a Schaghticoke. First, the exact words of the warner are recalled, and while they are not modern Abenaki, they are near enough to be intelligible, and they are not at all close to Stockbridge. Perhaps the oddness of the words helped to make them memorable. He said, "My friends, I am telling you. *ndapsizak, kedōdemōkawleba* (Abenaki: *nidōbak, kedōdokawleba*). I would warn you. *kwawimleba* (Abenaki: *kwawimkawleba*). They are going to exterminate you. *kedatsowi wakwatahogaba* (Abenaki: same)."

The following short extract from this second tradition contains an independent suggestion of the presence of Schaghticokes among the Stockbridge Rangers. It speaks of the day after the raid:

> The Indians, i.e., the Abenakis, returned looking for their friends, dead or living. And here on Louis Paul Road, suddenly off to one side they saw something lying. They went; there was a stranger lying. They took his hatchet to finish him off, when he spoke, "Don't kill me just yet. I want to be baptized. I am not baptized yet." They said, "That is not good. Then how are you called?" He said, "Samadagwis." They said, "You have no name?" [i.e., no Christian name for baptism]. "How then do you want to be called?" He said, "Sabadis" [i.e., Jean Baptiste]. They said, "Then to what people do you belong?" He said, "Mahigan." They said, "That is good. Now your name will be Sabadis." And they dispatched him with the hatchet.

This little vignette of the dying Samadagwis, while at first glance not of great significance, does seem to have the ring of truth. His name and the location are given, and Rogers tells us that he did indeed lose one Stockbridge Indian dead, or as it now seems, presumed dead, in that probably hurried 7:00 a.m. muster. His request for baptism is what suggests that he was a Schaghticoke. A group of them had visited Saint Francis five years before and had announced that they were well pleased with the French prayer and were then ready to accept it. By contrast, the Stockbridges were long-time disciples of Puritan Jonathan Edwards and his successors, the Sergeants. The thought keeps nagging me that Samadagwis might even have been the informer of the night before. If so, he was poorly rewarded for his trouble, but the grim irony of his baptism seems to have amused generations of Abenakis on winter evenings.

When the Harrington manuscript of 1869 turned up, two years after I had collected the above tradition, it proved to contain other stories about the raid current at Saint Francis a hundred years before my time. Although the warning is not specifically mentioned, it is implied by the fact that the ancestors of several of Harrington's informants were in hiding the night of the raid, and, between our versions, four specific hiding places can be made out. But most importantly, there is an account of how one Gabriel Annance escaped from his house with his little girl. It reads in part:

> Her father said to her brother, where is your gun? Her brother said, I don't know. Her father said to him, have not I told you to have your gun *always* ready? for you do not know when the enemy may come. Run, both of you, into the bush and hide. They were running along a little path, and there was in the path at one place a little depression with muddy water in it, and they turned a little out of the path, for a few steps, to shun the water; and an Indian was close to them and he said: Run, little girl, just as fast as you can. And she said: I will run just as fast as I can. The Indian saw one of Rogers' men coming from the bush in the path that the children were going to the bush in and he would meet the children. So the Indian went down on one knee and shot his gun at the man.

What is the point of this? The location of Gabriel Annance's house is still known. Just behind it, there was until recent years a year-round little pond or mud puddle. The path from Annance's house to the woods would skirt this little pond and is the same path which became graveled and is known today as Louis Paul Road. Again there is harmony between history and tradition and between one tradition and another: Rogers's one casualty, the man felled by the snap shot of the anonymous Indian by the path around the end of the little pond, and Samadagwis, who was found on Louis Paul Road and baptized with a hatchet, look most suspiciously like one and the same person.

The Abenakis have numerous historical traditions. The oldest one which I can date concerns an event which took place in 1637. There are some about the

Iroquois wars in the latter half of the seventeenth century and others about the period of the French and Indian wars, the American Revolution, and down to the present.

If there be a scholarly deduction to be made from this little demonstration, I think it is this: when traditions show good internal coherence and congruence with such historical data as we have, it seems to be a fair presumption that (1) the traditions are trustworthy and (2) they should be taken into account in our reconstructions of the past. But I am even more interested in a programmatic deduction which can be made, namely, that if so much really old oral tradition can be obtained from a superficially extinct culture such as the Abenaki, how much more there must be lying about in North America waiting to be collected. I come to much the same conclusion that Alan Dundes did in his recent overview of North American Indian folklore studies (Dundes 1967:69–70). I suggest that the time for obtaining oral tradition is not yet over, but we all know it is coming to a close. Field workers who already know a tribe and its culture and who have rapport with its traditionalists could salvage much valuable tradition in the next 10 or 15 years.

15

The Problem of the Openangos

Despite the fact that seventeenth- and eighteenth-century French and English documents refer to various groups and individuals within a broad geographical range by some variant of the name *Openango,* Day argues on linguistic grounds that the term probably designated the Penacooks, a Western Abenaki people located on the Merrimack River. Painstaking analysis of the name and its meaning allows Day to narrow the location of the group to a site near Concord, New Hampshire, and in so doing demonstrate how linguistic findings can be helpful in historical reconstructions. The paper was originally published in *Studies in Linguistics* 23:31–37 (1973).

The ethnohistorical literature of northeastern North America is littered with names for Indian groups—call them nations, tribes, bands, villages, or what you will—whose meaning is unknown and whose application is uncertain. Solving the puzzles presented by these names is no mere parlor game. Basic questions of identity are involved. It is probably not necessary to justify the fundamental importance of correct identities. One need only imagine an ethnohistorian trying to use a document from which all gentilic identifications were omitted. But it is hardly more satisfying for him to work with a document containing names whose identities have never been worked out satisfactorily. In this circumstance, attempting to draw conclusions about the locations and movements of peoples and about cultural trait attributions becomes a rather futile exercise. Although it may be impossible ever to learn the significance of some of these names, others may be expected to yield to further study. One which appears to fall in the latter category is *Openango.*

This name occurs only in the early French documents, and the references to it all fall within a span of 28 years. The Openangos were encountered from Michigan to margins of Acadia, but none of the writers using the name supplied us with any identification.

They made their appearance in history in the autumn of 1675 when the Jesuit Father, Henri Nouvel, encountered a group of "penneng8s," probably in the vicinity of Thunder Bay, Michigan, on Lake Huron (Thwaites 1896–1901 60:216; Nouvel 1957:14). Two days later he encountered a smaller group of "openeng8s" ("10 une autre Cabanne Doupeneng8s"), probably near Saginaw Bay. In 1679, Greysolon Dulhut reported, probably from Michilimackinac, that the "Openagos et Abénakis" were trying to divert the fur trade of his region from

136

Montreal to the English and the Dutch (Margry 1876–1886 6:22). The best known allusion to them is that in Baron Lahontan's *New Voyages to North America*. Having been assigned to Chambly in 1685, Lahontan wrote that the beaver trade there had decayed, but that formerly Indians, among them the "Openangos," "Used formerly to resort thither in shoals." He later listed them among the "Erratick Nations, who go and come from *Acadia,* to New-England." In an appendix, he listed them among the "Savage Nations" in Acadia (Lahontan 1905 1:90, 327, 339). The last occurrence of the name was in 1703. In that year, la Mothe Cadillac wrote from Detroit as follows: "Plusieurs cabanes et familles des Miamis se sont establies ici, aussi bien que des Népissiriniens; les uns se sont incorporés aux Hurons et les autres parmi les Outaouas et les Oppenago ou Loups" (Margry 1876–1886 5:304). After this notice, the primary historical documents are silent concerning them.

Who were the Openangos? The first historian to rediscover them and to tackle the question of their identity seems to have been William Williamson in his *History of the State of Maine,* which appeared in 1832. He took the name, which considering his spelling we may assume he got from Lahontan, to his Penobscot informant, Captain Francis Lola. I suspect that Captain Francis did not know the answer but took an amiable guess at it, since Williamson (1832:458) only claimed that they "are supposed to have been the inhabitants upon the Passamaquoddy Bay." Pressed for a meaning of the name, Captain Francis seems to have offered 'little sable' or 'marten' from the most similar Penobscot word he knew.

Frederic Kidder picked up Williamson's idea and, having prepared a Passamaquoddy vocabulary, entitled it *Vocabulary of the Openango or Passamaquoddy language,* which got printed in 1855 in Schoolcraft's *Indian Tribes* (Schoolcraft 1851–1857 5:689–691). Father Edward Jacker, in a biography of Father Nouvel published in 1861, made the Openangos out as Hurons from the circumstance that Nouvel mentioned the presence of Hurons in his party only after encountering the Openangos (Nouvel 1957:14). The *Handbook of American Indians* allows us three choices: in it, the Openangos of Lahontan are called "Passamaquoddies" following Williamson, Kidder, and Schoolcraft; the Openagos of Cadillac are called "Delaware," since his citation called them "Loups"; and in the appended synonymy of tribal names, Openango is regarded as a variant of Abenaki (Hodge 1907–1910 1:5, 2:1111). The latest writer to consider the question was Fannie Hardy Eckstorm of Brewer, Maine, who thought there were no Openangos and that the word was merely a corruption of Wabanakis (Eckstorm 1945:73–74). Her authority was Hodge.

We are entitled to ask again, this time a bit plaintively, Who were the Openangos? The Passamaquoddy and Huron solutions were pure guesswork with no real evidence to support them. The Abenaki solution was based on a phonetic resemblance which is not as close as one might wish, that is to say, *-ango* is not *-aki,* and we may note in passing that Dulhut spoke of Openangos *and* Abenakis, imply-ing a distinction, and that Lahontan likewise distinguished them in listing the Indians of Acadia. We need to try again. Far from its being a needle-in-a-haystack proposition, there seems to be enough information to identify them with considerable confidence if not with complete certainty.

We may start with the rather clear indications that the Openangos were New England Indians in spite of their middle western distribution in the late seven-teenth century. There are three: (1) The first Openangos, those met by Nouvel at Thunder Bay, were all men. They were married to Algonquin women whom Nouvel had known in the Tadoussac and Sillery missions, and their children had been baptized. This shows that both men and women were not only immigrants, but recent immigrants, from the east. (2) Cadillac called the Openangos "Loups." This is a term which the French applied eventually to all the nations from western Maine to Virginia, but at the time of his writing it was focused on and probably limited to those of western New England and the Hudson valley (Day 1975). (3) Lahontan placed them in Acadia and again as traveling between Acadia and New England, which at that time was present-day New England west of the Kennebec River, and informs us that prior to 1685 they were trading at Chambly on the Richelieu River.

When we direct our attention toward New England and scrutinize the con-ventional names of the Indian groups in this region, only *Penacook* seems to bear enough similarity to *Openango* to be worth investigating, apart from *Abenaki*, which has already been mentioned. This similarity is not very great, but the real question is, What native name did the French hear and reproduce as *Openango?* No writer on the subject has known the native name, and all attempts to deduce it from the English colonial spellings have been unsatisfying.

In 1856, Chandler E. Potter (1856a:26) in his *History of Manchester,* analyzed it by the system which C. G. Holland (1962:296) once termed "linguistic scrab-ble." He took *penayi* 'crooked' from Roger Williams's (1936) vocabulary from southeastern New England and changed it for convenience to *pennaqui;* then he took *auke* 'land' from Josiah Cotton's (1830) Massachusett vocabulary and put them together to make 'crooked land', which he thought appropriate for the intervale land along the meanders of the Merrimack River. Of course, it is the river which is crooked, not the land. Potter's etymologies, like Kidder's vocabu-lary, became included in Schoolcraft's magnum opus and were copied by several writers.

William Gerard provided an etymology for the *Handbook of American Indians* as follows: "cognate with Abnaki *pĕnâkuk,* or *penaⁿkuk* 'at the bottom of the hill or highland' " (Hodge 1907–1910 2:225). He probably meant *pen-,* interpreting it as 'at the bottom', *-aki-* 'land, ground', finished by the locative suffix *-k,* thus *penakik,* not *penakuk.* This etymology is faulty on four counts: *pen-* is not 'at the bottom', but rather 'downward moving' or 'falling'; the stem -*aki*- cannot be shortened to *ak* in order to add locative -*ek;* the form must be *penakik;* although *penakik* seems to have the elements in the right grammatical order, the word would not be accepted by a native speaker for 'falling land'. It is possible that Gerard, considering his use of 'hill' and the alternate form *pena^nkuk,* knew the morpheme -*ʒko* 'hill, bank'. This, it will be seen, would be much closer to the native form, but the translation is still wrong. The site of Penacook is not at the bottom of a hill or highland, but rather on the top of one! Gerard's etymology was picked up by Frank Speck (1940:18), however, and has some currency.

The facts of the matter are that Penacook was a village on the Merrimack River at Concord, New Hampshire, but the name has become, in common usage, the name of all the Merrimack River Indians. It is most probable that the speech of the Penacooks, at least until about 1690, was a Western Abenaki dialect. The only modern representative of the Western Abenaki dialects is Saint Francis, and at Saint Francis the place is remembered as *penʒkók* and the people as *penʒkoiák.* The Penacook village was located on Sugar Ball Hill at the edge of a high and steep sand bank which is continually eroding and sliding down into the Merrimack River. The name *penʒkók* means 'at the falling bank' and is so apt that one needs only to see the site to be doubly convinced of the identity. For me, *penʒkók* is the prototype of *Openango.* It is a better fit phonetically than either of the other candidates, *wʒbánáki* 'Abenaki' or the Eastern Abenaki *hépana'kess8* 'marten' (Râle 1833:383). Most of the recorded forms of the name commence with a vowel written *o*- and presumably weakly stressed. This probably represented the first element of the discontinuous morpheme *a . . . i* by which, in some Algonquian languages, the name of a place is transformed into the name of a person from or belonging to that place.

The historical data we have for the Penacooks and Openangos not only are congruent, but tend to strengthen the identity suggested by the names. Firstly, the Penacooks were among the New England tribes who shared the French name *Loups;* this makes it possible that they were the Loups of Cadillac. In fact, after the Mahicans of the Hudson River they were the first to bear the name. One statement dated 1735 indeed suggests that they were regarded then as *the* Loups of the French missions (Day 1975). Secondly, the Penacooks were among the earliest of the New England tribes to appear in the Canadian missions, where they could have married Algonquin women before 1675. Thirdly, there were Abenakis and nominal Loups of some sort around the southern end of Lake Michigan in 1680, and one Loup named Saget went with La Salle to the Illinois country in 1679, so there is nothing improbable about Penacooks being in that region to be seen by Nouvel, Dulhut, and Cadillac (Blair 1911–1912 1:364–365; Margry 1876–1886 2:139–141, 148–50, 158, 1:533–534, 538–539, 541; Terrell 1968:124–126). Finally, there is confirmation for the presence of

Penacooks on Lake Champlain and the Richelieu River in Lahontan's time. In 1687, Peter Schuyler mentioned a castle of Penacooks located somewhere between Montreal and Albany. In 1699, Schaghticokes, attempting to trap beaver near Winooski on Lake Champlain, were warned away by a party of "Boston Indians" who said it was their ground. And in 1700, it was reported in Albany that "there is a great Indian trade at Canada, many of the Pennikook Indians they see there, and on the Lake, going thither with their peltry" (O'Callaghan 1853–1887 3:482, 4:575, 662).

In résumé, the Openangos were probably New England Indians. The name resembles the correct form of the name *Penacook* more than it does any other New England tribal name. Cadillac called the Openangos "Loups," and the Penacooks were called "Loups." The history of Penacook migrations places them where Openangos were reported by Lahontan and, by elimination, makes it likely that they were the Loups who were met on Lake Michigan by Nouvel, Dulhut, and Cadillac. The only other possible candidates, considering the necessary previous association with the Saint Lawrence River missions, would be the Sokokis and the Mahicans. Neither of these groups has any name suggestive of *Openango*. Moreover, there is little evidence for the presence of Mahicans in the missions, and the Sokokis who were encountered in the Great Lakes mission were called *Sokokis*.

I believe the Openangos were Penacooks. There is no definite proof for this yet, but any alternate solution must satisfy the phonetic facts as well as does *penɔ́kók* and the historical circumstances as well as does the history of the Penacooks.

16

Missisquoi: A New Look at an Old Village

Until the end of the eighteenth century, the village of Missisquoi, located near present-day Swanton, Vermont, served as a political hub for Western Abenakis scattered through the Champlain valley. By the 1920s the site had been abandoned, although Abenakis continued to live in enclaves in the surrounding area and throughout the state. In recent decades, they have taken steps to reconstitute themselves formally as a band and have tried to gain recognition from the State of Vermont and the federal government as a tribe, with Swanton again serving as a political center. Day wrote the present paper just as these developments were getting underway and so it does not reflect them; rather, its usefulness lies in calling attention to a number of lesser-known sources—particularly French accounts—bearing on the history of the earlier community. One of these is the "Mots loups" manuscript of Jean-Claude Mathevet, which Day prepared for publication (Day 1975c). In the present paper he mines the "Mots loups" manuscript for phrases that shed light on everyday life at Missisquoi in the eighteenth century. The paper was presented at the Thirteenth Annual Meeting of the Northeastern Anthropological Association in Burlington, Vermont, April 27, 1973, and the informal remarks in the opening paragraph place it in the context of that conference. The paper was originally published in *Man in the Northeast* 6 (Fall):51–57 (1973).

When the first call for papers mentioned Canadian villages, I selected the abandoned Abenaki Indian village of Missisquoi, partly out of deference to our Vermont hosts, and I justify it as Canadian by virtue of the fact that it was generally regarded as being in New France until 1763. I say "generally regarded." The French asserted it, and the English did not strenuously deny it, although, of course, the Abenakis knew it as theirs. To orient you, if you will just go over the hill to Lake Champlain, turn right or north, and proceed about 35 or 40 miles downlake, you will come to the mouth of the Missisquoi River, flowing into Lake Champlain from the Vermont side. Up this river a few miles are long stretches of alluvial land which accommodated the successive sites of an Abenaki village known as Mazipskoik or to us as Missisquoi. This has been without a doubt the most famous and best-known Indian village in Vermont, which is not the same as saying that it has been either well or competently known.

Extensive archeological collections were made from the lower Missisquoi River valley, beginning in the last century, but these were rather unsystematic. Professional archeological research there in this century has focused largely on a site of Archaic people with no demonstrated connection with the historical Abenaki. It is very likely that Missisquoi was one of the beautiful inhabited valleys with rich corn fields which Champlain was told about but did not visit (Champlain 1922–1936 2:93).

To the English in Albany and in Massachusetts, the Missisquoi village, separated from them by 200 or 250 miles of hostile wilderness travel, was far away indeed, and their chances for observation were few. The Albany people were aware of the Missisquoi Indians as the fierce warriors who rendezvoused with King Philip at Schaghticoke and treated him rather contemptuously (Saltonstall 1913). They knew of the chief Sadochquis, who in 1685 brought his band down from Canada to settle at Schaghticoke, and of the Indians who ejected the Schaghticokes in 1699 when they tried to trap on the Winooski River (Livingston 1956:77–78; O'Callaghan 1853–1887 4:575). The Albany people also knew of the hospitable village which served as a stopover place for Peter Schuyler's Indians in 1687 and of the great war chief Gray Lock, who maintained friendly relations with Albany during Dummer's War while harassing Massachusetts (O'Callaghan 1853–1887 3:482).

From the viewpoint of the Massachusetts towns on the Connecticut River, Missisquoi was a truly legendary place. From it issued the warriors who posed a constant threat to the valley towns from the beginning of King William's War through the War of the Conquest (1689–1763), a period of about 75 years. Gray Lock, whose period of greatest activity was between 1712 and 1726, was a particular nuisance. He struck without warning, and Massachusetts levies, which had done so well in the past against King Philip and the eastern Indians, were quite unable to cope with him. Several expeditions were sent against him. Two went as far as Lake Champlain, but they never laid eyes on either Gray Lock or his village, although he observed them, followed them back, and struck again as soon as they reached home. When Dummer's War was over, Massachusetts chroniclers lost interest, and what little information they have to tell us about Missisquoi came from prisoners who passed through it and from what the Albany authorities learned from the Schaghticokes.

Volume 4 of Hemenway's (1868–1891) *Gazetteer,* that old standby of Vermont historians, does include some recollections of the first settlers of Swanton, and in Volume 1 of Crockett's (1921) *Vermont* there is a chapter which pulls together practically everything which could be gleaned from New England sources. None of these accounts helps us very much to *understand* the Abenaki village of Missisquoi. The best of them give us what we would expect to hear from enemies, victims, captives, and conquerors. It is that kind of dim, unsatisfying, ethnocentric, arm's-length picture of the Indians which practically constitutes a genre of nineteenth-century New England historical writing. Even Gray Lock, despite his importance, remained a figure of mystery to the English, and he simply disappears from the pages of their histories in 1727. To take a new look at this village we are going to need some new sources. Fortunately, they exist in two forms: French contemporary records and Indian traditions.

Not all of the sources I am going to draw on are absolutely new. Some are already known to historians, but some are quite unknown, and all have remained unknown to many interested readers because they are unpublished, because they appeared in little-known publications, or simply because they are in French. We would naturally expect that the Abenakis of Missisquoi were better known to their allies, the French, than to the English, and they were. Still, the better-known French documents, those which have appeared in collections in translation, are not especially helpful. They give us little more than estimates of the fighting strength of the village. But other French sources are very helpful in filling in the gaps in the history of Missisquoi. The French knew, for example, about the early appearance of Western Abenakis at Montreal and on the Saint Francis River. They knew of the withdrawal of southerly Abenakis to the foot of Lake Champlain following the bloody Iroquois wars in about 1665, of a further attack on them by the Iroquois in 1680, and of a short-lived mission among them in about 1682 (O'Callaghan 1853–1887 9:194). They knew of the thriving beaver trade which the Champlain Indians carried to Chambly (Lahontan 1905 1:90). And they knew of the setting-out and the composition of war parties, which the English in Massachusetts learned about only upon their arrival.

So far, so good, but these records fall short of putting us mentally inside the Missisquoi village. What we might hope for would be a long and detailed account of a Jesuit or other mission in the village, bringing, as it would, the detailed records and observations a missionary would make. I must hasten to state that such a record has not shown up and is not likely to show up. Nothing is known of the mission of ca. 1682 beyond the bare fact of its existence. But we are not totally denied missionary information. About 1743, French authorities began to take a special interest in Missisquoi for different reasons. Jutras-Desrosiers wanted to ship all the Abenakis there from Saint Francis to eliminate their use of his fief. The governor and the intendant saw an advantage in a French presence at Missisquoi to control the contraband trade in fur with Albany and of a mission there to strengthen the attachment of the Abenakis to the French cause. The English had been making moves to gain their friendship and assure their neutrality in case of war, and now the French proposed not only to secure the Abenakis, but also to try to win away from Albany the Schaghticokes, who lived on the upper Hudson (Charland 1961). To this end they proposed a missionary, a missionary's house, a chapel, and a sawmill. The Abenakis already had a fort. The Jesuit Father, Etienne Lauverjat, a veteran of the Penobscot and Saint Francis missions, was assigned there in 1744, a house was built for him, and he was at

Missisquoi until perhaps 1748. The mill was built probably in 1748, but in spite of Swanton local tradition, the church was probably never built. So far, no relation, record, or report of Father Lauverjat's stay at Missisquoi has come to light, but I don't think anyone has ever made a determined search for them. A real treasure-trove of information may await us in some Jesuit archive.

In 1731, Fort Saint-Frédéric was built at Crown Point, and a chaplain was assigned to it—a man who was to have many successors before 1758. These chaplains were presumably very busy men, and they do not seem to have been much given to literary efforts. But their records, beginning in 1732, have something to tell us, for they record some 60 baptisms and 20 burials of Abenakis, many of them from Missisquoi (Roy 1946:268–312). Indians frequented Fort Saint-Frédéric during its lifetime for various reasons—as a provisioning stop for war parties or passing through to visit the Schaghticokes or to trade at Albany. And here for the first time, in some fashion, the Missisquoi Indians become people, and we see them, with French baptismal names themselves, bringing children to be baptized, dying, and being buried. Family names I know at Saint Francis were known to the chaplains at Fort Saint-Frédéric 230 years ago. And not the least interesting items are some concerning Gray Lock, proving that he did not just fade away in 1727. He stayed around to beget a daughter, Marie-Charlotte, in 1737, and a son, Jean-Baptiste, in 1740. Both he and his wife had apparently been baptized, since they appear in the record as Pierre-Jean and Hélène respectively, and "Gray Lock" becomes in French *la Tête Blanche* 'the White Head'. There is independent confirmation that this is Gray Lock. The records suggest that Gray Lock died between 1744 and 1753, but his burial is not recorded. Possibly it will be found in Father Lauverjat's records someday.

Another new source of information on Missisquoi is a language manuscript in the archives of the Sulpician Fathers in Montreal (Day 1975). Although anonymous, it is the work of Father Jean-Claude Mathevet. Internal evidence strongly suggests that it was written between 1749 and 1755, either at Missisquoi or from the dictation of Indians who had been living recently at Missisquoi. We have seen that part of the French "grand plan" for Missisquoi in 1743 included the recruitment of Indians from the Schaghticoke village on the Hudson. This was a mixed village of refugees from King Philip's War—perhaps a Mahican substratum but overlain by Sokokis from Squakheag, who were Abenakis, and by Pocumtucks, Nonotucks, Agawams, and others, who were not. In 1723 Gray Lock had succeeded in attracting to his village a number of Schaghticokes, who had become disenchanted with their Dutch neighbors, and in 1744 another contingent arrived. There seems to have been a slow steady drift northward from Schaghticoke after 1700, and in 1754 the last 12 families abandoned the place and moved to Saint Francis (Stiles 1809a:105). It seems likely that Gray Lock's recruits were of the same Abenaki stock as many of the inhabitants of Missisquoi, but at least some of the later arrivals probably were not. We deduce this from the Mathevet manuscript, the language of which he termed "Loup," and which is a previously unknown central New England language, probably Pocumtuck.

Documenting the language is itself a step forward, but it gives us some other things to think about: one is the possibility that Father Mathevet may have been in residence at Missisquoi, at least briefly around 1750. Another whole dimension, although limited, is added by the insight into Missisquoi life found in the phrases recorded in this manuscript whose main purpose was the study of the so-called Loup language. Besides a stock of words and phrases for everyday use and phrases needed in his religious instruction, Mathevet recorded sentences which seem to grow out of current events. For example, "Did you kill the Frenchman's beasts?" suggests that when game was scarce the Indians might kill an occasional cow, perhaps from the seigneurie of Foucault on Alburg Point. "Do you think brandy is a food?" and many other sentences in the same vein indicate that the ubiquitous problem of the brandy trade did not pass Missisquoi by. "Be careful that your child doesn't fall in the fire" appears to be a common domestic admonition. One series of sentences may have grown out of a particular incident: "My little child is lost. Help me to find my child. I can't find him. You must find him." Some pages after he had recorded "Today is the first day of the year," he recorded the expression "A completely muddy village." One wonders whether this was not a comment on the situation inside the Missisquoi stockade that spring. And a number of sentences like "I am pursued by smoke" and "There are too many fleas" were most probably personal comments on the facts of life on which missionaries had been commenting eloquently for a century and a half. Many entries record what was probably commonplace for the time: "I sing the war song." "I want to buy some powder." "The young men go to war." "Of what are you making a feast? A bear." "There are not many animals in the woods." "Tomorrow I shall go to Montreal." One wonders what was the occasion for this personal document: "I wish I could see my child for the last time before I die." The following may be a comment on the state of the village during King George's War: "There are not many men. There are many women." And we learn their conventional greetings and replies: In the morning it was said, "Do you see the morning?" "I see the morning." Later it became "Do you see the evening? I see the evening." And this little vignette must have come from an actual incident in the life of the missionary: "I always tell you to baptize me. You don't listen to me. You are the cause of my killing the Englishman."

Along with these little personal glimpses is a fairly substantial collection of words and phrases which inform us about different elements in the culture of this Schaghticoke contingent at Missisquoi. Many of them confirm elements which we might have suspected—such as a knowledge of dugout canoes, corn agriculture, and the smoking of meat—but it is gratifying to have the confirmation.

Other items we could not have felt confident about—such as the knowledge of birch canoes, a negative reaction toward the practice of burning the forest, and the identity of some mythological personages which are mentioned.

After the English conquest of Canada, the Missisquoi Indians found themselves separated by the boundary line between New York and Lower Canada from their friends and relatives at Saint Francis, their allies the French, and their closest trading center at Montreal. Their reaction to this was to lease their agricultural land on the Missisquoi River and move to Saint Francis (Perry 1882). This removal was neither simultaneous nor complete. They never relinquished their claim to the region and collected rent on it until at least 1800, and many families returned to the Vermont shore of Lake Champlain until about 1922. With the departure of the bulk of the village about 1775, they practically disappear from New England history, but this move leads us to the last and most important source of our new knowledge of Missisquoi. The intermediate steps of the removal are not all clear. For example, there is evidence for a stopover on the Yamaska River, and the crowding they produced at Saint Francis brought about another reserve at Durham, Quebec, which was occupied between about 1807 and 1850. But whatever the factors involved, by the time all the Western Abenakis were united at Saint Francis, the censuses show that the great majority of the family names were of Missisquoi origin. This has meant that the twentieth-century ethnographer has been able to deal directly with descendents of Missisquoi families, many of whom returned regularly to Missisquoi until the 1920s, and in this way it has been possible to recover a considerable amount of information about the culture and way of life of the Abenakis at Missisquoi. Men only recently deceased recalled boyhoods and young manhoods spent at Highgate Springs, Grand Isle, Cedar Beach, Thompsons Point and elsewhere. We have just seen that the Mathevet manuscript gives us a glimpse into the life of the Schaghticoke group during their Missisquoi sojourn, and Saint Francis fieldwork has produced fairly full information on the traditional culture of the Abenakis, most of which can be, with considerable confidence, attributed to the Missisquoi band. What I am saying is that through the memory and traditions of a large element of the Saint Francis band, we have knowledge of Missisquoi ethnography in fair detail and covering a wide range of topics, such as house construction, costume, subsistence activities, annual round, life cycle, kinship, political organization, stories by which children were trained, plant medicines, dances, and so on. The most prevalent family dialect at Saint Francis is, in my judgment, one which came from Missisquoi.

It adds up something like this: Missisquoi is no longer some kind of legendary castle; our thinking about it is no longer confined to inconclusive speculation about the meaning of the name—about which McAleer (1906) wrote a whole book—or the problem of establishing a time sequence in the old archeological collections. The Missisquoi Indians did not just conveniently disappear into some unknowable Valhalla in the north just when Swanton settlers wanted their land. At Saint Francis one can still hear the language which was spoken at Missisquoi. One can hear trickster and transformer stories, whose setting is the Champlain valley. And old Gray Lock left numerous progeny under the family name of Wawanolet.

17

The Penobscot War Bow

All museum collections contain artifacts of dubious authenticity. The Canadian Museum of Civilization has in its ethnological collections a bow that appears to be a reproduction of one owned by a notorious nineteenth-century showman named Big Thunder from Old Town, Maine. The original, the so-called Penobscot War Bow, is an attractive specimen that has taken on a life of its own in the popular and scientific literature, but it turns out not to be based on the material culture traditions of the people to whom it is attributed; in short, it is a fraud. This paper shows the extent of Day's interest in material culture; his devotion to fact, whether material or nonmaterial; and the role his background in forestry played in his ethnographic pursuits. The paper was originally published as pp. 1–15 in *Contributions of Canadian Ethnology, 1975,* Mercury Series Paper 31, National Museum of Man, Canadian Ethnology Service, Ottawa (1975).

A scientist's sole justification as a scientist is his search for fact and truth, and, though truth remain elusive, he must persist in his search for fact. He should insist that only fact is grist for his mill, and, to the extent that his "facts" are uncertain, to that extent, at least, must his hypotheses and general propositions remain doubtful. This is elementary, perhaps trite, yet it will bear restating, since in both anthropology and linguistics the descriptivist handed over authority to the theorist decades ago, and we have no reason to be complacent about the existing data on North American ethnology and linguistics. It cannot be doubted that decades hence North American studies will suffer from the data famine that has been and is being created by this attitude.

There is, moreover, a greater fascination in the search for new fact than in checking and verifying old assumptions and in correcting old error. To this human trait must be attributed at least part of the well-known phenomenon by which tentative statements by an investigator are repeated in the literature without the original qualifications and are paraphrased or reproduced in abridged form until they are accepted as fact even by scientists. When the popular and popularizing media present these old assumptions with colored and calculated half-truth and untruth, the general public adds to its store of knowledge "facts" which never existed. In my opinion, the proper reaction of a scientist to this situation may be found in the prescription of the late great Maritime toponymist William Francis Ganong:

> In any genuine investigation, it is just as important to expose old error as to expound new truth . . . for, on the one hand, errors . . . have a wonderful vitality, and, on the other, if ignored, they are sure, sooner or later to be dug out and triumphantly displayed by the superficial student as the real truth overlooked by the investigator! The only logical way is for the investigator to recognize the error as a worthy enemy, and then proceed to demolish it by the same scientific methods which he used for the demonstration of the truth. (Eckstorm 1941:xiii)

Anyone who would reconstruct one of the North American cultures at the time of European contact must approach the facts by assessing historical documents and by attempting to distinguish aboriginal from borrowed traits in the data he acquires through his twentieth-century observations. Material cultures have been particularly subjected to European pressures, and their reconstruction is an area of ethnography in which it is easy to draw erroneous conclusions in spite of care and diligence. The character and even the very existence of a given artifact in a given culture around A.D. 1600 rests on three main classes of evidence: (a) its preservation in late prehistoric or contact-period archeological sites, (b) its recording in the writings of a very early observer, and (c) the inferring of its aboriginality at a much later time.

Requirement (a) eliminates that large fraction of a material culture which is subject to comminution and decay. Those who have worked with the extant writings of very early observers (b) know that their coverage of material culture is too occasional, too brief, and too incomplete for most purposes. Most of our conclusions about a material culture as it was about A.D. 1600 must be reached by process (c), and such inferences must depend on evaluations of native testimony, the character of the recorder, circumstantial considerations, and the evidence of distributional data.

Museum collections, which might seem to be a natural starting point for studies in material culture, contain almost nothing antedating 1750. The bulk of most collections postdates 1850 and, as museums continue to collect, an ever increasing proportion of their collections is being produced by twentieth-century natives according to what they think, and the collector hopes, are aboriginal patterns and materials. There are many obstacles in the way of establishing the authenticity, provenience, and aboriginality of artifacts found in museums. One encounters items collected or donated long ago without any documentation. Others may come from attics and have their origins two or more generations ago in a family which now remembers only that Uncle John traveled much and brought this piece back with him from "out West." There are artifacts acquired from twentieth-century Indians who know about their origins and uses only by hearsay. There are artifacts reproduced by Indians from memory at the ethnologist's request, artifacts which must carry an element of doubt unless they are accompanied by a full statement of the maker's qualifications. There are even occasional deliberate hoaxes palmed off on gullible collectors by Indians for money or sport.

This is not written to call into question the immense value of museum collections for the study of material culture or the high degree of confidence which we can place in those items and details which are confirmed by solid documentation, comparative studies, repeated collection, and the testimony of early observers. It is written rather to insist that items in collections may not be accepted uncritically but rather demand the most careful scrutiny and validation. It is written to reassert Ganong's dictum that students should recognize error as a worthy enemy and should systematically demolish it. It is written to provide a case history, demonstrating how a dubious item of material culture can, especially if it is attractive, become so entrenched in the popular media and in the minds of the public that it can finally achieve general acceptance. It is written particularly to reopen the question of the so-called Penobscot war bow.

The National Museum Specimen

In the collections of the Ethnology Division, National Museum of Man,[1] is an artifact (Number III-K-84) carried in the catalogue as a Penobscot war bow collected by G. A. Paul at Old Town, Maine, in 1913 (fig. 3). G. A. Paul was almost certainly Gabriel Paul, a Maliseet Indian living among the Penobscots and an informant of Frank G. Speck for whom Paul did considerable collecting (Speck 1935b:2).

Throughout the remainder of this paper, this artifact will be referred to as the National Museum specimen, bow terminology will follow Mason (1894), and arrow release terminology will follow Morse (1922).

The National Museum specimen is composed of a single stave, to the back of which is lashed a shorter piece, henceforth called the reinforcing piece. The ends of the reinforcing piece are connected to the ends of the stave, with pieces of rawhide, presumably to augment the action of the latter. The stave is slightly reflexed at the middle and strongly reflexed at the ends. As presently strung, it is 52½ inches (1.37 m) long. The reinforcing piece is reflexed somewhat more than the stave and is about 22⅜ inches (568 mm) long. Although the wood is aged and stained and the transverse grain is nearly covered with rawhide, there is little doubt that the bow stave is of sugar maple (*Acer saccharum* Marsh) and that the reinforcing piece is of red or black oak, probably red oak (*Quercus rubra* L.) (E. Little 1953). The stave is half-round in cross section, with a flat back and round belly. The reinforcing piece is also half-round, with its flat inner face

---

[1] [The National Museum of Man was subsequently renamed the Canadian Museum of Civilization. The collections of the Ethnology Division were consolidated with those of other divisions of the Museum in a centralized collection.—Eds.]

Fig. 3. The Penobscot War Bow in the Collections of the Canadian Museum of Civilization, Hull, Quebec. Catalogue number III-K-84; negative number J19212-10.

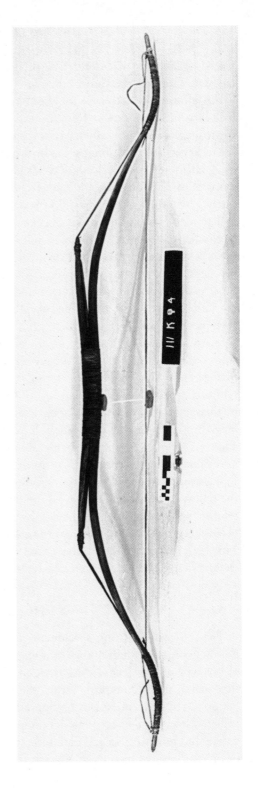

placed against the flat outer face of the stave so that, when wrapped with rawhide, they together form a handle grip about 1¼ inch (32 mm) in width (from left to right as seen by the user holding the bow vertically) and about 1⅜ inch (35 mm) in thickness (from front to back as seen by the user). The string is a single piece of rawhide which passes through holes bored in the stave just below the recurved ends and about seven inches (180 mm) from the tips. The stave has moderate notches on both edges about 1⅜ inch (35 mm) from each end, and the string is passed twice about these notches at each end and secured with a half-hitch. The most striking feature of the bow is a strip of rawhide, averaging about half an inch (13 mm) wide, which encircles the entire bow stave except that part of the belly which faces the main portion of the bowstring. Each end of the rawhide is secured by the bowstring, which passes through the rawhide where it lies along the inner face of the stave. The rawhide strip then extends along the inner (belly) face of the reflexed end, and passes over the end where it is secured by the projecting end, which penetrates a hole in the strip. The rawhide strip then passes back along the outer (back) face of the stave, the string again passing through a hole in the rawhide, to the ends of the reinforcing piece, where, by means of a longitudinal slit in the rawhide, it is carried around to the inner face of the reinforcing piece. It then runs between the flat opposing faces of the reinforcing piece and the stave to the other end of the reinforcing piece, around it, thence to and around the other end of the stave, being penetrated by the bowstring on both sides of the stave. It is held in place at each end of the stave by about a 5½-inch (148 mm) expanse of rawhide thong wrapping and at the ends of the reinforcing piece by a few turns of thong wrapping. At both locations, the thong wrapping is prevented from slipping by squared shoulders which represent the points at which the full size of the two components of the bow—stave and reinforcing piece—are each reduced by about ⅛ inch (3 mm) in width. This occurs about half an inch (13 mm) back from the tips of the reinforcing piece and about seven inches (180 mm) from the ends of the stave. The whole bow is cleverly designed and is executed in a neat, workmanlike manner.

History

The National Museum's specimen is not the first known bow of this type, and it is probable that others of the same general type still exist. The recorded history of this type of bow seems to have begun in the year 1900. On 12 December of that year Ernest Thompson Seton, the well-known writer on woodcraft and nature lore, attended the Boston Sportsman's Show and there met a Penobscot Indian who called himself Big Thunder and who showed Seton a two-piece compound bow with an extra reinforcing piece, which was attached to the bow in much the same manner as has just been described. It was 5 feet 6½ inches

(1.70 m) long and made of "hornbeam," probably *Ostrya virginia* (Mill.) K. Koch. The string, the handle lashing, and the cords connecting the extremities of the bow and of the reinforcing piece were of caribou hide. Seton's sketch is not perfectly clear, but the reinforcing piece appears to have been considerably shorter and the cords connecting its ends to the stave ends considerably longer than those in later models.

Big Thunder told Seton that this was the war bow of the Penobscots, that it had been in the tribe for over 200 years, and that it had been put in his charge by his uncle, the late Chief John Nepta. He was probably referring to the former Governor John Neptune, whose story has been written by Eckstorm (1945). Big Thunder also had a featherless arrow with a stone head and a very shallow nock which he pulled for Seton, using a thumb grip which Seton called the Mongolian. He told Seton that this was formerly the only grip used by his tribe, but that lately they used the secondary style. Seton sketched this grip, and his sketch shows a thumb pull but a grip otherwise not like the Mongolian. Seton thought the bow a very slow one and estimated that it pulled about 20 and not more than 25 pounds (between 9 and 11.5 kg). It is perhaps irrelevant that Big Thunder said that hornbeam practically never decays or loses its power with age, except perhaps to record what may have been an attempt to support his claim for the age of the bow. Actually, hornbeam is heavy, hard, strong and tough, but not particularly resistant to decay.

Seton may have made subsequent mention of Big Thunder's bow, but Seton's bibliography (Anonymous 1929) shows over a hundred titles which appeared after 1900, many of them in obscure periodicals, and the writer has not been able to make a thorough examination of them. A picture of Big Thunder with the bow is reproduced in John Francis Sprague's *Sebastian Rale,* published in Boston in 1906 (Eckstorm 1932:12) and in *The Museum Journal* (Speck 1911:22). The latter picture shows the details of the bow rather clearly, and generally confirms Seton's sketch. A comparison of this picture with the picture of Big Thunder in Speck (1940:fig. 59) seems to indicate that Big Thunder is holding the same bow in the latter picture, but the angle at which it is held obscures the details of the construction. The bow apparently remained for many years in Old Town, where it was seen in 1903 by an emissary of Miss Virginia Baker (Delabarre 1935:126) and, according to Eckstorm (1932:12), was purchased about 1928 for the Heye Museum of the American Indian in New York, although she could not obtain confirmation of this from the museum a few years later.

Speck (1940:113–114) mentioned Big Thunder's Bow in *Penobscot Man* and stated that at least a dozen reproductions of it had been made. He also reproduced an illustration of a bow of this type (Speck 1940:fig. 62), which according to Siebert (personal communication, 1968) was the only reproduction remaining at Old Town in 1935. The writer does not know the present whereabouts of any of the other reproductions excepting the specimen in the National Museum of Man, if this is a copy, as seems likely. It should be noted also that the bow described by Speck is neither the same one shown in his figure 62 nor the one described and drawn by Seton and is unlike them in several particulars. The Speck bow was of rock maple, the Seton bow of hornbeam. The bow in Speck's figure 62 exhibits further differences in the rawhide bracing from the Seton bow, from the National Museum specimen, and even from Speck's own description. The bow of the illustration shows only a piece of rawhide attaching each end of the reinforcing piece to the corresponding end of the bow, while the Seton bow was braced in the ingenious and intricate fashion described for the National Museum specimen, as was the bow described by Speck.

Since Big Thunder's original bow is the only one which pretends to aboriginality, and since it is unique, not only among the Penobscots but also apparently in all North America, it is appropriate to examine its credentials. Chief Big Thunder was a picturesque figure. Some information about his character and career may be found in Eckstorm (1932), Speck (1940), and Siebert (1941a), but the most detailed account is that of Delabarre (1935), from which most of the following remarks have been derived. His real name was Francis or Frank Loring, and he was known at Old Town as Big Frank Lola. Estimates of his birth date vary from 1821 to 1827, and he died on 7 April 1906. Lola is a family name at Old Town, and Big Thunder claimed that John Neptune was his uncle. Arthur Neptune, the oldest surviving Neptune and a direct descendent of old John Neptune, denies this relationship, and some Penobscots claimed that Loring was a full-blooded white man (Siebert, personal communication, 1969). Nothing definite has been written about his parentage, and by his own statement he was orphaned at an early age. He traveled with his sisters making and selling baskets, traveling as far as New York and Philadelphia, where he met and became associated for a time with P. T. Barnum. Estimates of the time spent traveling with Barnum's shows vary between eight months and 20 years, but no occupation other than showman has been attributed to him. It is known that in 1855 he gave a show at Brewer, Maine, and that in 1860 he visited Warren, Rhode Island. In his later years at Old Town, he sold—and apparently made—Indian relics with interesting stories attached to them. He was first and last a showman. All who knew him agreed that he was unscrupulous, a liar, and a rascal. Fannie Eckstorm, who knew him, and his Penobscot tribesmen, who were Speck's and Siebert's informants, were in agreement about this. There is no record of a contrary opinion.

Opinions regarding the authenticity of Big Thunder's bow have varied in tone, but they have been generally negative. Eckstorm stated flatly that it had no authenticity. Siebert, whose elderly informants were acquainted with Big Thunder, stated that the bow was not authentic but rather was one of Big Thunder's fabrications. Two lists of Big Thunder's marvelous relics and the stories he told about them may be found in Eckstorm (1932:12–13) and Delabarre (1935: 126–127). They included such treasures as a letter from Queen Isabella of Spain to the mother of Joe Polis, who lived into the nineteenth century, and a pictographic history of the Wampanoags on birch bark! When people wished to examine them, it was said that the first had been lost and the second accidentally destroyed by fire. Speck called the bow "Big Thunder's fabrication," pointed out that it rested on his "dubious tradition," and mentioned the possibility that it would prove to be an "ethnological fraud." Nevertheless, he included it in his description of Penobscot material culture on the chance that Big Thunder "could have been guilty of reproducing in his own fashion something actually described to him in youth by Indians then old" (Speck 1940:114). It is noteworthy that whereas Big Thunder told Seton that his war bow was 200 years old and had been inherited by him, Speck gained the impression at Old Town that he had inherited a tradition and had made a specimen according to it.

In earlier writings, Speck had made passing mention of the bow, which implied a measure of confidence in its authenticity. In his *Penobscot Transformer Tales* (Speck 1918:222), dictated by Newell Lyon, the culture hero Longhair was given his grandfather's ivory bow. Speck's footnote reads: "described [presumably by Lyon] as a composite bow made of three lengths of ivory lashed together." In his comparative study of Beothuk traits, he opposed in a table a "reinforced bow" for the Beothuk (based on Howley 1915:271) and a "reinforced composite bow" for the Penobscot (Speck 1922:44). It should be noted that the Beothuk bow was said merely to have had a strip of skin fastened along the outer side of the bow, a form of Mason's "veneer-backed" bow, for which numerous examples may be pointed out in North America, while the Penobscot bow (presumably Big Thunder's) exhibited a completely unique wooden reinforcing piece. Eckstorm (1932:13) criticized Speck for being too hasty in accepting Big Thunder's bow as an authentic Penobscot item, and this may have been behind his more cautious characterization of Longhair's ivory bow in 1935 (Speck 1935b:53). The latter footnote reads simply, "Supposed by narrator to be a double-backed affair known as the war bow." It is relevant here that Lyon's competence as an informant was a bone of contention between Speck and Eckstorm (Eckstorm 1945:40–41; Speck 1947:286–287), but it may be too late to validate either one opinion or the other.

Discussion

The question is whether Big Thunder's bow is an authentic item of old Penobscot material culture or not. The pertinent facts which were available to the writer may be summed up as follows:

First, there is no evidence in favor of the bow's authenticity except the unsupported testimony of Big Thunder and the oblique, perhaps secondary, testimony of Newell Lyon. Big Thunder was well known as a liar and as a professional maker and seller of Indian curios, and his reputation makes us doubt his testimony. Even a liar tells the truth occasionally, especially when there is no reason to lie, but in the case of his "war bow" Big Thunder did have reason to lie, since he was using it in his public appearances.

The opinion volunteered by Lyon, when narrating the transformer tales, that a bow (mentioned only in the text as an ivory bow) was a "double-backed affair known as the war bow" may have been independent of Big Thunder, or it may have been suggested by the presence of his bow in Old Town. Big Thunder died in 1906, the year before Speck commenced fieldwork at Old Town. The transformer tales were probably dictated between 1914 and 1918 (Speck 1940:4). There is no way to get behind Speck's footnotes on this question and learn how the information was elicited or volunteered, what prompted the statement by the informant, and how certain Lyon was of the identity of the war bow with the bow in the myth. We have already noted Eckstorm's low opinion of Lyon as an informant, an opinion which was shared by some but not all of his conemporaries, according to Siebert (personal communication, 1969) and to Speck's vigorous defense of Lyon's abilities and integrity. We are indebted to Siebert for what I believe to be the correct explanation. Two of his reliable informants told him that formerly the Penobscots had a "reinforced bow, made of any ordinary stave, reinforced on both surfaces with whale bone, with wood in the middle, wrapped together with sinew. . . . None of my informants say they ever saw one. This is apparently what Newell Lyon was referring to in his 'ivory bow' . . . but Lyon used his imagination to embellish it." Whether this was the ivory bow of the transformer tale or not, it explains how Lyon could have had an authentic personal tradition of a reinforced bow without validating Big Thunder's specimen in any way. In this connection, we should recall the magical properties accorded to articles of ivory and stone in Wabanaki tales and that, in Maliseet and Penobscot tales, both Gluskap and Mikumwes had ivory or stone bows, but there is no indication in these tales that the bows were of an unusual shape.

Second, not only does Big Thunder's testimony stand alone, his "war bow" also seems to stand alone. Speck said it was "thoroughly unlike any other American projector" (1940:114). The common and well-documented form of Penobscot bow is a single-curve self bow of hardwood. Speck described and illustrated it (1940:114–115). The Penobscot bows in the Heye Museum appear to be the same type (Eckstorm 1932:12) as were those collected by Siebert (personal communications, 1969). Other bows collected or described in the region are similar—the Beothuk (Howley 1915:271), Micmac (Wallis and Wallis 1955:31–32), and Saint Francis Abenaki (Canadian Museum of Civilization specimen III-J 28). At least some Beothuk and Micmac bows had a veneer backing of rawhide or sinew, but this is a totally different feature from the rawhide-braced wooden reinforcing piece of the "war bow."

There is some historical evidence for early bows in the Penobscot area. In 1583 Stephen Bellanger cruised the coast 200 leagues southwest from Cape Breton, and his observations on the Indians of that coast are among the earliest we have. Of bows, however, he mentioned only that they were two yards (1.8 m) long (T. Marsh 1962:250). In 1605, Rosier observed and tried bows near the mouth of the Saint George River below Thomaston, Maine. He said they were made much like the English bows, which he would not have said had the bows been like Big Thunder's bow (Purchas 1905–1907:343). Joseph Nicolar, a contemporary of Big Thunder, wrote a traditional account of Penobscot cosmology and history (Nicolar 1893) in which the origin of the bow and the making of the first bow were mentioned five times. Early warfare and weapons were discussed at some length, but there was no mention of an unusual war bow.

Third, Big Thunder's claim that the Penobscots formerly used the Mongolian arrow grip is another incongruity. Available published data (Morse 1922), Siebert's unpublished data (personal communication, 1968), the writer's unpublished data (Day 1962c), and the interpretations of Wissler (1926) and Kroeber (1927) all support a conclusion that the primary release (perhaps with secondary modifications at times) was used from the Micmac area to Massachusetts. We have not only the direct testimony concerning arrow release, but also the indirect evidence of Maliseet and Penobscot arrows modified for the primary release. Big Thunder's admission that the secondary release was used recently (Seton 1912:483) constitutes a kind of corroboration for the conclusion. Morse limited the distribution of the Mongolian release to Asia, while Wissler and Kroeber chose to regard the release of the California Yahi as a variant of the Mongolian. Big Thunder's grip as sketched by Seton (1912:483) was, however, neither one nor the other. It was a thumb pull without finger reinforcement, which is most curious in the face of Seton's statement that, because of the slight nock, the arrow would require a pinch grip. Where Big Thunder learned it remains a mystery, but it stands alone.

Fourth, the performance of Big Thunder's bow has some bearing on the question of its authenticity. There seems to be no record of any of the numerous "war bows" ever having shot an arrow. Big Thunder made claims for the original bow to Seton, but he did not demonstrate it in action. We may recall Seton's impression that the bow was a slow bow with about a 20-pound (9-kg) pull. Comparing this opinion with Speck's statement that the ordinary Penobscot self bows had a range of about 100 yards (90 m), one wonders why the Penobscots would take the trouble to fashion a complicated bow like Big Thunder's to achieve an apparent loss in effectiveness—and for war at that.

It does not seem prudent to test the performance of the National Museum's specimen, which is now more than 55 years old. A student of mechanics may speculate on the net gain or loss in force attributable to the reinforcing piece and transmitted by the rawhide bracing, lashed and braced as described above for the several examples. Each type would have to be estimated separately, however; that is to say, Big Thunder's compound bow with a single strip of rawhide passing from end to end; the National Museum self bow similarly braced; and the compound bow braced by two rawhide strips, one from each end of the reinforcing piece, as illustrated in Speck (1940:fig. 62). It appears to the writer that a fourth type might develop a greater force and cleaner action than any of the above, namely, a self bow braced with two strips like the last named. This has been drawn by artists, but no example is known from Old Town.

There has been no new evidence since 1940, when Speck, fully aware that the bow rested on the "dubious tradition" of an "unscrupulous showman," described it on the chance that it could have been genuine. There has never been a summing up of the evidence before, and the present summing up, in the writer's opinion, shows the "Penobscot war bow" was most probably a hoax.

The total and final impact of an Indian artifact may not be decided by anthropologists, however. Some items have a kind of intrinsic charm which causes the lay public, white and modern Indian alike, to take them to heart and not want to let them go. The now pan-Indian Plains war bonnet is the best-known example. The Penobscot "war bow" belongs in the same category, and it is enjoying a recrudescence centered outside the bourns of the anthropologist's domain. More than the usual artifact, it possesses that quality of vitality which Ganong attributed to error generally, and its dubious claims to authenticity have been discussed. Its emotional appeal for attention can only be diminished by demonstrating how it developed from totally unverifiable beginnings to nearly general acceptance.

Seton's description of Big Thunder's original war bow was printed in one of his books on woodcraft which had wide circulation among young people, but popular acceptance is difficult to trace until the appearance of Speck's (1940) *Penobscot Man*. One may suppose that many lay readers took Speck's anthropological prestige as adequate guarantee for the bow, but one must also suppose that they either did not read or did not heed his text. In spite of his admonitions about Big Thunder's character and his clearly stated reservations about the authenticity of the bow, it took the popular eye almost at once, and subsequent appearances of it outside the anthropological literature have shown no sign of doubts. Eight years after *Penobscot Man* appeared, a series of paintings of Indian life by Langdon Kihn was printed in *National Geographic Magazine* in association with a series of articles by Matthew W. Stirling, then Chief of the Bureau of American Ethnology (Stirling 1937). Plate VII of this series depicts a Penobscot Indian on snowshoes shooting a foundered moose with arrows from a bow reinforced with a wooden piece braced to the bow ends with cords. The legend stated that this reinforcement was used to strengthen a bow when first-class bow wood could not be obtained. This is a new idea in the literature of the "war bow," and the writer finds it difficult to imagine circumstances under which a Penobscot bowmaker could not find hornbeam or sugar maple. In this connection it may be recalled that known specimens of the reinforced bow were all of good bow woods. Soon after the appearance of the Kihn painting, the Boy Scouts of America (1959) brought out an issue of their *Indian Lore* booklet showing on the title page of the Northeast Woodlands section a drawing of an Indian shooting a deer with a reinforced bow. The costume and stance of the Indian and the action are very reminiscent of the Kihn painting.

In 1965 a museum was established on the Abenaki reserve at Odanak, Quebec. A copy of the Kihn picture was painted on one wall, and the white designer, who had access to a copy of *Penobscot Man,* caused an Abenaki to reproduce the variant "war bow" from figure 62 of that work. In 1966 a commercial artist prepared a drawing of an Abenaki in full costume, as he conceived it, pulling a "war bow." Copies of this drawing were passed out to Indians both at Odanak and at Old Town. In 1967, something of the bow's picturesque qualities won for it a prominent place in the display in the Indian Pavilion at Expo '67 at Montreal, where it was seen by millions of tourists, who had no reason to doubt its authenticity. Moreover, it was viewed by hundreds of Indians from across Canada, many of them deeply committed to the revival of Indian cultures. The possible feedback through these channels to the Indians of North America, thence to anthropologists, can only be imagined.

But if North American Indian ethnography is still studied two generations hence, it will not be astonishing if some bright-eyed student discovers the tradition of an ancient reinforced war bow among the Haida or the Dogrib or the Assiniboine, perhaps exemplified by a neat, recent facsimile. Surely the word has gone out and will spread farther and faster than this technical treatise.

18

From *The* Mots loups *of Father Mathevet*

In 1959, Day learned of the existence of an undated anonymous manuscript in the Sulpician archives in Montreal entitled simply "Mots loups" ('Wolf words'). When he was able to examine it first hand in 1961, he found that while the language was unmistakably Algonquian—and apparently Eastern Algonquian—it was not identical to any known language in the family. The possibility was raised that a substantial primary source had been uncovered for the interior of New England, which Day liked to characterize as a linguistic and ethnographic "no man's land." The manuscript itself, which is presented in facsimile and retranscribed form on facing pages in the monograph, is omitted here. Included are the three final sections of the introduction, which focus on establishing the linguistic identity of the manuscript. They exemplify Day's integrated approach to resolving problems. Also omitted are earlier sections of the introduction on the history of the Sulpician missions in Quebec, the identity of the author of the manuscript, the preparation of the manuscript for publication, and the range of meanings the name *Loup* has in the early French records. Day's references to original manuscript page numbers have been preserved in the body of the text, but not the footnotes relating to his analysis of the manuscript; for these, the publication itself should be consulted. The excerpted sections are from pp. 44–64, *The* Mots loups *of Father Mathevet,* Publications in Ethnology No. 8, National Museum of Canada, National Museum of Man, Ottawa (1975).

The Loups of Father Mathevet

Who were the Loups of Father Mathevet's manuscript? Hanzeli (1961:123, 230) placed the language in the Lower Tier of the Central Algonquians in the classification of Voegelin and Voegelin (1946), with Fox, Menominee, Miami, Potawatomi, and Shawnee as putative near-relatives, but this was frankly provisional. The foregoing history of the name demonstrates that, even before Mathevet's arrival in Canada, it was a group term in French usage, with broad and sometimes vague denotations, and cannot identify Mathevet's Loups for us. It apparently limits us to only the Algonquian tribes between the Kennebec River and Virginia. We cannot be satisfied by the conventional associations of Montagnais "maigan" and Algonquin "maingan" and "mahingan" with Mahican, or of French "Loup" with Mahican and Delaware. In fact, even a cursory examination of Mathevet's manuscript reveals that the language, although unquestionably Algonquian, is neither Mahican nor Delaware. As shown in Table 1, the Loup of the manuscript is not the same as the specimens we have of the Unami and Munsee dialects of Delaware; nor does it resemble the varieties of Mahican

Table 1. Loup and Mahican-Delaware vocabularies

	man	woman	fire	water	tree	bear	star	ten	corn
Loup[1]	ilin8	8inai	8te	nipi	metag8is8 'arbre fêlé'	a8ass8s	alag8s	paiak8ᵉ	8iatchimanĕs
Stockbridge Mahican[1]	neemanâoo	p'ghainoom	'thtouw	m'ppeh	—	—	anauquauth	—	—
2	nemannauw, enin	—	—	nbey	metooque 'wood'	mquoh	—	—	—
3	nĩ manaú	paXa´num	stáu	mbai	matuk'	ma´ᵴkwᵃ	náXu´s	mdá´nat	cká´mõnan wosak·k·amonman 'her corn'
4	nemanak (pl.)	p'hánam	—	nebïk (loc.)	mar·ók 'a stick'	—	—	—	—
Moravian Mahican[5]	—	oXkwéo	stáu	ahmen	wastachquaam	machquò	anakusàk (pl.)	wimbat	onúkquask
Delaware (Munsee)[6]	li·n·nwak (pl.)	ochqueu[7]	—	—	mi·'Xtuk	maXk	ala´ŋgwe	—	Xwathkwi·'ïmkan 'corn ripening'
Delaware (Unami)	lenno[7]	aquahang,[8] hac-qua-kytch[9]	tindey[7]	m'bee[5]	mehittuk[7]	machqu,[5] machque[7]	allanque[7]	wimbat,[5] metellen[5]	chasquem,[7] chasquemi[5]
Nanticoke	iin,[8] linni[9]	cutsseneppo	tind[9]	nep[8]	pduk,[8] ptuqu[9]	winkpen[8]	pumwiye,[8] pum-wia[9]	met-ty[9]	cà-in[9]
Powhatan[10]	nimatewh		bocuttaow	suckquahañ	meihtus	monnonsacqueo 'female bear' (?)	attaugwassowk (pl.?)	koske	pacussacan

1. Konkapot in Holmes 1804
2. Edwards 1788
3. Michelson 1914
4. Prince 1905
5. Zeisberger 1887
6. Speck and Moses 1945
7. Brinton and Anthony 1888
8. Heckewelder in Speck 1927
9. Murray in Speck 1927
10. J. P. Harrington 1955

Table 2. Loup and New England Algonquian vocabularies

	man	woman	fire	water	tree	bear	star	ten	corn	fish
Loup	ilin8	8inai	l8te	nipi	metag8is8 'arbre fèlé'	a8ass8s	alag8s	paiak8e	8iatchimanĕs	namens
Eastern Abenaki[1]	arenañbé	phañnem	skôtai	nebi	abási	a8éss8s	8a'ta'8éss8	mtára	skam8n	namés
Western Abenaki[2]	alnôba	phanem	skweda	nebi	abazi	awasos	alakws	mdala	skamôn	namas
Massachusett[3]	ninnu	squáas	chikkoht, nootau	nippe, nuppe	mehtug	mosq, moshq, masq, mashq	anogqs	piuk, piog	weatchimin	nâmâs, namohs
Narragansett[4]	nnin	squàws	sqûtta, nòte, yòte	nupp	mihtúck	mosk	anóckqus	piùck	ewáchimneash (pl.)	nammaùus
Mohegan-Pequot	i:n[5]	shkwá,[5] wínâi 'old woman'	wí yû'ṭ[6]	nuppe[6]	metoog, mi'tû'g[6]	awasus[5]	—	biog, bâ'iŏg	wewaútchemins[3]	pi'âmâ·g[6]
Naugatuck[7]	rinh	wenih	ru'uh-tah	nuppeh	tookh	awasuso	—	—	—	—

1. Râle 1833
2. Day 1956–1979
3. J. Trumbull 1903
4. R. Williams 1866
5. Speck 1928a
6. Prince and Speck 1904
7. De Forest 1851

recorded for Stockbridge and in the Moravian writings; nor, for that matter, is it similar to Nanticoke or Powhatan.

We are not concerned at this point with affinities or with whatever degree of relationship this Loup dialect may ultimately prove to have had with other Eastern Algonquian languages, but only with identifying the language or dialect of the manuscript and the tribe or band that spoke it. The elimination of Mahican and Delaware directs or attention toward New England, the only other known home of nominal Loups, but another cursory examination suffices to show that the dialect of the manuscript differs from all recorded New England languages (see Table 2). Herein lies not only the possibility that the manuscript will prove to be a work of considerable significance, but also the likelihood that specific identification of the tribe and the language will prove difficult. In earlier papers I called attention to the linguistic and ethnographic no man's land that has always existed in central and northwestern New England, that is, in what is now Vermont, New Hampshire, western Maine, and western and central Massachusetts (Day 1962b:28, 1965:365–374, 1967a:244, 1967b:107–109). The statement I made in 1961 to the effect that substantial and unambiguous linguistic data from the region were wholly lacking is still true. Therefore, if a work as substantial as the "Mots loups" could be proven to originate in this hitherto unknown region and if it could be correctly classified as to tribe, locality, and date, it would be of great value in clearing up the tissue of surmise that has always characterized attempts to extend classifications into this region. At the same time, unless we can establish positive identification from the manuscript itself or from historical data, the very lack of linguistic information that would make the manuscript valuable will make its identification difficult.

One approach that suggests itself is to study the known facts of Mathevet's Canadian career. These facts place time limits on the composition of the manuscript, namely, between 1740, when he arrived in Quebec, and 1778, the year in which he suffered the paralytic stroke that preceded his death.

Practically nothing is known of Mathevet's whereabouts between 1740 and 1747. It has been assumed that he was at Quebec, since in 1740 he began teaching Latin, presumably there, and in 1747 he was ordained there (Faillon n.d.: Y268). From 1747 to 1778 he was associated chiefly with the Lac des Deux-Montagnes mission at Oka. His only recorded absences were a brief expedition to Lake George in 1757 as chaplain for his Nipissings; his service as pastor of Sainte-Anne-de-Bellevue in 1757, Oka in 1760–1777, and the Cedars in 1766 and 1767; and a period of service, perhaps intermittent, at the mission of La Présentation from 1758 to 1760. None of the pastorates would have demanded prolonged absence from the Lac des Deux-Montagnes. We must assume either that the Loups of his manuscript were members of one of the groups with which he had sustained contact between 1740 and 1778 or that he took at least one moderately lengthy trip that we have not been able to discover in the records. It seems reasonable to assume that these Loups were a group of some size, since it is unlikely that Mathevet would have invested so much time studying the language of an individual or of a handful of persons.

We can probably eliminate Mathevet's short wartime expedition to Lake George in 1757 as the occasion on which he composed the manuscript. The whole trip occupied only a little over a month, and his time must have been pretty well filled with travel, the preparations for battle, and its aftermath. Furthermore, there were listed among Montcalm's approximately 1,800 Indians only 5 "Loups" from the Ohio River, most probably Delawares or Mahicans (O'Callaghan 1853–1887 10:607; Bougainville 1924b:282).

Mathevet's service at La Présentation presents a more likely occasion for the composition of the manuscript. He did baptize one so-called Loup at La Présentation in 1758 (Cuoq 1898:13), and there is a hint of the presence of Loups at that mission in the existence of a small vocabulary entitled "Langue des Loups," bound in with Father Terlaye's French-Onondaga dictionary (Magon de Terlaye n.d.). When the missionaries at the Lac des Deux-Montagnes spoke of Iroquois they commonly meant Mohawk, if we may judge by the linguistic remains, but the population of La Présentation was predominantly Onondaga and Cayuga (Beauchamp 1905:291; Colden 1902 1:221). As Terlaye was at La Présentation from 1754 to 1759 or 1760, he presumably compiled his Onondaga dictionary at that time (Cuoq 1894:173; Pilling 1888:160). There is no definite evidence to show where the "Langue des Loups" was written, however, and, in any event, the language is different from that of the "Mots loups" and the handwriting is not Mathevet's. The author of "Mission du Lac des Deux-Montagnes" stated that when Fathers Terlaye, La Garde, and Mathevet were at La Présentation, they "allaient souvent loin du village exercer leur zèle" (Notre-Dame de Montréal, Archives n.d.:14), but it later appears that he referred only to Île des Galots and Île Picquet in the Saint Lawrence River, a few miles away.

The weakness of the argument favoring La Présentation as the place where Mathevet found his Loups directs our attention back to the main scene of his activity, the Lac des Deux-Montagnes. We have already noted the unidentified Loups who were present at the old Mission of the Mountain in 1683, but they appear to have been few in number, perhaps captives along with the Sioux, Pawnees, Foxes, Flatheads, and Menominees, in a mission dominated by Iroquois, Hurons, and Algonquins—in all a total of only 210 persons (P. Rousseau n.d.:106, 110; Shea 1881:299). It is likely that these Loups would have lost their identity before Mathevet's time as a result of intermarriage and the attrition of wars and epidemics. In 1720, the mission was said to have 150 warriors of the Iroquois, Algonquin, and Huron nations (Faillon n.d.:B21). The author of the census of 1736 knew only of Iroquois, Algonquins, and Nipissings at the Lac des

Deux-Montagnes, and the only "Loups" he recognized were in the English colonies (Faillon n.d.:B50; O'Callaghan 1853–1887 9:1052–1053). This is not conclusive evidence that there were no Loups at the Lac des Deux-Montagnes, however, since it is known that there were Loups in the nominally Abenaki villages of Bécancour, Saint Francis, and Missisquoi, but Loups are not mentioned in the census (Bacqueville de la Potherie 1753 1:309; Public Archives of Canada n.d.b 49:598; Bois 1883–1885 3:112; La Chasse 1929:347; O'Callaghan 1853–1887 9:937, 945, 1108; Kellogg 1744). No Loups were included in O. Maurault's (1930:26) description of the Lac des Deux-Montagnes population of 1742—only Iroquois, Algonquins, Nipissings, Ottawas, Mississaugas, Tête-de-Boules, Flatheads, Foxes, Pawnees, and Negro slaves. Lafontaine (n.d. 1:130) spoke of Hurons, Iroquois, Algonquins, and Ottawas in separate villages on the Lake. In 1752, Franquet (1889:42) was definite that the mission comprised four nations, namely, the French, Iroquois, Algonquins, and Nipissings, each living in separate areas; and Bougainville (1924a:50, 1924b:270), who visited the Lac des Deux-Montagnes with Montcalm to sing the war song, reported the same composition for the village in 1757. Sir William Johnson's enumeration of the Indians within the Northern Department in 1760 recognized at the Lac des Deux-Montagnes only the Onondagas, Arundacs, and Algonquins (O'Callaghan 1853–1887 7:582). In short, no Loups were reported as residents of the Lac des Deux-Montagnes mission through 1760; nor did they appear in the enumeration of the war party of Picquet and Mathevet that joined Montcalm at Fort William Henry (Bougainville 1924b:278). If there were Loups at La Présentation, as was suggested above, they could have moved to the Lake when La Présentation was abandoned in 1760, but no evidence has been found to justify this assumption.

There are other possibilities. For example, there is the remark of Beauharnois concerning Abenakis domiciled at the Lac des Deux-Montagnes in 1745 (Faillon n.d.:H171). We might entertain the idea that these nominal Abenakis were actually Loups, and that Mathevet, contrary to the suppositions of his biographers, was at the Lake at this time rather than at Quebec. Or we might guess that these Abenaki Loups were still at the Lake upon his arrival in 1747. Abenakis of Bécancour and Saint Francis were visitors at the Lac des Deux-Montagnes in 1752 (Franquet 1889:46, 52). Their visit could have been related to the presence of other Abenakis resident there since 1745, but it is unlikely that Mathevet ever ministered to any Loups at Bécancour or Saint Francis, since these missions were adequately served by Jesuits, who were unlikely to need to call on the Sulpicians for assistance.

We should also consider the possibility that Mathevet's Loups lived at some station near enough to the Lac des Deux-Montagnes mission for him to minister to them, and that he made a visit or visits to them for which no records have been found. The station that best fills the requirements, and perhaps the only one that does, is Missisquoi on the lower end of Lake Champlain. Although this village was generally regarded by the French as an Abenaki village, and Abenakis undoubtedly lived there, Loups were also there at least as early as 1723 (Temple and Sheldon 1875:203; Charland 1961:323; Roy 1927–1929 5:252; Vaudreuil de Cavagnal 1938; O'Callaghan 1853–1887 9:1052; Wraxall 1915:149). In 1743 it was decided to establish a mission at Missisquoi, and a Jesuit priest, Étienne Lauverjat, was assigned there (Public Archives of Canada n.d.c:78). He had arrived by at least the autumn of 1744 (Kellogg 1744). The village was disrupted by the war of 1745–1748 (Public Archives of Canada n.d.b:93; Charland 1961: 329), and this would provide a plausible explanation of the presence of Abenakis at the Lac des Deux-Montagnes in 1745 (Faillon n.d.:H171), but not, as we shall see later, for Mathevet's encountering Indians from Missisquoi. In 1747 Father Lauverjat was at Saint-Michel-de-Bellechasse near Quebec (Thomas-M. Charland, personal communication, 1970), and in 1749 at Pointe à Lacaille below Quebec (Public Archives of Canada n.d.b:93), and the records tell us no more about missionaries at Missisquoi though the village was occupied for several more decades. During the Seven Years' War, the Indians withdrew temporarily to Saint Francis and Bécancour (Anonymous 1931:412). The last of the Loups at Schaghticoke removed to Saint Francis in 1754 (Bois 1883–1885 3:515–516; Stiles 1809b:105), and they were still there in 1757 (J. Johnson 1757, 1902:6; Kalm 1966 2:map). Faillon, citing the king's memoir of instructions of 1749 (Public Archives of Canada n.d.c:89), observed that all missions were under the Jesuits at that time except that of the Lac des Deux-Montagnes (Faillon n.d.:H192). Nevertheless, it is noteworthy that Lauverjat had to abandon Missisquoi, leaving unserved a mission that was considered important at that time.

The records permit the assumption that Mathevet visited Missisquoi, possibly after the departure of Lauverjat, but nothing in the records confirms that he did. It is also possible that some of the Loups from Missisquoi removed to the Lac des Deux-Montagnes, where they could have encountered Mathevet during the Seven Years' War, rather than to Saint Francis, Bécancour, or the French camp on Île-aux-Noix, but so far documentary confirmation is lacking. There is one further possibility, namely, that some Loups settled at the Lake after the Conquest and after the census of 1760 instead of returning to Missisquoi.

We must regretfully conclude that the details of Mathevet's career and the movements of Loups, as worked out so far from the documents, do not clearly indicate the time and place of Mathevet's association with an identifiable group of Loups. It remains for the manuscript itself to bear witness to its origins, if it can. Unfortunately, the manuscript does not seem to contain any incontestable evidence for identifying these Loups. It contains a number of suggestive clues rather than positive identification, and while this also is regrettable, we can only make use of what there is.

Mathevet's Loup lexicon contains several rather obvious loans from English. Examples, with their probable English derivations, are:

abel (pp. 6, 106) 'apple'
poul (pp. 8, 108) 'bull'
choup (pp. 5, 105) 'soap'
ch8gat (pp. 23, 92) 'sugar'
pils^e (p. 35) 'pins'
ahni (p. 41) 'honey'
pis (p. 89) 'pease'
boutel (p. 93) 'butter'
chix (p. 93) 'cheese'
ag8tchas (p. 93) 'goats'
sips (p. 97) 'sheep' (dialect or substandard 'sheeps')
paneg8g (p. 99) 'pancakes'

However, these loan words indicate no more than that these Loups had been in contact with the English before 1740, an experience that had been shared by all the eastern tribes the French knew as "Loups."

A small handful of words appear to be loan words from Dutch:

k8°i (p. 8) and *k88i* (p. 108) 'cow', probably from Dutch *koe*
kipkip 'chicken' (pp. 12, 14, 58, 61, 112, 114), probably from Dutch *kip*
plas^e 'bottle' (p. 82), probably from Dutch *fles*
sat 'salt' (antefolio recto, p. 100), probably from Dutch *zout*
probably *kible* "un minot" (p. 84)
mesch8 'iron' (p. 36), probably from *mesje* 'little knife'

These must testify to some association with the Dutch on the Hudson or the lower Connecticut River.

The manuscript contains only wispy clues to the date of its composition. On page 50a verso appears a word whose French equivalent can be translated as 'I cut off his head, for example, an Englishman's'. This could be considered an indication that the manuscript was written during the war, that is before the Treaty of Paris in 1763, rather than in Mathevet's later years. It may be noted here that, when the revision on page 100 was written, the same word was put in a general context 'I cut off his head, for example, my enemy's', suggesting, if we wish to follow this line of thought, that the revision was made after the English had ceased to be the enemy. On page 59 is an untranslated entry, *nibike nangitlan eglescheman,* which I have translated tentatively as 'Soon at least I kill an Englishman'. An entry on page 67 reads in translation 'I always tell you to baptize me. You do not listen to me. You are the cause of my killing an Englishman'. This is so specific that it appears to be a verbatim quotation of a reproach made by an Indian, rather than a phrase Mathevet might have framed to elicit a Loup equivalent. It appears to refer to an actual incident, and succeeding entries indicate that the Indian was hired to do the killing. One might conclude that this part of the record, at least, was made during a period of peace, possibly either between 1748 and 1754, that is, between King George's War and the Seven Years' War, or immediately after the British conquest of Canada.

There are several indications in the manuscript that Montreal was the French town nearest to the location of the Loups when Mathevet was writing. The French equivalent of a Loup entry on page 21 meaning 'Tomorrow I want to go to town' actually reads 'Tomorrow I will go to Montreal'. On page 54, a Loup entry *m8liang* 'to Montreal' is translated by *en ville* 'to town'. Page 65 carries a statement about people having departed from Montreal, and page 69 the phrase 'Would to God that I could see Montreal'. (One wonders in passing whether the latter reflected the feelings of a homesick missionary or the wish of a new Loup convert who had never seen the wonders of Montreal.) In a rather obscure entry on page 60, which I have interpreted as 'I go to the Frenchman's country', the term 'Frenchman's country' in the Loup entry is translated as 'Montreal'. This implies that the Loups were then outside of the Frenchman's country, and hence probably south of Montreal. Page 8 carries an entry, repeated on page 108, 'Have you killed the domestic animals of the French?', but this is hardly diagnostic, since this could have happened at any of the Indian settlements around Montreal, on Lake Champlain, or even in the vicinity of Fort Saint-Frédéric. On page 73 is an entry that may be translated as 'When the land is burnt, there will be nothing'. This appears to me to prove only that at the time of writing the Loups were north of Fort Saint-Frédéric, where the southerly practice of deliberately burning the woods prevailed.

There are several references to Negroes (pp. 1, 101), which might at first seem to provide a clue, but upon close examination are not very helpful. The Indians of both New England and New York had known Negroes for many years before Mathevet's time. Roger Williams recorded a Narragansett word for "cole black man" before 1643 (1866:80), and in 1671 the Reverend John Russell of Hadley, Massachusetts, had a Negro slave (Wright 1949 1:25). The New York census of 1737 listed 1,630 Negroes in Albany County alone (O'Callaghan 1853–1887 6:133), and there were Negroes at the Lac des Deux-Montagnes (O. Maurault 1930:26).

There are abundant indications that Mathevet had access to one or more Abenaki speakers while he was writing his "Mots loups," but it is not clear whether he was working in a mixed Loup-Abenaki village, at a Loup village where Abenakis were occasional visitors, or at a village where both were visitors. On page 38, *8liteng8at* is labeled "abnaquis." On page 81, *nimitang8ssena* for 'le Pater' differs from the Loup form given elsewhere for 'father', but corresponds with modern Saint Francis Abenaki *nemitōgwsena* 'our (exclusive) father'. On pages 80, 81, and 89, Abenaki *nia* 'I' occurs in otherwise Loup sentences. Pages 58–64, which we have concluded were bound out of order and were part of the original notebook, contain many words labeled "abnaquis" that closely resemble modern Abenaki forms for the same words. They contain other words that, although not so labeled, resemble Abenaki and differ from Loup forms of the same words given elsewhere in the manuscript; thus, one may deduce that they also were "abnaquis." Sometimes "abnaquis" and Loup words are contrasted by listing them side by side or alternately in a column. The four common Catholic prayers—the Our Father, Hail Mary, Apostles' Creed, and Confiteor—are given in "abnaquis." Although they are not so labeled, their resemblance to Abenaki versions is obvious, and at the end of the Our Father, after the "abnaquis" Amen, the author added "= (loup) ni alak." It is plain that Mathevet took these prayers down from the dictation of an Abenaki. They are in his hand; they are unlike the extant versions of the same prayers recorded by earlier or contemporary missionaries in the Abenaki field, thus weakening any notion that they were copied; and comparison with modern versions shows that he did not well comprehend what he was writing. Therefore, we must conclude that the Abenakis of Mathevet's acquaintance had already received the attentions of a missionary.

On the bottom of page 58 appears the sentence *saagat alni alnanbak kel8zangan* 'l'abnaquis est difficile a apprendre', that is, 'Abenaki is hard to learn'. We might like to read into this entry a comment on the degree of mutual intelligibility of Loup and this dialect of Abenaki, but this would be forced. It is more likely that the Abenaki informant was indicating the difficulties of Abenaki for a Frenchman. It is also noteworthy that the Loup word for Mass, *alamessi kemix^e,* which must be originally from French 'à la messe', has the same form as the Saint Francis Abenaki word for 'chapel, Mass enclosure', making it likely that the Loups got the word from the Christian Abenakis. Along with this goes the presence of a Loup name (pp. 15, 114) for All Souls' Day, which takes the same form as the Abenaki word.

The most definite clue in the manuscript to the location of these Loups may be found in the juxtaposition of two entries on page 25, which are repeated on page 40. They are *tak8aangan* 'moulin a scie' ('sawmill'), followed by *mak8sem* (pl.) *mak8semak* Loup 'de nation'. *tak8aangan* was probably the Loup word for a 'corn-grinding mill'. We may compare Saint Francis Abenaki *tagwahōgan,* originally a corn-grinder consisting of a hollowed tree stump and a wooden pounder, and the following Loup entries: *nitak8ans* 'je pile' and *tak8ahank* 'pilon' (p. 90); *nitak8am* 'je pille dans un pillon' (p. 93). *mak8sem* is probably the Loup word for 'wolf' (*Lupus* sp.), but it is clear that at the time of writing Mathevet thought it was the name of the Loup nation. The significance of the juxtaposition of these entries lies in two facts:

1) *tak8aangan* is given as 'sawmill', a secondary meaning it has also acquired in Saint Francis Abenaki; moreover, the French sawmill and settlement on the lower falls of the Missisquoi River at Swanton, Vermont, was known as Taqua-hunga in the eighteenth century (Crockett 1921 1:facing p. 41), and is still so known to the Saint Francis Abenakis (Day 1956–1979).

2) The sawmill at Swanton was planned in 1745 and probably built in 1748 or early 1749 (Charland 1961:322–323, personal communication, 1969).

Mathevet's association of the name of the Missisquoi settlement with what he thought was the name of the Loup nation strongly suggests that either he was writing at Missisquoi or his Loups had recently come from Missisquoi and he therefore identified them with the village. Should this suggestion be valid, then we have a clue to the date of his writings, since Missisquoi would not have been called *tak8aangan* until the mill was built.

One Loup entry in the manuscript is particularly noteworthy in relation to the origin of Mathevet's Loups: *miskagantakil* 'perdrix des savannes' on page 19. The Loup name is a cognate of the Saint Francis Abenaki name *mskagōdagwihla* 'black-spruce-branch bird', with the dropping of the final syllable that we have noted in some other Loup names. If this is a proper Loup word and not a loan from Abenaki, it would seem to place the homeland of the Loups within the range of the spruce grouse, which is at present limited to the northern parts of Maine, New Hampshire, Vermont, and New York (Chapman 1901:180). Tak-ing into account its natural habitat—the northern coniferous forest—it is doubt-ful that the spruce grouse occurred in southern New England even in Mathevet's time. The Pocumtucks might have known the bird from travel in the northern Berkshire Hills.

Two statements that might positively identify the Loups if one were able to decipher them are found on page 97 of the manuscript:

> *8miskan8ag8iak.* 'Les Loups'

(and immediately below it)

> *nimiskan8ag8i.* 'Je suis de la nation loupe. (On les appelle ainsi a cause qu'ils ont leur village sur le bord d' une terre fort elevée.)'

Here we have the name by which Mathevet knew his Loups and which was probably the Loups' own name for themselves! Unfortunately, this name seems not to exist elsewhere in our literature. Nor does the explanation 'They are so called because they have their village on the edge of very high ground' enable one to confidently identify a particular village, since, for one thing, it is ambiguous. It could mean that the village was on the brink of an escarpment. It could also mean that it was at the foot of a hill or mountain or on the edge of an expanse of high country. Villages were frequently built on the edge of escarpments for defensive purposes. The Penacook village on Sugar Ball Hill at Concord, New Hampshire, is a classic example: the Squakheag village sites in the vicinity of Northfield, Massachusetts, are others. Several other New England Indian villages could also be described as being on the edge of hilly country.

Moreover, the question arises, Why did Mathevet use the present tense, "ils ont leur village . . ."? Was he actually visiting them at the village from which their tribal name was derived? Or did he employ "ont" as a historic present? If we assume the former, it becomes increasingly difficult to find a village within the range of Mathevet's activities that fits the topographical description. Surely, Missisquoi does not, nor La Présentation, nor any known Indian village in the vicinity of Montreal except the Lac des Deux-Montagnes mission itself. It is located at the foot of two mountains, and there is the precedent of the Iroquois converts in this village who were renamed for the village Kanadasagaronon, which was translated by Cuoq (1882:10) as 'au bas de la côte'. We recall, however, that the several listings of tribes at the mission did not include any Loups after mention of what was probably a handful of captives at the old Mission of the Mountain in 1683. It is conceivable that some Loups took up temporary residence at the Lac des Deux-Montagnes without being detected by the censuses, as some Abenakis evidently did in 1745. But if his Loups had renamed themselves after the mission, Mathevet would hardly have let this fact pass unnoticed.

It is more probable, on the face of it, that the name was derived from an earlier home of these Loups, which was unknown to Mathevet. Taking into account the concentration of Loups at Schaghticoke who migrated to Canada between 1699 and 1754, the site of Schaghticoke merits consideration, but its location does not fit the topographical requirements (Niles 1912; Robert E. Funk, personal communication, 1964; P. Schuyler Miller, personal communications, 1965; U.S. Geological Survey, Cohoes, N.Y., quadrangle, n.d.). This is in one way fortunate, since it keeps open the possibility that if the name leads us to a village it will be the ancestral home of Mathevet's Loups, and will thus fix their identity.

Since Mathevet's translation leaves the location of the Loups unsettled, we are thrown back on an analysis of the name for a clue to use within the framework of what we know about the historical locations and movements of the groups known to the French as Loups. The name has resisted attempts to break it down into meaning something like 'at the edge of very high ground' in the sense of either at the top of an escarpment or at the foot of mountainous terrain. The manuscript gives us examples of the Loup equivalents for 'bord' *k8alissit* (p. 99), 'montagne' *8ach8* (p. 78), 'déclin d'une terre élevée' *eska8ang8a* (p. 97), and 'd'en haut' *ag8ta8i* (p. 34). None of these forms seem to contribute to the analysis of *8miskan8ag8iak,* but it is recognized that a fuller knowledge of the language might permit an analysis into something like 'foot-of-the-mountain people'.

In the absence of definite and verifiable information and with the knowledge that Mathevet's notebooks only represent his initial efforts to learn the language, it is legitimate to speculate about what his informants might actually have said, in contrast with the forms that the missionary heard and recorded.

On page 97, the entry that immediately follows the two related to the Loup nation is *eska8ang8a* 'declin d'une terre elevée'. The sequence may indicate either that Mathevet thought *eska8ang8a* was related to *8miskan8ag8iak,* or that he obtained *eska8ang8a* while trying to elicit component parts of the tribal name. In any event, *eska8ang8a* appears to have only one morpheme in common with *8miskan8ag8iak,* namely -*ang8-,* which is probably cognate to Abenaki -*ōko-* 'bank', and neither Natick nor Abenaki sheds any light on *eska-, eska8-* in the sense of 'déclin: declivity, downslope'. The appropriate Abenaki stem is *pen-,* as is the Massachusett (J. Trumbull 1903:123), an element that is also present in Loup, as shown by the entry *pinipagat* 'les feüilles tombent' (p. 19). To assume that *eska8ang8a* was the basis of the tribal name would require an explanation for the replacement of the residual *eska8-* by *eskan8-,* which could be done by assuming the *n* to be a nasal vowel indicator not heard in recording *eska8ang8a.* It would also require an explanation of the *m* in the tribal name. Since it occurs after the pronominal prefix *ni-* in *nimiskan8ag8i,* this *m* is presumably part of the stem. It is doubtful that the tribal name is derived from *eska8ang8a.*

The manuscript contains one other stem that should be mentioned in passing, namely, *miska8-* 'good, beautiful', as seen in *miska8inang8s8* 'beau' (p. 79); *miska8ateng8at* 'c'est aimable' (p. 38); and *miska8elindam8k* 'ils sont bien aises' (p. 80). *miska8ang8* 'good or beautiful bank' is a possibility, but does not appear to be in the tradition of Algonquian place-nomenclature. Another possibility, this one requiring that *n* be heard as *m* and that Loup shared the morpheme *wanask-* with Saint Francis Abenaki, is suggested by Abenaki *wanaskōkoiak* 'tip (or point, or end)-of-the-bank people'. This meaning might satisfy Mathevet's gloss, but the phonetic resemblance is not close.

Although no positive identification of Mathevet's Loups may be possible with the data at hand, I wish to advance a tentative solution that I believe does no violence to the known facts and that is favored by a convergence of internal evidence and the historical circumstances already noted.

Limiting our search to the rather generous area over which the French in Mathevet's time were willing to spread the name *Loup,* we can eliminate, by lexical comparisons, the tribes of the Mahican-Delaware area and all the tribes from New England for whom linguistic documentation exists. This is not a comment on the direction or degree of affinity that Mathevet's Loup language has with known languages or dialects, but is simply an observation that it is not identical with any Eastern Algonquian language I am familiar with. Our attention must therefore be directed to the undocumented and little-known region of northwestern and central New England in which history has placed the names of such putative tribes as the Pigwackets, Ossipees, Piscataquas, Quoboags, Nipmucks, Nashaways, Penacooks, Winnipesaukees, Woronocos, Agawams, Nonotucks, Pocumtucks, Squakheags, Cowasucks, Missiassiks, and others. For few of these groups do we have linguistic data more substantial than tribal names, personal names, and place-names—usually untranslated. The only exceptions are 13 names of months, presumably in the Agawam dialect (Day 1967a), and 3 names of fur-bearing animals from the middle Connecticut valley but of uncertain tribal provenance (Judd 1857). A minor indication that we may be on the right track is that the "Mots loups" records an *l*-dialect, and most of the northwestern-central New England problem area was probably an *l*-dialect area in which the reflexes of Proto-Algonquian *θ and/or *l is *l* (Haas 1967).

Since the name *Loup* does not yield to attempts to interpret it as 'the edge of mountainous country, the edge of an escarpment', or the like, we might try a more analytical approach. The following solution is proposed tentatively, since no meaningful solution with more exact phonetic correspondences could be found:

Loup	*8misk*	-	*an8*	-	*ag8*	-	*i*	-	*ak*
Saint Francis Abenaki	*amiskw*	-	*ōlo*	-	*ōko*	-	*i*	-	*ak*
English	beaver-		tail-		bank		people		
					(or hill)				

Confronted with *8miskan8ag8iak* as a tribal name, we can be confident that -*ak* is an animate plural suffix and that -*i*- is a gentilic suffix; thus, freely, -*iak* 'people'. In the entry that immediately follows the two related to the Loup nation on page 97, the occurrence of -*ang8*- in *eska8ang8a,* probably cognate with Saint Francis Abenaki -*ōko*- 'bank', permits the tentative assumption that -*ag8*- was a mishearing or misspelling of the same stem, hence -*ag8(ang8)iak* 'bank people'.

Admittedly, -*an8*- is not -*ōlo*-, and my assumption is not that the Loup form showed *n* where one would expect *l,* but that the informant said -*ōlo*- and Mathevet misheard it as -*ōno*-. Linguists with field experience know how easy it is to mishear a segment in a long word, even when the study of a language is farther advanced than Mathevet's apparently was. The assumptions are that Mathevet wrote *a* for the lower back [a] or the lower mid [ɔ], which is still a characteristic of French-Canadian speech, and that he interpreted the nasal quality of the vowel and the apico-alveolar articulation of the *l* as *n.* This does not seem to be an unreasonable set of assumptions, and we may recall that Mathevet made a practice of representing the nasal vowel by *an,* not even by *aï,* as the missionaries to the Eastern Abenakis were wont to do.

Interpreting *8misk-* as 'beaver' requires that Loup—unlike Abenaki, but like Cree, Ojibwa, and Delaware (J. Trumbull 1903:7)—drop the final *-wa* of Proto-Algonquian **ameθkwa* 'beaver' (Siebert 1941b:300). This is not a problem, but the initial *8-* needs some explanation, especially since Mathevet wrote *nimis-kan8ag8i* 'I am a Loup', implying that the stem commenced with *m* and that the initial *8-* in *8miskan8ag8iak* was a third-person prefix, the third-singular form being presumably *8miskan8ag8.* If this were the case, however, the tribal name would most probably be *miskan8ag8iak,* not *8miskan8ag8iak.* This suggests that the initial vowel—whether *8* or *a* misheard as *8*—was part of the stem. My surmise is that Mathevet, either by reason of mishearing or through the habit acquired in writing many paradigms and assisted by a weakly stressed first sylla-ble, wrote the first-person form as *nimiskan8ag8i* when it should have been *n8miskan8ag8i.*

All these assumptions seem reasonable to me, all the more so since I have not been able to find a more suitable explanation of the name, not even in Saint Francis Abenaki, which, unlike the southern New England languages, is still alive, and for which I had abundant resources, including repeated access to good informants. It may be repeated that *amiskwōlowōkoiak* is still a perfectly good form in Abenaki and means 'beaver-tail-hill people'.

Even if we assume the correctness of this solution, however, it does not seem to tell us much about the location of the village. Where was Beaver-Tail Hill? I have not been able to locate a hill of this name in the proximity of a known Indian vil-lage, but the answer may reside in Sheldon's history of Deerfield, Massachusetts:

> The Pocumtuck range, according to Indian tradition, is only the petrified body of a huge beaver, which used to disport itself here in a pond of corresponding dimen-sions. This animal, by continued depredations on the shores, had offended Hobomuck, who at length determined to kill it. Accordingly, armed with the trunk of an enormous oak, he waded into the water and attacked the monster. After a desperate contest, the beaver was dispatched by a blow across the neck with the ponderous cudgel. The carcass sank to the bottom of the pond and turned to stone. Should any skeptic doubt the truth of this tradition he is referred to the beaver itself. Wequamps is the head, north of which the bent neck shows where fell the fatal stroke; North Sugar Loaf, the shoulders, rising to Pocumtuck Rock the back, whence it tapers off to the tail at Cheapside. All this is now as plainly to be seen by an observer from the West Mountain as it was the day this big beaver pond was drained off. (Sheldon 1895 1:29)

That is to say, Pocumtuck Mountain in profile resembles a beaver, with the head at the south end and the tail at the north end, and this, to the Pocumtuck Indians, was the Great Beaver that was killed by their transformer in the formative period of the world and turned to stone. The physiographic details may be seen in the Greenfield and Mount Toby quadrangle maps (U.S. Geological Survey n.d.). Further, according to Sheldon (Young 1969:113), the early concentration of Pocumtuck settlement was around the north, or beaver-tail, end of this range, near the junction of the Deerfield and Connecticut Rivers. Their last historic fortified village was located on Fort Hill, a bluff "about a mile and a half northeast of the Common in Deerfield," that is, at the foot of and just opposite the beaver's tail on the west side of the mountain (Sheldon 1895 1:69).

Here then is a mountain that resembled a beaver and that had a historic Indian village near the tail. Moreover, this particular beaver figured prominently in an important cosmological tradition, which would account for any importance attached to it. The name *amiskōlowōkok* does not occur in the surviving Pocumtuck deeds in the Deerfield region, but there was no necessity to name it when the boundaries of the parcels were described (Wright 1905:61–62, 65–68, 74–75). The Pocumtucks originally lived within the region across which French writers and cartographers spread the name *Loup*. After their removal to Schaghticoke on the Hudson in 1676 or 1677, they certainly shared the name *Loup* with the other fugitives who made up the village. In fact, they do not seem to have been referred to again in history by the name Pocumtuck, probably as a consequence of their merger with closely related river tribes into the new Schaghticoke tribe, with English and Iroquois alliances under the Covenant Chain. In fact, Sheldon wrote, "Never again do we find in recorded history a single page relating to the unfortunate Pocumtucks" (Young 1969:121).

Are we justified in accepting Sheldon's origin tale for the Pocumtuck Range as an authentic Pocumtuck tradition? It would certainly be reassuring to have confirmation of it from another source, but there is no known collection of oral traditions from either the Pocumtucks or any of the other river tribes. The Micmacs, Maliseet-Passamaquoddies, and the Penobscots have similar origin tales featuring animals, including the Great Beaver, that were turned to stone by the transformer, in this case, Gluskap. Sheldon was a careful historian, and there is no reason to suppose he would invent a myth merely to adorn the physiographical chapter of his town history. It is much more likely that he was repeating a local tradition known to him. Donald R. Friary, of the Heritage Foundation at Deerfield, wrote: "A good deal of oral tradition in this area has died since Sheldon's time. Sheldon was born in 1818 and it could be that he was in touch with some very early tradition" (personal communication, 1969).

Sheldon's naming the Pocumtuck transformer "Hobomuck" is curious, since, to most of the early New England writers, Hobbomuck, variously spelled, was thought to be the Devil. The Puritan mind did not admire the Algonquian cosmology and pantheon, and it may be doubted whether any of the writers, even the sympathetic Roger Williams, ever really understood it. Winslow's statement is especially interesting: "Whom they [the Indians near Plymouth] call *Hobbamuck,* and to the northwards of us, *Hobbamoqui;* this, as far as we can conceive, is the Devil" (J. Trumbull 1903:27). Here Winslow not only concedes that he is not sure that Hobbomuck is the Devil (any being with supernatural powers who was not the Puritans' Jehovah was likely to be identified with the Devil), but gives us a spelling in "Hobbamoqui" that closely resembles Saint Francis Abenaki *ōbamakwit* 'the wanderer', which brings to mind the inevitable wanderings of Algonquian transformers as they modified the face of the earth. Therefore, Sheldon's tale cannot be condemned as a careless retelling of a half-understood tradition on the grounds that he brought in Hobbomuck, the Devil, in the wrong context. Rather, it may be the first clue to the real character of Hobbomuck and to the identity of the transformer in central New England. It is difficult to make a more certain judgment of the authenticity of this tradition, although we may hope that clarifying documents will come to light. If, however, this was a genuine Pocumtuck transformer tale, it would surely have been remembered by Pocumtucks at Schaghticoke, Missisquoi, or elsewhere in the time of Mathevet, only 75 years after their dispersal from Deerfield.

But did Mathevet ever come in contact with Pocumtucks? The known facts that the Pocumtucks migrated to Schaghticoke, that Schaghticokes on more than one occasion moved to Missisquoi, and that Missisquoi was well within the reach of Mathevet's mission station make a meeting between Mathevet and the Pocumtucks entirely possible. No one has ever attempted to identify the native groups inhabiting the refugee village of Schaghticoke, their relative proportions at specific dates, or their proportional representations in the sequence of partial withdrawals that finally left the village empty in 1754; nor is it certain that this can be done with the documents that remain. We know that there were Loups at Missisquoi, those from Schaghticoke having arrived as early as 1724, if not before. It appears possible, even likely, that there were Pocumtucks among them. Definite proof is so far lacking, but the data permit the working assumption that Mathevet knew Pocumtucks.

Where they may have met is less clear. The several clues already mentioned linking Mathevet's Loups to Missisquoi strongly suggest that they were at Missisquoi at the time Mathevet was studying their language, or had been there long enough to become associated in his mind with the place. These clues are: the repeated juxtaposition of the entries for 'Loups' and 'sawmill', which became the name of the Missisquoi Falls settlement about 1748; the several references implying the proximity of the Loups to Montreal; the indications that Mathevet was dealing with a mixed Loup and Abenaki community, together with the fact that Missisquoi was a mixed Loup and Abenaki village after 1738, and perhaps earlier (Roy 1927–1929 2:252; Charland 1961:323); and the reference implying care in the use of fire in the woods, which was characteristic of the Indians at the foot of Lake Champlain but not of the Iroquois or of those at the head of Lake Champlain. The removal of the missionary Lauverjat from Missisquoi in 1747, the year of Mathevet's ordination, in spite of the importance attributed to the mission by the French government after 1743, would have permitted the young Mathevet to visit Missisquoi as a substitute missionary between 1747 and the beginning of the Seven Years' War, when the Indians withdrew from Missisquoi for the duration. Three prior years' work by Father Lauverjat could explain how Mathevet's "abnaquis" informants learned their prayers.

There is nothing in the above, however, to prevent one from holding rigidly to the known facts of Mathevet's career and assuming that the Loups came to him at Oka during the same period. We recall that his biographers are silent about the period 1747–1757, and, at the time of the temporary withdrawal from Missisquoi, some Loups and Abenakis could have moved temporarily to Oka. In making this assumption, however, one must take into account that no Loups or Abenakis were mentioned at the Lac des Deux-Montagnes in 1752 by Franquet (1889), in 1757 by Bougainville (1924a), or in 1760 by Sir William Johnson (O'Callaghan 1853–1887 7:582). Moreover, there is no evidence that the Missisquoi Indians withdrew anywhere other than to the French fort at Saint-Jean on the Richelieu River, to Île aux Noix (Renaud 1929:85), or to Saint Francis and Bécancour (Anon. 1931:412). It is doubtful that Mathevet's Loups were the Abenakis who were mentioned as resident at the Lac des Deux-Montagnes in 1745, because of the likelihood that he knew the Loups only after Missisquoi had become *tagwaõgan* 'the mill' in 1748 or 1749. Assuming a change of locale from Missisquoi to the Lac des Deux-Montagnes for the actual composition of the manuscript does not affect the assumption that the Loups in question were Pocumtucks from Schaghticoke via Missisquoi. The important question, of course, is where Mathevet's Loups came from originally, and the argument in favor of Pocumtuck can be put forward independently, without reference to where Mathevet encountered them.

Notes on the Loup Language

The language of Mathevet's manuscript gives an initial impression of a northeastern Algonquian language most closely related to the reasonably well documented languages of Massachusett, Narragansett, and Saint Francis Abenaki. This general impression is confirmed by a preliminary survey.

The phonological isoglosses of Eastern Algonquian languages indicate a developmental position for Loup between Saint Francis Abenaki and Massachusett, and show Loup sharing the general pattern of Massachusett and the other southern New England languages. This fact was first given public mention by Goddard (1970). The occurrence of *l* in a language with these apparent relationships suggests a language from the so-called Nipmuc region that was contiguous to the Western Abenaki dialects, to Massachusett, Narragansett, and Mohegan-Pequot. It was also contiguous to either the Mahican or the Connecticut River dialects, depending on whether the latter were themselves Nipmuck.

Pending a comprehensive study of the lexical isoglosses, we may determine by inspection that most of the Loup lexicon is shared with other New England languages. The presence of eastern, rather than central, Algonquian nouns, where they differ, is noticeable; for example, eastern *sancheman* 'chief', rather than central *okima*. Having in mind the hypothesis derived above from internal and historical evidence, namely, that the language of the "Mots loups" was Pocumtuck, it is appropriate to compare its lexicon with the fragments we have from the middle Connecticut valley (Day 1967a). The topographical terms found in John Pynchon's deed to Agawam are not considered here, since they are suspect as a Connecticut valley sample because the deed was drawn with the help of Ahaughton, a Massachusetts Bay Indian (Wright 1905:11–12). Although the sample presented by the Connecticut valley fragments is too small for satisfying conclusions and introduces the problem of unsophisticated transcriptions into an English orthography, something may be learned from it (see Table 3).

Nothing can be said about the two animal names and seven Agawam morphemes that do not occur in Mathevet's work, except that they are rather low-frequency forms and their nonappearance needs no comment. Thirteen of the 14 morphemes that occur in both lists appear to agree. The one that does not— *papsa-* 'half' (no. 4)—finds a cognate in Saint Francis Abenaki for the Agawam root, and the Loup word agrees with the Massachusett. A by-product is confirmation of what had been a doubtful element in the Agawam list, namely, *lowa-*, which I had assumed meant 'middle'. The initial *l* was questionable in the light of Abenaki *nōwi-*, Massachusett *nôeu*, and other similar forms, but Mathevet's independent recording of Loup *lan8i* [lōwi] seems to confirm it.

It is unlikely that Mathevet's work contains sufficient material for a comprehensive grammar of his Loup language, but even the observations incidental to editing the manuscript are very suggestive. There are indications of the double paradigms for transitive animate direct verbs and transitive inanimate verbs that characterize the Eastern Algonquian languages (Goddard 1967), but contrasting pairs are generally lacking. See, for example, on page 44, *8anisau 8iaux nitanten* 'je cherche de la viande perdue', and *8anisa8an nichahag8a* 'mon couteau est perdu'. Loup shares with Massachusett and Narragansett a second person singular imperative in *-s*, and its plural indicator for inanimate nouns, *-s*, is reminiscent of Massachusett and Narragansett *-š*. The Loup locative, however, is the *-k*, -vowel + *k* that is usual for New England languages, rather than the Massachusett *-t*, -vowel + *t*, and it possesses the generalized locative *-sik* that is more prominent in the Abenaki languages. Loup syntax agrees generally with Saint Francis Abe-

Table 3. Comparison of Connecticut valley and Loup words and morphemes

Connecticut valley		Loup
wallaneg,		
woollaneag	'fisher, blackcat'	*8lanig8a*
openach	'marten'	——
nottamag	'mink'	——
papsa-	['half']	*pansi8ai*
-apquoho	['he passes, goes by']	——
lowa-	['middle']	*lan8i*
-pon-	['winter']	*pipon*
-assik	[generalized locative]	*-sik*
squann-	['spring']	*sig8an*
-i-	[genitive]	*-i-*
-kesos	['moon, month']	*kiz8s*
moonesquann-	['weed, cultivate']	——
-imock	[infinitive ending]	——
towwa-	['hill a crop,' verb root]	——
matterllawaw	['ripe, mature flowers']	——
micheen-	['eating']	*mitchi-*
pahqui-	['early']	*p8k8i* 'moitié'
-taqunk-	['autumn']	*tag8ang8*
pepewarr	['white frost']	*t8p8* 'gelée blanche'
quani-	['long']	*k8ni*
squochee-	['thawing']	——
wappicummilcom	['stepping on it']	——
namassack	['fishes']	*namensak*

Note. Glosses in brackets are putative.

naki, syntax, and, one suspects, students of the southern New England languages will find that Loup agrees in syntax with them as well. Mathevet's Loup displays the diminutive suffixes *-s, -is,* and *-sis* that are common in New England languages, the negative imperative *ak8i* shared by both northern and southern New England languages, and the negative particle *mat* characteristic of southern languages only.

Mathevet recorded only one form for the conjunction 'and', namely, *8ank,* and gave it the additional meanings 'encore, davantage, plus, par dessus, aussi'. It may be queried whether this was really the simple conjunction 'and', whether it was the only Loup form for this function, or whether it was not properly the form for 'and also, and further', which Mathevet may have acquired early in his studies and continued to repeat. These queries are made in view of Abenaki *ta* and *ni* 'and' and *atsi* 'and also', as well as Massachusett *ka* 'and' and *wonk* 'also, again, moreover'. On the other hand, it is curious that another form for 'and' did not develop in context somewhere in the manuscript if *8ank* was not the correct form. Deficiencies in some of the simple tenses are possibly characteristic of Loup, but are more probably the consequence of Mathevet's employing the present tense for other tenses during what was certainly the early stage of his Loup studies.

Among the grammatical problems posed by the manuscript are Mathevet's implying a vocative form on page 85, after having stated on page 12 that the vocative was identical with the base form of the noun, and the perhaps unique interrogative particle *kā* on pages 15, 60, and 115. Its similarity to Mohawk *kā* suggests the possibility that it was borrowed from Mohawk, perhaps during the years when Schaghticokes and Iroquois met at Albany under the Covenant Chain. Mathevet understood it as a Loup, not an Iroquois, form, since he used it in Loup phrases (pp. 7, 8, 11, and elsewhere).

In sum, the preliminary indications are that Loup is a southern New England language with close affinities to the Connecticut valley dialects and perhaps to Nipmuck, if indeed it is not itself a representative of the still undocumented Nipmuck language. Thus, these indications from the language itself do not contradict, and do in some measure confirm, the hypothesis erected on the internal evidence in the manuscript and on our incomplete knowledge of Sulpician missionary activity.

Conclusions

The designation "loups" in the title of Mathevet's manuscript, taking into account contemporary French usage, tells us only that the language it records was an Algonquian language spoken somewhere between the Kennebec River and Virginia. That it is an unknown language has been established by inspection and comparison of existing vocabularies, and the concentration of undescribed languages in central and northwestern New England inclines one's expectations toward that region. This assumption is supported by the fact that the "Mots loups" is in an *l*-dialect, and it is generally held that central and northwestern New England was a region of *l*-dialects. A preliminary survey of the language of the manuscript indicates that it is probably a southern New England language, with some affinities to the Connecticut valley languages.

We look in vain for a statement by the author that would identify the specific people that spoke this language, so we must fall back on internal evidence and on what we know of Mathevet's career and the history of the time. The manuscript testifies clearly that Mathevet was in contact with Abenakis at the time he was writing the "Mots loups," these Abenakis having previously received the attentions of a missionary; that the Loups had been in contact with the Dutch and the

English; and that the Loups were living near enough to Montreal to regard it as the centre of their dealings with the French. It contains a suggestion that the manuscript was composed either during the period of peace between 1748 and 1754 or after 1760. It suggests further that the Loups either lived at, or had recently come from, Missisquoi after the construction of the French sawmill there in 1748 or 1749.

In one place, Mathevet gives the name of these particular Loups, probably their own name for themselves, as *8miskan8ag8iak*. He explains that they were so called because they had their village on the edge of very high ground. The name appears to be unique in our literature, and the explanation is ambiguous. It is proposed here, on reasonable but uncertain grounds, that Mathevet's Loups were Pocumtucks. These grounds are (1) an analysis of *8miskan8ag8iak* as 'beaver-tail-hill people' and (2) Sheldon's identification of the location of the main Pocumtuck population as around the "tail" end of Pocumtuck Mountain, which was regarded as the petrified remains of a great beaver killed by the Pocumtuck transformer.

Our knowledge of Mathevet's life is sketchy, and the only documented contact between him and any Loups is his baptism of a Loup at the mission of La Présentation in 1758. The numerous migrations of the New England Indians placed most of the nominal Loups from New England, including the Pocumtucks, within a day's travel of Montreal by the time of Mathevet's ordination in 1747. Whether Mathevet visited the Loups at their village or whether they came to reside temporarily near one of Mathevet's missions or parishes is unclear. The village of Missisquoi has been singled out as a probable site for residence by his Loups, and I incline toward the solution that Mathevet visited them at Missisquoi between 1749 and 1754. This position rests on the following circumstances: Mathevet was less likely to have been sent on a missionary journey before ordination. He was ordained in 1747 and sent to the Lac des Deux-Montagnes. His biographers have no details for the years 1747–1757. The manuscript seems to associate Mathevet's Loups with some Abenakis and to link them with Missisquoi, a place of known Loup and Abenaki populations, under the name of *tak8aangan* 'moulin à scie'. Missisquoi was known to the English as Taquahunga, but it could not have been so called until the sawmill was built, an event that probably took place in the autumn of 1748 or in early 1749. By 1749, Missisquoi was reestablished after three years of war, but was without a missionary. This could have provided a motive for a missionary to visit the village and reduces the likelihood that any considerable number of Indians forsook Missisquoi for the Lac des Deux-Montagnes. The failure of the several existing accounts of the Lac des Deux-Montagnes mission to mention any Loups there in 1742, 1752, 1757, and 1760 should be noted. This is not proof positive that no body of Loups ever resided at the Lake, since it has been noted that a group of

Abenakis took up residence there in 1745 without receiving mention in any census or traveler's account. The most telling data may be these: that the Indians who were dislodged during the war of 1745–1748 were reestablished at Missisquoi by 1748, the earliest year Missisquoi could have been known as Taquahunga; that they were not in evidence at the Lac des Deux-Montagnes when Franquet visited there in 1752; and that there were evidently no Loups present at the Lake when Bougainville recruited a war party for the Fort William Henry campaign, which Mathevet accompanied.

Other possibilities can be considered: that some of the Missisquoi Loups and Abenakis sojourned at least briefly at the Lac des Deux-Montagnes during the 1745–1748 war or after the Conquest, and these were possibly the same Abenakis mentioned by Beauharnois as resident at the Lake in 1745; that there were more Loups at La Présentation than we have evidence for; or that Mathevet visited Loups from Saint Francis after their removal to Saint Regis in 1759. So far, however, none of these possibilities are supported by known documents.

It would be interesting to know definitely where Mathevet made his study of this Loup language. Hopefully, a document may yet be found that will tell us. The location, however, may be irrelevant to the main question of the identity of his Loups. It is this question in particular that I hope will be clarified by future documentary research so that the Pocumtuck hypothesis may be tested. If this Loup language is really Pocumtuck, then it may also be a representative of the mysterious Nipmuck language, equated by some writers with Pocumtuck (Michelson 1912; Voegelin and Voegelin 1946; Gahan 1941a, 1941b). Whether or not it is Pocumtuck, it is probably the first substantial linguistic specimen from the terra incognita of central and northwestern New England.

The manuscript "Langue des Loups," which is bound in with Terlaye's Onondaga dictionary, and the scattered Loup words in the dictionaries of Aubery and Nudénans still lack detailed study. Probably we shall be able to more confidently identify the language of the "Mots loups" when this has been done and when all Loup data have been considered in relation to the known northeastern Algonquian languages and the locations and migrations of the peoples that spoke these languages.

19

The Western Abenaki Transformer

A review of the extensive literature on the ubiquitous culture hero Gluskap among eastern Algonquian-speaking groups serves as background for an examination of the Western Abenaki transformers Bedegwadzo and Odzihozo, who appear to be entirely distinct from Gluskap. Day's characterization of the Western Abenaki transformers is drawn in part from the ethnographic literature and in part from his own folkloric investigations at Saint Francis. Elsewhere, Day (1971a, 1981b) uses the oral traditions relating to Odzihozo along with other evidence to support a claim that the eastern shore of Lake Champlain in Vermont north of Vergennes was Western Abenaki territory. This paper was originally published in *Journal of the Folklore Institute* 13(1)75–89 (1976).

Students have long been concerned with the problem of world origins in North American mythology, and the literature is substantial. Algonquian mythology has come in for its share of attention. There exist collections of tales from several Algonquian groups and some analytical and comparative studies, all reflecting the state of collections in their times (Brinton 1885b; Chamberlain 1891; Hewitt 1910; Dixon 1909; Lowie 1909; Fisher 1946; Róheim 1952; Radin 1956). In the eastern part of the Algonquian area, the Micmacs, Maliseets, Passamaquoddies, Penobscots, and Abenakis have been sometimes regarded as the Wabanaki tribes, and linguistic, cultural, and even physical resemblances have been observed or inferred for these tribes (Leland 1884; Michelson 1912; Speck 1915a, 1926). Likewise the mythologies of these Wabanaki tribes have been looked upon as a group of related mythologies (Dixon 1909:3), much of the unity ascribed to them being provided by the ubiquitous culture hero named Gluskap. Speck gave the several linguistic and dialectic variants of the name as Micmac, Maliseet-Passamaquoddy *Glúskap;* Penobscot *Gluskábe;* Wawenock (Bécancour) *Gluskábe;* and Abenaki *Gluskǫbá* (Speck 1918:187 n. 2, 188 n. 1). There are numerous orthographic variants of these forms, but for the sake of simplicity, Gluskap will be used here. This paper will be concerned with Wabanaki mythologies and especially with the figures appearing in myths about world origins—creator, trickster, transformer, and culture hero to use terms familiar

Data for this paper were drawn from field research supported by the Spaulding-Potter Trusts of Manchester, New Hampshire, and the National Science Foundation, with the cooperation of Dartmouth College.

from the literature. Also a brief review of past work in the field of Wabanaki mythology is in order.

Little of value appears in the missionary, military, and travel accounts of the seventeenth and eighteenth centuries, except for one tale in Le Clercq's *New Relation of Gaspesia* and one in John Giles's captivity narrative. Both are copied in Mechling (1914:91–95, 114–115), and neither concerns a culture hero. Vetromile (1866:62–68) recorded a Penobscot account of Pamola, the spirit of Mount Katahdin. Serious collection of Wabanaki mythology probably began with Silas Rand's (1894:xxi) collection of Micmac tales in 1847, and he has been called the discoverer of Gluskap. In 1882 there began an efflorescence of Wabanaki folklore and folklorists, a phenomenon which itself deserves study since it had parallels among the Iroquois and other tribes. In this year Charles Godfrey Leland (1884) commenced to collect Passamaquoddy folklore and subsequently published his own stories together with selections of Micmac, Maliseet, Passamaquoddy, Penobscot, and Abenaki stories which he obtained from Rand, Edward Jack, Mrs. William Wallace Brown, and Abby Alger. During the decade of the 1880s, Brown (1890) and J. H. Fewkes (1890) were collecting among the Passamaquoddies; Jack (1895) was collecting among the Maliseets, and both Alger (1897) and Joseph Nicolar (1893), who had begun some 30 years before, were collecting among the Penobscots, but their results did not appear in print until later, and some of their tales have never been printed. The 1890s saw Hagar (1895, 1896, 1900) adding to Micmac mythology and J. D. Prince (1899, 1901) beginning to collect among the Passamaquoddies. In the next decade, although some earlier work was printed, there was a general lull in the study of Wabanaki mythology marked chiefly by the appearance of the first Abenaki tales (M. Harrington 1901; Deming 1902), a significant Micmac tale in native language text (Prince 1906), and the collaboration of Leland and Prince (1902) to produce metrical versions of Leland's (1884:ix) myths and some Abenaki tales, the latter perhaps collected by Alger. The next decade saw the revival of important collecting activity among the Maliseets, Micmacs, and Penobscots (Mechling 1914; Speck 1915b, 1917, 1918, 1935b; Stamp 1915). Speck (1928b) made the only collection of tales at the Bécancour Abenaki reserve in 1914, and substantial additions were made to Micmac mythology by Michelson (1925), Parsons (1925), and Wilson Wallis and Ruth Wallis (1955). Prince's (1921) complete Passamaquoddy tales were brought out in native language text, and Eckstorm (1924) added some legends about Katahdin to our knowledge. Since this period of activity, the only published additions to Wabanaki mythology have been those of Beck (1966) and Ives (1964), the latter including the Maliseet tales of E. Tappan Adney. Laszlo Szabo, however, is building a substantial collection of Maliseet tales (Archives, Canadian Museum of Civilization, Ottawa), and we look forward to Frank T. Siebert's collection of Penobscot tales in native language text, begun in the 1930s.

There has been some discussion of the character of Gluskap, of his possible origins and transmission as culture hero within the Wabanaki area, and of the problems posed by the multiple heroes in Maliseet and Penobscot tales (Speck 1935b; Fisher 1946). Speck (1928b; Speck and Tantaquidgeon n.d.) prepared a comparative study of Wabanaki transformers which remains unpublished, but no comprehensive treatment of Wabanaki transformers exists in print.

Wabanaki Culture Heroes

The Gluskap of the Micmacs is a powerful being who came to them from the sea in a stone canoe accompanied by an old woman whom he addressed as grandmother. He taught the Micmacs all they knew. "He was always sober, grave, and good; all that the Indians knew of what was wise and good he taught them." He transformed the landscape, and in time he departed toward the west. There he has been sought out by men who wished favors, but they had to make a very long and difficult journey before they found him in a beautiful land, living with Kuhkw the Earthquake, and Coolpŭjôt, the boneless one, who controlled the seasons (Rand 1894:232–237). As Fisher pointed out, his benevolent concern for mankind is demonstrated in the myths themselves, not merely in statements about him. In one version from Cape Breton, the creator Ktčĭn'sxam shaped Gluskap of earth, breathed on him, and he was made (Speck 1915b:59), but most versions of the Gluskap story commence with him already living with his grandmother or mother and a younger brother. Another powerful personage among the Micmacs is known as Kitpusiagana, whom Rand and the Wallises assign to an inferior position.

The Gluskap of the Maliseets bears a strong resemblance to the Gluskap of the Micmacs. He first came to the Maliseet country in a canoe, which was an island, together with his mother, or in some versions his grandmother. He worked his way up the Saint John River modifying the landscape and was soon joined at Kennebecasis Bay by his elder brother Mikumwesu (Mechling 1914:1–2). He had a series of adventures, partly by himself and partly shared by Mikumwesu, who had adventures of his own in the Maliseet country. Gluskap finally retired to a place in the south with his grandmother and a blind medicine man who has to be turned over every seven years to expose the medicinal plants growing under him. There is an obvious analogy here to Coolpŭjôt, companion of the Micmac Gluskap, who has to be turned over to change the seasons.

One version collected by Jack characterizes Gluskap as the Good Twin, whose Evil Twin brother, Malsum the Wolf, kills their mother by deciding to be born by bursting through her side. There is a widespread impression that this episode is a bona fide Wabanaki episode accounting for Gluskap's origin. It appeared first in Rand's (1894:339–340) Micmac legends, not as a tale but as a paraphrase of information given him by a Maliseet, Gabriel Thomas of Saint Mary's Reserve, and from Jack (1895:196–197), who recorded it from a certain Gabe of Saint Mary's, probably the same person. Jack claimed that Gabe was a very old man at the time and that he considered him a reliable source. Leland (1884:15–17) retold the episode from Rand's manuscripts before they were published, and Leland and Prince (1902:43–49) retold it in verse. Leland (1884:106–109) printed a second and better version collected by Jack at Fredericton, New Brunswick, presumably from Gabe Thomas like the others, but for some reason Leland labeled it a Micmac story. This was sufficient to put the episode into general circulation among students of the Wabanaki. Mechling (1914:44, 1958–1959:26) reprinted Rand's version and later mentioned it as a reflection of the Maliseet attitude towards twins, as did Wallis and Wallis (1957:33).

There is reason to question whether this episode really belongs in Wabanaki mythology, and the student who eventually attempts to settle the question should consider the following points among others. No one ever collected this episode among the Micmacs. It struck Rand as incongruous with the Micmac material he had collected, and he questioned whether it really referred to Gluskap. When Leland made it the first story in his book, however, he did not mention Rand's doubts. Its existence among the Maliseets, attested by both Rand and Jack, appears then to rest on the authority of a single informant. No one ever collected it among the Penobscots, Passamaquoddies, or Abenakis. This general ignorance of the episode cannot be explained away easily as the result of our incomplete knowledge of the several Wabanaki mythologies, since there are other and different accounts of Gluskap's origin (Speck 1915b:59–60; Nicolar 1893). Moreover, the structure of Gluskap's family in the principal Maliseet version, in which Gluskap's elder brother is the good, wonder-working Mikumwesu, is an implicit contradiction of the twin-birth episode (Mechling 1914).

Speck (1935b:9, n. 2) observed that the episode had a distinct Iroquois flavor, and although the Good and Evil Twin motif is widespread (Count 1952), Speck's hunch is worth further consideration. The appearance of the episode among the Maliseets, but not among the tribes to the east and west of them could be explained by a borrowing from the Hurons at Lorette, Quebec, in the eighteenth or nineteenth century. There was, moreover, considerable contact between the Maliseets and the Iroquois at Caughnawaga, Quebec, prior to 1850 at meetings of a confederacy to which both nations belonged. However the story came to Gabe Thomas, it did not appear again among the Maliseets until Ives (1964) obtained it from the Tobique Reserve. Was this a genuine old Maliseet motif coming to the surface again or was it derived at some point from a literate informant who knew the printed versions of Leland and Prince?

Among the Penobscots, Gluskap is best known as a benevolent transformer like his Micmac and Maliseet counterparts, who makes his appearance as a small boy under the care of his grandmother, Woodchuck (Speck 1918, 1935b). Another rather grander character appears in Nicolar's version as the first man-like being, the object of a special creation by the creator who proceeded to instruct mankind in all that it knows. Students have been inclined to accept Speck's judgment that Nicolar's account was much influenced by Christian ideas (Speck 1935b:6, n. 1). The similarities may be the result of Nicolar's use of biblical language when describing the creation, but the bulk of the narrative is Indian in nature and constitutes a contradiction to the biblical story of creation. It is noteworthy that Nicolar made a long effort to collect the stories from traditionalists beginning about 1850, and it is conceivable that he himself was the carrier of a Norridgewock tradition from his grandfather. Still a third type of Penobscot Gluskap is found in a single tale collected by Alger (1894). In Speck's Penobscot tales a large number of personages are involved in transformer-like episodes or have transformer-like characteristics: Snowy Owl, Long Hair, Froth, Fond-of-Traveling, Fast Runner, White Weasel, and Abandoned Boy, each represented by a single tale.

All we know of the Bécancour Abenaki transformer comes to us in four stories collected by Speck (1928b).

Western Abenaki Transformers

It has been generally assumed that the Abenakis at Saint Francis, who are the Western Abenakis by linguistic criteria, shared Gluskap as their culture hero, but a dearth of material from them has been noted (Speck 1918:128, 188, 1935b:5–6; Fisher 1946:228, 235). The Western Abenakis have always been something of an unknown entity to ethnographers. Their location prevented encounters with the earliest explorers. The few travelers who encountered them in the seventeenth century left either very scanty accounts of them or none at all. The withdrawals of the Western Abenakis from New England in the seventeenth and eighteenth centuries restricted the opportunities of the English to know them, and the French, for whatever reason, left only fragmentary observations on their culture. Except for a handful recorded by Rowland Robinson on Lake Champlain, no tales were collected from any of the component Western Abenaki groups in their original location, that is, before they joined the mixed refugee village at Saint Francis. Of the Western Abenaki tales in print from Saint Francis, many are historical or anecdotal in nature rather than mythological, and none of the mythological tales refer to a named culture hero (Wzôkhilain 1830b; J. Maurault 1866; Robinson 1896, 1901, 1905; M. Harrington 1901; Deming 1902; Leland and Prince 1902; Masta 1932; Speck 1945). In 1908 or 1912, Speck obtained the plots of two Gluskap stories from an Abenaki living at the Huron village of Lorette, Quebec, each only one sentence long, and by 1918 he had obtained a Western Abenaki cognate of the name, namely, Gluskǫbá, but concluded that it was already too late to secure a Western Abenaki version of the Gluskap myth (Speck 1918:188 n. 1, 1935b:6 n. 2, n.d.). In the 1920s, Hallowell was unsuccessful in finding anyone at Saint Francis who knew any Gluskap stories (Speck 1935b:6 n. 2; Fisher 1946:256; Hallowell, personal communication, 1961).

The purpose of this paper is to reexamine the Western Abenaki culture hero in the light of information which has turned up during the course of new fieldwork (Day 1956–1979). My beginning assumption was, like that of my predecessors, that the Western Abenaki culture hero was naturally Gluskap, and I hoped that with luck I might uncover a trace of him even though they had not.

In spite of the general moribund condition of Abenaki culture in 1956, mingled with the general population whose knowledge of their culture ranged from slight to considerable, there was a double handful of conservative individuals who retained a firm grasp on the old way of life. Much of the oral tradition had been passed from grandparent to grandchild in two steps from the mid-eighteenth century, and some of it was repeated to me with a remark to the effect that this was just the way grandmother used to tell it.

For five years, during the course of rather broad ethnographic and linguistic research, I searched diligently for some memory of Gluskǫbá. I found and recorded a fair assortment of mythological tales not previously suspected, tales in which some of the characters associated with Penobscot and Maliseet transformer tales appear, sometimes under the same names, sometimes under other names, engaged in episodes both familiar and new, but no amount of enquiry produced any memory of even the name Gluskǫbá. The fact that the Western Abenaki remembered a respectable body of mythology gave a new edge to the question, why they seemed to have forgotten the central figure in it.

In the winter of 1961–1962 I first heard stories of a wonder-working hero named Bedegwadzo "Round Mountain" or sometimes Bedegwadzois "Round Hill," who was described as a great *medawlinno* or shaman who lived long ago on Lake Champlain. Hallowell (1932) had heard this name but had been given the impression that it was merely a family name. Some of Bedegwadzo's exploits, however, such as taming a whirlwind and subduing the Thunderers, seem to lift him out of the ranks of ordinary shamans and place him among the transformers. I heard other stories of transformer-like feats in which the central character was left unnamed. These would start, "Long ago an Indian. . . ." At least one such tale with an anonymous hero but a clearly transformer-type episode, the creation of Otter Creek Falls, has appeared in print (Robinson 1905). At this point I began to speculate whether Bedegwadzo was not the Western Abenaki Gluskap under a different name, but gradually over a period of four years, the most conservative traditionalist, Théophile Panadis, fed me bits of the tale which put Western Abenaki mythology into proper perspective. He died before he was ready to record the whole tale on tape, but later I was able to record a version by Ambroise Obomsawin, who knew it from Mr. Panadis. This version, which is reproduced below in translation, is not so much a tale as an incomplete synopsis of the main transformer cycle.

> This story—this strange story—it was told by the late Simon Obomsawin and the late Louis Tahamont. Very long ago there was a being who made the mountains and the hills, the rivers and the lakes, and the weather. For beginning, at first, he had his body and his arms, but his legs were too short for him to be able to walk, and so he could not move around he had to sit, and he used his hands to be able to travel about. And he gathered it—he filled his hands with earth to make the mountains and hills, and in order to travel, then he had to drag his bottom on the ground to make rivers, and as he dug the water followed and it kept coming. He made the lakes, and to make the big lakes then he had to turn sitting, and then he made a deep hollow here sitting. And it happened afterwards that he grew his legs like a tadpole [does]. Then he placed his leg once here, again the other there, to make rivers, to place tributaries to the main river.
>
> And at one place, he came upon a river fork where there grew the White Pine Fungus, and there he stopped to talk with it. And that Fungus was a very great medicine. It was an important medicine.
>
> And afterwards he [the river-maker] became old, and probably he was tired, then he made Bitawbakw (Lake Champlain). And then he sat on a rock in that Lake, and he changed himself, he himself [did it], on that rock. That rock can be seen from Burlington [Vermont], and it is called Odzihozo, because of the fact that the one who made the Lake, he made himself into a rock, and from that time to be seen from Burlington. Some now still know it [Burlington] as Odzihozek ['at Odzihozo']. The Bostonians [Americans] call it Rock Dunder.
>
> For hundreds of years the Abenakis, while travelling there on Bitawbakw, always there they left tobacco and pipes for him, so he could smoke and also so the wind would not blow strong, so they could cross and so they go to Grand Isle. From this they think—some believe that he is called Odziho [a fortune, a chance] like drawing a straw. There is another similar stone that is there near the end of that Grand Isle that is called Odzihozo's wife, at the end of the island.
>
> Long ago the old men ended stories this way: "Our old ancestor, he said that. He made that. He wanted it that way."

It seems clear that the Western Abenaki transformer present in the early days of creation was named Odzihozo. Odzihozo was grotesque and extraordinarily powerful, but as far as existing stories go, he had no concern at all for mankind. A fuller version of his encounter with the White Pine Fungus exists.

Although the text is a bit obscure on this point, Odzihozo is the name of the river-maker, not of the rock, since it means 'he makes himself from something' and refers to his self-creation, which is not mentioned in this version. If the name had referred to his act of transforming himself into stone on top of the already existing rock in the lake, it would have to have been Ōdzihozo 'he makes himself over, changes himself'. Reference is made in the text to the false etymologies of the name current in this century among Indians who did not know the myth and confused the name with *odzihós* 'a chance'. This notion, probably suggested by the similarity of the names, was strengthened by the fact that the rock was one terminus of the long, dangerous crossing of Burlington Bay. Its name and reputation as the spirit in charge of this crossing were well known even to the Iroquois in the seventeenth century who, however, had trouble making a folk etymology to fit the name (Lounsbury 1960:60–62). Hallowell (n.d.) had obtained an oblique reference to the rocks from an informant who named them *djios* and *djiosskwa* respectively and called them simply deities, male and female. Robinson (1892a:6 n. 1) heard the Abenaki name of Rock Dunder as *Wohjahose,* which he thought erroneously meant 'The Forbidder', together with the idea that he was the guardian spirit of Lake Champlain to whom tobacco offerings must be made in passing.

Once aware of the existence of this story, I enquired about it of other informants and obtained further details. It became apparent that it had been common knowledge to the adult generation of about 1900–1910. It was known to a number of men who died in the 1950s and 1960s and to one (Edward Hannis), who died in 1972. All of these men who knew the story denied that the river-maker was Gluskǫbá, but no one was willing to assign the primeval transforming of the landscape to Bedegwadzo. It seems then that, instead of no Western Abenaki transformer, we have two, namely Odzihozo and Bedegwadzo. Neither of these names is known among any of the other Wabanaki tribes. If the Western Abenaki did not know Gluskap, it remains to explain how Speck obtained the cognate form of the name and the two Gluskap themes from a Saint Francis Abenaki. The themes are no great problem. An Abenaki married to a Huron woman and living at Lorette could easily have learned them from either Bécancour Abenakis or Maliseets. The Western Abenaki cognate Gluskǫbá did not appear in print until after Speck had visited Bécancour in 1914 and obtained stories of Gluskǫbá there. It is possible, even probable, that the cognate originated with the studious Abenaki Henry L. Masta, who accompanied Speck to Bécancour and later translated François Neptune's stories into the western dialect, converting the name into "Glusk8ba," 8 being Masta's symbol for the lower midback nasal vowel [5]. The name has been somewhat reinforced among some younger Abenakis by an event in 1965. After Théophile Panadis and I had been discussing Gluskǫbá for several years, he dictated a short French version of the Odzihozo myth to a young lady and for some unknown reason he chose to use the name Gluskǫbá for Odzihozo. My notes show that the next year he was quite explicit on two occasions that Gluskǫbá was not Odzihozo, but his whimsy has achieved some circulation.

It is clear from this sketch of the Odzihozo cycle and from the related episodes and remarks I obtained that Odzihozo is not the Gluskap of the Micmacs, Maliseets, and Passamaquoddies or of the better known Penobscot versions. His definite origin, his self-creation, his early grotesque appearance and gradual spontaneous growth, his coexistence with the unformed world and perhaps his more pervasive influence in shaping it, and, so far as we know, his lack of concern for mankind sets him apart from the more human, noble-minded, generous Gluskap. Gluskap had his own family and a concern for mankind. He came to the Micmacs and Maliseets from the sea and was already a boy at the outset of most of the Penobscot stories. We may observe here that Nicolar's (1893:12) derivation of the name of his hero, *Klose-kur-beh,* was 'the man from nothing'. Whether we make much or little of this etymology, it is clear from Nicolar's account that Klose-kur-beh did not create himself, that he rose from the dust as a complete man, that his career exhibited Gluskap's typical altruism, and therefore he too had little in common with Odzihozo.

Nevertheless, a transformer very like Odzihozo makes two appearances in Wabanaki literature. One appears in a Bécancour Abenaki tale collected by Speck. This transformer created himself, and, at least in the beginning, moved around in a sitting position. His origin was coeval with the creator's creation of mankind; his power was derived from earth touched by the creator; and he engaged in a trial of personal power with the creator himself. The other three tales collected at Bécancour do not continue the career of this character. Rather they are episodes well known in Gluskap stories. The other Odzihozo-like character appears in a single short tale collected by Alger (1894). This person made himself out of earth left over from the creation of man and was a character of such power that the creator consulted him on basic questions of shaping the earth and the waters. Both of these characters were given the name Gluskap by their narrators, but both, like Odzihozo and unlike Gluskap elsewhere, were self-creating and present at the original shaping of the earth. This raises the question of the appropriateness of applying the name Gluskap to them. The familiarity of the Bécancour Abenakis with the name Gluskap could be explained by their contacts with Eastern Abenakis and especially by the substantial presence of Maliseets in the band. Similarly, it is possible that Alger's informant, or even Alger herself, applied the familiar name Gluskap to the unique Penobscot appearance of an Odzihozo-like character.

Bedegwadzo, on the other hand, bears much more similarity than Odzihozo to the Gluskap we know from the main Wabanaki tradition by reason of his more human nature, his concern for the welfare of human beings, his more recent existence, and the nature of his exploits.

Discussion

It seems that the Western Abenaki material, slender as it still is, may contain a clue which will be helpful for reexamining Wabanaki mythologies, namely, the existence of two orders of transformers. Credit for perceiving the possibility of this in Algonquian mythologies must go to Fisher. She was led to speculate that, in addition to the better-known Algonquian culture heroes, as Gluskap and Nanabozho, there might be an older concept, and that this older concept might be represented by the Cree-Naskapi Tcikapis (Shikabish). One Cree account, called to her attention by Hallowell, is explicit in making Tcikapis much earlier than Nanabozho (C. Gordon 1925). It was Fisher who pointed out the resemblance between the dwarf Tcikapis with his deceptive power and the Maliseet Mikumwesu, the elder brother of Gluskap, a tiny man with a tiny but very powerful bow and great personal power. Two Micmac traditions seem to confirm the priority of Mikumwesu, one making "Megumooweco" the father of Gluskap and one making "Mekmues" the oldtime Micmac good spirit of the creator (Hagar 1895; Prince 1906).

Fisher was unwilling to invest great confidence in the theory of two orders of transformers on the basis of these scattered indications, but there are further arguments to recommend it. For one thing, besides the similarities between Tcikapis and Mikumwesu noted by Fisher, the primacy of Mikumwesu over Gluskap is not only stated but clearly borne out by events of the myth. This is best seen in the most complete, coherent version of a Wabanaki transformer cycle, namely, the Maliseet version recorded by Mechling (1914:1–40) from Jim Paul of Saint Mary's Reserve in 1910. This version provides chronology and purpose for many episodes which have been collected elsewhere merely as isolated tales. Another character not mentioned by Fisher who seems to belong with Tcikapis and Mikumwesu is the Micmac Kitpusiagana, who, like Tcikapis, was born in Caesarian fashion and remained child-sized for at least most of his adventures (Rand 1894:62–80; Wallis and Wallis 1955:338–343).

The Western Abenaki material sets forth two transformers who, being distinct in both time and characteristics, constitute a further example of the existence of two orders. One transformer, Odzihozo, is ancient, grotesque, so powerful as to be self-creating and the primary transformer of the landscape, endowed with the property of growth reminiscent of the Passamaquoddy Mikumwesu, who could increase his stature at will (Leland and Prince 1902:12). He might be assigned to the primal period of mythology together with Tcikapis, Mikumwesu, and Kitpusiagana. The other, Bedegwadzo, might be regarded as a later transformer comparable to the Gluskap of most stories and to the numerous minor Penobscot transformers. He might be grouped with Nanabozho and Wiskejak with respect to relative chronology but not with respect to character, since Bedegwadzo, as he appears in the existing stories, has none of the trickster about him. In fact, transformer and trickster cycles are essentially distinct in all Wabanaki mythologies. This can be taken as one distinguishing characteristic of the cultures south of the Saint Lawrence River and east of Iroquoia. The absence of the earth-diver theme is another distinguishing characteristic, and the absence of the Good and Evil Twins may prove to be still another.

This brief exposition of Odzihozo and Bedegwadzo is by no means the whole existing corpus of Western Abenaki mythology. A fair number of tales are on hand, and there is some hope of obtaining more. There is a further possibility of turning up a collection told by James Annance to Moses Williams about 1840 (Parkman 1947:36). When all these Western Abenaki materials become available, it will be appropriate to reconsider the whole matter of Wabanaki mythologies. Their assumed uniformity and even the existence of a Wabanaki group should be reexamined. A general knowledge of Gluskap by Wabanaki tribes can no longer be assumed, and it will be appropriate to examine the natures and distributions of the several Wabanaki transformers. It will also be appropriate to consider their origins and possible borrowings of their names and characteristics by one tribe or another. Fisher has already cited a statement which Jack had from the Maliseets that they got Gluskap from the Micmacs. I have had the same statement from a Maliseet, but other Maliseets claim Gluskap is theirs.

Fisher's hypothesis of two orders of transformers is worth following up. If we disregard Bécancour because of the paucity of information, the evidence is weakest for the Penobscot, Alger's tale being the unique manifestation of the older order; but this "Gluskap" clearly belongs with the Bécancour "Gluskap" and with Odzihozo. Without this tale, they alone would lack the kind of distinction seen in the Micmac Kitpusiagana-Gluskap contrast, the Maliseet Mikumwesu-Gluskap contrast, and the Western Abenaki Odzihozo-Bedegwadzo contrast. We might postulate that the Odzihozo-type transformer, in a more strict sense, had only a western distribution, possibly no farther east than the Kennebec River, but we should keep in mind the possibility of Kennebec influences on Penobscot culture in the eighteenth century and of Passamaquoddy influences after that.

Wabanaki mythologies contain many problems beyond the scope of this paper. Fisher thought that even the earliest Gluskap materials showed evidence of weakened native tradition. This may be queried, but it is obvious that the different tales, as they come to us, are very uneven with respect to the qualifications of the narrator, the literalness of the recording, and the ability of the recorder to understand and express the significance which a tale had to the narrator. All the Wabanaki literature should be reassessed with the utmost care.

My experience with recovering Western Abenaki myths and the work of Beck and of Ives suggest that the time for productive collecting in this field is not yet over. An intensive effort should be made to record what remains, but special care should be taken at this late date to determine the provenience and genealogy of each tale collected. The time for the definitive study of Wabanaki mythologies is not yet, but we begin to glimpse the form it could take.

20

Indian Place-Names as Ethnohistoric Data

Day's interest in Western Abenaki place-names amounted to a minor passion, and this paper is a useful compendium of do's and don't's in a field characterized by much fanciful speculation. When the proper care is exercised, place-names with analyzable or reconstructible meanings can provide important clues regarding earlier locations and events and thus serve the larger ends of ethnohistory. This paper was originally published as pp. 26–31 in *Actes du huitième congrès des algonquinistes,* Ottawa, Carleton University (1977).

Let us admit at the outset that Indian place-names are fun. They combine the romance of history, real or spurious, with the challenge of a detective story. And this is part of the trouble. Indian place-names seem to have had a greater attraction for the untrained than for competent students of ethnolinguistics and ethnohistory. As a result we have all too many examples—both amusing and exasperating—of names which have been enthusiastically analyzed by the following procedure: (1) Assuming that the name as spelled on a modern map and pronounced by the analyst himself is just what the Indian said; (2) segmenting this name in any way which seemed most convenient; (3) assigning a meaning to the segments so obtained by appropriating words or even arbitrary parts of words from dictionaries of an Indian language in the same region, assuming that it is the same as the language of the place-name; and, (4) having ignored the Indian grammar altogether, rearranging the bits of English meaning into a grammatical phrase. This procedure was dubbed "linguistic scrabble" by Holland (1962:296).

Since this naiveté may sound farfetched to an audience of scholars, let me cite a single example. In New Hampshire on the southern edge of the White Mountains is a beautiful lake now known as Squam Lake. This name seems to have no documentary history, and we shall probably never know its meaning unless a fuller form is found in an early document. It means nothing in the Western Abenaki language once spoken in the region, but a local historian, nothing daunted, analyzed it as follows. She asserted that Squam is an abbreviation of "Wonneasquam sauke," for no apparent reason unless it was suggested by the name of neighboring Lake Winnisquam. This was broken down into *winne,* said to mean 'smiling', which it does not; *asquam,* said to mean 'big water', which it does not; and *auke,* said to mean 'mountain', although it means 'land'—and the

195

whole was said to mean 'smiling big sheet of water surrounded by mountains' (Speare n.d.:53). Some local residents have appropriated the Indian name of the nearby Baker River for Squam Lake. This name is *Asquamachumauke,* and the same kind of analysis has given us a meaning 'crooked water from high places', which does not suit the lake. Actually, *Asquamachumauke* itself is probably a rather corrupt form, and my guess is that it started life as Abenaki *skamésk-wamaákw,* which names the sticks which the female beaver has gnawed for the bark in the house and let float to the top. This notion is supported somewhat by the fact that the Baker River was famous as a beaver grounds. In any event, you now recognize the sort of scholarship I was referring to.

Indian place-names can be ethnohistoric data, however, and there are some linguists and ethnohistorians who are interested in them. It is the serious study of place-names I want to talk about.

Before a place-name can become an ethnohistoric datum, it must meet several conditions (Lounsbury 1960). One must determine the place to which the name belonged, the time period during which it was used, the language from which it came, and the meaning. The place, the time, and the language have often been assumed without much thought, and determining the meaning of a name has prerequisites which have proven to be stumbling blocks for much place-name analysis.

First, in order to ascertain the meaning of a place-name, one needs the actual form which the Indian used, not a version garbled by whites who had difficulty pronouncing the Indian name and were not strongly motivated to pronounce it correctly. When there are native speakers of the language who still call the place by the same name, the correct form can usually be obtained directly from informants, although Indian languages are subject to change with time as are other languages. When there are no native speakers, or none who know the name, or when the modern name for the place in the native language is now different from the one under study, one must resort to reconstructing it as well as one can from the historical record and a knowledge of the language. To do this, one must treat the sources of the name like other historical data and approach them with the same care. One must at least consider the age of the historical source, the integrity of the recorder, the native language of the recorder, and the recorder's ability to hear and record an Indian language.

Second, a knowledge of the Indian language to which the name belongs is the indispensable prerequisite for determining the meaning of the name. This should be obvious, but incompetence of writers in the relevant Indian language is the reason behind most unsatisfactory place-name analysis. The best solutions are sometimes produced by that rather rare native speaker who has a full command of "the old language" and at the same time has an interest and an analytical bent. Lacking such an informant, the analysis must be supplied by a linguist who is acquainted with the phonetics, lexicon, and grammar of the language, and few linguists know an Indian language well enough to be completely independent of a native speaker.

Although the original name and its literal meaning are enough to satisfy the purposes of a writer of a place-name article, the ethnohistorian must have one more piece of information before the name is useful. He needs to know the significance of the name, that is, the connotation of the name when used as the name of a particular place. There are many purely descriptive, self-obvious names, many "Bald Mountains," many "Round Islands," and the like. But if a place is named, for example, 'the outlet of Lodeno's river', which is the Abenaki name for Three Rivers, we have not merely the linguistic form, but the information that this river was the hunting territory of one Lodeno, a fact attested by tradition (Laurent 1884:213).

This somewhat pedantic listing of prerequisite conditions needs illustrating. The futility of trying to extract further ethnographic or historical information from even a correctly analyzed name attributed to the wrong place should be obvious. When analysis is difficult, as is often the case, no help can be had from topography or other associations if we are looking at the wrong place. In fact, they can confuse the analyst and cast doubt on a correctly analyzed name. For example, *skwaméskwamaákw* is appropriate to Baker River but inappropriate to Squam Lake and hence questionable even without further knowledge. Students had trouble with the name Saratoga, because they assumed it to have been the name of present-day Saratoga Springs, until Beauchamp showed that it was originally a locality on the Hudson River (Beauchamp 1907:196–197).

Knowing the time when a name was applied to a place is equally essential, since it has a bearing on the language of the name. For example, there is a river which flows into the Saint Lawrence River from the south which is now called the Yamaska. Since the Abenakis have lived in and controlled this region for about 300 years, it is natural to look for a meaning in the Abenaki language. Modern Abenakis make the same assumption, but since there is no word *yamaska* in Abenaki, they fall back to *mamaská,* the modern word for 'toad'. The old word for 'toad', however, was simply *maská,* and *mamaská* seems to have come into use only late in the last century to avoid a sexual homonym. One Abenaki postulated an imaginary conversation, perhaps giving travel directions, thus: "This is the Saint Francis River, and that the Toad River" (Masta 1932: 102). In Abenaki this is *Yó Alsígôntégw, ni yá Maská Zibó.* This is quite unsatisfying and reminiscent of the local Maine explanations of the names Matanawcook and Annabessacook, which postulated two Indians named Matty and Anna and saying that Matty was no cook but Anna was "besser" cook (Eckstorm 1941:xvi). The modern Abenaki explanation of Yamaska becomes pointless, however, when we take into account the fact that the name of the river on a map of 1713 is

Ouramaska and further that the Lower Algonquins occupied that stretch of the Saint Lawrence River even before the Abenakis settled in the region (Anonymous 1713). If we convert the *r* of Old Algonquin into the *n* of modern Algonquin, we have *o:namaska*. This suggests, at least to me, the Algonquin word *ondimuŝki*, which may be translated 'this way into the bush', a descriptive phrase used for a small river striking off through the woods (Day 1970). The geography lends plausibility to this solution, and history increases its probability, since the small Yamaska River was indeed used as a shortcut between the Saint Lawrence River and Lake Champlain, thereby avoiding the Richelieu River, the main route of Iroquois war parties and white armies. At the very least, this solution relieves us of having to rely on empty late Abenaki etymologies for tentative solutions and points up the necessity for dating a place-name.

This example also illustrates the futility of trying to analyze a place-name through the vehicle of the wrong language, but there are many examples of this, and Indians are among our worst offenders. Secure in their knowledge of their own language and often willing to assume the similarity of other Indian languages to it, they sometimes confidently attempt to analyze a name from a totally different language. An extreme example of this procedure is Pushaw Lake in Maine, which was named for a white settler named Pushaw (Eckstorm 1941:33). This did not prevent an Abenaki from deriving it from *passabákw* 'rising lake water' (Masta 1932:95). This sort of myopia is much like that of Reider T. Sherwin (1940), who, having persuaded himself that the Algonquian languages descended from Old Norse, mistook the Iroquoian name Niagara for an Algonquian name and promptly produced a Norse etymology for it.

It would seem self-evident that to determine the meaning of an Indian name, one needs to know the language in question, but those who have not known the language have filled the literature with horrible examples. A good native speaker is an adequate source for current Indian place-names. For old names which have, or are suspected of having, undergone corruption, a skill in finding and interpreting old sources is also essential. And for the sizeable proportion of old names whose earliest and best form is still not transparent, the ultimate resource is the native speaker whose knowledge of the language and the old way of life is exceptional and who at the same time has an interest in the problem of names. Such native speakers are rare, but such a one will have at his command a stock of forms, which are neither in the head of the linguist nor in the lexicons available to him, as well as a sense of what is and is not an appropriate name for a given place.

As an example of the difference between meaning, which is the minimum product of place-name study, and significance, which makes a place-name usable for ethnohistory, we may take the Lamoille River in Vermont, for which the Abenaki name is *wíntégw*. This word certainly means 'marrow river'. But why it was named Marrow River is quite unknown from history, tradition, or geographical circumstance, so the name tells us nothing about either the culture or history of the Abenakis beyond the obvious fact that they knew the river well enough to name it.

Perhaps the most common use of place-names, however, has been to locate and delimit the homeland of a given people, and this exercise can be performed without knowing the significance of the names but only their location and meaning. A classic demonstration of this use is Jackson's (1955:129–165) locating within Scotland the country of the Picts at the time of Roman contact. This is a valid and useful application of place-names. There remain a number of caveats and limitations to this use, however, even if we overlook the deficiencies and uncertainties of the names one has to work with. (1) For one thing, peoples often have names for places which they do not occupy but have merely visited or heard about. Take as examples the names for Washington and Philadelphia still surviving in Mohawk (Lounsbury 1960:26). (2) We should not expect boundaries necessarily to be sharp. Rather we should be content with a definite core area and a more or less sharp margin. The reasons for this are essentially two. Boundaries between tribes were often boundary zones, rather than boundary lines, which makes for double naming of features within this zone that each tribe might claim and exploit as it was able. Moreover, one would expect double naming of features along a boundary line, since the features would be known to the people on both sides, and some of them, at least, would be important as landmarks or boundary markers. (3) Place-names are not ageless documents. They were given at a point in history which is seldom determinable, but they cannot be used by themselves to demonstrate an occupation much earlier than the earliest date of their recording. (4) Given the same quantity and quality of data, it should be easier to establish a boundary line between peoples speaking different languages than between political groups speaking dialects of the same language.

Some place-names add to the historical record. Let me give two examples from the Abenaki country. The Missisquoi River in Vermont perpetuates the name *Mazipskoík* 'at the flint', which was originally the name of a place near the river, rather than of the river itself (Day 1956–1979). This calls attention to Abenaki knowledge and use of an important chert quarry discovered by archeologists only 50 years ago (Bolton 1930a). In the Richelieu River is an island now known as Ash Island. The Abenakis know it as *Odepsék* 'where the heads are, the place of heads'. This name locates the place where about 1694 an Abenaki war party was surprised by and killed the warriors of a Mohawk party and stuck their heads up on poles around the island. The location, taken together with the Abenaki oral tradition of the event, gives us a fairly detailed knowledge of an event about which history alone tells us next to nothing.

Some descriptive names tell us something about the aboriginal environment or about the use of significance of the place for the Indians. For example, on Lake Champlain south of Burlington is *Megezóidolká* 'Eagle Cliff', testifying to a nesting place of bald eagles, a fact one might have suspected but which is not recorded in any naturalist's notes. A little river flowing into the Saint Francis River in Quebec is called *kawásenitégw* 'wind-throw river' and fixes the place of forest destruction by a tornado which is remembered in oral tradition. The name of the Winooski River in Vermont is also significant ecologically. *Winoskí* means 'wild-onion land'. One might jump to the conclusion that the whole valley was characterized by the growth of wild onions. Actually, the name *Winoskík* was restricted to an early historical village, most probably situated at the foot of the lower falls of the river. The lowlands here are suitable grounds for *Allium Canadense,* the wild leek, and the testimony of the name should probably be restricted to this area. Along the Great Oxbow of the upper Connecticut River lie the Coos Intervales, meadows famous in history. The Abenaki name for this area is *Kowasék* 'place of white pines', which gives the ecologist a clue that although white pine is a subclimax species, it was dominant here centuries ago. Not all descriptive names are helpful. For example, *onegíkwizibó* 'otter river', now Otter Creek, testifies to a former noteworthy abundance of otters, which is not especially astonishing and happens to have been documented in an early natural history (Thompson 1842:33).

Some descriptive names are not sufficient testimony to an event or a use or a characteristic taken by themselves. There is, for example, a crossing in Lake Champlain which has been long known to whites as Sandbar Bridge. The Abenaki name is *Kíileságwôgán.* It is not clear from the name alone that this is not merely a translation of the white man's name for the crossing. *Kíileságwôgán* must be taken in its basic meaning 'land crossing' and considered in conjunction with the Abenaki tradition of a war episode, which supplies the significance of the name as a secret fording place known only to the Indians at one time.

Some place-names have relevance for the mythology of a people. For example, there are many names in the Northeast which locate and identify a physiographic feature which was transformed by a culture hero in the early days of the world. In addition to shedding some light and interest on the myths themselves, the grouping of these features tells us something about the home territory and migrations of a given tribe. One might suppose that these names would be preserved with a clear form and meaning because of their importance to the people who gave them. This is not always the case, and in these latter days the names of places important in the mythology must be collected with the same care and scrutiny as any other. Let me close with one of my favorite examples.

In Lake Champlain is a rock which no longer bears an Indian name among whites. It is called Rock Dunder. However, I know from informants now dead that it was once familiarly known to them as *Odzihózo,* the name of the great transformer whose living remains it is. For centuries the Abenakis have left tobacco offerings there, asking for safe crossing of Burlington Bay. This custom continued for a generation after the knowledge of *Odzihózo* was lost, and this later generation assumed that the name was *dzihósek* 'a chance, a gamble', which provided them with a folk etymology appropriate to the site. Given only this form, we should be quite unable to arrive at the true form and significance of the name of Rock Dunder, which may be a borrowing from Iroquois *rotsî'yo,* which is difficult to etymologize (Lounsbury 1960:60–62).

I think it is fair to conclude that Indian place-names, although potentially valuable, are difficult to use and that before one can place reliance on a name, it must be validated every step of the way.

21

Western Abenaki

In this encyclopedia article, Day provides what is unquestionably the most comprehensive summary of Western Abenaki history and culture in print, particularly from the perspective of Saint Francis (Odanak), where he did the bulk of his fieldwork. The article was originally published as pp. 148–159 in Vol. 15, *Northeast*, of *Handbook of North American Indians*, Washington, D.C., Smithsonian Institution (1978).

Language

The Western Abenaki are usually called Abenaki (ˌăbəˈnăkē) in English from their own name *wǫbanakii* and sometimes Benaki (ˈbenəkē) from French *abénaquis*.[1]

The existence of a group distinguishable as the Western Abenaki is known from a language that was documented at Odanak, Quebec, in the early nineteenth century (Wzôkhilain 1830a, 1830b) and in Vermont and New Hampshire place-names of the seventeenth and eighteenth centuries. This language, which was still spoken in 1973 by the Indians at Odanak on the Saint Francis River in Quebec, is distinguished from the Eastern Abenaki language of Maine by differences in phonology, grammar, and lexicon. It is not an evolutionary development from the Kennebec dialect after 1679, as Prince (1902) supposed. The geographical boundary between the Eastern and Western Abenaki languages is not clear, since data from the boundary zone between the Merrimack and Kennebec Rivers are inadequate. Eastern Abenaki is documented as far west as the Kennebec River, and it is probable that Western Abenaki was spoken by the Indians of the upper Merrimack River, the upper and middle Connecticut River, and Lake Champlain. The intermediate dialect of Bécancour may have stemmed from the Androscoggin River. The dialect of the Pigwacket on the upper Saco is unknown, and the speech of the Almouchiquois on the lower Saco, wrongly called Sokoki by nineteenth-century writers, may have belonged with the dialects of coastal Massachusetts.

[1] The orthography used for the Western Abenaki language follows the phonemicization of Day (1964), with the omission of the largely predictable accent and the substitution of ə for e and ǫ for ō (a slightly centralized, optionally rounded, low back nasalized vowel).

Component Groups

The geographically central tribe of the Western Abenaki region, the one that formed the beginnings of the village of Saint Francis (Odanak), was the Sokoki of the upper Connecticut River. The name Sokoki was wrongly shifted to the Saco River Indians by nineteenth-century historians, and writers came to regard Squakheag, the southernmost Sokoki village at Northfield, Massachusetts, as an isolated and independent group. Seventeenth-century documents treat the Sokoki as the inhabitants of the entire upper Connecticut River, which would extend the name Sokoki to the Cowasucks at Newbury, Vermont. The tribes of the upper Merrimack River, the Winnipesaukees and the Penacooks at Concord, New Hampshire, were Western Abenakis. Downriver were other bands at Amoskeag (Manchester, New Hampshire), Souhegan, Nashaway, Pawtuckett (Lowell, Massachusetts), and Naamkeek (Salem, Massachusetts). It is uncertain whether any of these were Abenakis, and all were probably under the overlordship of Passaconaway, whose chief residences were at Amoskeag and Pawtuckett. Wood's (1634) map shows Penacook as a fortified village under the chief Mattacomen, which may indicate that he was coordinate with Passaconaway and independent at this time. The Vermont shore of Lake Champlain was probably occupied by Western Abenakis from prehistoric time (Day 1971). Villages at the mouths of the Winooski, Lamoille, and Missisquoi Rivers, on Grand Isle, and elsewhere are known; but in the eighteenth century, their population gradually concentrated at Missisquoi, and the Missisquoi tribe came to stand, in most writings, for all the Champlain valley Abenakis. The tribes of Lake Champlain and the Connecticut and Merrimack valleys appear to have been always friendly during the historic period. They were frequently allies; they settled in the same refugee or mission villages, and they gave other evidence of being essentially one people.

It appears that all the inhabitants of the country from the Merrimack River to Lake Champlain, that is, the Western Abenakis, found their way eventually to the Saint Francis River. Some Eastern Abenakis from the Chaudière mission and some southern New England Indians, probably mostly Pocumtucks and Nipmucks, were incorporated in the village at one time. For convenience, therefore, the Saint Francis village and all its contributory groups will be considered together here. This means consideration of some peoples who, before their removal, were part of the southern New England culture area and who may have contributed some southern traits to the culture observed at Saint Francis in the nineteenth and twentieth centuries.

Territory and Environment

The territory of the Western Abenaki lay within the New England–Acadian physiographic province. The principal subdivisions of the territory are, from west to east, the Champlain Valley, the Green Mountains, the Connecticut River valley, and the White Mountains, whose bordering uplands to the south contain Lake Winnipesaukee and the Merrimack River valley. This territory has abundant precipitation fairly evenly distributed throughout the year. Summers are warm, and winters are cold, with four or five months of snow cover. Most of the known Abenaki villages were situated where the growing season was 140 days or more.

The original forest of the lowlands was a mixture of central and northern hardwoods and hemlock with white pine occurring as occasional large individuals or dominating stands on light soils and old fields. The hills and lower mountain slopes were dominated by northern hardwoods and hemlock and the upper slopes by red spruce and northern hardwoods. Swamps were characterized by balsam fir and swamp hardwoods and bogs by black spruce, tamarack, and white cedar. The upper-slope types were found at lower elevations in the northern part of the region (Westveld 1956; Braun 1950:422–440). The large game animals were moose, deer, and black bear, and there were many furbearers— beaver, muskrat, otter, mink, marten, fisher, raccoon, foxes, and skunk. Wolf and bobcat were numerous, lynx and mountain lion less so. Wolverine were rare. Hare, rabbit, weasel, squirrels, and many species of birds occurred. The northern part of the region was differentiated by the occurrence of more moose and fewer deer, by sporadic occurrences of woodland caribou, and by more beaver. The Western Abenaki territory had an abundant flora and fauna as a consequence of its latitudinal position and the environmental variety created by its mountain and valley topography.

Those southern New England Indians who removed to Saint Francis probably came mostly from the Connecticut valley in Massachusetts and the lakes of the highland in eastern Massachusetts and northeastern Connecticut. This region has a somewhat milder climate, that is, a longer average growing season and a shorter period of snow cover. Sharing the forest cover of the lowlands farther north, it constituted a kind of transition from the characteristic northern to more southerly fauna.

History

The Western Abenaki have always been something of an unknown quantity to historians and ethnographers. Their interior location prevented encounters with the earliest explorers. The few traders and other travelers who were among them in the seventeenth century left either very scanty accounts or none at all. Their withdrawals from the southern periphery of their country and the long colonial wars restricted the opportunities of the English to know the Western Abenaki, and English testimony concerning them features battles, treaties, and captivities. The Dutch knew them through the Iroquois. The best early information on them comes from the French, who knew them as converts and allies, but French preoccupations with conversion and defense seem to have prevented even those missionaries who knew the Abenaki best from leaving a reasonably comprehensive account of their culture. Moreover, French practice of referring to both Penacooks and Sokokis as Loups, originally their name for the Mahicans, tends to confound their record. As a result, the Western Abenaki have moved through the pages of New England history under the names of their villages, regarded as tribal names, and through the pages of Canadian history under group names of vague denotation. They stand in works of secondary history characterized largely by stereotypes growing out of the errors of certain influential nineteenth-century historians.

Their prehistory likewise largely remains to be unraveled. Considerable material has been collected from sites such as Missisquoi, Cowasuck, Squakheag, Winnipesaukee, Namaskik, and Massabesic, and smaller amounts from other sites, generally without documenting even relative age. The Fort Hill Squakheag site is the only systematically excavated site that can be connected with a historic Western Abenaki group (Thomas 1971).

Only glimpses of the Western Abenaki can be gained from the writers of the early seventeenth century. About 1617 Ferdinando Gorges's men at the mouth of the Saco learned of the Sockhigones to the west and southwest, who were probably the Sokokis on the Connecticut River. They also learned of a country between the Sockhigones and the Eastern Abenaki called Apistama, possibly Winnipesaukee, one of whose early names, Winnipistogee, bears some resemblance to Apistama. John Smith was told that there were 30 habitations on the Merrimack River, but those on the lower river under Passaconaway were probably Massachusett rather than Abenaki in speech and culture. The English on Massachusetts Bay had contact with Passaconaway as early as 1632. Massachusetts Bay surveyors penetrated to Penacook and perhaps up the Pemigewasset River in 1638 and to Lake Winnipesaukee in 1652. Richard Walderne knew the details of the Merrimack River from the Indians at Dover as early as 1635, and Peter Weare may have seen it in the company of Indians in 1637 (Kimball 1878). A party of Gorge's men visited a Pigwacket village in 1642 (Winthrop 1853 2:67).

The Dutch traded with the Indians of the lower Connecticut River soon after Adriaen Block's discovery in 1614, established a post at Hartford in 1633, and in 1634–1635 made contact with the Agawams at Springfield. After 1636 William Pynchon at Springfield, Massachusetts, and his traders became well acquainted with the Connecticut River Indians in Massachusetts—the Agawams, Woronocos, Nonotucks, and Pocumtucks—but achieved only slight acquaintance with the Sokokis above Deerfield (NYCD 13:308). The "Northern Indians" at King Philip's Hoosick River rendezvous in 1676 were probably Western Abenakis from Lake Champlain (Lincoln 1913:87–88), and it is not unlikely that the Dutch had some trading connections with the Indians in the Champlain Valley.

The French first encountered the Western Abenaki in 1642 when the upper Algonquins, returning from war against the Iroquois, brought to Trois Rivières a Sokoki whom they had mistaken for an Iroquois. The French released him, and, the next spring, the grateful Sokokis tried to buy the freedom of Father Isaac Jogues from the Iroquois. The Iroquois kept their presents without releasing Jogues, and this grave breach of protocol may mark the beginning of the new Sokoki-Iroquois enmity, but there were no open hostilities for several years. About this time, two Sokokis were killed by the Montagnais near the Iroquois country, and in the fall of 1645, they evened the score by killing three Montagnais from Sillery. They used their scalps to try to arouse the Mohawks against the Canadian Indians, but the Iroquois had hostages among the French at the time and were angling for a peace with the Algonquins that would allow them to hunt safely in the north (Thwaites 1896–1901 55:183, 193, 31:35ff.).

In 1651 Father Gabriel Druillettes induced the Penacooks, Sokokis, Pocumtucks, and Mahicans to form a solid front with the French against the Iroquois. They do not appear to have attacked the Iroquois at this time, but Druillettes's visit was probably responsible for the Sokokis' renewing their former friendship with the Algonquins. There seems to have been an uneasy peace while the Iroquois were turning their attention to the Eries and harassing the Ottawa River fur traffic, but in 1651 the Iroquois attacked the Sokokis (NYCD 9:5). In 1663 the Iroquois launched an attack on the Sokokis that proved to be disastrous for both sides. The Dutch tried to patch up a peace the next spring, but when the English took over New Netherland from the Dutch in 1664 and held their first council with the Iroquois at Albany, the Iroquois regarded themselves still at war, not only with the Sokokis but also with the Pocumtucks and Penacooks (NYCD 13:297–298, 308–309, 355–356). The 1663 war may have been the beginning of the major exodus from Squakheag, but Sokokis were still in place to participate in the unsuccessful joint attack by the southern New England Indians on the Mohawks in 1669, and some were still close enough to Squakheag to participate in King Philip's War in 1675 and to sell land in 1686 and 1687. The Iroquois also attacked Penacook sometime before 1668, and, probably as a consequence, before 1670 many Penacooks moved to Pentucket above Lowell Falls on the Merrimack.

Some Sokokis moved to the Saint Lawrence River, and Sokoki names began appearing in Canadian church registers in 1662. Others arrived during King Philip's War. At the end of the war in 1676, the River Indians of Massachusetts fled to the Hudson River, and the next year Gov. Edmund Andros started a settlement for them at Schaghticoke near the mouth of the Hoosick River. There were perhaps some Sokokis among the early settlers of this village, and a number were found there in 1735 to deed land (Thwaites 1896–1901 60:135; Livingston 1956:40; Wright 1905).

In 1644 Passaconaway made a treaty of peace with Massachusetts, and the Merrimack River Indians remained at peace until Capt. Samuel Moseley's unprovoked assault on Penacook in 1675. Most of the Penacooks went to Canada, and in 1677 they persuaded Wannalancet to follow, but he returned later to the Merrimack. By 1670 there were Sokokis settled near Montreal and near Trois Rivières, and the Sokoki and Penacook removals caused by Philip's War certainly augmented the village at Missisquoi, which had probably already received Sokokis after the Iroquois attacks. Together they brought a vigorous fur trade to Chambly for a few years. A short-lived mission was established among them by the French, and in 1680 they were again attacked by the Iroquois. From this time on, the Western Abenakis in Canada were allies of the French, particularly in the colonial wars that commenced in 1689. At the same time they maintained communication and friendly ties with the Schaghticokes, who were nominal English allies; with those Penacooks who had fled to the Androscoggin River in Maine; and with the Indians on the Merrimack River. Their relations with the French were not always perfect. In 1688 one group suddenly quit the Saint Lawrence and moved south, leaving their standing crops and even pillaging and burning French communities on the way (NYCD 9:194, 195).

About 1695 a village of Western Abenakis on one of the forks of the Saint Francis River moved downriver after an Iroquois attack to swell the population at Saint Francis (Paquin 1833:220). Father Jacques Bigot established a mission at Saint Francis in 1700 to which came in that year Sokokis and Penacooks who had been sharing the mission on the Chaudière River with Eastern Abenakis (Bacqueville de la Potherie 1753 1).

Western Abenakis figured prominently in the early history of New France. Some Penacook men intermarried with mission Algonquin and Nipissing women and followed the fur trade to Lake Huron, where they were seen by Father Henri Nouvel in 1675 (Thwaites 1896–1901 60:214–218). One group of Sokokis and Penacooks accompanied René-Robert Cavelier de La Salle down the Mississippi in 1682. Some Sokokis accompanied Joseph-Antoine Le Febvre de LaBarre against the Senecas in 1684, and Sokokis made up most of Joseph-François Hertel de la Fresnière's war party against Salmon Falls, Maine, in 1690. They participated in the attack on Schenectady in 1690 and the destruction of the Mohawk villages in 1693, and they accompanied Louis de Buade de Frontenac against the Onondagas in 1696.

By 1698 many Schaghticokes had become dissatisfied with their situation, and by degrees they began to move into the French zone, first to Missisquoi, later to Saint Francis.

The Cowasuck territory on the upper Connecticut River was abandoned briefly in 1704 after an attack by men from Northampton, Massachusetts, but was probably reoccupied after the Treaty of Utrecht in 1713, and Joseph Aubery's map of 1715 called it a former mission. The Pigwackets, who had been attracted to Saint Francis about 1706, likewise returned to Pigwacket in 1714 (Thwaites 1896–1901 67:30–32).

Relations between the Western Abenaki and the English began to deteriorate again in 1717, and in 1723 a war broke out between them that did not include the French. One of the most celebrated incidents of this war was John Lovewell's battle in the Pigwacket country, but the principal action took the form of repeated raids by Gray Lock of Missisquoi on the Massachusetts towns in the Connecticut River valley. Massachusetts, through the Penobscots, finally persuaded the Saint Francis Indians to accept peace, and the Saint Francis Indians compelled Gray Lock to desist (Temple and Sheldon 1875:191–215). A treaty was signed in Montreal with the Saint Francis Indians, but Gray Lock was absent. English settlements had crept up the Connecticut and Merrimack valleys during the peace and were struck by Abenaki raids during King George's War (1745–1748). After this war, the Indians were disturbed by rumors that the then-vacant Coos Intervales were going to be fortified by the English, and at a conference at Montreal in 1752, the Abenakis reasserted their claim to the land and threatened war if it were occupied (NYCD 10:252–254).

The last colonial war, 1754–1763, occasioned still another withdrawal of the Western Abenakis from locations that were too exposed to English attacks. The last remaining families at Schaghticoke took advantage of a raid into the Albany region by Bécancour Abenakis to return to Canada with them. The Missisquoi withdrew for the duration of the war to François-Charles de Bourlamaque's army at Île-aux-Noix in the upper Richelieu River and to Saint Francis and Bécancour. One group on the upper Connecticut River who favored the English cause withdrew to the Clyde River in northern Vermont, where they remained until 1763. The Abenakis fought with the French at the battles of Monongahela, Oswego, Lake George, William Henry, Quebec, and elsewhere and conducted their own raids against the New England and New York frontiers. After the Treaty of Paris, they returned as usual to reoccupy their lands, but this time they encountered the first wave of English settlers pushing northward to settle the lands of the Indian allies of the French; and, for the next decade or so, returning Indians and advancing English mingled in frontier regions from Lake Champlain to the upper Androscoggin River (Hemenway 1868–1891).

The American Revolution was a source of confusion to the Western Abenakis, accustomed for generations to wars between the French and the English. During the early years of the war, some took the part of the Crown while some assisted the Americans. The Missisquoi tribe withdrew from the scene of the conflict again, and later the Saint Francis Indians lapsed into a species of neutrality that the British authorities thought was a cloak for American intelligence activities. After this war, the Western Abenakis did not return to any of their former locations in force but rather united or reunited with their brethren at Saint Francis. When they deeded northern New Hampshire in 1798, they did it in the name of the chiefs at Saint Francis, and a competing land company could find only one man and two women still resident on the upper Connecticut River to give an opposing deed. Missisquoi families returned and collected rent on their land, which they gradually abandoned, but they never relinquished claim to it (New Hampshire Historical Society 1795–1810; Hemenway 1868–1891 4: 998–1000).

In 1805 the English Crown granted new lands at Durham, Quebec, on the Saint Francis River to accommodate the population increase brought about by the influx of new arrivals (Public Archives of Canada n.d.a 94:9). The Durham Reserve was settled not only by new arrivals but also by families that had been long at Saint Francis. By 1850 most of this band was absorbed into the Saint Francis village. The tribe at Saint Francis continued to be known in official documents as the Sokokis and Abenakis of Saint Francis until at least 1880, but by 1900, the practice of referring to the whole group as Abenakis (which may be noted as early as 1736) became general. It has been adopted by the Indians themselves, who in the 1970s think of themselves as Abenakis, which is linguistically correct.

In the War of 1812, the Abenakis of Saint Francis and Bécancour furnished two companies for the British forces, and they now refer to their participation as "the last time the Abenakis went to war," although many saw service in the two world wars. After the War of 1812, parts of the Eastern Townships were granted to white veterans and settled, and their value to the Abenakis as hunting and trapping grounds was diminished. Most of the tribe turned to new hunting grounds north of the Saint Lawrence, to a territory belonging to the Algonquins of Trois Rivières but abandoned by them in the 1830s. However, certain Abenaki families returned to ancestral locations in the United States to hunt, fish, and guide surveyors and sportsmen.

In 1774 Levi Frisbie had journeyed to Saint Francis and brought back from there four Indian students for Eleazar Wheelock's Indian Charity School, which had recently moved from Connecticut to Hanover, New Hampshire. This was the beginning of a long-lived relationship between Dartmouth College and the Saint Francis Indians, who supplied most of Dartmouth's Indian students for the next 80 years. One of the first students, Francis Annance, established a Protestant school on the Durham Reserve, and several young women were sent to Burlington, Vermont, and to Boston for training (Wheelock 1775:44–54). Between 1829 and 1858 another Dartmouth graduate, Pial Pol Wzôkhilain, conducted a Protestant church and an English-language school at Saint Francis. An Anglican mission was founded in 1866, and an Adventist congregation existed between 1884 and 1915. Father Joseph DeGonzague, son of one of the last life chiefs, served as Catholic missionary from 1895 to 1937. From about 1865 to about 1950, the ash-splint basket industry brought a considerable number of Abenakis back to the resort areas of northeastern United States. By the end of the nineteenth century, some Abenakis were combining their hunting and trapping with the guiding of sportsmen. Guiding gradually replaced hunting and trapping, and the last parties abandoned their hunting territories about 1922. Guiding at sportsmen's clubs continued until about 1970. Beginning with World War I, the lure of industrial employment started small Abenaki communities in several northeastern U.S. cities, and in the 1970s these far outnumbered the parent community.

Population

Data are lacking for a reliable estimate of early Western Abenaki populations. Epidemics of European diseases, which reduced native populations to one-tenth or one-twentieth, struck at the mouth of the Saco in 1617 and progressed down the coast and up the Connecticut River by 1635. Gov. Thomas Dudley estimated the Merrimack River Indians at 400 or 500 men in 1631 (Bouton 1856:18), and Druillettes reported 10 towns on the Connecticut River in 1650, of which probably only a few were Abenaki (Druillettes 1857:322). The Iroquois wars were responsible for undetermined mortality between 1650 and 1680, as were the almost continuous hostilities between the Western Abenakis and the Massachusetts colony after 1675, and there were repeated losses by epidemics after settling in Canada. A reasonable guess for the preplague population of the Western Abenakis may be 5,000 persons on the upper Merrimack River, the upper Connecticut River, and Lake Champlain.

There is a reasonably good sequence of statistics only for the mission village of Saint Francis, but it must be remembered that this village never included all the Western Abenakis. Until about 1790 there were sizeable bands at Missisquoi and the upper Connecticut and Androscoggin rivers, and between 1807 and about 1850 there were numerous families at Durham, Quebec. By the middle of the nineteenth century a number of families had left the reserve more or less permanently. It was estimated that 200 persons were absent in 1904, and many families left during World War I. Charland (1964:341) has assembled the census data for the Saint Francis village:

1783	342
1810	418
1828	380
1848	306
1874	266
1888	330
1904	370

An Indian Affairs census in 1965 of band members, not village residents, gives 576. "Band members" under Indian Affairs rulings comprise only descendants in the male line and do not include persons of predominantly Abenaki blood from the mother's side or individuals living away who have not made an effort to be kept on the band rolls. In 1973, out of a probable 900 to 1,000 persons with a significant amount of Abenaki blood, only about 220 lived at Odanak.

Culture

The Western Abenaki culture area lay north of a line running roughly from Portland, Maine, through Manchester, New Hampshire, and Northfield, Massachusetts, to the tops of the Green Mountains, thence northward to Otter Creek, which it followed to Lake Champlain. North of this line were Abenaki-speaking moose hunters with an important agriculture, patrilineal tendencies, and relatively weak chiefs. South of this line were non-Abenaki-speaking agriculturalists whose principal game animal was deer, with some matrilineal tendencies, and strong hereditary chiefs.

Since the Saint Francis village at Odanak, Quebec, appears to be a village of immigrants and not older than 1660, reconstructing the earlier cultures of these immigrants would require identifying and characterizing the several components of the village and tracing them back to their earlier locations and habitats. It is probably too late to do this thoroughly and with confidence, so for the purposes of this sketch, the assumption has been made that the Western Abenaki were essentially homogeneous culturally. The main elements of Western Abenaki culture have been reconstructed from the data of history and from the language, oral traditions, and memory ethnography at Saint Francis. Most of the following is taken from Day's (1956–1979) field notes. The majority of the family names at Odanak in the earliest census, in 1829, came from or were associated with Missisquoi. In other words, Saint Francis cultural traits identifiable as Indian in the nineteenth and twentieth centuries are essentially Missisquoi cultural traits of the eighteenth century. This pushes back the question of their ultimate provenience but does not settle it, since Missisquoi had received increments from the same tribes that contributed to Saint Francis directly.

The earliest known Western Abenaki villages—Penacook, Squakheag, Missisquoi—were palisaded for defense, as was Saint Francis. Villages were typically located on the edge of a bluff close to (1) a sizeable alluvial meadow suitable for corn culture and (2) a supply of water. All villages were close to a river or lake that served both as a source of fish and as a travel route. Their houses were rectangular structures of bark with arched roofs, a smoke hole for each fire, and room enough for several families. Sweat lodges were round and dome-shaped.

Subsistence

Although local diversity in the annual round was imposed by the differences in local resources, a common round can be reconstructed. The first activity in the spring was tapping maple trees and making syrup and possibly sugar, both for immediate eating and storage. Maple and birch trees were tapped by making a slanting gash in the bark, then inserting an elderberry twig with the pith bored out in the lower end of the gash. The sap was collected in a birchbark container and was boiled into syrup consistency in either a birchbark pail or a clay pot. In later times iron trade kettles were substituted, and this may have been the beginning of maple-sugar making. Then followed the catching of spring runs of fish in large quantities for immediate eating and for smoking. Fish were taken by weirs and fish traps, by spearing from shore or from canoe by day or by torchlight, by hooks on night lines or hand lines, and by nets. Spring greens and especially groundnuts or wild potatoes were gathered. Spring flights of passenger pigeons were shot and netted. In May, fields were planted with corn, beans, and squashes, and tobacco was planted in small separate gardens. Summer subsistence activities consisted of weeding the corn fields, fishing, and picking berries as each species became ripe. Blueberries were especially prized. A lengthy sojourn on one of the larger lakes for the fishing and to escape forest insect pests was broken by return trips to the village to weed the fields. The Sokokis even traveled to the seashore in summer. In late summer, medicinal plants were collected, dried, and stored. Nuts were collected also, butternuts and the now-extinct chestnut being the most important. In the fall they shot and netted the abundant waterfowl and killed quantities of passenger pigeons as they gathered for their southward migration. Eels were caught and smoked for winter. Deer were hunted by stalking rather than by snaring and driving as in southern New England. Bears were killed after they had denned up for the winter. Moose were hunted by calling during the rutting season in the fall and by running them down on snowshoes or shooting them in yards in the winter. Muskrat, beaver, otter, and other furbearers were taken in the fall and winter, both for food and pelts. All furbearers were trapped; beavers and muskrats were taken in their lake houses, and muskrats were additionally dug or driven out of their riverbank dens. Spruce grouse and porcupine could be taken when other game was scarce.

The mainstays of their subsistence were probably moose, fish, corn, and beaver in that order.

Clothing and Adornment

The basic male costume was a breechclout and belt, both of tanned skin. The belt was wrapped around the waist two or three times and knotted at the hip with the fringed ends hanging at the side or in front. Moosehide moccasins were worn in winter and often in summer. Two patterns are known, the beavertail and the rabbit nose (Hatt 1916:171–178, 167–169). In winter, foot wrappers of tanned skin or of rabbit fur were worn under the moccasins and an outer pair of moccasins with higher tops was added. The moose-hock moccasin boot, which was nearly waterproof and was considered especially good for snowshoeing, was sometimes worn. Leggings, with feet, reaching to the thigh and tied to the belt were worn gartered below the knee. A long sleeveless coat of two panels of moosehide, front and back, was worn by both sexes in cold weather. It was probably painted like the Penobscot coat, but no museum specimens are known. The sleeves were separable. The young male wore his hair long and loose, sometimes secured by a headband, and the married man's hairdo was a coil or knot on the crown of the head held by a thong. The female wore the hair long and loose or secured by a band or, characteristically, in two braids with a flat coil on the crown of the head tied by a thong with pendant ends. Hair ornaments might be attached to this coil. Both sexes might go bareheaded or with the head covered with a blanket in cold weather, but a variety of caps were made for both warmth and dress. A man's pointed hoodlike cap falling to the shoulders was documented in the eighteenth century but may not have been aboriginal. The woman's cap was conical, and both might bear feathers at the point. Males sometimes wore a fur cap made from the skin of a young buck deer with the antlers left on. Another cap was made from the shoulder skin of a moose, the long white hairs of the moose hump forming a natural crest, which might be left white or dyed. This cap had an opening in the back for the hair knot and feathers if feathers were worn. It may be that this was the prototype of the widely distributed deer-hair roach. There is an Abenaki tradition that no more than two feathers were worn by the men.

Robes were of fur, with beaver preferred. It is possible that kilts were also worn by the Western Abenakis, since they were worn by the Iroquois and the Eastern Abenakis, but there is no evidence for them. A knife was customarily worn in a sheath on the breast suspended about the neck; a wooden cup and a small skin bag containing the fire-making kit, pipe, tobacco, and guardian spirit keepsake were tucked under the belt. The basic female costume was moccasins, leggings, a knee-length skirt, and a blouse reaching to midthigh.

Abenaki costume began to be modified early by European example and trade goods, but even after 1850 some older people wore a traditional costume consisting for men of moccasins; leggings; breechclout, with the addition of a pocket for pipe, tobacco, and fire-making kit; belt; a cloth shirt worn outside the belt, hanging to midthigh; and long hair. Women wore moccasins, leggings, skirt, blouse, long hair, and often a blanket.

Technology

Hunting weapons were bow, arrow, knife, and spear. War weapons included these items plus a characteristic war club with a ball head made from the root crown of a hardwood with projecting sharpened root bases. Fishing equipment included hooks and lines, nets, and fish spear. The man's tool kit included crooked knife, awl, hand ax, gouge, and adz; and his chief materials were wood, bone, rawhide, moose sinew, birchbark, spruce root, and the inner bark of basswood and leatherwood. The woman's tool kit included awl, needles, wooden skin scraper, stone scrapers, stone grinders, and corn pounder, and her chief materials were tanned hides, furs, birchbark, spruce root, paints, porcupine quills, and moosehair.

Moccasin tops, garters, belts, pouches, belt cups, pipes, canoes, and containers were decorated, but the data of decoration are scattered, a study of motifs has never been made, and pottery design of sure Western Abenaki provenience is practically unknown. Geometric designs were rendered on woven surfaces by weaving and false embroidery; geometrical and curvilinear designs were rendered by paint, porcupine quill, and moosehair.

The Western Abenaki were dependent on the snowshoe for winter travel and on the birchbark canoe for summer travel. The wooden dugout canoe was also known. Loads were transported in winter on toboggans and on the back by blanket pack and tumpline. Splint pack baskets, which were very common in the nineteenth century, are probably postcontact, but the woven basswood-bark pack basket with chest strap may be aboriginal. Summer overland foot travel occurred, and the locations of some of the historic foot trails are known. Babies were carried in a cradle board, but a blanket hammock was used in camp.

Life Cycle

Abenakis were affectionate parents, and children were not struck. In general, education and discipline consisted of traditional stories often repeated, grave admonitions, and the pressure of group disapproval. Punishment often took the form of blackening the child's face and putting him or her outside the wigwam for a time. Disobeying an order affecting survival might receive prompt, fitting punishment. Through necessity or convenience, children were often reared by grandparents or paternal uncles, and the paternal uncle was often the boy's tutor and the paternal aunt the girl's tutor. The instruction of girls in household skills commenced early. The evidence for first rites is inadequate, but a boy was given a small bow and arrow at age five or six, and at 10 or 12 he began to go hunting with his father or uncle. At puberty, boys might seek a guiding vision, and there was menstrual seclusion for girls.

Marriage was proposed by a young man through an intermediary, the proposal being accompanied by a present or token and, in the eighteenth century at least, by a wampum string. The girl could reject the suitor by returning the gift. Some cases of child betrothal are remembered. There is an eighteenth-century record of the proposal being made by the parents of the boy placing a blanket on the shoulders of the girl's mother. A courtship dance around the secluded hut of a marriageable girl is also remembered. The variety of remembered proposal procedures may be survivals from the several components of the Saint Francis tribe. If the young man's proposal was accepted—one writer has the girl reciprocating by placing an ear of corn in the young man's wigwam—he made the girl's mother the present of his first game and then departed on a hunt and did not return until he had a suitable bride present. There was then a period of trial cohabitation during which the couple slept head-to-foot; if the trial was unsuccessful, the couple separated and the man lost his presents. Marriage was celebrated in the presence of the chiefs and parents and normally was followed by feasting and dancing.

The dead were always buried when possible, since spirits of unburied dead remained around the corpse as the dreaded Ghost Fire. Those who died in winter were placed on a scaffold until it was possible to bury them. The coffin was a full-length roll of bark tied with a cord, and the grave was covered with a tent-shaped structure of wood with an upright board at one end bearing the identification of the deceased. Weapons and utensils necessary for their support in the other world were buried with them as well as food sufficient for the journey over the Ghost Trail. Graves were oriented facing the east, and the graves of chiefs were anciently planted around with an oval of tree seedlings. Children were especially mourned, the mother cutting her hair and painting her face black. Presents were customarily offered to mourning parents who responded with a feast. A widow wore a hood for one year during which time she could not participate in festivities or remarry.

Social Organization

Hunting, fishing, warfare, and the fabrication of houses, canoes, and the implements of war and hunting were the responsibilities of the Abenaki men. Child care, cooking, preparation of skins and clothing, cultivation of agricultural crops excepting tobacco, and the gathering of food plants were the responsibilities of the women and children.

Western Abenaki society was patrilineal. The basic unit was the household, one to several nuclear families of the same patrilineage living together in one long bark house. The formal unit was a patrilineal totemic descent group regarded as the descendants of a remote male ancestor, not of the totem animal, together with their wives and children. The tribe was denoted 'all the households together'. In 1736 turtle, bear, beaver, otter, and partridge totems were reported at Saint Francis (Chauvinerie 1928). Family names in the early nineteenth-century censuses suggest the presence of turtle, bear, beaver, partridge, raccoon, hummingbird, and muskrat totems, with fisher, eagle, and partridge totems represented by Eastern Abenaki residents. Morgan's (1877:179) list of Abenaki gens, which Speck (1935c) rejected as Penobscot, is not from Saint Francis and may possibly have been from Bécancour. The winter hunting group was a convenient nonpermanent grouping selected from the sons and brothers of one mature hunter and their families, and sometimes a daughter and her husband. The nature and degree of exogamy prior to Christian influence are difficult to determine, but there is evidence for cross-cousin marriage in the kinship nomenclature as well as special relations with paternal grandparents and uncles. Turtle and Bear moieties, representing Sokoki and Abenaki proper respectively, functioned in the council and on the ballfield. The totem animals may have been those of the most prominent clans. A constant and characteristic feature of the society was the special lifelong relationship of two male partners formed in early youth.

Patrilocal residence was the norm, but when practical considerations favored it, a daughter's husband might live for a time with his father-in-law. Removal of discrete groups to Saint Francis caused some adjustments in their territorial claims and use, but families remembered their places of origin in the nineteenth century (e.g., Kendall 1809). After about 1830, the Western Abenaki took over the hunting territory north of the Saint Lawrence River abandoned by the Algonquins of Point-du-Lac (Trois Rivières) extending from the Assomption River on the west, north to the Vermillon River and the vicinity of Coucoucache, and east to include the Saint Maurice drainage. This territory they organized into family hunting territories (Hallowell 1932), and there are indications that a family-hunting-territory system was in effect in their New England homeland. Rights to these territories seem to have been transmitted within the family of a male, but it is noteworthy that deeds and leases for agricultural land at Squakheag and Missisquoi bear the names of both men and women.

Political Organization

Each Western Abenaki nation had a civil chief and a war chief. A chief was selected for outstanding ability and installed in a chief-making ceremony in which he received a new name. His influence was considerable because of his prestige and personal powers, but the extent of his absolute authority is uncertain. Chiefs held office for life unless they were deposed for bad behavior. The civil chief usually presided at the Great Council of the Nation, which was composed of the war chief and the elders of the several families. At Saint Francis the council consisted, by the eighteenth century, of a grand chief and several chiefs, probably as an accommodation to the diverse elements that had come together there. The wampum complex probably reached the Western Abenakis in the early seventeenth century about the time it reached the Iroquois and the upriver Mahicans, and belts and strings were used to commemorate treaties and the decisions of councils. The bag of wampum records at Saint Francis was entrusted to a group of six men and seven women in 1771 (J. Maurault 1866:571). The best orator, at Saint Francis usually chosen from among the chiefs, held the office of "The Advisor," whose duty it was to recall to the attention of the council the needs of the nation. The Great Council sat as a court and decreed all punishments, even to banishment or death.

The Great Council settled all national and international affairs except the question of war, which was decided at a general council attended by men, women, and young people and at which both men and women addressed the council. When the general council decided for war, the war chief rose with the ceremonial red war club in his hand and asked who would volunteer. A war leader would rise and urge the young men to follow him, and when a party was raised, there would be a feast followed by a war dance. A group or groups of 10 men, each under a leader, comprised a party capable of independent action. Ten parties required a grand leader, but control was exercised by example, persuasion, and the loyalty he could inspire through his reputation and ability rather than by military discipline. Warriors painted their faces red and their bodies with their totems and with marks showing their war records. During the historic period, both prisoners and scalps were taken, and young warriors were given new titles in recognition of outstanding exploits. J. Maurault (1866) attributed the full range of the torture complex to the Western Abenakis, but the historical record, including the captivity narratives, provides no support for this idea. Prisoners were escorted by their captors between two rows of warriors who placed their hand on each passing prisoner's shoulder to indicate his captive status. During the colonial wars prisoners from New England were held for ransom or were occasionally adopted.

The only Indian enemies of the Western Abenakis during the historic period were the Iroquois, and this enmity predated European contact. The Western Abenakis appear to have been on friendly terms with the Algonquian-speaking tribes in New England and had anciently a treaty of friendship with the Algonquins. The position of the Western Abenakis in precontact trade has not been worked out.

Games

The ability to run was much esteemed. Among the boys, games requiring much running were played at an early age and races were frequent. Archery practice and contests likewise commenced at an early age and continued throughout life. The handball game, recorded among them by Lafitau (1724 2:76) is probably the one recorded in detail on the lower Merrimack by Wood (1634:86), and lacrosse, played at Saint Francis in the nineteenth century, was probably aboriginal among them. Specimens of the ring-and-pin game have been collected from them, but the game is no longer remembered. In the nineteenth and early twentieth centuries, boys played a kind of snow snake and slid downhill on a single upturned stave, but by 1900 all these pastimes had been largely replaced by baseball and card playing.

Cosmogony

The Western Abenaki physical world was not created. It always existed under the supervision of *Tabaldak* 'the Owner', who created the living beings. Only one, *Odzihozo*, was so powerful that he created himself from some dust that the Owner had touched. *Odzihozo* became the transformer who reshaped the surface of the earth to his liking, finally changing himself into a rock in Lake Champlain to watch over his handiwork. Man was created by *Tabaldak* in two efforts. First he created a man and a woman out of stone, but, not liking the result, he destroyed them. Then he created a couple from living wood who pleased him and who became the ancestors of the Indian race. This exemplifies the concept of stone as the substance of primeval power and of wood as the substance appropriate to man. In ancient times, a man of great power was born, *Pədəgwadzo*, who became the lesser transformer whose deeds tamed the elements in favor of mankind. In the world of the Western Abenaki, many things are alive that whites commonly regard as inanimate, and every living thing has its own peculiar power, more or less specific in kind and limited in quantity. Man seeks to increase his power and to acquire other powers through the dream vision quest and the acquisition of a guardian spirit, tokens of whom were formerly preserved. A few individuals are born with unusual spiritual powers. Such a one is a *mədawlinno*. The most common acts of northern shamanism are found among the powers of different Abenaki *mədawlinnos*—divination to locate game, far seeing and seeing into the future, sinking their footsteps into rock, and curing by mental power. For the solution of difficult oracles, the *mədawlinno* retired into a small dome-shaped hut, but the shaking tent was not used. The drum is the *mədawlinno*'s instrument, and missionary disapproval may have been the reason it fell into disuse until it was revived as a dance accompaniment in the mid-twentieth century. The basic organizing principles of the Western Abenaki world view are the animate world; the concept of personal power; the earth, Our Grandmother, which is the tangible source of the life force; and the Owner's concern for the game animals and the medicinal plants, out of which grow the rituals of harvesting and recycling by tobacco burning, prayer, conservative harvesting, respectful treatment of bones, the grease incense offering before eating, and the interdiction against food waste.

Myth

Western Abenaki myth and cosmology clearly belong to the genre of the Wabanaki region, rather than to that north of the Saint Lawrence River. In it, the trickster is *Azɔban* 'the Raccoon', and the trickster cycle is completely divorced from the transformer cycle. It shares with Eastern Abenaki mythology the dread flying creature *Bmola* 'the Wind Bird'; the benevolent Thunders, who are a group of brothers, seven in number, as with the Iroquois; malevolent underwater creatures; and curious little underwater people, the *manɔgɔmasak*. Besides myth, their corpus of oral narrative comprises many stories that were repeated to teach and preserve the values of the culture. Sacred stories could be repeated only in winter when man's natural enemies, the underwater monsters, could not hear them. Secular and teaching stories, as well as oral historical traditions, of which the Abenaki are very tenacious, can be told at any time.

Ceremonies

Certain occasions were marked by public ceremonies, each with its own dance and ritual. The principal occasions were weddings, greeting visitors from another village or tribe, chief making, first corn harvest, declaration of war, and funerals. Numerous social dances were performed at most of these ceremonies and are still performed for pleasure in an impromptu gathering. A number of borrowed dances are now performed—the Eagle Dance and the women's Blanket Dance from the Iroquois, the Knife Dance from the Hurons of Lorette, and the Pipe Dance that descends from the Calumet Dance introduced by the Fox in 1719 (LeSueur 1952). The music for dancing is supplied by a singer who accompanies himself on a rattle.

Curing

Although a *mɔdawlinno* might be called on to treat a mysterious or stubborn illness, the use of plant medicines was highly developed and persisted in the 1970s. Certain common remedies were widely known, but a few individuals, both men and women, were highly skilled and knowledgeable and were recognized as professionals. The reputation of Abenaki doctors spread to surrounding white communities in colonial times, and their influence can be traced in colonial herbalism. The men of one family have simultaneously practiced plant medicine and collected medicinal plants for pharmacies for at least the last hundred years.

Sociocultural Situation in 1970

The Western Abenaki band at Odanak is governed under the rules of the Canadian Department of Indian Affairs by an elected chief and three elected councilors and managed by an Indian band manager. The majority of the population belongs to the Roman Catholic mission of Saint François-de-Sales, which has a resident missionary, and a smaller number belongs to the Anglican mission conducted from Sorel. There is very little subsistence agriculture and no trapping, and guiding has disappeared. Most men are employed off the reserve. Some native artifacts are produced for tourists, but ash splint–sweetgrass basketmaking has ceased being an important industry. All school children are transported to white schools off the reserve, and a fair proportion continue to secondary and university levels.

In 1974 the language survived with 21 elderly, fully competent speakers and an undetermined number of young and middle-aged persons with varying amounts of knowledge of the language, mostly passive. Young people were being raised speaking French as a first language. Odanak is superficially like the surrounding Canadian villages, and practically nothing can be observed of the traditional or contact-traditional culture in the areas of subsistence, political organization, social organization, or ceremony except the occasional performance of social and ceremonial dances for audiences. In spite of this, there existed in the 1960s in the minds of the older people a nearly full recollection of the elements of the traditional way of life, either from youthful participation or from tradition. Many Abenaki attitudes persist in the areas of child rearing, social relationships, and world view.

Synonymy

Abenaki: probably from Montagnais *8abanǎki8ek* 'dawn land people' (Fabvre 1970:208–209) through Champlain's French as Abenaquioicts. It has an Abenaki cognate *wǫbanakiiak,* which seems to have been adopted by the missionaries at Sillery and brought by them to Saint Francis. The supremacy of this name over those of the more numerous Sokoki and of the other tribes at Saint Francis is probably a historical accident assisted by the fact that most spoke Abenaki dialects.

Sokoki: from their own name *ozokwaki,* plural *ozokwakiak* 'the ones who broke up, broke away'. Some variants encountered are French Assok8ekik, Soko-kiois, Sokoquiois, and Sokoquis; English Sowquachick, Squakeys, Suckquakege, and Zooquagese; and Dutch Soquackicks. The Mohawk Onojake appears to be a translation of the Abenaki name.

Penacook: from *pənəkok* 'at the falling bank', the name of the village site at Concord, New Hampshire. The people were *pənəkoi,* plural *pənəkoiak* 'falling bank people'. They appear in French sources as penneng8s, Oupeneng8s (Thwaites 1896–1901 60:214–218), Oppenago (Margry 1876–1886 5:304), and similar forms (Day 1973).

Cowasuck: from *goasək* 'white pine place', the name of the Lower Coos Intervales at Newbury, Vermont. The people were *goasi,* plural *goasiak* 'the ones from the white pines'. Variant forms for the place are French Koés and English Cohass, Cohoss, Coos, and for the people Cohassiac (Kendall 1809 3:191).

Missisquoi: from *mazipskoik* 'at the flint', referring to the chert quarry near Swanton, Vermont. The people were *mazipskoi,* plural *mazipskoiak* 'flint people'. Some of the variants are Michiskoui, Misiskuoi, Missiscoui, Masiassuck, Missisque, and Missisco.

The name Arsigantegok (variously Arrasaguntacook, Ersegontegog, Assagunticook, and Anasaguntacook) was applied to the Saint Francis River and Arsigantegwiak to the Saint Francis Indians in the eighteenth century. Some writers have mistakenly thought that this was the original name of the Androscoggin River tribes and that they were therefore the first to settle Saint Francis. Saint Francis was actually settled by Sokokis, and Arsigantegok seems to have its origin in Eastern Abenaki *arsikaïntekw* 'empty cabin river', perhaps so called (Aubery 1715b) because upon the arrival of the Abenakis from Sillery, many houses had been emptied by the smallpox (Gill 1886:13). This name was adopted by the Western Abenakis as *alsigəntəgok,* and several folk etymologies developed to account for it. The Mahican called the people of Saint Francis Wtanshekaunhtukko (Hopkins 1753:77).

Sources

There is no comprehensive historical or anthropological treatment of the Western Abenaki. J. Maurault (1866) is an attempt at a comprehensive history, but, except for three chapters and some of the footnotes, it relies on secondary sources. Charland (1964) is a painstaking work from primary documents, but it is focused on the Saint Francis village. Some information about the Saint Francis band is contained in two histories of the French parish Saint-François-du-Lac (Sulte 1886; Charland 1942) and in the several captivity narratives. The most readily accessible local sources on the Western Abenakis in New England are, for the Penacooks, Bouton (1856); for the Squakheags, Temple and Sheldon (1875); for the Cowasuck, Thompson (1842); and for the Missisquoi, Crockett (1921). These works are all mixtures of primary and secondary materials and contain some dated assumptions. Hemenway (1868–1891) preserves numerous testimonies of first settlers concerning the local Abenakis. Two little-known sources are the biography of Henry Tufts (1807), who was among the bands between Lakes Memphremagog and Umbagog in 1772–1775, and the papers of Henri Vassal (1811–1889), who was agent for the Abenakis at Saint Francis in the late nineteenth century.

The only extensive ethnographic data are contained in the field notes of Hallowell (1918–1932) and Day (1956–1979) and in Hallowell's (1928) study of kinship. This classic study should be considered in the light of knowledge that Western Abenaki nomenclature has an independent history and is not derived from the Eastern Abenaki terms. A fairly complete collection of Western Abenaki material culture specimens could be assembled from the combined collections of the Canadian Museum of Civilization, Hull, Quebec; La Société Historique d'Odanak; the McCord Museum, McGill University, Montreal; the Museum of the American Indian, Heye Foundation, New York; Dartmouth College Museum, Hanover, New Hampshire; and University Museum, University of Pennsylvania, Philadelphia. The language has been documented by three native writers, Pial Pol Wzôkhilain, Sozap Lolô, and Henry L. Masta (Day 1961).

22

Arosagunticook and Androscoggin

Although the population of Saint Francis undeniably represents a mix of groups arriving from various locations in New England at various times, the earliest settlers were not from the Androscoggin River area in Maine, as some historians have supposed, but were Sokokis from the middle Connecticut River valley. The notion that the Androscoggin people were the first settlers is attributed in part to a confusion of their name with the early names of the Saint Francis River and the inhabitants of the Saint Francis mission. As in other papers, Day's painstaking approach to place-names yields significant findings for ethnohistory. This paper was originally published as pp. 10–15 in *Papers of the Tenth Algonquian Conference,* Ottawa, Carleton University (1979).

On the north bank of the Saint Francis River in Quebec, about four miles from the place where it empties into Lake Saint Peter, stands an Indian village called Odanak. It is better known in history as Saint-François and Saint Francis. The beginnings of this village are not recorded, but it has been at or near its present location for over three centuries. Uncertainty and controversy have characterized all discussion of its origin.

In the Saint Francis Indians we have a group which probably was not at Saint Francis at the time of French exploration and first settlement on the Saint Lawrence River, and whose origins and movements in and out of Saint Francis have never been adequately explained. The usual view of New England historians has been that of a mysterious tribe into which at one time or another the local tribes were said to have disappeared. Canadian historians have known only of the arrival of increments of Indian emigrants from unknown locations in New England and New York, usually identified only under broad and misleading group names. Linguists and anthropologists have followed the historians and have been satisfied to present their data under the rubrics "Abenaki" or "Saint Francis Abenaki" without inquiring effectively into the ancestral identities of the various components of the village. This is, of course, unsatisfactory. Linguistic and ethnographic data which cannot be assigned to a definite, named group at a definite time and place are at best useless and at worst a fruitful source of confusion and false theory.

History has not been silent about the identity of the Saint Francis Indians, but there has been no consensus. Rather, secondary writers repeating earlier writers have developed several explanatory traditions. We can detect one tradition among Maine historians which attributed the earliest and principal settlement at Saint Francis to the Indians of the Androscoggin River. Another can be detected among Quebec historians which attributed the major settlement to Indians from the Kennebec River. This tradition can be traced to Abbé Joseph Maurault (1866:173–174, 272). Some writers seem to be unaware of any settlement at Saint Francis before the arrival of the mission of Saint-François-de-Sales from the Chaudière River in 1700. Not until James Mooney's article in the *Handbook of American Indians North of Mexico* in 1907 was a multiple origin for the village stated (Hodge 1907–1910 2:410–411). At present the multiple origins of the village are generally accepted, and herein lies the problem which has been in the back of my head since the beginning of my work there in 1956. The language and culture there were already moribund, but the problem was not that there was no Saint Francis culture, but that there was seemingly only one culture and one language in a village said to have been made up from 10 or a dozen bands. Whose culture and language was it? Or if it was a composite, who contributed what?

This year I am undertaking a study of the peopling of the village with the goal of identifying if possible the movements of the several contributory tribes and their subsequent fate—migration out of the village, losses to epidemics and war, replacement and intermarriage. This is being done from historical sources at first; the testimony of language and comparative ethnography will constitute different approaches later on (Day 1977b). Here I want only to take a quick look at one of the theories for the peopling of the village, one which has become rather commonly accepted by anthropologists, namely, that the Indians of the Androscoggin River were the first to settle at Saint Francis, were the most numerous there, and hence were the source of the culture and language which later predominated. If this be true, the whole problem is solved, but I have come to disbelieve some of this solution and to doubt most of it.

This tradition seems to have had its origin with James Sullivan, the pioneer historian of the District of Maine. He spoke in 1804 of the "Androscoggins or Anasaguntacooks on Brunswick River" (Sullivan 1804:210). In 1828 Thomas Hutchinson, a Massachusetts historian, wrote that the Indians on the Saint Francis River were the "Aresaguntacooks" and "Weweenocks" (Wawenocks) who had gone first to the falls of the Chaudière (Hutchinson 1936 1:384). In 1832 William D. Williamson followed with a statement in his history of Maine that the Anasagunticooks occupied all the Androscoggin River and were the first to go to Saint Francis (Williamson 1832:466). In 1859 Frederic Kidder called the Androscoggin Indians the "Assagunticooks" and said they left Maine in 1750—which could deny them the role of first settlers at Saint Francis—but stated that they were the most numerous at Saint Francis and therefore it was probable that their dialect became dominant (Kidder 1859:235). In 1864 Nathaniel Tuckerman True wrote that the Indians on the Androscoggin were known under the general name of "Anasagunticooks" and that at a late period the name "seemed to extend to the scattered remnants on the river and at St. Francis in Canada" (True 1864:150–151). In 1907 the first volume of the *Handbook of American Indians North of Mexico* appeared, and in it James Mooney amalgamated the earlier writings and wrote of Saint Francis, "Here the Arosaguntacook were still the principal tribe and their dialect was adopted by all the inhabitants of the village, who were frequently known collectively as Arosaguntacook." Considering the circulation and prestige of the *Handbook,* it is not surprising that the idea was adopted by anthropologists. It appears in the writings of Frank G. Speck, A. I. Hallowell, Fred Johnson, and others.

But there are difficulties with this notion. Jean Crevier, the first seigneur of Saint Francis, settled there about 1671, and there are indications that there were Indians in the vicinity already. There is no direct evidence for Androscoggin Indians, however. Rather, there is a record of an organized band of Sokokis, complete with chiefs, near and probably on the Saint Francis River in 1669. Sokoki names had begun to appear in church registers at Montreal, Sorel, and Trois Rivières by 1658, but no Abenaki names appear until a single baptism at Sorel in 1687 and in 1690 at Saint Francis. In 1678 Crevier spoke of his trade only with the Sokokis, and in 1684 Father Bigot spoke only of Sokokis in the vicinity of Trois Rivières (Charland 1942:16–17, 1964:16–21).

The first, and so far the only, definite reference I have found to Androscoggin Indians in Canada occurs during King Philip's War. The war broke out in June of 1675 between the English in Massachusetts and the southern New England Indians and quickly spread into southern New Hampshire and southern Maine, involving Penacooks, Piscataquas, Saco Indians, and Amarascoggins. The end of this war in 1676 has been the occasion for New England historians to comment on the disappearance of local tribes and remnants into Canada, frequently assuming that their destination was Saint Francis. In the first summer of the war, a certain Francis Card was captured by the Kennebec Indians and after his escape in the fall he made a deposition which included this statement: "There is a great many Indians in *Canada* that have not been out this Summer, both of *Kennibeck* and *Damarascoggin,* therefore a great many of these Indians at *Kennibeck* do intend to go to Canada in the Spring to them." Thus we have Kennebec and Androscoggin Indians somewhere in Canada in the summer of 1675 and more planning to join them in the spring of 1676, since the Indians on the Kennebec at that time included Androscoggin and Saco River Indians under Squando (Hubbard 1865 2:204). We can probably pick up their destination in Canada from the Jesuit Relations which recorded the arrival before the war of some Sokokis who went to Trois Rivières and some Abenakis who went to Sillery. It is likely that the first Androscoggins were in the latter contingent (Thwaites 1896–1901 60:233). By October 1676 there were 150 Abenakis at Sillery. At Saint Francis, the Sokokis who "took the Road to three Rivers" found some of their countrymen who had preceded them, and most if not all moved to Saint Francis in 1702 at the urging of Father Bigot. In 1699 the Intendant Champigny called Saint Francis a mission of Sokokis (Thwaites 1896–1901 60:131–135; Charland 1964:21). In short, there is no evidence to support the idea that Androscoggin Indians formed the nucleus of the Saint Francis village, but rather some contrary indications.

The first sizeable number of Androscoggin Indians to arrive at Saint Francis may have been part of the contingent which removed there from the Chaudière mission in 1700. There has been much confusion among secondary writers on this subject. Some begin the foundation of Saint Francis with the arrival of these Chaudière Abenakis. Maurault cited a tradition that it received 1,500 warriors, or a population of some 7,500 persons. Actually the population of the Chaudière mission the year before the move was only 355 souls, and of these only a part came to Saint Francis. This part included Sokokis and Loups as well as Abenakis, while the other part, all Abenakis, moved farther up the Chaudière in order to be nearer their kinsmen in Maine (J. Maurault 1866:282–283; Charland 1964:40; Bacqueville de La Potherie 1753 1:309). It is possible that those who moved up the Chaudière were all or mostly from the Kennebec and Penobscot Rivers and that the Abenakis who came to Saint Francis with the Sokokis and Loups may have been mostly Androscoggins. In lieu of facts we might guess that this contingent was no more than half of the total population of the Chaudière mission and that the Abenaki part no more than half of that, or perhaps some 90 persons.

The subsequent arrivals at Saint Francis which can be identified up to 1772 are largely from Pigwacket, Maine; the Merrimack River in New Hampshire; the upper Connecticut River; and Missisquoi on Lake Champlain. I have not yet found either a French or an English document testifying to a movement of Indians from the Androscoggin River to Saint Francis. That they did go there at some time is almost certain. Kendall, in his travels of 1807 and 1808, found Indians at Saint Francis who came from Sagadahoc at the mouth of the river (Kendall 1809 3:143). The Indians had apparently all gone from the upper Androscoggin by 1775, although they may have been the Indians Henry Tufts knew at Lake Umbagog between 1772 and 1775 (Lapham 1891; Tufts 1807:chs. 7–9). These together with related bands on the upper Connecticut River and at Lake Memphremagog did remove to Saint Francis soon afterwards, and in 1798 their head chief, Manawalemit Swassin, was one of the chiefs at Saint Francis who sold northern New Hampshire to the Bedell Land Company. If the Androscoggin Indians ever had a dominant role at Saint Francis, it must have come after the arrival of these last groups toward 1800, but considering the other bands that arrived at the same time from Cowas, Lake Memphremagog, and Missisquoi, there seems to be no compelling reason to think the Androscoggins were dominant even then.

Then where did the notion come from? I suspect that it came from an association of the name of the Androscoggin River Indians and that of the Saint Francis village. The early writers called the Androscoggin River Indians Amascoggin, Amanoscoggin, Amarascoggin and the like. About 50 years after this name appeared in the literature, a tribe variously known as Assagunticook, Arosagunticook, Anasagunticook, and the like began to appear in the Massachusetts colonial records, beginning with the treaty of Arrowsic in 1719, and later writers have assumed that these Indians were from the Androscoggin River. I have not found a contemporary statement linking the two, and I can only imagine that they became associated through a fancied resemblance between the two names—Amarascoggin and Arosaguntacook. The resemblance is not close. They share only an initial *a* and, somewhere in the middle, *s, r, n, k,* and *g* sounds. But Nathaniel Tuckerman True asserted that not only these two words but one other—Amascontee—were from the same roots and had the same meaning (True 1864:150). Swanton grouped them in his synonymy and for good measure added a fourth name from the Androscoggin River beginning with *a:* Amilkôngantegwok (Hodge 1907–1910 1:89).

Once Arosaguntacook was identified with Amarascoggin, it was reasonable to postulate an important presence of Androscoggin Indians on the Saint Francis River, because the old name for Saint Francis River was Arsikôntegok! One could easily leap to the conclusion that the village was named for its first or most important group of inhabitants. But the anonymous author of the *Dictionnaire abnaquis-françois* stated clearly that Arsikôntegok was the name of the Saint Francis River and that it meant 'empty cabin river' (Aubery 1715a:14). This was a plausible name for the village, which had suffered from epidemics, casualties during King William's War, and in particular an attack by the Iroquois in 1690. The census of 1692 gave it only 25 inhabitants (Charland 1964:20). Incidentally, Arsikôntegok appears in the record as the name of the village 10 years before Arosaguntacooks appear at conferences in Maine. We have at least one contemporary testimony for the distinction in the 1726 census of Jacob Wendall, which lists the "Ammoscoggon" Indians with the other Maine tribes, then adds the "Arresaguntacooks of St. François" as one of the new tribes in Canada (Wendall 1866:9).

Therefore, until and unless I see new evidence to the contrary, I favor the position that (1) the Androscoggin River Indians were the Amarascoggins, not the Arosaguntacooks; (2) Arsikôntegok was the name of the Saint Francis River and village, derived from its characteristics, not from the founding tribe, and probably given by the Eastern Abenakis from the Chaudière in 1700; and (3) the Arosaguntacooks who appear in the Maine treaties were merely delegations from Saint Francis, whose ethnic composition at that time was probably predominantly Western Abenaki.

23

Abenaki Place-Names in the Champlain Valley

This article, Day's most comprehensive treatment of Western Abenaki place-names, appeared in an issue of the *International Journal of American Linguistics* dedicated to Floyd G. Lounsbury, who provided a similarly comprehensive treatment of Iroquoian place-names in the Champlain valley (Lounsbury 1960). Since Iroquoian (Mohawk) place-names predominate in the southern part of the valley, the Lake George area, and the western side of Lake Champlain, and Western Abenaki place-names predominate on the eastern side of the lake north of Vergennes, Vermont, the papers complement each other and reinforce the idea that the lake formed a boundary between the two groups (cf. Day 1971a). Day draws on his more than 20 years of collection and analysis of Western Abenaki names and establishes his authority by separating carefully derived etymologies from the guesswork that pervades so many past treatments of the subject. This paper was originally published in *International Journal of American Linguistics* 47(2):143–171 (1981).

Introduction

In conjunction with the celebration of the 350th anniversary of the discovery of Lake Champlain in 1609, Floyd Lounsbury wrote a paper, which was a model of method and lucidity, entitled *Iroquois Place-Names in the Champlain Valley* (Lounsbury 1960). A companion paper, treating the Abenaki place-names in the Champlain Valley, seems to be the most appropriate contribution I can make in Lounsbury's honor, inasmuch as I am not an Iroquoian linguist.

Since Lake Champlain lay between the Iroquois and the Abenakis throughout the historic period, there are place-names in the valley from both peoples. It appears from Lounsbury's study that most of the Iroquois names were in the language of the Mohawks, the easternmost Iroquois nation and the one nearest the lake. The Abenaki names are all in the Western Abenaki language which was spoken by those Abenaki tribes native to the Champlain Valley, the upper Con-

The grammatical terminology used in this article differs at some points from that familiar to Algonquian linguists. A paper on place-names may expect to find at least as many readers among nonlinguists as among linguists, and a simplified and descriptive terminology is more serviceable to them than the elaborate one developed by structuralists since Boas to account for the complexities of Algonquian grammar. Linguists should have no difficulty with this terminology. They will recognize the elements called here possessible bound noun roots as dependent noun stems and the unmarked bound noun roots as elements usually appearing as concrete noun finals. The elements called here general roots are known in many instances as prenoun and preverb particles.

necticut River, the upper Merrimack River, the upper Saco River, and perhaps the upper Androscoggin River. These tribes are known in historical and anthropological literature, under the names of their local bands or aggregations, as Missisquoi, Winooskik, Penacook, Cowasuck, Sokwaki, Winnipesaukee, and Pigwacket. This language is related to, but distinct from, the Eastern Abenaki language spoken originally in Maine and surviving to the present day in one dialect, Penobscot.

By 1800 practically all the members of the several Western Abenaki tribes had moved to the village of Saint Francis on the river of the same name in Quebec. We have four books written at Saint Francis in the Western Abenaki language (Wzôkhilain 1830a, 1830b, 1832, 1845), and if we assume that the author's parents' generation spoke the same way, this carries the language back at least into the eighteenth century. The incidental vocabulary included in Father Mathevet's so-called "Mots loups" manuscript from about 1750 appears to be essentially from a Western Abenaki dialect, except for the prayers which are in Eastern Abenaki (Day 1975). A still earlier record of the language exists in the place-names of northwestern New England, and there is no reason to believe Prince's (1902) theory that Western Abenaki diverged from Penobscot after 1679.

In my opinion, Western Abenaki occupation of the Champlain Valley was prehistoric (Day 1971). It was long customary for writers of Vermont history to assert that there were few or no permanent Indian residents within the state, although it is easy to demonstrate that this was incorrect (Day 1965). There were historic villages on the Missisquoi and Winooski Rivers and probably on South Hero Island, and the abundance of prehistoric evidence is only recently being uncovered. The southern limit of Abenaki occupation in the valley probably coincided with the northern boundary of Mahican territory. We do not know just how far north the Mahicans hunted, but there is record of one claim as far north as the southern tip of Lake Champlain at Whitehall (Johnson 1921–1965 8:256). Iroquois hostility may have caused Abenaki withdrawal from their more southerly locations in the seventeenth century and even temporary abandonment of the Champlain Valley during French and English intercolonial wars. The last village in the Champlain Valley to be occupied by the Abenakis was Missisquoi, and this seems to have been abandoned during the American Revolution. From then until about 1960 there was more or less continuous visiting and short-term residence by Abenakis from Saint Francis to old familiar locations in the valley. There were similar visits and even extended residence in other parts of northern New England. Some families even moved into the Adirondacks, which had probably never been Abenaki territory, because of the hunting to be had there. One consequence of this continued contact was the preservation among the Abenakis of a knowledge of the geography, mythology, historical traditions, and place-names of the Champlain Valley. This knowledge was extensive enough so that it was possible for me, between 1956 and 1978, to obtain names for the principal places on Lake Champlain from native speakers who knew the places, the names, and the reasons for the application of the names (see map).

Most of the names appearing in this article come from my own field notes taken at Odanak and elsewhere between 1956 and 1978. My principal informants were William Simon Obomsawin, Marian Obomsawin, John Watso, Théophile Panadis, Mathilde DeGonzague, Edward Hannis, Ambroise Obomsawin, and Oliver Obomsawin. All of these informants were fluent speakers of the Western Abenaki language, were acquainted with the Lake Champlain region, and had the advantage of having received traditional knowledge from their elders. In addition to the place-names they knew and still used, these informants were able in many cases to furnish me with the correct forms and meanings of names found in the literature in more or less garbled forms and accompanied by incorrect meanings or no meaning at all. It is noteworthy that almost no recorded forms have been found which were not still in use during the period of my fieldwork. Modern usage corresponds for the most part with old documentary forms and with names obtained from informants a century ago. Moreover, the store of names held by my informants was larger than that collected from literature. Therefore, my approach for the most part differs somewhat from that of Lounsbury (1960:27), who limited his study to the old place-names and their traditional etymologies. The knowledge of my informants allows me to treat not only the identity and analysis of the names, but also the reason for their application to particular locations.

The primary documents for the study of Abenaki place-names in the Champlain Valley are largely eighteenth-century maps and nineteenth-century writings. I have found no Abenaki place-names in documents earlier than 1713, although it is possible that some early French names and one Mohawk name may have had an Abenaki original. Other names began to appear in early works of local history and geography (S. Williams 1794; Allen 1798; Kendall 1809; Thompson 1842; Coolidge and Mansfield 1859; Hemenway 1868–1891). The most important single source of Abenaki names in the Champlain Valley is the papers of Rowland E. Robinson. Robinson became acquainted with Abenakis from Saint Francis who frequented the vicinity of his home in Ferrisburgh, Vermont, and commenced recording place-names before 1860. Some of these names appeared in print in prose works (Robinson 1867, 1892a, 1892b) and were repeated in his stories and sketches. He first obtained names from John Watso. In 1881, his nephew William G. Robinson in Montreal recorded a list of names from four Abenakis, then elderly, and the next year Rowland Robinson recorded

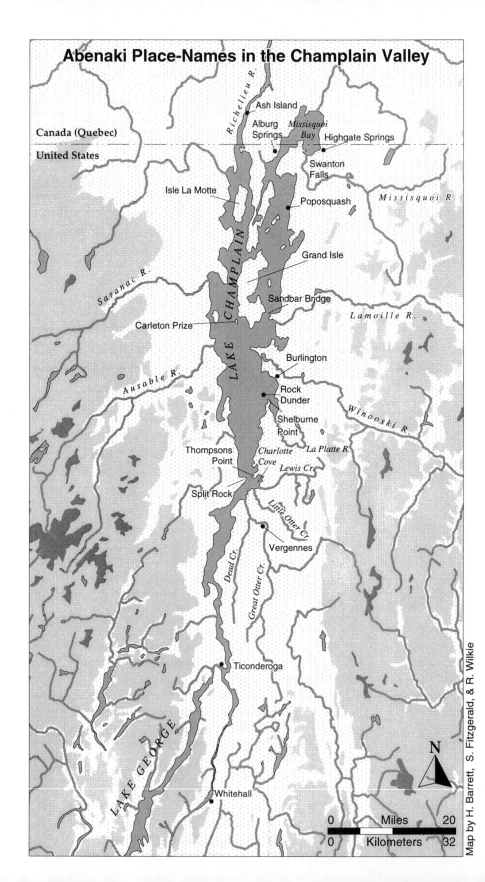

Abenaki Place-Names in the Champlain Valley

Richelieu R.

Ash Island

Canada (Quebec)

United States

Alburg Springs

Missisquoi Bay

Highgate Springs

Swanton Falls

Isle La Motte

Poposquash

Missisquoi R.

Grand Isle

Saranac R.

LAKE CHAMPLAIN

Sandbar Bridge

Lamoille R.

Carleton Prize

Ausable R.

Burlington

Rock Dunder

Winooski R.

Shelburne Point

Thompsons Point

Charlotte Cove

La Platte R.

Lewis Cr.

Split Rock

Little Otter Cr.

Vergennes

Dead Cr.

Great Otter Cr.

Ticonderoga

LAKE GEORGE

Whitehall

N

0 ———— Miles ———— 20

0 ———— Kilometers ———— 32

Map by H. Barrett, S. Fitzgerald, & R. Wilkie

some names from Louis Tahamont and Joseph Taksus. The originals are pre-served at Rokeby, Robinson's old home, and I am indebted to Stephen Loring for a copy of Robinson's Indian material made by Ted Williams, a former curator at Rokeby. Some names were recorded from two Abenaki hunters who became famous guides in the Adirondacks. They were known as Sabele and Sabattis, but their full names were Sôbial (Saint-Pierre) Benedict and Mitchell Sabadis (Saint-Jean-Baptiste). Both were interviewed about 1850 by Holden (1874:23–24), and better forms of some of the names were obtained from Sabattis by Prince (1900), who had an interest in Abenaki languages. A few Champlain Valley names appeared in two books by literate native speakers of Western Abenaki (Laurent 1884; Masta 1932) and a few more in a letter from Henri Vassal, superintendent of the Saint Francis Agency (Vassal 1885).

Ordinarily there is little profit in rehearsing secondary writings, but one good purpose may be served in the case of place-name literature, namely, to disprove the false forms and etymologies which otherwise achieve common acceptance. These are discussed under particular names, but it is useful to mention briefly the principal secondary writings on Champlain Valley names. Beauchamp (1893) discussed a few names from the New York side in his *Indian Names in New York,* and more are to be found in his later compilation *Aboriginal Place Names of New York* (Beauchamp 1907). McAleer (1906) devoted an entire book to the name Missisquoi and its varieties. A considerable number of names were compiled by Douglas-Lithgow (1909). Crockett (1921 1:68–70 reproduced Robinson's names with some errors in copying. Lake Champlain names received little atten-tion after this until Huden (1957) published a booklet entitled *Indian Place Names in Vermont* which added to the existing store of names from a wide variety of sources. It suffers from the lack of a bibliography, however, which would enable the student to retrace his sources, and both the Abenaki names and their etymologies are unreliable. Some additional names were given in Huden's (1962) larger work, *Indian Place Names of New England.*

Procedure

Lounsbury's exposition of the indispensable requirements for a satisfactory etymology of a place-name is now classical (Holland 1963). These are given as (1) the sound of the name in the original language, (2) the meaning of the name, (3) the grammatical makeup of the name in the original language, and (4) the geographical or historical circumstances behind the choice of the name. My task was simplified by the survival of the names in the living language, which made the determination of sound, meaning, and grammatical structure straightfor-ward matters of linguistic field method and analysis. The reason for applying the name was also known to my informants in most cases, and when it was not, it could usually be worked out with considerable confidence from the meaning of the word and a knowledge of the geographic feature being named, together with Abenaki use of and attitudes toward their environment.

The common problems of field method were incurred during the acquisition of the data. It was necessary to ascertain the credentials of the informants as carriers of a valid tradition of Lake Champlain geography and history and personal acquaintance. It was further necessary to distinguish with care between names which were generally accepted old names of places for at least two or three generations and those which an informant might coin as an appropriate descriptive name. Names obtained from one informant were routinely checked with other informants on matters of form, meaning, referent, and reason for applying the name. Only Saranac, Ticonderoga Falls, and Whitehall come to us in shapes so distorted that certain or highly probable reconstruction and etymology were not possible. These names will give the reader of Lounsbury's paper a further appreciation of the difficulties inherent in place-name study beyond those of linguistic analysis alone (Day 1977a). No attempt at an exhaustive documentary search has been made, and one may feel certain that at the time of Abenaki occupation of the Champlain Valley many more place-names were in use.

Structure of Abenaki Place-Names

Although the grammar of the Western Abenaki word (like Algonquian words generally) is complex, place-names have, for the most part, relatively simple construction. The simplest type is composed of a free noun root plus a locative suffix; for example, *menahán* 'island' plus *-ok* (locative suffix) gives *menáhanók* 'at the island'. Another simple construction consists of a free noun root plus the situative suffix *-sek,* which may be translated 'where (the noun) is' or 'are'. For example, *goá* 'white pine tree' plus *-sek* gives *goasék* 'where there is a white pine tree' or 'where there are white pine trees'. Many place-names are simply compounds of noun roots, either with or without connective *-i-.* These compounds may be made up of two free noun roots, that is, roots which may stand by themselves without prefixes or suffixes, for example, *magwá-i-zibó* 'Iroquois River', where *magwá* and *zibó* may occur independently, or of a free noun root and a bound noun root, for example, *goa-tégw* 'white pine river', where the element *-tegw* must always occur with a prefixed element. Another common construction consists of a general root plus a noun root, either free or bound, again with or without connective *-i-,* for example, *gwen-i-tégw* 'long river'. General roots are a class of roots which take different sets of inflections to form nouns, stative verbs, and adverbs. They occur in place-names only prefixed to a noun root to characterize it or to a verb root to qualify it, for example, *gtá-adén* 'great mountain' and *bal-itá-n* 'wrong way flowing'. A few place-names are formed by a verb stem plus the third singular ending of the conjunct mode, which is typically used for dependent clauses and, in some cases, is preceded by the compound adverb *adáli* 'place where'. An example is *adáli masípskwooík* 'where it is flinty'. Some less common kinds of place-name construction are found among the Champlain Valley names.

Orthography

The following letters will be used in writing Western Abenaki place-names and related words in this paper: *a b d e g h i k l m n o o ô p s t w y z.* The following guide will permit English speakers to approximate the pronunciation of the names: *a* is pronounced much like the *a* in *father,* as *asmá* 'not yet'. *e* is pronounced when unstressed somewhat like the unstressed vowels of English, as the *a* in *above* or the *o* in *connect.* When stressed, it ranges from this central position to something like the vowel sound in *took,* but with the lips unrounded, as *spemék* 'above' adverb. *i* is pronounced much like the vowel sound of the word *peak,* as *wizí* 'gall'. *o* is pronounced like the *o* in *poke,* as *odóllô* 'his kidney'. *ô* is a nasal vowel and is pronounced like the vowel in French *ton.* English speakers may approximate it by nasalizing the *o* in *on.* The consonants may be more easily understood when they are organized into groups: stops (*b p, d t, g k*), sibilants (*s z*), nasal continuants (*m n*), a lateral (*l*), and a spirant (*h*). There are two semivowels (*w y*).

Unlike some other Algonquian languages, Western Abenaki has not one, but two stops in each position of articulation—*b* and *p* in the labial position, *d* and *t* in the alveolar position, and *g* and *k* in the velar position. One stop in each pair (*p, t,* and *k*) is a fortis stop. This means that it is pronounced with greater tension of the vocal tract than other stops, but otherwise they are much like English *p t k.* Fortis stops are always voiceless and may occur in any position in a word. *b d g* are lenis stops. This means that they are made with less muscular tension of the vocal tract. They are voiceless at the beginning and end of words and in clusters with any voiceless consonant (*p t k s h*). In other positions, they are voiced and pronounced like English *b d g.* Many Western Abenaki words are strongly stressed on the last syllable, and when this happens final *b d g* become not only voiceless, but fortis as well. The sibilants *s* and *z* behave like the stops. *s* is always tense and voiceless. *z* is voiced except at the beginning and end of words and before a fortis consonant (*p t k s*) and is lenis except when it closes a word with a strong stress on the final syllable.

The lateral *l* is pronounced much like English *l* but with a bit more force in final position, which is particularly noticeable when the final syllable is *-il* and the tongue is consequently raised to form the *l.* Under certain conditions, *l* has the variant *ł,* which is voiceless and pronounced with more friction. Since this variant only occurs after *h* and before a vowel, and *l* never does, one symbol *l* is used to represent both varieties.

The nasal continuants *m* and *n* are pronounced exactly like English *m* and *n*, except at the beginning of words when they are followed by a fortis consonant, where *m* and *n* become voiceless and thus are often very hard to hear.

h is pronounced as in English, being usually voiceless although tending toward a voiced sound between vowels.

w is pronounced in most cases as in English. At the beginning of a word and followed by a voiceless consonant (*p t k s h*), it becomes voiceless. In the middle of a word between voiceless consonants and at the end of a word after a voiceless consonant (it only occurs after *k*), it becomes voiceless. When it follows a vowel and closes a syllable, it is a semivowel, so Abenaki *paw-* is given the sound of *-ow* in English *powwow*. Two rare affricated sounds occur which are represented by sequences of two letters. These are the sound of *ch*, as in *church*, which is represented by *tš*, and the sound *j*, as in *judge*, which is represented by *dž*. Only *dž* occurs in these place-names.

In addition to the 19 letters given, the vowel of a syllable receiving strong stress is marked by an accent mark over it, thus *á*. Although stress is predictable in many cases, it is marked throughout this paper to help the reader to pronounce the names correctly. A strongly stressed syllable is also longer and slightly higher in pitch. When the strong stress falls on the last syllable, the pitch of that syllable rises a bit higher than that of other strongly stressed syllables. In this article, a long syllable is sometimes marked by a following colon.

Champlain Valley Place-Names

This article is limited to a consideration of the names for Lake Champlain itself, its islands, shores, tributary streams, and outlet. These names are presented commencing with the outlet at the north end of the lake and working southward along both shores to the southern end of the lake and its southernmost tributaries.

Richelieu River

Lake Champlain drains northward through the Richelieu River into the Saint Lawrence River, which it enters at Sorel, Quebec. I have found no Abenaki names for the Richelieu River in the early literature, but there are four modern names for it. They are:

(1) *bitawbágwizibó* may be translated as 'Lake Champlain River'. The parts of the word are *bitawbágw*, 'Lake Champlain' (see the further analysis of this in the "Lake Champlain" section); *-i-*, a connective; *zibó*, a free noun root meaning 'river'. Since the first *b* is initial and the *g* precedes a voiceless *w*, they are pro-

nounced approximately like English *p* and *k*, respectively. The *aw* is a diphthong pronounced like the *ow* in *how,* not like the *aw* in *law.* Thus, *pitawbákwizibó.*

This was probably the original Abenaki name for the Richelieu River, since it was the outlet of the lake, and the name was suitable for use by traffic in either direction.

(2) *magwáizibó* 'Iroquois River' was so called because it was the most direct route between the Iroquois country and the Saint Lawrence River. The parts of the word are *magwá,* a free noun root meaning 'Iroquois'; *-i-,* a connective; *zibó,* a free noun root meaning 'river'. This name is seen to be a compound noun with connective *-i-* between two free noun roots.

There is an early equivalent in the French *La Rivière des Iroquois,* and it seems likely that the Abenaki name was taken over in translation from the French by the Abenakis who settled on the Saint Francis River in the middle of the seventeenth century, when war traffic was heaviest. It is also possible that both French and Abenaki took over an older Montagnais or Algonquin name. It is further possible that *magwáizibó* was an old Abenaki name applied by the Sokwakis, who may have been occupying the east bank of the Richelieu at the time of French contact (see Day 1981).

(3) *masisóliantégw* may be translated as 'Sorel River'. This name may have originated with the Abenakis on Lake Champlain, who used the Richelieu River to reach Sorel at its mouth, but it would have been equally appropriate for the Abenakis at Saint Francis to identify the turning place into the river by the settlement at its mouth. The parts of the word are *másisolián,* the usual Abenaki name for 'Sorel'; *-tegw,* a bound noun root meaning 'river'. *másisolián* is made up of *mas-,* a general root meaning 'big'; *-i-* a connective; *solián,* the Abenaki pronunciation of an old Algonquian word for 'money'.

In this word, the connective *-i-* is reduced to a weak schwa, the *g* before *w* is voiceless, and the name is pronounced *masəsóliantékw,* the final *w* being voiceless.

The reason for naming Sorel *másisolián* 'big money' was not known to any of my informants. It is likely connected somehow with the trade conducted at Sorel, and this would seem to date the name after the establishment of the fort in 1665, rather than at the time of the short-lived defensive structure built in 1642.

A letter from William G. Robinson of Montreal dated January 14, 1880, gives the spelling *Ma sis liau tŭkw,* which is probably a misspelling of *Masisóliantégw* or a misreading of his handwriting (Robinson 1860–1881). He gave as a meaning 'The mandrake river', which is not a translation and is most probably a comment on the utility of the river. Mandrake or May Apple, *Podopyllum peltatum* L., is an Abenaki medicinal plant.

(4) Vassal (1885:29) wrote "masipskouitegon—from Missisquoi Bay" as a

name by which the Abenakis at Saint Francis knew the Richelieu River. The *n* is probably a misprint for Vassal's handwritten *u*, and I would spell his form *masípskwitégw*. The analysis of this is *masípsku*, a free noun meaning 'flint, chert, or other flintlike rock' (speakers of another dialect at Saint Francis say *mazípskw*); *-i-*, a connective; and *-tegw*, a bound noun root meaning 'river'.

The name, pronounced *masípskwitékw*, means 'flint river'. It does not mean 'from Missisquoi Bay', and one wonders whether Vassal did not confuse a description of the Richelieu River with its name. *masípskwitégw* is rather a name for the Missisquoi River.

Chambly

Chambly is situated at the falls of the Richelieu River and a widening of it called the Basin. In the seventeenth century, the French regarded this as the foot of Lake Champlain and the beginning of the Richelieu River. Prior to 1685, Western Abenakis had an active fur trade at Fort Chambly and must have had a name for the place. Lounsbury (1960) found a Huron name for Chambly in the writings of Father Pierre Potier which meant 'The bulge in the waterway', essentially the same as the Mohawk name for Lake Champlain. The Abenakis call a lake formed by the widening of a river *pkwábagá* and name the basin in the Saint Francis River this way, but so far I have learned no name for Chambly either from the written record or from tradition.

Ash Island

Ash Island is in the upper Richelieu River, or by former reckoning in the outlet of Lake Champlain, opposite the mouth of the Lacolle River and about seven miles north of Rouses Point, New York. It is known in historical tradition as Head Island and is well known to the Abenakis as the location of an encounter with the Iroquois, which probably took place in September 1690. It is the best known and most often told tradition in their history (Day 1976), and they call Head Island *odébsék*. This can be translated as 'where his head is' or 'where their heads are', but as the name of Head Island it should be translated as 'where their heads are'.

The analysis of the word is *o-*, third-person prefix, singular or plural, before a noun translated 'his, her, their'; *-deb*, possessible bound noun root meaning 'head'; *-sek*, situative suffix indicating the place at which, or time through which, the preceding noun exists. This suffix must be distinguished from locative suffixes.

An Algonquian linguist might query why the definite third-person prefix *o-* is used to possess the root for 'head' when the indefinite possessor *m-* might seem to be required by the fact that the heads are anonymous. A provisional answer might be that in the last century there was a strong trend, now almost complete, for *m-* to be replaced by *o-* even in the case of genuinely indefinite possessors. In this case, however, the heads placed on poles around Head Island did not belong to unknown possessors. They were the heads of Iroquois placed there by the Abenakis who originated the name and the ancestors of those who carry it on. Since in this word *b* is followed by a fortis consonant *s,* the *b* is voiceless and the name is pronounced *odápsək.*

Lake Champlain

The Abenakis have apparently had only one name for Lake Champlain, but a number of forms have been heard and written down, together with a variety of seemingly contradictory meanings. Thompson (1842:5) wrote, "The name of this in the Abenâqui tongue was Petawâbouque, signifying alternate land and water, in allusion to the numerous islands and projecting points of land along the lake." Thompson did not give his source. Watson (1852) gave *Petaonbough,* signifying "a double pond or lake branching out into two," probably referring to its connection with Lake George, on the authority of R. W. Livingston. This is repeated in Watson (1869:3). A note in the Robinson Papers reads, "They called Lake Champlain Pe-tou-bouque. Wadso's defination [*sic*] of the word is: The Waters that lie between the two countries of the Abenakis and the Iroquois. Others of the tribe with whom I have conversed give a different interpretation of the word, but cannot give it an intelligable [*sic*] translation." The Robinson Papers also contain a letter written in 1880 from Montreal by his nephew, William G. Robinson, who obtained names from four "old Wobanakis." He gave *Pe two boroke* with the meaning 'The double lake'. The Wadso mentioned by Robinson was John Watso, with whom Robinson was acquainted in 1860, since he cited him in the sketch of the history of Ferrisburgh (Robinson 1867) he wrote by 1860. Holden (1874:31) quoted Watson and gave a new form from Sabele, namely, *Petowahco,* without giving any meaning. Holden (1874:163) also gave *Pittowbagonk* 'The dividing waters between the east and west and north of the Hudson' from Sabattis. Palmer (n.d.:14) wrote, "The original Indian name of Lake Champlain has been a subject of much speculation and research. By some it is supposed to have been called Peta-wa-bouqe meaning *alternate land and water,* in allusion to its numerous islands and projecting points of land. Among other names ascribed to the lake are . . . Petowpargow, the *great water."* Palmer's own confusion is suggested by his final statement, "These names, however, seem to have been selected more from the peculiar aptness of their meaning than from any known application to the lake itself." Vassal (1885:29) gave *Sitoâmbagook* 'Double Bay'. The *s* was probably an editorial misreading of a handwritten *p; sitoâm* is meaningless. Vassal may have misheard *sitaôbagak,* which means 'contiguous bays, bays together and touching'. Robinson (1892a:6) wrote, "Petow-bouk, interpreted by some 'Alternate Land and Water,' by others, 'The Water that Lies Between,' is the Waubanakee name of Lake Champlain." Robinson wrote essentially the same information to Manley Hardy of Brewer, Maine, on February 24, 1896: "Petowbowk is the name that all St. Francis Indians give Lake Champlain; translated by . . . Wadso, 'the lake that lies between,'" with Watso's explanation that it meant the lake which lay between the countries of the Abenaki and the Iroquois (Eckstorm 1941:67). These are the basic references and they have been quoted or followed by Douglas-Lithgow (1909:92). Beauchamp (1907:73, 240), Crockett (1921:69), and Huden (1957:14, 1962:184).

If one were dependent solely on the forms of the name in the literature, it would be very difficult even to arrive at the Abenaki word. Fortunately, the name is still well known to Abenakis at Saint Francis. It is *bitawbágw,* usually heard in the locative form *bitáwbagók,* which means respectively 'between-lake' and 'at between-lake'. The analysis is *bitaw-,* a general root meaning 'between in any spatial sense'; *-bagw,* a bound noun root meaning 'water at rest, body of water, bay, pond, lake'; *-ok,* a locative singular suffix which follows a consonant and usually suppresses the *w* or noun stems ending in *-gw. bitawbágw* is pronounced much like *pitawbákw* since the *g* becomes voiceless before a voiceless consonant (*w*) and also fortis in stressed final position. All of the literary variants of the name may be taken as badly transcribed, even mutilated, versions of this name. The principal confusion has arisen out of the semantic complexity of the general root *bitaw-.*

bitaw- carries the basic meaning 'between in any spatial sense' as, for example, air space between the double walls of a house, a fallen tree lying between the forked branches of another tree, a layer of water between two layers of ice, a board or boards lying between other boards in a lumber pile, a middle layer of bark on a birch tree, or a lake lying between any two places or topographical features. From this basic meaning and the known historical situation, the original meaning of the name was probably 'between-lake' or 'lake between', implying that it was the lake lying between the Abenaki and the Iroquois. This was appropriate to the early geographic situation when the lake separated Mohawks in the Mohawk valley from the Abenakis living on the eastern shore of the northern part of the lake. It was even more appropriate when the Abenakis were reduced to the one village of Missisquoi on the extreme northeastern corner of the lake and still more appropriate when they moved to Saint Francis. It was true in terms of land titles by which the Abenakis owned the eastern shore of the lake and the Iroquois claimed the western shore as far north as Rock Rogeo (see "Rock Dunder" section). It would have been an appropriate name for use by the Algonquins and Montagnais along the Saint Lawrence River, but it is not known whether they used it. *bitaw-* is still used with its basic spatial meaning in the word *bitáwôgamá* which employs the bound noun root for 'lake'—*ôgama.* This means a 'lake (or bay) between (two other features or things)'.

bitaw- also has a secondary meaning 'double'. It is easy to reconstruct how this probably came to be. An Abenaki general root carries only a broad general meaning. It is limited and made more precise only by the element(s) which follow(s) it. When one item is between two other items, the latter are doubled in number and in position, and the focus of *bitaw-* sometimes shifts from the item which is between to the items which it is between. Some examples of *bitaw-* used in this way are *bitáwôwdí* 'double road', that is, a modern highway with a median strip between the lanes; *bitáwsá* 'he goes the double', that is, a second parallel route; and even in a further semantic extension in *bitáwinosís* 'my double grandchild', that is, 'my great-grandchild'. Nowadays, the adverb *bitáwiwí* is more often thought of as 'double' than as 'between'. Therefore, *bitawbágw* can also be understood as meaning 'double lake', and the Abenakis explain this by the fact that the upper widest part of the lake is split in two by the land masses of Grand Isle. Since the two parts are about equal, this permits the free translation Twin Lake.

There is a still further semantic extension. Since an item which lies between two other items constitutes with them layers, *bitaw-* has come to mean, in some contexts, 'layered, in layers'. One may speak of a pile of lumber as *bitáwitá* 'it is layered (horizontally), it is piled up'. In counting the pages of a book one might say *negwedátegwá gassíbitáwatá* for '100 pages', literally '100 many times it is layered'. It is this extended meaning of *bitaw-* which made it possible for native speakers who knew the lake to translate *bitawbágw* as 'alternate land and water', a perfectly appropriate term since east-west cross sections of the lake cut across two, three, or four channels of the lake. It is a coincidence that three variant meanings of the same root were all appropriately descriptive of Lake Champlain, even though in translation they strike an English speaker as being quite different. This coincidence accounts for the confusion about the meaning of the name.

Grand Isle

Both North Hero and South Hero Islands are known as *gitsímenahán* 'big island', pronounced like *kitsímenahán*. The parts of the word are *git-*, a general root meaning 'big, great'—before *i* the *t* is palatalized to *gits-* (pronounced *kits-*), but it remains *git-* before other vowels; *-i-*, a connective; *menahán*, a free noun root meaning 'island'. This refers to the land mass of the two islands which divide the lake. They can be distinguished by several terms, but I could not obtain any consensus on separate names.

Isle La Motte

I have never found an old name for Isle La Motte. An obviously modern name for the island, among Abenakis who returned to Missisquoi in this century, was *azíbidžízikók*, pronouncing *dž* like *j* in English *jeer*. This means 'at the little sheep droppings'. The parts of the word are *azíb*, a free noun root meaning 'a sheep', a loanword from English *sheep*, pronounced *azíp:; -i-*, a connective; *-dži*, a bound noun root meaning 'a piece of dung, a dropping'; *-z*, a diminutive suffix; *-ikok*, locative plural suffix.

Highgate Springs

The mineral springs in the town of Highgate near the shore of Missisquoi Bay are still known to the Abenakis, who frequented the locality well into this century. They called the place *nebízônnebík* 'at the medicine water', from *nebi-zŏn*, a free noun root meaning 'medicine' in the sense of a curative substance, not of psychic or spiritual power; *nebi-*, a free noun root meaning 'water'; *-k*, locative singular suffix which follows a vowel.

An area of flat ground north of Highgate was known as *dáwskodasék* 'where the open meadow is'. An alternate accent pattern is *dáwskodásek*. The first *d*, being the initial sound of the word, is pronounced like a lax *t*, and *aw* is pronounced like the *ow* in *how*. The parts of the word are *daw-*, a general root meaning 'open in a general sense'; *-skoda*, deverbal bound noun root derived from the free noun *mskodá* 'meadow, unforested land'; *-sek*, situative suffix which can be translated as 'where (the preceding noun) is'.

Alburg Springs

The mineral springs across Missisquoi Bay in Alburg were also known to the Abenakis, who called them *nebizônnebizék* 'at the little medicine water'. The analysis of the name is the same as that for *nebízônnebík* except for the addition of the diminutive suffix *-z* which is suffixed to *nebi* 'water' before the locative suffix, which here is *-ek* since it follows a consonant.

Missisquoi

Missisquoi is now the name of a bay in Lake Champlain, a river in Vermont, and a county in Quebec. It has been the subject of much debate and controversy. McAleer (1906) made an earnest effort to determine its meaning, starting with 31 different recorded spellings of the name, consulting many likely authorities, and coming up with eight interpretations but no conclusion in a book of 143 pages. His study best demonstrates that there is little profit in attempting to resolve place-name problems from the variant corrupted spellings and solutions from a random choice of Algonquian languages.

The name originated from an aboriginal chert quarry between the lower Missisquoi River and Missisquoi Bay described by Bolton (1930b:457–465). Robinson learned over a century ago from John Watso that "Missisque is a corruption of Masseepsque, The place of arrow flints; and applies only to the bay of that name," and Abenakis in this century know that the name originated with the chert quarry. Two native writers, both native speakers of unquestioned competence, have left us clear testimony as to the shape and meaning of the Abenaki name. Laurent (1884:216) wrote, "MISSISQUOI, comes from: *Masipskoik,* (Abenakis), where there is flint." Masta (1932:89) wrote, "Missisque from Massipsqui meaning flint." Laurent's form is correct, and Masta's *massipsqui* was a concession to the form he started with—*Missisque,* since elsewhere (1932:56) he gave in his lexicon *massipskw* as 'flint'. Moreover, as Masta certainly knew, *massipsqui* is an incomplete form consisting as it does of the noun *masipskw* plus the connective *-i-* but no following noun to complete a compound word. Laurent's Abenaki name and translation are the ones still in use, but the analysis is not immediately obvious because the full form has undergone some syncope.

The full form is *adáli masípskwooík,* which means 'the place where it is flint, where it is flinty'. The parts of the word are *masípskw,* a free noun root meaning 'flint, chert, or other flinty rock'; *-oo,* a verbalizing suffix which signifies 'be something' or 'be like something' ('something' being the substance of the preceding noun); *-ik,* third-person singular ending of the conjunct mode which is used primarily for dependent verbs. It carries several meanings including 'when' and 'where' even without the identifying adverb *adalí* preceding the verb. Modern descendants of families from Missisquoi say rather *mazípskwohoík* with *z* for *s* and with *h* between the *os. adalí* is commonly dropped and *masípskwooík* 'where it is flint or flinty' is freely translated by Laurent and others as 'where there is flint'. Most speakers coalesce the *-oho-* or *-oo-* with the preceding *w,* giving *masípskwoík* or even *masípskoík.* McAleer erred in rejecting this name, which was given him by Laurent, on the ground that there was no flint in the vicinity, not realizing that the Abenaki term was not restricted to flint proper in the geologist's terms.

Missisquoi Bay

Missisquoi Bay is called *masípskwbí* which means literally 'flint water'. The parts of the word are *masípskw,* a free noun root meaning 'flint, chert, or other flinty rock' (also *mazípskw*); *-bi,* a deverbal bound noun root meaning 'water', from the free noun root *nebí* meaning 'water'. *nebí* and *-bi* usually mean water as a substance and help to form such words as 'river water', 'sap', 'wine', and 'spring water'. One would expect the name of Missisquoi Bay to be *masípskwibágw,* since *masípskwbí* suggests water which is somehow flinty, but it is a good grammatical form and is established by usage.

Missisquoi River

The usual name for the Missisquoi River is *wázowategók,* which can be freely translated as 'at the river which turns back'. The parts of the word are *wazowa-,* a general root meaning 'backward, turning back, reversing, doubling on its course'; *-tegw,* a bound noun root meaning 'river'; *-ok,* a locative suffix which follows a consonant and usually suppresses the *w* of noun stems ending in *-gw.*

This name refers to the course of the river which at first flows north by east, then southwest, and finally makes two sharp bends before flowing into Lake Champlain. Robinson (1867:32) heard this over a century ago. He wrote, "Azzasataquake was their name for the Missisque River, signifying, The stream that turns back." And there is a similar statement in some notes found in his papers. In the transcription I have it reads, "Assasatquake, their name for the Missisqui River, signifying the Back-Wood running (shine?), that is, that turns in from itself." "Back-Wood running (shine?)" is probably a misreading for "backward running stream," which is how Crockett (1921 1:68) read it. Robinson's note of March 4, 1881, attempted further explanation but produced statements which themselves need explanation. He wrote, "Their name for the Missisqui River is 'The Stream that runs against itself, or Two Stream(s) battling each other' or Tocksoose says, 'Two streams mouthing into each other.'" These reflect the difficulty the Indian experienced in expressing in English two different concepts, both of which can be expressed by the general root *wazowa-.* The "Stream that runs against itself" is one way of describing the course of the Missisquoi doubling upon itself. "Two streams battling each other" refers to a situation in which the current of a stream or lake eddies or returns in the opposite direction. But the right word to express this is *wazowádzoán* 'a returning current, a back current'. "Two streams mouthing into each other" appears to be an unsuccessful attempt to express the same situation, as *wázowategók* says nothing about any junction or confluence of two streams.

A French map of 1713 (Anonymous 1713) bears a puzzling name for a stream which appears to be the Missisquoi. It is a stream rising just east of the headwaters of the Yamaska River, flowing south, then making a sharp bend to flow northwesterly into Lake Champlain, and it is given the name *PetagoubKy.* The names on this map appear to be bad copies of names which originated in an Eastern Abenaki dialect. It has been said that Joseph Aubery, the missionary at Saint Francis, was the authority for them. It is possible that Western Abenaki speakers in his congregation gave him names which he transcribed badly because they were foreign to him. *PetagoubKy* seems to me to resemble most *bédegwibágw* 'round bay', but it is clearly applied to a river. Possibly it was meant to represent *bedegítegók* 'returning river', which would describe the Missisquoi and be in harmony with the name we know, but this is no more than a guess.

The Missisquoi is also referred to as 'flint river', and this is expressed both by *masípskwizibó,* using the free noun root for 'river' *zibó,* and *masípskwitégw,* using the bound noun root for 'river' *-tegw.*

Swanton Falls

Swanton is located at the lower falls of the Missisquoi River. In 1748 or 1749 the French built a sawmill at the falls, and the place became known to the Abenakis as *dagwáhôganék* 'at the mill' or as *dagwáhôgánizék* 'at the little mill'. The name stuck and appears in English documents after the withdrawal of the French as Taquahunga and Taquahunga Falls. (See, for example, the map reproduced in Crockett 1921 1:facing page 40.)

The analysis of *dagwáhôganék* is *dagwa-*, a verb root meaning 'grind by pounding'; *-hôgan,* a nominalizing suffix meaning 'implement'; *-ek,* locative suffix. The literal translation is 'at the grinding implement'. The primary meaning of *dagwáhôgán* is a grinding mill consisting of a hollowed-out stump and a wooden pounder. Obviously by the eighteenth century it had been extended to include a 'sawmill', probably by analogy to the double usage of French *moulin,* and it is still used in both senses.

dagwáhôgánizék contains the same elements but with the addition of the diminutive suffix *-iz.*

Poposquash

Poposquash is a small and low rocky island north of Saint Albans Bay. The name is an English corruption which has so effectively concealed the original name that it would probably never have been deciphered without the testimony of Théophile Panadis, a Missisquoi Abenaki. The most obvious solution would employ the word *popokwá* 'cranberry', and this was suggested by Huden (1957: 19), but the use of *-skw* for *-kw* and the final *-sh* must be explained. Huden further volunteered *Pamapskak* 'rocky place', *Pop-e-qua-tuck* 'broken land', and *Wab-ees-qua* 'white, bubbly water'. *Pamapskak* does mean 'rocky place', or better 'rocky area', but it does not sound much like *Poposquash*. *Pop-e-qua-tuck* sounds more like *popokwátegw* 'cranberry river', and in any event 'broken land' is not appropriate to the site. In old New England usage, 'broken land' was applied to a tract of land which was too irregular in topography for easy cultivation and would not be appropriate for a small rocky island. Huden must have obtained *Wab-ees-qua* from one of the Abenaki speakers he knew, but for some reason failed to extract the real significance.

The Abenakis knew the island as *wábeskwasék* 'where the bladder is', and it was so called because, when viewed at a little distance across the water, it suggested to them a floating fish bladder. A nearby island is called Fish Bladder Island on the Geological Survey map, so it is probable that the name has gotten transferred. The analysis of the word is simple: *wabeskwá,* a noun, apparently a free noun root meaning simply 'blister, bubble, bladder', is used in this name with the understanding that the air bladder of a fish is meant, but this is not specified; *-sek,* situative suffix indicating 'the place at which, or time through which' the preceding noun exists. (Cf. Ash [Head] Island.)

Sandbar Bridge

North of the outlet of the Lamoille River is a sandbar which stretches from the mainland to the opposite shore of South Hero Island. On this sandbar a bridge has been built. The Abenakis call the bridge *kíileságwôgán* 'land bridge', from *ki,* a free noun root meaning 'land, earth' (the fuller form *akí* is usually used following a personal possessive); *-i-,* a connective; *le-,* a lexicalizing prefix which has the function of making a word out of a bound root; *-sagw-,* a bound verb root meaning 'step upon'; *-wôgan,* nominalizing suffix variously translated according to context as 'thing, substance, action, (etc.)' and at times by an English verb ending such as the *ing* in *working.* In this word the final *w* of *-sagw* and the initial *w* of *-wôgan* coalesce. The word *leságwôgán* means literally 'what one steps on', that is, a bridge on which one can cross by stepping on it rather than by wading.

The sandbar figures in the Abenaki oral tradition of an event in their old wars. It was the secret route by which the population of a whole village made their escape in the night from an approaching enemy. A ford is called *adáli pkágôzógamék* 'place where there is a foot crossing', and even without either tradition or historical evidence one feels almost certain that this would have been the old name for the crossing place. A sandbar is *ôgwaômkwitán.* The parts of this word are *ôgwa-,* an infrequent general root with the meaning of 'piling up, accumulating'. It is found also in *ôgwábônsén* to name 'snow ridges formed by the wind'; *-ômku,* a bound noun root meaning 'sand'; *-ita,* a bound verb root meaning 'flows'; *-n,* a substantizing suffix. *-itan* may be translated as 'current' and *ôgwaômkwitán* as 'sand accumulated by the current'.

Carleton Prize

This rocky islet off the southwestern end of South Hero Island was regarded as being part of the long and hazardous canoe crossing, at right angles to the prevailing westerly winds, from Shelburne Point to South Hero. The Abenakis named it *odzihózoiskwá* or 'Odzhihozo's wife'. (For Odzihozo, see "Rock Dunder" section.) The analysis of the name is *odzihózo,* a personal name; *-i-,* a connective; *-skwa,* unpossessible bound noun root meaning 'woman, wife'. Although the full form is *odzihózoiskwá,* it is commonly syncopated in the spoken language by coalescing the final *o* of *odzihózo* and the connective *-i-* into a schwa, which often drops out to bring *z* and *s* together. This devoices the *z* and the resulting word is pronounced *odzíhosskwá.*

Lamoille River

The name of the Lamoille River, which flows out of Vermont into Lake Champlain opposite the southern end of South Hero Island, has been the subject of considerable inconclusive discussion. The English traveler Edward Augustus Kendall (1809 3:274–275) seems to have originated the controversy, and his statement is worth repeating as a good summary of the problem:

> Lamouëlle or Lamouëtte is one of the small number of topographical names which has been mentioned above, as received by Vermont from the French. The word is at present a stumbling-block to the Vermontese orthographists. Dr. Williams writes it Lamoille, and Mr. Dean, in his Alphabetical *Atlas,* (a well-contrived gazeteer [*sic*], but a most barbarous piece of geographical literature) writes it Lamoil, Dr. Morse has sometimes La Moelle, and sometimes La Moille. In Charlevoix's map, it is la rivière à La Mouëlle.
>
> Of none of these words is it easy, however, to give any interpretation; and I venture, in consequence, to submit, that the true name of the river is not à la Mouëlle, but à la Mouëtte. A map-engraver might more pardonably omit to cross his tt, than to make the river DeChasy, in this lake, the river *Blazy;* or the *Ile aux Erables* or Isle of Maples, in Lake Superior, the Isle of Naples; and, yet, both the latter mistakes, with a hundred others, occur in Mr. Carleton's Map of the United States, published in Boston, in the year 1806. The mouëtte is in English the *mew* or *gull,* of which more than one species frequents Lake Champlain and the mouths of its rivers, particularly the Little White River Gull. Among the other rivers of the Lake, one was called by the French *Au rat,* another *Aux Castors,* and a third *Aux Loutres;* and it was equally natural that they should denote a fourth to the mouëtte.
>
> (It may be further worthy of remark, that the name Lamouëlle or Lamouëtte is applied, in the map cited not to the river now called Lamoille or Lamoëlle, but to the Onion River or Winooski; while the Lamouëlle or Lamouëtte is there called *Rivière du Sud*—that is, South River.)

Kendall's suggestion has been followed by a number of other authors, but Charlevoix's word, now spelled *la moelle,* is not, as Kendall suggested, difficult to interpret. It means 'bone marrow'. And to this day the Abenakis name the river *wíntegók* 'at marrow river', composed of *win,* a free noun root meaning 'bone marrow'; *-tegw,* a bound noun root meaning 'river'; *-ok,* a locative singular suffix which follows a consonant and usually suppresses the *-w* of noun stems ending in *-gw.* The lower reaches of this river thaw out in spring before the lake. This enabled the Abenakis to get an early start on building their canoes. Canoe building required that a moose be killed for marrow and tallow to mix with spruce gum for gumming the seams, hence the name 'marrow river'. Robinson also obtained this name from his Abenaki informants. He wrote it *win tŭkw,* and the copy I have from his papers gives as a meaning 'the narrow river', which is not a possible translation.

The lower reach of the Lamoille River was known to the first settlers as *Scodogua, Scodoqua, Scodaqua,* and *Scadagua* (Vermont 1939 5:67, 78, 93, 137, 230). These variant spellings were attempts to record the Abenaki name *mskitegwá,* which means 'a reach' or 'quiet stretch of river, dead water'. The parts of this word are *msk-,* the initial element of *mskitégw,* probably a general root meaning 'still' referring to water, but never heard except in this word. If the final *-i-* is the connective; the root may be just *msk-,* but without additional examples of this element, the full root could be *mask-, maski-, mesk-, meski-, misk-, miski-, mosk-,* or *moski-.* Some of these are known but with other meanings; *-tegw,* bound noun root meaning 'river'; *-a,* definitive suffix, often translated as English 'the'.

Essentially the same word in a different dialect was the name of the Concord River in Massachusetts, and Thoreau (1950:113) mentions getting an equivalent from Indians in Maine, one of whom was Swassin Tahamont from Saint Francis. He spelled what he heard as *Musketicook* showing that he heard the locative *mskitegók* rather than the independent definite *mskitegwá.* His Penobscot guide, Joe Polis, gave him *Muskeeticook* 'dead-water' (Thoreau 1950:337).

It is likely that the locative of this word *mskitegók* was also the origin of *Schaghticoke,* the name for the Indian village near the mouth of the Hoosick River and opposite the village of Stillwater, New York. Although this name has usually been derived from the root meaning 'off to the side, branching', *beska-* in Western Abenaki, Asa Fitch (1870:386) got for it the meaning 'quiet water' from a Saint Francis Indian a century ago.

Saranac River

This river is known to all Abenakis as *zalônák:tégw.* All my informants, including several who were familiar with Saranac River and the Saranac Lakes and some who were born before 1880, agreed on this. The parts of the word are *zalón,* a free noun root meaning 'sumac cone'; *- ak* an animate plural suffix; *-tegw,* a bound noun root meaning 'river'. The word is pronounced *salônák:tékw,* in which the initial *s* is voiceless but not fortis and the final *w* is voiceless. The segment preceding the *w,* although phonemically *g,* is voiceless because of its position in the final cluster and also fortis by reason of its ending the final strongly stressed syllable.

zalón is not 'sumac tree' as the Robinson Papers had it, or 'sumac bud' as reported by Prince (1900:125). *zalón* is the large, red, conelike fruiting body of the sumac. 'Sumac tree' is *zalónakwám,* in which *-akwam* is a bound noun root meaning 'woody plant, tree, or shrub', but *zalónák* is often used for sumac trees as a substitute for the full form. This practice may be compared with a similar English practice which permits us to refer to a clump of blueberry bushes as blueberries. Therefore, *zalónák:tégw* may be freely translated as 'sumac trees river'. Moreover, in modern usage at least, Saranac Lake is called *zalônákinebés* 'sumacs lake' (Masta 1932:32), and the region of the Saranac Lakes is called *zalônakík* 'at sumac land'. The parts of this word are *zalôn*, free noun root meaning 'sumac cone'; *akí*, free noun root meaning 'land, earth'; *-k*, locative singular suffix used after vowels.

Robinson recorded another name for the Saranac River which seems to be no longer in use, namely, *Sadustuk*, which he understood to mean 'the river of saplings'. The final element is almost certainly *-tegw* 'river', but there is no form *sadus* which means 'saplings'. I suspect that Robinson heard *zedíiztégw* 'little evergreen river', which is pronounced *sədíistékw*. The analysis of this word is *zədí*, free noun root meaning 'evergreen tree or shrub, evergreen branches'; *-iz*, a diminutive suffix; *-tegw*, bound noun root meaning 'river'. It is likely that Robinson's informant knew some French and may have translated *zedíiztégw* as Sapin River, *sapin* being a French term for a number of coniferous species. Robinson could have heard this as Sapling River.

Although the modern names for the Saranac River are quite definite and clear, this cannot be said about the names in the older records or the relationship, if any, between the older forms and modern usage.

The following forms are selected from eighteenth-century sources: *Sataramec*—about 1752—Franquet (1889:171); *Serindac*—1755—Map of French grants (Beauchamp 1907:45); *Salasanac*—1779—Sauthier map (O'Callaghan 1849–1851 1:facing page 774); *Savaniac*—before 1800—journal of Gilliland, the pioneer of Willsboro, New York (Watson 1863:117); *St. Aranack* (see *Savaniac*).

These names exemplify most of the problems which plague students of place-names. No meaning accompanies any of these names. They are just enough alike to suggest that they may have been derived from the same original name, but they are not enough alike to give even a rough idea of what that name might have been. Allowance must be made for the vagaries of cartographers and map engravers. For example, the Sauthier map copied the French name of the Winooski River—*Ouinouski* or *Ouinouskik*—as *Ouiuonschick*, thus transposing two sets of sounds and introducing a nonexistent second *w* sound. One does not even know in what language to look for the original of these names. They are commonly assumed to be in an Algonquian language, but Beauchamp (1907:45) suggested that *Saranac* might come from Iroquois *saranne* meaning 'to ascend'. The original may even have been French. The Saranac River is named the *St. Amant* on the Lery map of 1748 (O'Callaghan 1849–1851 1:facing page 556), and Watson suggested that Gilliland's *St. Aranack*, which was applied to the nearby Salmon River perhaps by error, might be a corruption of *St. Amant*. *St. Aranack* also bears some relation to Franquet's *Sataramec*. The name *Serindac* converted into acceptable Abenaki sounds gives *salintak*, which sounds much like *zalôna-tékw* 'sumac stake' or perhaps in earlier times 'sumac tree', since the cognate of

-atekw means 'tree' in some other Algonquian languages. *salintak* also resembles *zalôntégw* 'sumac river'. And there it seems we must leave the earliest names until further evidence can be brought to bear on them.

The nineteenth century produced a set of names which are definitely related to each other. They are *Senhaneenapay* 'Saranac Lake' from Elijah Benedict (Emmons 1841:127); *Senhanelac-tuk* 'River of sumac trees' from John Watso (Robinson 1867:32); *Sinhaloneinnepus* 'Upper Saranac Lake', 'large and beautiful lake' from Mitchell Sabattis (Holden 1874:33), obtained "years ago"; *Sinhalannacktuk* 'River of sumach trees' from John Watso (Robinson 1860–1881); and *S'nhalô'nek* 'entrance of a river into a lake' from Sabattis (Prince 1900:124). Prince also got *Salônak* 'sumach buds' from some Abenakis (1900:125), but this will be kept separate from the set above for the present.

It is apparent that these names bear a strong resemblance to each other but their alleged meanings are contradictory. *Sinhaloneinnepus* does not mean 'large and beautiful lake'. Prince accepted Sabattis's gloss 'entrance of a river into a lake' and with the assistance of Reverend Michael O'Brien, a good student of Penobscot, produced an ingenious etymology to support it. He made *s'n-* to be a modern or slovenly pronunciation of *sôgda-* 'mouth of a river' plus *h'la* 'come' plus *-nek* in analogy with Rasles's Abenaki *ari-'rannek* 'the place where one goes by canoe' to give a locative form 'the place where it comes in'. This explanation would require that Sabattis used the same "slovenly" pronunciation to different recorders about a half-century apart and that Robinson's informant and Elijah Benedict did the same thing. This and the modern variant explanation must be viewed in the light of the fact that the word for the 'mouth' or 'coming in' of a river is still *zôgedahlá,* and I have never heard it pronounced otherwise by anyone. Although Robinson gives 'river of sumac trees', the Abenaki names which accompany this meaning are like the rest of the set and unlike the modern *zalônák:tégw,* which does mean 'river of sumac trees'. We may believe that some, possibly all, of the meanings given were descriptions of a feature rather than a translation of the name.

The most troublesome feature of this set is the first syllable, which differs from that of the modern Abenaki name, even in those names which were translated identically as 'river of sumac trees'. *Senhan-, senhanel-, sinhalon-, sinhalann-,* and *s'nhalôn-* are not *zalôn.* It cannot be dismissed as incompetent transcription since, in addition to agreement in all versions, Robinson had a rather good ear for dialect and Prince's Abenaki transcriptions were good. Was 'sumac' *sinhalôn* in the early nineteenth century? This is unlikely. Wzôkhilain wrote *salôn* in 1830 (1830b:47). Moreover, the *senhalôn* names were being obtained about the time my informants must have been learning *zalônáktégw* from their elders. One could compose a grammatically acceptable name, namely, *sazálônak:tégw.* The initial *sa-* is a reduplication of the first syllable and adds the force of 'sumacs in

general, sumacs everywhere, many sumacs'. This has the right number of syllables, but it does not resemble the first syllable of the set.

The key to the puzzle may reside in the fact that a name similar to the others of
this set appears twice as the name, not of the Saranac River, but of Plattsburgh at
its mouth. Sabattis gave *Senhalone* as the name for Plattsburgh (Holden 1874:
33), and the Abenaki chief Joseph Laurent named Plattsburgh *Sôn-Halônek*
(1884:52). The definition that Sabattis gave Prince, 'entrance of a river into a
lake', is more appropriate for Plattsburgh than for the Saranac River. Beauchamp
(1893:15, 1907:45) toyed with the idea that it might be an Oneida word but
finally concluded that it was Algonquian because it came from Sabattis. Sabattis
did have connections with Saint Regis and apparently knew some Mohawk, but
it does seem unlikely that both he and Laurent would use an Oneida name for
Plattsburgh. If we assume that the names of the *senhalon-* set were names for
Plattsburgh rather than the Saranac River and take Laurent as our best authority
for the shape of the name, we are presented with a ready-made and quite different explanation. *Sôn Halônek* means 'at Saint Helen' and is the name by which
the Abenakis know Île-Ste-Hélène near Montreal. And if Plattsburgh was *Sôn
Halônek,* the Saranac River could have been logically named *Sôn Halônektégw,*
'Saint Helen's River', a plain unambiguous translation requiring no adjustment
of the phonetic shape. This solution would require that Watso was giving one
Indian name and the English translation of another and that Benedict was
calling Saranac Lake *Sôn Halôninebi* 'Saint Helen's Water'. This is no more than a
tentative solution of a set of seemingly contradictory data, and I could place
more confidence in it if I had confirming testimony that Plattsburgh was really
named *Sainte-Hélène* at one time.

Ausable River

The Ausable River is so named from the early French name *La Rivière au Sable*
'Sandy River'. It flows into Lake Champlain from the west, entering north of
Port Kent, New York. A few miles upstream it flows through a deep gorge known
to tourists for a hundred years as Ausable Chasm. The Abenakis name the river,
from this feature, *nágwiadzoák,* which may be freely translated as 'underground
stream'. The parts of this word are *nagw-,* a general root meaning 'under, underneath'; *-i-,* a connective; *-a,* substantizing suffix (hence *nagwiá* 'the underneath');
-dzoa-, bound verb root meaning 'flows, be a current'; *-k,* third-person singular
conjunct ending. The literal translation is '(where) it flows underneath', that is,
'underneath the ground'.

Another, and possibly older, name was current in the last century. Holden
(1874:30) recorded from Sabattis *Papaquanetuck* translated as 'the river of cranberries'. Robinson (1860–1881) recorded, probably from Watso, *Poproquama-
netuk* 'the cranberry river'. I take this from a transcript of Robinson's notes, so the

r may be a misreading. Both names should be *popokwáimenitégw,* which indeed means 'river of cranberries'. This name analyzes into *popokwá,* a free noun root naming the 'cranberry plant' *Vaccinium oxycoccos* L. and V. *macrocarpon* Ait.; *-i-,* a connective; *-men,* bound noun root meaning 'berry, berrylike fruit'. If the river were named solely for the cranberry plants rather than the berries (which an Indian would be unlikely to do), the name would be *popokwáitégw.*

Winooski River

The Winooski River flows into Lake Champlain from the east, entering north of Burlington, Vermont. It has appeared under various versions of the same name since the eighteenth century. It appeared on the *Carte du Canada* (Anon. 1713) as *R. Ouisnouski.* Kendall (1809 3:273) wrote of it, "The name *Onion River* is translated from *Winooski, Winooskeag* or *Winoostiquoke,* meaning the banks of a river on which there are onions, or, rather, wild garlic." This free translation may have been given to him at Saint Francis, which he visited, but he recorded three different words. *winoskí* is 'onion land'; *winoskík* is 'at onion land'; *winóstegók* is 'at onion river'.

The Abenakis usually refer to this river as *winóskitégw* 'onion land river', and the locality is usually referred to as *winóskitegók* 'at onion land river' or sometimes simply as *winóstegók* 'at onion river'. The river is also called *winóskizibó* 'onion land river', employing the free noun root *zibó* in place of the bound noun root *-tegw.* The parts of these words are *winós,* a free noun root designating 'the wild onions, the genus *Allium* L.'; *ki,* a free noun root meaning 'land'; *-k,* a locative suffix; *-tegw,* bound noun root meaning 'river'; *zibó,* a free noun root meaning 'river'.

Burlington

In this century at least, the largest city in Vermont on the shores of Burlington Bay is called by the Abenakis *balitén.* Since this has no meaning, it is most probably a loanword, simply Burlington with an Abenaki pronunciation. Some speakers, however, believe that *balitén* was originally *balitán,* which is a good Abenaki word with a meaning not inappropriate to the locality. It means freely 'wrong way current', a handicap often encountered by canoeists crossing Burlington Bay when a favorable surface current may suddenly shift to a contrary one. The analysis of the word is *bal-,* a general root meaning 'wrong, erroneous, false, other'; *-ita-,* a bound verb root meaning 'flow, be a current'; *-n,* a substantizing suffix. Thus, *balitán,* pronounced *palitán* with a voiceless but lenis *p,* means 'a wrong current'.

There is another and ancient name for the vicinity of Burlington. It is *odzíhozsék,* pronounced *odzíhossék* or *odzihóssek* in different dialects (see next section).

Rock Dunder

Rock Dunder is a rocky islet in the lake about a half-mile from the tip of Shelburne Point. Vermont historians have been intrigued by this rock but are generally unfamiliar with its background. The reason for its being called Rock Dunder is unknown. To the Abenaki, however, this is the most significant feature of the lake, since, in their mythology, the supernatural figure who shaped the face of the earth made Lake Champlain his masterpiece and at last climbed onto Rock Dunder and there changed himself into stone. The impression of someone sitting on the rock is heightened by its geological formation, which is a short cylinder of horizontally bedded dark slate resting on slanting strata of lighter-colored limestone.

This Abenaki Transformer was unique among Abenaki supernatural figures in that he created himself, and for this reason he is named *Odzíhozó* (pronounced also *Odzíhózo* in one dialect) which signifies 'he makes himself from something'. Therefore, since Rock Dunder is regarded as the Transformer himself, it is also called *Odzíhozó*. Some Abenakis who do not know the old lore thoroughly think the name is *ôdzíhozó*, interpreted as 'he changes himself into something'. This would be an appropriate descriptive term based on the Transformer's last action, but his proper name was given for his earlier unique accomplishment of self-creation. The analysis of *odzíhozó* is *odz-*, a general root meaning 'from, out of'; *-i-*, a connective; *-ho-*, a verb suffix signifying 'make, accomplish'; *-z-*, a transitive animate reflexive verb final; *-o,* third-person singular transitive animate verb ending.

ôdzíhozó has a similar analysis, except for the general root *ôdz-*, which carries the meaning of 'adding to, increasing'; the nature of the increase may be specified by a following general root, as *ôdzíólihozó* 'he makes himself better'. Thus, *ôdzíhozó* really means 'he adds something to himself'. It can infer 'change', but to specify 'he changes himself' one must say *ôdzibílowihozó* or *obílowihozín.*

Some younger Abenakis have deduced a false etymology from the circumstance that when canoe travel on the lake was common, which is to say until about 1920, Abenakis would make an offering of tobacco and/or pipes either to *odzíhozó* or to *odzihóziskwá* for a safe crossing (see "Carleton Prize" section). Furthermore, the word *odzíhós* means 'a chance', such as one might take by cutting cards or drawing a straw in a lottery. A set of long and short drawing sticks becomes *odzíhosák* by adding the animate plural suffix *-ak,* and one may say, for example, *nadonôda ndzíhosák* 'let us draw chances'.

The Robinsons had gotten a sketchy idea of the nature of Rock Dunder from three or more Abenakis by 1881 and recorded it variously as *Wa-ju-hose, Wo ge hose,* and *Wohjahose* (Robinson 1860–1881). Rowland introduced it into some of his fiction, and in his history of Vermont he wrote, in connection with the French and Indian expedition against Schenectady in 1690, "Wohjahose, signifying the Forbidden, is the Waubanakee name of Rock Dunder, which was supposed to be the guardian spirit of Petowbowk. Some dire calamity was certain to befall those who passed his abode without making some propitiary offering" (Robinson 1892a:6). Robinson's gloss was a partial characterization, not a translation. Crockett (1921 1:63) reproduced *Wujahose* 'the Forbidden' and Huden (1957:6, 1962:292) twice gave *wojahosen* as 'Forbidder's Rock, Guardian's Rock'. *odzihózoisén* would be 'Odzihozo's Rock', which would have to refer only to the base strata of Rock Dunder on which *Odzihozo* sits, not to the entire rock. I have never happened to hear this form, but it would be accurate and appropriate if properly applied. Possibly it was suggested by *Wuchowsen,* the wind bird in Penobscot mythology.

Although the Abenaki name of Rock Dunder and its meaning are now clear, there remains a problem of relating it to a rock or rocks frequently mentioned in seventeenth- and eighteenth-century documents and discussed by Lounsbury (1960:60–62). As he observed, at one time or another a rock, an island, a point, and a lake or part of a lake have borne similar names, variously spelled, which he assembled under the rubric "*Rogeo.*" A definitive study of the numerous Iroquois names and their appropriate topographic referents might produce a paper longer than this one and would be a paper I am not qualified to write. I should like here merely to point out the possibility that the Iroquois original of the variants of *Rogeo* might be a borrowing from Abenaki *Odzíhozó* and the apparent proliferation of rocks, islands, and so on may have grown out of the existence of two rocks with the similar names *Odzíhozó* and *Odzihózoiskwa.* In support of what is no more than a notion, I point out that one of the fullest Mohawk names in this series, *Rogiochne,* which Lounsbury (1960:62) identifies as *rotsi²yô:(h)ne* 'at the place of Rotsî:²yo', stripped of its locative ending and the initial *r,* which is necessary in Mohawk but not in Abenaki, leaves *-otsî:²yo,* which is superficially close indeed to *Odzíhozó.*

Shelburne Point

Shelburne Bay lies south of Burlington. It receives the La Platte River at its southern end and is largely separated from the main body of the lake by Shelburne Point. The better-known writers on Vermont place-names have created some false impressions which must be corrected if the place-names of this locality are to be understood. Crockett (1921 1:68), apparently following Robinson, wrote, "The La Plotte River appears on an old map as the Quineaska, and was called by the Indians Quineska-took, from the name given to Shelburne Point, meaning Long Joint, as it was supposed to represent a man's forearm." Huden (1957:20, 1962:208) was probably following Crockett when he wrote, "*Kwini aska:* The LaPlatte River: from Abnaki *Kwini,* 'long' plus *eskuan,* 'joint' or 'elbow'. Probably refers to long arc of riverbed. Spelled also Quinneaska."

The errors, chronologically considered, are as follows: (1) *Quineaska* on the Sauthier Map contains one syllable too many; (2) Crockett apparently misread Robinson's gloss 'the long point' as 'the long joint'; (3) and both Crockett and Huden attempted unnecessarily to explain 'long joint'. Having introduced an error by writing 'point' as 'joint', Crockett made a plausible explanation, referring it to 'forearm'. Huden's interpretation of a long elbow is rather farfetched and an unlikely Abenaki concept. Finally, 'a long elbow' is not *kwini eskuan*. It would be *gwenígeskwán*. This cannot be shortened to *-eskwan* without ambiguity, even though deverbal roots are sometimes formed from full noun roots. *-eskwan* leaves the listener uncertain whether *-geskwan* 'elbow' or *-beskwan* 'back' is meant. Robinson (1860–1881) had almost the correct form when he wrote *Quineska* 'the long point'. In fact, he may have had the completely correct form and his transcriber simply miscopied it, considering his letter of 1895, probably to Manley Hardy of Brewer, Maine, which reads, "The Wabanaki called the Point [in Shelburne] 'Quinaska,' the Long Point" (Eckstorm 1941:205–206). *Quineaska*, analyzed by Huden as *kwini aska* 'long elbow', is grammatically correct. The connective *-i-* can be used between a general root ending in a consonant and a bound noun root commencing with a vowel. I have only heard this word, however, without the connective, and ease of pronunciation does seem to urge dropping the connective here.

The correct name for Shelburne Point is *gwénaská* 'the long point'. The parts of the word are *gwen-*, a general root meaning 'long in distance or dimension or time'. This root is polymorphic and has also the shapes *gwin-* and *gwan-*; *-ask*, a bound noun root meaning 'a point of land'; *-a*, definitive suffix often translated by English 'the'; hence, *gwénaská* 'the long point'. This is pronounced much like *kwánaská* with a voiceless but lenis initial *k*. This name was known and corroborated for Shelburne Point by informants in recent years.

The cliffs around the tip of Shelburne Point are called *megezóidolká* 'the eagle's breast' and are sometimes called in English Eagle Cliff. These names refer to it as a former nesting site of eagles. The analysis is *megezó*, a free noun root meaning 'eagle'; *-i-*, a connective; *-dolka*, bound noun root meaning 'chest, breast'.

La Platte River

Robinson gave the correct name of this river and the correct meaning of the name, "Quinaskatook, Long Point Stream" (Eckstorm 1941:205–206). To be consistent with the orthography used here, this should be spelled *gwenáskatégw* and pronounced *kwenáskatékw* with the initial *k* voiceless and lenis and the last *k* voiceless and fortis. This is the same name as that for Shelburne Point except for the addition of the bound noun root *-tegw* 'river'.

The La Platte River is known to the Abenakis by yet another name, *senipôgán:izibó* 'stone pipe river'. The parts of the word are *sen*, free noun root meaning 'stone'; *-i-*, connective; *-pôgan*, bound noun root meaning 'pipe for smoking'; *-i-*, connective; *zibó*, free noun root meaning 'river'.

Since the river was named from the point which, as Zadock Thompson tells us (1842 3:102), the French named *Pointe au Plâtre*, one may surmise that the French made pipes there from local pipe clay (*pipes de plâtre*). The Abenaki name may be only a translation of a French name.

Split Rock

Split Rock is a rocky cliff, now bearing a lighthouse, on the west side of the lake south of Essex, New York. It is opposite Thompsons Point on the Vermont side, and together they form the deep narrows which constrict the main body of the lake at its southern end. The usual Abenaki name for Split Rock, as well as the English name, is derived from a split which goes down to the water line in high water isolating the northern tip of the rock. It is called *zôbapská* 'the through rock'. This name is formed from *zôb-*, general root meaning 'through in space or time'; *-apskw*, bound noun root meaning 'rock' and usually applied to ledges, boulders, or considerable expanses of rock rather than to smaller stones; *-a*, definitive suffix which converts *zôbápskw* 'a through rock' to 'the through rock'. The literal translation is awkward in English, but the implication of the Abenaki composition is 'the go-through rock', although no part of the word is explicitly 'go'. The initial *z* is pronounced as a lenis *s*. Crockett (1921 1:69) gave the form *Tobapskwa*, which is probably Robinson's (1860–1881) *So baps kwa* 'the pass through the rock' miscopied. There is an Abenaki word *togapská* which does mean 'a rock which has been split as by frost', but I incline to the view that this is coincidence.

Split rock is well known to the Abenakis for the great number of rattlesnakes there and for the natural figure resembling a snake on the rock for which they have an origin myth. For these reasons they refer to the main rocky mass as *sizikwáimenahán* 'rattlesnake island' and as *alídegwômék:sén* 'rock where there is a picture' or 'rock where there are pictures'. The parts of *sizikwáimenahán* are *sizikwá*, a noun not yet etymologized, probably not a free noun, meaning 'rattlesnake'; *-i-*, a connective; *menahán*, a free noun root meaning 'island'. The parts of *alídegwômék:sén* are *al-*, general root meaning 'like, as, how, because, the way that'; *-idegw(a)*, bound noun root meaning 'face'; *-ômek*, animate intransitive infinitive ending; *sen*, free noun root meaning 'stone'. *alídegwômék*, which is literally 'like-being-a-face', is the usual equivalent of 'portrait' or 'picture'. Therefore, the whole name may be translated 'portrait rock' or 'picture rock'.

Thompsons Point

This point extends from the eastern shore opposite Split Rock. It was named by Robinson (1860–1881) as *Kozo wa ap ska* 'the long stony point'. Crockett

(1921 1:69) apparently repeated this as *Kozoapsqua* 'the Long Rocky Point', which Huden (1957:8) respelled as *Ko-zo ap-skwa* 'Stony Point'. This name, which is still in use, should be *kwazôwáapskák* 'at the extended rock'. The parts of this word are *kwazô-*, general root meaning 'extended, stretched, drawn out'; *-w-*, intervocalic glide; *-apskw,* bound noun root meaning 'rock'; *-a,* definitive suffix which often suppresses the final *w* of *kw* and *skw* clusters; *-k,* locative singular suffix. I have also heard Thompsons Point called *gwénapskák* 'at the long rock' and *kwazôwáhômék* 'at the extended point'. The only new element in these names is *-ahôm-,* a bound noun root meaning 'point of land'.

Charlotte Cove

Robinson (1905:221) heard the name "Pawn bowk" for Charlotte Cove and commented on the abundance of Indian pottery once found on its shores. This was probably meant for *bôbágw,* pronounced *pôbákw* with voiceless lenis *p* and voiceless fortis *k,* which means 'pond, bay, basin'. This word consists of *bô-,* an initial element, perhaps a general root, but its real nature has not been determined yet. It bears superficial resemblance to three other roots and may possibly be related to one of them—*bam-,* 'place where' or 'time when'; *ben-* 'downward moving', which appears in some combinations as *bôn-,* and *bôkw-* 'shallow'; *-bagw,* bound noun root meaning 'water at rest, body of water, bay, pond, lake'. One may surmise that Robinson got this name from local Indians who were referring to Charlotte Cove nearby simply as 'The Bay' rather than naming it distinctively.

Lewis, Little Otter, and Great Otter Creeks

These three streams all empty into Lake Champlain in the town of Ferrisburgh, and we owe most of our knowledge of their nomenclature to the historian and most famous native son of Ferrisburgh, Rowland E. Robinson. The earliest literary references to their names are found in Robinson's (1867) *A Sketch of the Early History of Ferrisburgh,* published in 1867, but it appears likely that his data, obtained from John Watso, originated before 1860, according to the *Sketch* itself and Edward D. Collins's foreword to *Uncle Lisha's Outing* (Robinson 1934b:9–10). It is convenient to discuss them together.

We have but one name for Lewis Creek and that obtained from a single informant, Watso. Robinson's notes read "Their names of Rivers in Ferrisburgh were, of Great Otter Creek: Pecunktuk, or The Crooked River; of Little Otter Creek, Wonakakituk, or the River of Otters, and of Lewis Creek, sungahnetuk, the Fishing Place. This was told me by John Wadso, or Wadhso, an intelligent Indian of St. Francis, who also gave the names of some other rivers of the Champlain Valley—."

This is the only name we find for Lewis Creek, although Robinson (1867:32

and elsewhere) also spelled it *Sungahnee-tuk*. He changed the translation to 'River of Fish Weirs' in 1892 (Robinson 1892b:576) and in subsequent writings. The name *Sungahnetuk* suggests the Abenaki word *senigánitégw* 'stone works river', and *senigán* 'stone works' would be a tolerable descriptive term for the permanent stones in a fish weir which was planned to be used year after year, but it is not restricted to this kind of structure. Such weirs were found at the outlet of Lake Winnipesauke in New Hampshire, for example. It appears to me, however, that Robinson's name more probably represents his hearing of *kwsénôgán* 'fish weir'. I have never obtained this word in a Saint Francis dialect, but Speck (1940:90) got Penobscot *kwse'nαgan,* which would be the Penobscot analogue of it.

Robinson's notes give the name *Wonakakituk* 'the River of Otters' for Little Otter Creek rather than for Great Otter Creek, and he repeated it as *Wónakáke-tuk* (1867:32). By the time he wrote his essay "Along Three Rivers" in 1894, he wrote, "Its Waubanakee name is Won a kaka tuk-ese, or Little Otter River, while that of Great Otter is the same with the omission of the diminutive 'ese' " (1905: 221), and he continued with this form. We can conclude that his association with Abenakis after 1867 produced the distinction. His ultimate name for the Little Otter should be spelled *onegígwtegwíz* or *wnegígwtegwíz,* which is pronounced *onəgíkwtegwís* and means literally 'little otter river', that is, a 'little river of otters' not a 'river of little otters'. The parts of the word are *onegígw* (or *wnegígw*), free noun root meaning 'otter'; *-i-,* connective; *-tegw,* bound noun root meaning 'river'; *-iz,* diminutive suffix. I have heard this name from informants.

Robinson's notes give only *Pecunktuk* 'The Crooked River' for Otter Creek, which he repeated in print (1867:31–32). In 1880 his nephew, William G. Robinson, sent him from Montreal a list of names which he had obtained from four elderly Abenakis. This list included *Wina ka ka tŭkw* 'the otter river' and *Pe cenk tŭkw* or *Pkonkwe tŭkw* 'crooked river', without identifying the river in either case. Robinson's own notes from Joseph Tocksoose in 1881 include the name *Won-a-kake-tukw,* again without identifying the river. One is left to guess which river was the original and rightful subject of the name *Wonakaketuk*. As noted above, Robinson had by 1894 distinguished Little Otter from Great Otter by recognizing the first with a diminutive. He also added that Great Otter was sometimes called *Petonk-tuk* 'the crooked river', probably a misprint. And in 1899 he recognized both *Peconk-took* and *Wo-na-ka-te-took* for the Great Otter (1934a:245, 1905:102).

Crockett (1921 1:69) reproduced Robinson's names with changed spellings as follows: Otter Creek as *Wonakake-took* 'Otter River' and *Pecouk-took* 'Crooked River'; Little Otter Creek as *Wonaketookese* 'Little Otter River'. Huden limited his names to those in Robinson's earliest notes from Watso and revised the spellings according to his understanding thus: *Wo-no-ka-kee-took* 'The Little Otter River' and *Pe-con-took,* for which he proposed the meaning 'The Swift River'. Also, quite unnecessarily, considering Robinson's testimony, he proposed a variant *Pecon-auk-took* with the supposed meaning 'a small enclosed field near the river'. This meaning is impossible, because Abenaki grammar would make this the name of a river, not a field. *onegígwtégw* has already been explained under *onegígwtegwíz.* Robinson's *Pecunktuk* is *bikŏ́g:tégw* 'crooked river'. The parts are simple: *bikŏ́g-,* general root meaning 'crooked'; *-tegw* bound noun root meaning 'river'. I have heard both names for Otter Creek and also *onegígwizibó* 'otter river', pronounced *onəgíkwizibó,* in which the free noun root for 'river' *zibó* is substituted for *-tegw.*

Vergennes

The little city of Vergennes is located at the lower falls of Otter Creek. In 1881 Robinson obtained two names for these falls from Joseph Tocksoose, namely, *Ne-tah-me-Puntukk* 'The First Falls' and *Ne-tah-me-kan-neek* 'The First Carrying Place'—in the orthography used here, *nitámibôntégw* and *nitámonigánek,* respectively. These names are general terms, not restricted to the falls at Vergennes but applicable to the lower falls or the lower carry of any river. The falls at Vergennes, however, had special significance since Robinson apparently got an origin myth for them which he worked into *Out of Bondage and Other Stories* (1905:114–116). The parts of these names are *nitam-,* general root meaning 'first in a series'; *-i-,* a connective; *bôntégw,* a word meaning 'waterfall'. The last element of the word is the familiar bound noun root for 'river' *-tegw.* The first element appears to be an unusual variant of the general root *ben-,* which means 'downward moving' as in falling or sliding downward; *onigán* or *wnigán,* a word meaning 'a portage or carry', that is, a place where in canoe travel it is necessary to take canoes and baggage out of the water and carry them around rough water. It is composed of a nominalizing suffix *-n,* which makes a noun out of a verb stem *onigá* 'he carries, carry thou'. The analysis of *onigá* is not clear to me yet. It may not be an irreducible form.

Dead Creek

Dead Creek is a small tributary which joins Great Otter Creek just before the latter flows into Lake Champlain. It is known to the Abenakis as *píbegantégw,* with the final *-gw* cluster pronounced voiceless as *-kw.* This means 'roily water river'. The name is formed from *pibegán,* noun meaning 'roily water' (I am unable to analyze this word with certainty); *-tegw,* bound noun root meaning 'river'. Rivers with roily water are not rare, and the name *píbegantégw* is applied to more than one river in Western Abenaki territory.

Ticonderoga

Ticonderoga was known as *tsitôtegwihlá* which may be freely translated as 'the waterway continues'. The parts of the word are *tsitô-*, general root with the meaning 'continuing'; *-tegw*, bound noun root meaning 'river'; *-i-*, a connective; *-hl*, bound verb root with the general meaning of 'progress, move, become', but allowing a variety of other English equivalents in different contexts; *-a*, a third singular verb ending.

The spelling of this name is a good guide to its pronunciation except for the *l*, which after *h* has a sound not found in English. It is formed by placing the front of the tongue against the alveolar ridge behind the upper front teeth and forcing air around it without vibrating the vocal cords; that is, the *l* is a voiceless bilateral fricative like the *ɫ* of Welsh.

This name bears so much resemblance to the English form Ticonderoga as to raise the question whether it may not be formed in imitation of it. On the other hand, it is so appropriate to the locality and so in line with Abenaki naming practice that it may very well be an original name and the resemblance only coincidental. *tsitôtegwihlá* is a fairly common topographical term applied to the continuation of a river or waterway from a lake or widening in a waterway. When it is applied to the river itself, it is restricted to the part which flows out of a lake or wide place, hence downstream. When it is applied to a waterway as a travel route, it may be used for the narrowed watercourse either upstream or downstream from the lake or basin, depending on the direction being traveled at the time.

This name could be applied appropriately to Crown Point, south of which Lake Champlain is narrower. As applied to Ticonderoga, it conveys both this meaning and takes notice of the alternate route to the Hudson River by the Ticonderoga River and Lake George. At Ticonderoga, either way the water route continues. I find it interesting that this name combines by implication the concepts found in the Iroquois names for Lake Champlain and Ticonderoga. It recognizes Lake Champlain as a bulge in the important waterway which the Mohawks saw from the south as a bulge forming and the Abenakis saw from the north as a bulge narrowing (Lounsbury 1960:38). It recognizes implicitly the junction of two waterways at Ticonderoga (Lounsbury 1960:49) which is specified in Mohawk. I am inclined to believe that *tsitôtegwihlá* is an old Abenaki name.

Holden (1874:27) obtained a name for the falls of the Ticonderoga River from Sabattis: "Huncksoock. The place where everybody fights. A name given by the nomadic Indians of the north to the upper falls on the outlet of Lake George." *Huncksoock* is not an Abenaki word as it stands, and it may never be possible to determine just what Sabattis said. The magnitude of the problem presented by this name may be indicated by the solutions which have suggested themselves to me.

(1) The Abenaki way to express 'place where they (many) fight as in war' (distinguished from fighting between individuals or small groups for personal reasons) is *dáli aodóldimék*. This does not sound at all like *Huncksoock*.

(2) The final syllable *-soock* suggests the Abenaki situative suffix *-sek* 'where something(s) is (are)'. *Hunck* cannot be the beginning of a word. It might represent the genuine Abenaki sound *-ôk,* which by itself cannot be a noun or noun stem, but no pertinent initial suggests itself.

(3) Since the outstanding feature of Ticonderoga since 1756 has been a fort, one might consider the word for 'fort' as a starting point. 'Fort' is *wakwólozín* (to some speakers *wakólozín*), and 'at the fort' is *wakwólozinék*. This could have been mistaken by an untrained recorder as *Huncksoock*. There can be no certainty about this, but it is one guess at integrating Sabattis's distorted form with his statement of its meaning. One must keep in mind, however, that in some other instances Sabattis characterized a place rather than translating the name he gave.

Whitehall

Whitehall is at the point where Wood Creek flows into East Bay at the southern tip of Lake Champlain. Holden (1874:35) has given us a name from Sabele for this place, namely, *Wompachookglenosuck.* No translation accompanied this name.

Conclusion

Modern Abenakis know few names for places south of Otter Creek. One can only speculate on the reason for this, since during the eighteenth century they were quite familiar with the country all the way to Albany both by Lake George and by the southern end of Lake Champlain and Wood Creek. In the early and middle nineteenth century a handful of Abenaki hunters became famous as guides in the Adirondacks. From these men we have a considerable number of names for places in the Adirondacks and some on Lake Champlain which I have noted. One suspects that these names were coined by these guides or by their parents, since the interior of the Adirondacks was not traditional Abenaki hunting territory. Even in the twentieth century, some Abenakis lived at Lake George and others sold baskets at Saratoga Springs. Since there is little evidence for Abenaki occupation, but some for Mahican use south of Otter Creek, one might surmise that the names for features on the southern part of Lake Champlain known to warriors and travelers in the eighteenth century were new coinages, less firmly fixed in Abenaki vocabulary, and therefore became lost in this century after their contact largely ceased. Apparently, no names have survived for such prominent places as Crown Point, the Drowned Lands, and Wood Creek. It would be easy to construct apt descriptive names for these places, some of which may have been in actual use. The hazard of doing this is that enthusiasts will take them up and pass them on until they become fixed as the historical Abenaki names for those places. Against this hypothesis are the facts that two names for Ticonderoga have come down to us. The Abenakis still know two names for Albany, perhaps preserved by the large number of them who have moved to that city since World War I, and they knew Schaghticoke and several places on Lake George. It is possible that I missed by only a few years informants who had a full nomenclature for the southern end of the Champlain Valley.

24

From *The Identity of the Saint Francis Indians*

The village of Odanak on the Saint Francis River in Quebec is home to the Saint Francis Indians, whose ancestors took refuge there at different times from various points in northwestern New England following the wars and epidemics of the seventeenth and eighteenth centuries. Sorting out the tribal, cultural, and linguistic origins of the Saint Francis people was a major focus of Day's research for two-and-a-half decades, and the *Identity* monograph represents a synthesis of the diverse lines of evidence he brought to bear on the problem. The excerpts below include only the introductory and concluding sections of the monograph. Omitted are the middle sections detailing the history of the identity problem, the history of Odanak itself from the mid-seventeenth century to the 1970s, and an analysis of family names, which Day hoped to collate with information on dialect variation. The excerpted sections were originally published as pp. 1, 5–6, and 107–117 in Mercury Series Paper 71, National Museum of Man, Canadian Ethnology Service, Ottawa (1981).

The Problem

On the north bank of the Rivière Saint-François in Quebec, about four miles from the place where it empties into Lac Saint-Pierre and immediately adjacent to the village of Pierreville, stands an Indian village called Odanak by the Indians whose village it is. It is better known in history as Arsikantegouk and Saint-François or Saint Francis.

Arsikantegouk was an early Abenaki name for the village. Father Joseph A. Aubery, who was a missionary there between 1709 and 1756, signed the preface of his French-Abenaki dictionary "Arsikanteg8k dari," that is to say "at Arsikanteg8k" (Aubery 1715b:540). The author of the anonymous Abenaki-French dictionary, probably Father Jacques LeSueur, wrote, among the examples illustrating the element *arsi-* 'empty': "arsi-kantek8, rivière où il n'y a plus personne. C'est la Rivière de St-François" (LeSueur 1720:14). The translation is free, and the name means literally 'empty cabin river'. The reason for so naming the river was apparently not recorded by Aubery or his contemporaries. Charles Gill (1886:5, 13–14), who pointed out these facts, made two suggestions: the Abenakis may have arrived at Saint Francis after the Iroquois massacre of the French colonists in 1691 when few inhabitants were left, or they named it for the condition of the village after the heavy mortality caused by a plague soon after 1700. A third possibility is that when the Abenakis emigrated from the Chaudière River in 1700 they may have called the Indian village already existing

263

on the Saint Francis River 'empty cabin village' because of the depredations in 1690 (not 1691), not on the French settlement at the mouth of the river but on the Indian settlement upriver. I like this better for two reasons. Since Arsikantegouk became the name of the Indian village, it was probably named for the condition of that village rather than that of the French village, and this particular attack by the Iroquois became fixed in Indian tradition at Saint Francis more firmly than any other event (Day 1976). [. . .]

In this paper, the Indian village will be called Odanak, except in quotations or paraphrases of other writers. It is the name the Indians have long used for the place and means simply 'at the village'. It became the official designation by the Bureau de Poste in 1916.

The beginnings of Odanak were not recorded, but according to Indian tradition it has been at or near its present location for over three centuries. Uncertainty and controversy have characterized all discussions of its origin.

In the Saint Francis Indians we have a group which probably was not at Odanak at the time of French exploration and settlement of the Saint Lawrence River and whose origins and movements in and out of Odanak have never been adequately explained. The view still current among New England historians is that of a mysterious tribe into which at one time or another the local New England tribes were said to have disappeared. Canadian historians have known only of the arrival of increments of Indian emigrants from unknown locations in New England and New York, usually identified only under broad and misleading group names. They came to be referred to as "Abenakis" but, since the whole purpose of this work is to attempt to identify the Indians of Odanak, the neutral term "Saint Francis Indians" will be used. Linguists and anthropologists have generally followed the historians and have been satisfied to present their data under the rubrics "Abenaki" or "Saint Francis Abenaki" without inquiring effectively into the ancestral identities of the various components of the tribe at Odanak. Linguistic and ethnographic data which cannot be assigned to a definite group at a definite time and place have at best very limited usefulness and at worst are a fruitful source of confusion and ill-founded theory.

It is particularly unfortunate that this should be the case of the Saint Francis Indians, because they are heirs to a significant history and cultural tradition. They originally occupied a territory which would be a blank on the linguistic and ethnographic maps of North America if mapmakers did not extend tribal and trait boundaries through a region for which they had only the slenderest information. Our ignorance of this region derives from the fact that it is an interior region which remained practically unknown to early English, French and Dutch observers. In addition to presenting us with a tantalizing gap in the record, this region has special significance. It was a transition zone between the Algonquian hunters of the boreal forest and the agricultural Algonquians of New York and

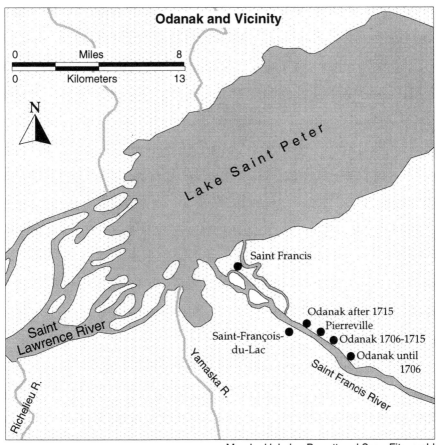

Map by Halvdan Barrett and Sean Fitzgerald

southern New England, so that one may suppose that its inhabitants represented a subsistence type of mixed hunting and agriculture for which we do not have enough information. They also formed an interface for contact phenomena between the Iroquois and the eastern Algonquians, and as such deserve study. They might serve, among other things, as a test of the conventional view that shared phenomena generally moved from the Iroquois to the Algonquians. The Saint Francis Indians played an important role in the history of New France, which has been partly misunderstood because of the prevailing ignorance about their background before their arrival at Saint Francis.

It has been generally agreed that Odanak was a refugee village and that more than one tribe contributed to its population. As the writer's ethnographic and linguistic data accumulated over the past 23 years, it became a matter of increasing urgency to identify the provenience and relative contributions of the several donor tribes in order that this data might take its proper place on an ethnographic map of eastern North America in the contact period, say 1600–1650. Reconstructing the culture of a refugee mission village without known antecedents would have much less value. [. . .]

Discussion

The identity of the Saint Francis Indians at different stages of their history should be of interest to historians who are concerned with the Indian and colonial wars, and it is essential information for ethnologists of the eastern woodlands.

This monograph brings together most of the available evidence bearing on this problem, but documents which would provide evidence on some crucial points have not been found. Although the historical record is incomplete, it nevertheless gives a different picture of the peopling of Odanak from that commonly presented in most historical and anthropological writings. The primary sources contradict a number of commonly held beliefs, which had their origins in secondary writings. They destroy the conventional view that Odanak was founded in 1700 by Eastern Abenakis from the Chaudière mission. It was really settled by Sokwakis about 1670 and received more than one addition of Sokwakis and some Loups and even a few Algonquins. The impact of the immigration from the Chaudière in 1700 has also been misunderstood. This migration contained all the Sokwakis and Loups in the Chaudière mission but only part of the Eastern Abenakis, the remainder withdrawing up the Chaudière River to be closer to their people in Maine. There were subsequent additions of Sokwakis, Abenakis, and Algonquins and, for a time, the whole Pigwacket tribe, from which a few probably remained at Odanak. The Norridgewocks took refuge at Odanak and Bécancour at least twice, and, although they departed, extensive intermarriage had taken place by 1750.

During the eighteenth century the tribes of northwestern New England and adjacent New York exhibited a high degree of mobility. Odanak appears to have been only one of several villages to which these Indians moved and at will moved out again. Norridgewocks, Amesacontees, Pigwackets, Penacooks, Sokwakis, and Missisquois still existed in their original locations in some numbers at this time, and movements between them and the refugee villages of Odanak, Bécancour, and Schaghticoke were commonplace. After 1730 the populations of Odanak and Missisquoi were probably more closely related to each other than formerly, because of mass movements in both directions. By this time the population of Missisquoi was heavily infiltrated by the same elements that largely made up Odanak—Sokwakis; Penacooks; and, more recently, Schaghticoke elements, which likewise included Sokwakis and Penacooks after 1685. Social and cultural interaction among these groups must have been considerable.

The northern New England Indians tended to be allies of the French, and the long series of colonial wars saw them execute a series of withdrawals to Canada in wartime followed by a series of return moves to reoccupy their old territories. Odanak and its feeder villages probably fluctuated in both absolute and relative size with a trend for the original feeder villages to decrease and for Odanak to increase. There is evidence for several more or less short-lived intermediate stations which ultimately disappeared as their populations removed to Odanak or, remaining in place, gradually disappeared as an Indian community by mingling with the white population. Individuals and families appear to have moved with considerable freedom between the feeder villages and the smaller, less well-known intermediate stations and between both these and Odanak. It may never be possible to trace all these movements because of inadequate records, but probably the main trends have now been detected.

Over the whole period of its existence Odanak suffered losses to war, disease and emigration, but there is no information which permits us to apportion these losses among the several tribal elements of the Odanak village, with the exception of the apparently final withdrawals of the Pigwackets and Norridgewocks.

Rogers's raid on the village in 1759 did not destroy the tribe, as has been commonly supposed, but it did disrupt it so severely that it was not fully reestablished until 1767 or 1768. Again, we can only guess at the proportions of the several tribal components which remained and returned, but reviewing the events of those troubled years makes it likely that a number of families present in 1759 were not present in 1768. A controversy brought into the record the presence of refugees from Odanak among the Saint Regis Iroquois, but it is possible that others joined the Algonquins of the Ottawa River, in whose territory they hunted in the winter of 1761–1762, and the tribes of Acadia, where they hunted for several winters after 1762. We can only speculate that most of these returned by 1800, when all the outlying bands and a few Algonquins had settled at Odanak. After 1775 all the Schaghticokes; all or nearly all of the Missisquois; nearly all of the Indians on the upper Connecticut, Androscoggin, and Sandy Rivers; and possibly some Norridgewocks made a final removal to Odanak, although Bécancour and the Penobscot River were probably more congenial for the Norridgewocks.

Most, perhaps all, of the tribal groups which came to live at Odanak at one time or another can be identified from the record. The record also gives us fair estimates of the total population from time to time but no more than hints of the proportions of the several tribes in the village at any one time. Nothing like a census by tribes exists for any stage of the village's history, and we are left to infer the proportional composition of Odanak as well as we can. The story told by the documents is incomplete, uncertain in spots, and sometimes even misleading. With these limitations understood, I propose the following reconstruction as the most probable one that can be reached from the records of tribal movements and losses.

The original Sokwaki village was strengthened by repeated increments of Sokwakis and the addition of some Penacooks and other Merrimack River peoples. A few Algonquins appear to have been included in the village around 1700. The net contribution of the Pigwackets was probably small. A sizeable number of Eastern Abenakis, probably mostly from the Kennebec, were added in 1700 by way of the Chaudière mission, and frequent contacts between 1722 and 1750 brought some Norridgewock blood into the village.

The composition of Schaghticoke presents a problem nearly as complex as that of Odanak, but we know it was originally and principally composed of Indians from the middle Connecticut River between Squakheag and Agawam. A little later, the Penacooks were referred to as relatives of the Schaghticokes and were in frequent communication with them. The Schaghticokes probably had contacts with the Canadian tribes soon after they settled on the Hudson River, and years of involved migrations finally brought all the Schaghticokes to Missisquoi and Odanak. Missisquoi itself may have been made up principally of Penacooks and Sokwakis, and most of them, together with the Schaghticokes whom they had taken in, removed to Odanak after 1775.

It is unclear whether the Indians of the upper Connecticut River, the Cowasucks, had lived at Odanak before their first recorded migration there in 1763. In any event, by 1800 all but a handful of them, together with the Indians remaining on the upper Androscoggin, had arrived at Odanak.

It appears that the nucleus of the Saint Francis Indians was always composed of Sokwakis and Penacooks, who were reinforced repeatedly during the eighteenth century. Three other tribes or groups were added to make the "complete" village of 1800. These were some Eastern Abenakis by way of the Chaudière and later from Norridgewock, the upper Connecticut and Androscoggin River Indians, and the tribes from the middle Connecticut River by way of Schaghticoke. Closer study of the fates of certain New England tribes, such as the Nipmucks and Piscataqua, might tell us more about their contributions to the early population, but they appear to have been minor elements, who themselves were absorbed by other tribes and went to Canada with them.

It is possible that a number of the groups which were named as tribes were actually so closely related that tribal distinctions would be unnecessary if we but knew the relationships. Alliances and cooperation were apparent between the Penacooks, Sokwakis, and Cowasucks; between the Sokwakis, Penacooks, and

Pocumtucks; between the Pocumtucks and the tribes farther down the Connecticut River; between the Sokwakis, Pocumtucks, and Mahicans; and between the Penacooks, Winnipesaukees, and Pigwackets. Alliances and cooperation in war need not be indicative of close cultural or linguistic relationships, but they do suggest it. There is, moreover, some evidence for genuine kinship shared by the Sokwakis, Cowasucks, and Penacooks.

Vague tribal nomenclature has confused these relationships. The historical literature abounds in overlapping, duplicating, and inconsistent nomenclature. All of the tribes in western Maine, New Hampshire, Vermont, and Massachusetts, the region from which Odanak drew most of its population, were at one time or another referred to by French writers as "Loups," forcing the student to deduce, and sometimes to speculate about, the identity of a particular group of Loups from the context. Somewhat later, French usage extended the name "Abenaki" to cover descendents of the same tribes. Because of a common head chief, the Wamesits and other groups on the lower Merrimack River came to share the name "Penacook," which properly belonged only to those living at Penacook.

Family names found at Odanak provide additional clues to the composition of the village. They do this by virtue of the language of the name or by a recorded association of the name with an earlier place of residence. However, there does not seem to exist anything like a complete list of families in the village for the time which would be most useful, namely, about 1800. The registers of the mission prior to 1848 have disappeared, and the earliest census I have found is for the year 1829. Nevertheless, the occurrence of certain names in older documents establishes the presence of certain families in the village in the eighteenth century. Some useful conclusions can be drawn from a roster of veterans of the War of 1812, since according to local tradition all the warriors, which is to say all able-bodied males 14 years of age or more, went to this war. The roster is not a full listing of all who served in the war—only of those veterans who had heirs in the village in 1844—but it is useful nevertheless.

Some family names point quite clearly to origins at Missisquoi and Schaghticoke and on the Connecticut, Androscoggin, and Kennebec Rivers. Others can be identified as the names of white prisoners, Algonquins, and Maliseets. The relative representation as determined from the names corresponds rather well with the indications of the history of tribal movements. Sixty percent of those names for which a plausible origin can be determined appear to be of Western Abenaki origin, from either the language of the name or the place of origin. Twelve percent are thought to be of Eastern Abenaki origin; 13 percent are from non-Abenaki Indians; and 15 percent are from whites. Thus, the names prove to be helpful by confirming what the record of tribal movements predicted, and they permit the tribe to be largely reconstructed after 1829 and followed until the present time, overlapping and connecting with the genealogies of twentieth-century members of the tribe.

The following chronology gives what appear to be the most significant events in the peopling of Odanak.

Date	Tribal Composition
1670	Sokwakis at Odanak
1676	More Sokwakis arrive
1684–1697	Substantial losses by war, disease, and emigration
1692	Population nadir: 25 persons
ca. 1695	More Sokwakis arrive, plus Loups and Algonquins
1700	Abenakis arrive with more Sokwakis and Loups
1702	More Sokwakis, Abenakis, and Algonquins added
1707	Entire Pigwacket tribe arrives; population peaks at about 1,100
1714	Nearly all Pigwackets leave
1723	Schaghticoke immigration has begun by this date, i.e., central New England tribes, Sokwakis, and Penacooks
1730	Entire Missisquoi tribe added for a few years
1738	By this date Missisquois have departed
1749	Population peaks at about 1,000
1752	Population perhaps about 920
1754	Last of Schaghticokes arrive
1759	Important losses by war and partial dispersal
1768	Village reestablished; population about 400
1778	Odanak plus Cowas about 1,100 persons
1798	By this date most of the Missisquois have arrived, including Sokwakis, Penacooks, and Schaghticokes; also some 700 Indians have arrived from the region between Lake Memphremagog and Lake Umbagog, that is, Cowasucks, Penacooks, and Androscoggins; population about 1,100
1805	17 families are granted land in Durham; emigration out
1821	Population 360, plus about 150 at Durham
1830s	Cholera epidemic
1830–1832	First numerical census: population 383

This information has relevance for historians of the period and as background for ethnologists, but it is not sufficiently detailed for a culture history.

The cultural identity of the Saint Francis Indians has special significance, because they are practically the only source of information on the cultures of the refugee tribes that composed them. By the time students began to study their homeland, no communities remained in it. Data on the culture of the several contributing tribes while still in place are largely restricted to incidental, usually very sketchy, observations by historians, plus archeological information which is beginning to accumulate. For example, nothing like a reasonably full ethnographic description of Penacook culture exists. What remains of it must be looked for among the Saint Francis Indians, but even by the time Joseph Maurault set down his first limited observations, all elements of the population had been in, or associated with, Odanak for over 50 years. The question arises, How distinct were the cultural boundaries even at that date? To retrieve Penacook traits, for example, it would be necessary first to separate Penacook traits from the total of Saint Francis data.

There remains the problem of determining the relative contribution of each tribe to the data collected by anthropologists from the Saint Francis Indians in this century. When I wrote earlier of the need to identify the Saint Francis Indians in order to place their traits on an ethnographic map, I seemed to imply a temporally constant homogeneity. This was not intended, because the heterogeneity of the Odanak population is well known, and some cultural change over time should be taken for granted. In terms of family names alone, the composition of the tribe in 1812 was different from that of 1900, which was still different from that of 1960, and the tribe of 1960 is the one from which most of the ethnographic data were obtained. Family names alone are only a partial indicator of tribal representations and the traditions they may have handed down. Ideally, one would like to trace the ethnologist's informants backward genealogically, identifying the important modifying influences on their ancestors, that is, the predominating influence of one parent, grandparent, or foster parent on their speech and other cultural traditions (e.g., mythology, oral tradition, technology, hunting practices, and medicine). When the genealogy is traced it is seen that a single informant's heredity includes not only the expected number of ancestors increasing backwards in geometric progression, but apparently several tribal ancestries as well.

A theoretical distinction may be made between the actual culture of the tribe in the 1800s and that which appears in the notes of twentieth-century ethnologists taken from informants whose parents and grandparents lived at that time. Circumstances required that the ethnologists' work be limited to a selected fraction of the tribe. No informant could transmit a full account of a culture, and it is likely that altogether they did not transmit a cross section of the culture of their grandparents' time. This distinction may be only theoretical, however, because each informant's ancestors represent several families, and together they could represent most of the earlier population.

In any attempt to work out the culture or cultures that dominated at Odanak, one is confronted with the whole problem of cultures in contact—tendencies toward persistence, loss or modification, dominance and subordination. No formulas have been worked out for these phenomena. Anthropologists are still studying them case by case. Lacking rules for these processes, recourse must be had to a purely pragmatic approach.

If we had full information on the cultures of the tribes that contributed to the Odanak population, the obvious procedure would be to compare the culture at Odanak item by item with that of each of the contributing cultures, thus documenting in detail the relative influence of each tribal component on the culture of the Saint Francis Indians. Since relatively little is known about the original cultural inventories of the contributing tribes, one would have to fall back on determining as well as one could the identities of the immigrant groups and assigning to each the very partial inventory of their cultural baggage that is known. This is not an effective procedure. Too little is known about each tribe for comparative purposes and, as one might expect, the more obvious characteristics that received mention by seventeenth-century observers were in large part shared by several of the tribes.

This much was so apparent at the beginning of my fieldwork that I early conceived a reverse plan for fixing cultural traits by projecting twentieth-century data from specific informants back to the place of origins of their respective ancestors. The inadequacy of the genealogical data so far seen has caused this plan to be laid aside also, although I still hope that the family dialects at least can be traced to their seventeenth-century origins.

Two salient facts form the background of the problem: the village had mixed origins, but in the twentieth century it apparently had but one language and culture. This uniformity must be assumed to be the result either of an original uniformity among all or most of the contributors of the mixed group or of the evolution of a new culture from the ingredients of the mixture, probably with the dominance of one of the ingredients. Culture convergence in a mixed community may take many routes, and what actually took place at Odanak to bring about the twentieth-century uniformity is unknown. If all the contributing tribes were culturally distinct, our prospects for disentangling the confusion would be small unless the culture of the Eastern Abenakis, which is rather well documented, prevailed, and this does not seem to be the case. If, on the other hand, most of the contributors to the village, whom we know with few exceptions by distinct names or the names of their villages, shared the same culture, the solution would be much simpler. This possibility is not unlikely and should be examined.

Since language is an item of culture as well as the principal medium for transmitting other elements of culture, it could be regarded as the most profitable single criterion available to us for examining this possibility. There happens to be more information on the language than on other elements of culture. Obviously, it cannot be assumed that other cultural traits will change as language changes, since the forces for change operating on different traits are not identical. Nevertheless, language can at least be taken as a tentative indicator of what happened at Odanak.

All available indications are that the Saint Francis Indians have spoken the same language since at least 1800. The chief showpiece in this argument is the work of Pial Pol Wzôkhilain, which consists of four books published between 1830 and 1845. Wzôkhilain was born in 1800, and it may be presumed that he was writing in the language he learned from his parents, who lived in the previous century. These books are perfectly intelligible to Saint Francis Indians today. It would be possible to argue that Wzôkhilain spoke only one of several languages at Odanak in 1800, the one which just happened to predominate. Although this is theoretically possible, one would then have to admit the coincidence that this language, preserved by chance in written forms, was the one which was universally used in midcentury. Additional evidence for linguistic homogeneity in the nineteenth century are cases like that of Mitchell Sabattis, whose father, born before 1800, was an Abenaki from Saint Regis. Sabattis's language as recorded by John Dyneley Prince before 1900 was, nevertheless, identical with that now spoken at Odanak. My interrogation of informants about the origins of variant speech characteristics led to ancestors living in the first part of the eighteenth century, who spoke in the identical manner. The Missisquoi chief, Gray Lock, was allegedly from Woronoco, but his descendants, bearing the name Wawanolet, speak a standard Western Abenaki.

It seems probable that homogeneity had already been achieved by 1800. And once the community had become essentially uniform in speech, individual Maliseets, Bécancour Abenakis, Algonquins, and French would perforce adapt to the dominant culture in a generation or two, as a result of social pressures as well as intermarriage. That this was actually the case is demonstrated by informants who descended from foreign ancestors, such as the Maliseet Joachim Denis, the Algonquin Ursule Wawa, and the French Toussaint Masta. Their speech is quite like that of the rest of Odanak.

Questions remain. How long had linguistic uniformity existed? Which language was it that became the language of the tribe? It has sometimes been assumed that the current speech at Odanak is a direct descendent of that found in the early eighteenth-century dictionaries of Aubery, LeSueur, and Nudénans (Nudénans 1760; J. Maurault 1866:37 fn. 2, passim; Gill 1886:12; Hallowell 1928:101–102). The presence of *r* in these dictionaries where modern speech has *l* has been noted but attributed to change over time. The attention of linguists, however, has produced an awareness that the speech at Odanak is significantly different from that of the old dictionaries and from modern Penobscot, which is much closer to the language preserved by the old dictionaries. These differences are found in the phonology, grammar, and lexicon, and their sum justifies regarding it as a separate language or very different dialect, depending on how one defines these imprecise labels (Goddard 1970; Siebert, personal communications, 1965, 1966; Teeter 1973:1145). It is now customary to name the speech at Odanak Western Abenaki to distinguish it from the dialects of the Eastern Abenakis in Maine. The current practice of calling the Saint Francis Indians Abenakis is therefore correct linguistically. It becomes misleading only if one assumes that all Abenakis came from Maine.

The first missionaries at Odanak had spent their Abenaki apprenticeship in "Acadia," where *r*-dialects of Eastern Abenaki prevailed, and it was natural for them to continue writing at Odanak the language they were familiar with, especially since in the first years after 1700 Eastern Abenakis formed a substantial part of the population of Odanak. The missionaries' orthography outlived the Eastern Abenaki language at Odanak, even in the writings of literate Indians. For example, Pial Pol signed his name Osunkhirhine but wrote it Wzôkhilain in his books. The Wôlinas family came from an *l*-language area on the middle Connecticut River and was recorded in 1735 as Wollenus and Wallenas (Wright 1905:124, 128, 129, 130, 132). Orthographic habit at Odanak changed it to Warinan until local spelling caught up with the spoken language when it came to be written Wanlinas. This persistence of *r* could be taken as evidence for the continuing dominance of Eastern Abenaki, but no support for this can be found in the history of tribal migrations or the family names. It seems safe to assume that some 200 Eastern Abenakis arrived from the Chaudière River in 1700 and that until 1728 these, plus the recurring visits of the kindred Norridgewocks, constituted a substantial Eastern Abenaki influence on the culture of a predominantly Sokwaki-Penacook village. About this time, however, important numbers of Schaghticokes and Missisquoi Indians began to arrive. This must have tended to dilute the Eastern Abenaki influence, and all subsequent important immigrations would strengthen the influence of Western Abenaki elements.

Hence it does not appear that homogeneity always prevailed, but it is possible that most of the arrivals at Odanak after 1728 spoke Western Abenaki dialects. The prevailing cultures of the Schaghticokes and the Androscoggin River Indians at the times of their arrival at Odanak are uncertain. The original population of Schaghticoke came from villages of uncertain linguistic associations, and the boundary between Eastern and Western Abenaki is not known with certainty. Siebert (1980:114) places it west of the Saco River and thus includes the Androscoggin valley in the Eastern Abenaki region. But even if the aboriginal language on the Androscoggin River was Eastern Abenaki, the late arrivals from there probably contained some Penacook and Cowasuck descendants from Penacook residence on the river in the seventeenth century and from eighteenth-century association in the headwaters country.

Tribal movements show that more or less related Algonquian languages were in contact at least by 1676 at Sillery, the Chaudière River, Norridgewock, the Androscoggin River, Penacook, and especially Schaghticoke and Missisquoi, so the stage was set for the beginning of change in what became the feeder villages for Odanak. If, as seems likely, the Sokwaki, Cowasuck, and Penacook were Western Abenaki in speech, their presence at Schaghticoke, Missisquoi, and the upper Connecticut River locations, which furnished the last and largest contingents into Odanak, points to the prevalence of Western Abenaki in these contingents before they arrived at Odanak just before 1800. In other words, it was almost inevitable that some convergence of speech would have taken place in more than a century of contact, and we need not try to explain the nineteenth-century uniformity as having all developed at Odanak.

It does seem likely that most of the population of Odanak from its beginning spoke Western Abenaki dialects, but the proposal just sketched is only the simplest solution for the nineteenth-century homogeneity. It is to some degree speculation, being derived indirectly from historical relations and movement, whereas the early linguistic data which would establish or disprove it beyond doubt are missing. Exhaustive study of the data which do exist should clarify the picture considerably, even though data of indisputable provenience in central New England are scarce indeed. Until this is done, the most likely conclusion about the linguistic history of Odanak is that linguistic homogeneity was probably achieved about 1800, and we may use this with caution as a clue to the situation respecting other cultural elements.

The perseverance of four slightly different variants of the same language at Odanak points to the probable existence of at least four different dialects at an earlier time. It will take further study to determine their most probable provenience.

Although we should not expect that all cultural traits should always and everywhere change hand in hand with language changes, it is reasonable to expect that the language and culture of a group which is greatly superior numerically will predominate in the main. There are repeated indications in history that the Sokwakis, Penacooks, and Cowasucks were related, and the prominence of these tribes at Odanak is evident in the record. Their representation there becomes all the more striking when we note the presence of Sokwakis and Penacooks among the Schaghticokes and Missisquois, the presence of Penacooks among the Androscoggins, and the numerical prominence of the Cowasucks among the latest arrivals at Odanak.

The numerical predominance of the Sokwakis, Penacooks, and Cowasucks together with the linguistic uniformity which had developed by the nineteenth century point to these three groups as the most probable source of the language and culture which has been described in this century.

Conclusion

The village of Odanak, or Arsikantegouk, on the Saint Francis River was settled by Sokwakis about 1670. The original Sokwaki village was strengthened by repeated increments of Sokwakis and some Penacooks. In 1700 it received all the Sokwakis and Penacooks from the mission on the Chaudière River and some of the Eastern Abenakis. There were subsequent additions of Sokwakis, Abenakis, a few Algonquins, and the whole Pigwacket tribe, which arrived in 1707 and left in 1714. The Norridgewocks took refuge there twice but returned to the Kennebec River. Between 1696 and 1754, the entire population of the refugee village of Schaghticoke on the Hudson River moved to Odanak, some directly and some after a stopover at Missisquoi.

Rogers's raid in 1759 did not destroy the tribe, as has been commonly supposed, but it did disrupt the village severely until 1767 or 1768. By 1800 practically all of the Indians originally living in Vermont, New Hampshire, western Maine, and the Connecticut valley in Massachusetts, excepting the Pigwackets, had moved to Odanak. The newer arrivals, who were Cowasucks, Penacooks, Androscoggins, and Missisquois, considerably outnumbered the residents already there.

A study of the families found in the village after 1800 points to a predominance of Western Abenaki origins and so tends to confirm the conclusion drawn from the history of the migrations. The indications are that Western Abenaki has been the language of Odanak since at least 1800. This is not unexpected, since the population appears to have been dominated from the beginning by Sokwakis and Penacooks, and the late additions from Missisquoi, Schaghticoke, and the Memphremagog-Umbagog region contained additional Sokwakis, Penacooks, and Cowasucks.

The simplest explanation for the dominance of one language is numerical superiority of one group of speakers, and the historical indications of the numerical predominance of the related Sokwakis, Penacooks, and Cowasucks does point to these tribes as the most likely source of the Western Abenaki language currently spoken at Odanak.

One cannot assume that the factors which produce uniformity of language in a mixed community will operate identically on all other cultural traits. One would expect certain cultural traits of the less numerous groups to persist for one reason or another. Nevertheless, one would ordinarily expect the greater part of the culture of the numerically superior group to prevail.

Therefore, the most probable conclusion from the information we have is that the language and culture of the Saint Francis Indians are essentially those of the related Sokwakis, Penacooks, and Cowasucks. It is reasonable, however, to expect the persistence of some traits from the Androscoggin River, which may or may not have been significantly different, and from the middle Connecticut River in Massachusetts, which probably was in a different culture area.

Works Cited in Day's Papers

Adams, J. T.
  1935   *The Epic of America.* Boston: Little, Brown.
Alger, Abby L.
  1894   The Creation. A Penobscot Indian Myth Told by One of the Tribe to Abby L. Alger. *The Popular Science Monthly* 44(December):195–196.
  1897   *In Indian Tents: Stories Told by Penobscot, Passamaquoddy and Micmac Indians.* Boston: Roberts Brothers.
Allen, Ira
  1798   *The Natural and Political History of the State of Vermont.* London: Printed by J. S. Myers, sold by W. West.
"An American"
  1939   *American Husbandry* [1775]. H. J. Carman, ed. New York: Columbia University Press.
André, Louis
  1688–   Préceptes, phrases, et mots de la langue algonquine outaouaise pour un missionnaire
  1715   nouveau. (Manuscript in Jesuit Archives, Montreal.)
Anonymous
  1661   Dictionnaire algonquin. (Manuscript in the Archives of Notre-Dame de Montréal.)
  1662   Racines de la langue ŏtăŏise et algonquine. (Manuscript in the Archives of Notre-Dame de Montréal.)
  1680   *Carte d'une grande partie du Canada.* H11/902–1680. Map Division, Public Archives of Canada, Ottawa.
  1713   *Carte du Canada avec partie des côtes de la N(ouv)elle Angleterre et de l'Acadie.* H2/900–1713. Map Division, Public Archives of Canada, Ottawa.
  1906a   A Shorte and Briefe Narration (Cartier's Second Voyage, 1535–1536) [1600]. In *Early English and French Voyages, Chiefly Out of Hakluyt, 1534–1608,* edited by Henry S. Burrage, 33–88. Original Narratives of Early American History. New York: Charles Scribner's Sons.
  1906b   Relation of a Voyage to Sagadahoc, 1607–1608. In *Early English and French Voyages, Chiefly Out of Hakluyt, 1534–1608,* edited by Henry S. Burrage, 395–419. Original Narratives of Early American History. New York: Charles Scribner's Sons.
  1906c   A Relation or Journall of a Plantation settled at Plimouth in New England and proceedings thereof [1625]. In *Hakluytus Posthumus or Purchas, His Pilgrimes,* 19:312–343. Glasgow: J. MacLehose and Sons.
  1909a   Narrative of a Journey into the Mohawk and Oneida Country, 1634–1635. In *Narratives of New Netherland, 1609–1664,* edited by J. Franklin Jameson, 135–162. Original Narratives of Early American History. New York: Charles Scribner's Sons.
  1909b   Journal of New Netherland, 1647. In *Narratives of New Netherland, 1609–1664,* edited by J. Franklin Jameson, 265–284. Original Narratives of Early American History. New York: Charles Scribner's Sons.

1909c The Representation of New Netherland, 1650. In *Narratives of New Netherland, 1609–1664,* edited by J. Franklin Jameson, 285–354. Original Narratives of Early American History. New York: Charles Scribner's Sons.

1929 *Ernest Thompson Seton. A Biographical Sketch Done by Various Hands, to Which is Attached a Complete Bibliography of the Works of This Author.* New York: Doubleday, Page.

1931 Mémoire sur les forts de la Nouvelle-France. *Bulletin des recherches historiques* 37(1): 408–426.

n.d. Registres de Notre-Dame. (Manuscript in the Archives of Notre-Dame de Montréal.)

Archer, Gabriel
1843 The Relation of Captain Gosnold's Voyage. *Collections of the Massachusetts Historical Society,* 3d ser., 8:72–81.

Arnaud, Charles
1880 Mission montagnais du Lac St-Jean. *Annales de la propagation de la foi pour la province de Québec* 11:145–154.

Ashburn, Percy Moreau
1947 *The Ranks of Death.* New York: Coward-McCann.

Ashe, Thomas
1808 *Travels in America Performed in 1806.* London: William Sawyer.

[Aubery, Joseph]
1715a [Dictionnaire abnaquis-françois.] (Manuscript in the Société historique d'Odanak [Pierreville], Quebec.)

1715b Dictionnaire françois-abnaquis. (Manuscript in the Société historique d'Odanak [Pierreville], Quebec.)

1715c *Carte pour les hauteurs de terre. . . .* H3/900–1715. Map Division, Public Archives of Canada, Ottawa.

Bacqueville de la Potherie, Claude C. Le Roy
1753 *Histoire de l'Amérique septentrionale [1722].* 4 vols. Paris: Nyon.

Bailey, Alfred C.
1933 The Significance of the Identity and Disappearance of the Laurentian Iroquois. *Transactions of the Royal Society of Canada,* 3d ser., 27(2):97–108.

Bakeless, John Edwin
1950 *The Eyes of Discovery: The Pageant of North America as Seen by the First Explorers.* Philadelphia: J. B. Lippincott.

Baker, Frederick Storrs
1950 *Principles of Silviculture.* New York: McGraw-Hill.

Ballard, Rev. Edward
1866 Indian Mode of Applying Names. *Collections of the New Hampshire Historical Society* 8:446–452.

Bancroft, George
1885 *History of the United States of America.* New York: D. Appleton.

Barney, George
1882 The History of the Town of Swanton, in Franklin County. In *The Vermont Historical Gazetteer,* edited by Abby M. Hemenway, 4:989–1144. Burlington, Vt.

Baxter, James Phinney
1893 *Christopher Levett, of York, the Pioneer Colonist in Casco Bay.* Portland, Maine: Printed for the Gorges Society.

Bear, Firman Edward
1951 Soil Scientist Tells What Has Happened to Our Soil. *New Jersey Agriculture* 33(4):4.

Beauchamp, William M.
1892 *The Iroquois Trail, or Foot-prints of the Six Nations, in Customs, Traditions, and History, in Which Are Included David Cusick's Sketches of Ancient History of the Six Nations.* Fayetteville, N.C.: H. C. Beauchamp.

1893   *Indian Names in New York With a Selection from Other States. . . .* Fayetteville, N.C.: H. C. Beauchamp.

1905   *A History of the New York Iroquois, Now Commonly Called the Six Nations.* New York State Museum Bulletin 78. Albany, N.Y.

1907   *Aboriginal Place Names of New York.* New York State Museum Bulletin 108, Archaeology 12. Albany, N.Y.

Beck, Horace P.

1966   *Gluskap the Liar and Other Indian Tales.* Freeport, Maine: Wheelwright.

Bell, Robert E.

1951   Archaeology and Anthropology, 1950. *American Scientist* 32(2):289–294.

Bergeron, Arthur

1960   *Pierreville 1853–1953: Un siècle de vie paroissiale.* Pierreville, Quebec: Comité du centenaire.

Bigelow, Timothy

1876   *Journal of a Tour to Niagara Falls in the Year 1805.* Boston: J. Wilson.

Biggar, Henry P., ed.

1922–   *The Works of Samuel de Champlain.* 6 vols. Toronto: The Champlain Society.
1936

Biggs, W.

1893   Drake's Great Armada [1600]. In *Voyages of Elizabethian Seamen,* edited by E. J. Payne, 230–272. Oxford: Oxford University Press.

Blair, Emma H., ed.

1911–   *The Indian Tribes of the Upper Mississippi Valley and Region of the Great Lakes, as De-*
1912   *scribed by Nicolas Perrot, French Commandant in the Northwest; Bacqueville de la Potherie, French Royal Commissioner to Canada; Morrell Marston, American Army Officer; and Thomas Forsyth, United States Agent at Fort Armstrong.* 2 vols. Cleveland: Arthur H. Clark.

Blane, William Newnham

1918   A Tour of Southern Illinois in 1822. In *Pictures of Illinois One Hundred Years Ago,* edited by M. M. Quaife, 39–81. Chicago: R. R. Donnelley.

Bloomfield, Leonard

1925   On the Sound System of Central Algonquian. *Language* 1(4):130–156.

1946   Algonquian. In *Linguistic Structures of Native America,* edited by Harry Hoijer, 85–129. Viking Fund Publications in Anthropology 6. New York.

Bois, Louis-Édouard, ed.

1883–   *Collection de manuscrits contenant lettres, mémoires, et autres documents historiques relatifs*
1885   *à la Nouvelle-France,* 4 vols. Quebec: A. Coté.

Bolton, Reginald P.

1930a   Indian Remains in Vermont. *Indian Notes* 7(1):57–69.

1930b   An Aboriginal Chert Quarry in Northern Vermont. *Indian Notes* 7(4):457–465.

Bougainville, Louis-Antoine de

1924a   Mémoire sur l'état de la Nouvelle-France [1757]. In *Rapport de l'Archiviste de la province de Québec, 1923–1924,* 42–70. Quebec: Imprimeur du Roi.

1924b   Le journal de M. de Bougainville. In *Rapport de l'Archiviste de la province de Québec, 1923–1924,* 202–393. Quebec: Imprimeur du Roi.

Bouton, Nathaniel

1856   *The History of Concord, from its First Grant in 1725, to the Organization of the City Government in 1853, with a History of the Ancient Penacooks, ...* Concord, N.H.: B. W. Sandborn.

Boynton, Eben Moody

1898   Introduction to *New Englands Prospect* [1634], by William Wood. Boston: Published by the author.

Boy Scouts of America
    1959   *Indian Lore.* New Brunswick, N.J.: Boy Scouts of America.
Bradford, William
    1908   *Bradford's History of Plymouth Plantation, 1606–1646,* edited by William T. Davis.
            Original Narratives of Early American History. New York: Charles Scribner's Sons.
Brant-Sero, John O.
    1901   Dekanawideh: The Law-giver of the Caniengahakas. *Man* 1(134)166–170.
Braun, Emma L.
    1950   *The Deciduous Forests of Eastern North America.* Philadelphia: Blakiston.
Brereton, John
    1843   A Brief and True Relation of the Discovery of the North Part of Virginia. *Collections of
            the Massachusetts Historical Society,* 3d ser., 8:83–94.
    1906   A Briefe and True Relation of the Discoverie of the North Part of Virginia ... Made this
            Present Yeere 1602. In *Early English and French Voyages, Chiefly from Hakluyt, 1534–
            1608,* edited by Henry S. Burrage, 325–340. Original Narratives of Early American
            History. New York: Charles Scribner's Sons.
Brinton, Daniel G., ed.
    1885a   *The Lenâpé and Their Legends; with Complete Text and Symbols of the Walam Olum, a
            New Translation, and an Inquiry into its Authenticity.* Library of Aboriginal American
            Literature 5. Philadelphia: D. G. Brinton.
    1885b   The Chief God of the Algonkins, in His Character as a Cheat and a Liar. *American
            Antiquarian and Oriental Journal* 7(1):137–139.
Brinton, Daniel G., and Albert Anthony, eds.
    1888   *A Lenâpé-English Dictionary.* Philadelphia: Historical Society of Pennsylvania.
Bromley, Stanley Willard
    1935   The Original Forest Types of Southern New England. *Ecological Monographs* 5:61–89.
    1945   An Indian Relic Area. *Scientific Monthly* 60 (April):153–154.
Brown, Raymond H.
    1943   *Mirror for Americans.* New York: American Geographic Society.
Brown, Mrs. W. Wallace
    1890   Wa-ba-ba-nal, or Northern Lights. *Journal of American Folk-Lore* 3(10):213–214.
Browne, George Waldo
    1906   The Merrimack River: Story of Its First Survey. *Granite State Magazine* 1:133–140.
Budd, Thomas
    1865   *Good order established in Pennsilvania & New-Jersey in America* [1685]. E. Armstrong,
            ed. New York: William Gowan.
Burnaby, Andrew
    1904   *Travels Through the Middle Settlements in North America in the Years 1759 and 1760*
            [1775]. London: A. Wassels.
Byers, Douglas S.
    1946   The Environment of the Northeast. In *Man in Northeastern North America,* edited by
            Frederick Johnson, 3–32. Papers of the Robert S. Peabody Foundation for Archaeology
            3. Andover, Mass.
Canada. Department of Indian Affairs and Northern Development. Indian Affairs Branch
    1967   *Linguistic and Cultural Affiliations of Canadian Indian Bands.* Ottawa: Queen's Printer.
Canada. Dominion Forest Service
    1949   *Native Trees of Canada.* Dominion Forest Service Bulletin 61. Ottawa.
Carrière, Gaston
    1958   *Le Roi de Betsiamites: Le Père Charles Arnaud, O.M.I. (1826–1914).* Ottawa: University
            of Ottawa Press.
Cartier, Jacques
    1906   The first relation of Jacques Carthier of S. Malo, of the new land called New France,
            newly discovered in the yere of our lord 1534 [1580]. In *Early English and French*

Voyages, Chiefly Out of Hakluyt, 1534–1608, edited by Henry S. Burrage, 1–31. Original Narratives of Early American History. New York: Charles Scribner's Sons.

Carver, Jonathan
  1796 *Three Years Travels Through the Interior Parts of North America.* Philadelphia: Key and Simpson.

Chamberlain, Alexander F.
  1891 Nanibozhu Amongst the Otchipwe, Mississagas, and Other Algonkian Tribes. *Journal of American Folk-Lore* 4(14):193–213.

Champlain, Samuel de
  1922– *The Works of Samuel de Champlain* [1626]. Henry P. Biggar, ed. 6 vols. Toronto: The
  1936   Champlain Society.

Chapman, Frank M.
  1901 *Handbook of Birds of Eastern North America.* New York: D. Appleton.

Charland, Thomas-Marie
  1942 *Histoire de Saint-François-du-Lac.* Ottawa: Collège Dominicain.
  1961 Un village d'abénaquis sur la rivière Missisquoi. *Revue d'histoire de l'Amérique française* 15(3):319–332.
  1964 *Histoire des Abénakis d'Odanak (1675–1937).* Montreal: Éditions de Lévrier.

Charlevoix, Pierre F. X. de
  1866– *History and General Description of New France* [1744]. John G. Shea, ed. 6 vols. New
  1872   York: John G. Shea.

[Chauvinerie, Maray de la]
  1928 Dénombrement des nations sauvages qui ont rapport au gouvernement de Canada; des guerriers de chaque nation avec les armoiries, 1736 [1726]. *Bulletin des recherches historiques* 34:541–551.

Coffin, Charles C.
  1878 *The History of Boscawen and Webster, from 1733 to 1878.* Concord, N.H.: Printed by the Republican Press Association.

Colby, William George
  1941 *Pasture Culture in Massachusetts.* Massachusetts Agriculture Experimental Station Bulletin 380. Amherst, Mass.: Massachusetts State College.

Colden, Cadwallader
  1902 *The History of the Five Indian Nations of Canada.* 2 vols. New York: New Amsterdam Book Co.

Cook, Frederick
  1887 *Journals of the Military Expedition of Major General John Sullivan Against the Six Nations of Indians in 1779.* Auburn, N.Y.: Knapp, Peck, and Thompson.

Coolidge, Austin Jacobs, and John Brainard Mansfield
  1859 *A History and Description of New England, General and Local.* Boston: Published by A. J. Coolidge.

Cooper, John M.
  1939 Is the Algonquian Family Hunting Ground System Pre-Columbian? *American Anthropologist* 41(1):66–90.
  1945 Tête-de-Boule Cree. *International Journal of American Linguistics* 11(1):36–44.
  1946 The Culture of the Northeastern Indian Hunters: A Reconstructive Interpretation. In *Man in Northeastern North America,* edited by Frederick Johnson, 272–305. Papers of the Robert S. Peabody Foundation for Archaeology 3. Andover, Mass.

Cotton, Josiah
  1830 Vocabulary of the Massachusetts (or Natick) Indian Language. *Collections of the Massachusetts Historical Society,* 3d ser., 2:147–259.

Count, Earl W.
  1952 The Earth-Diver and the Rival Twins: A Clue to Time Correlation in North-Eurasiatic and North American Mythology. In *Indian Tribes of Aboriginal North America,* edited by

Sol Tax, 55–62. Selected Papers of the 29th International Congress of Americanists. Chicago: University of Chicago Press.

Crawford, John G.

1898   Indians of New Hampshire: Etymology of their Language. *Collections of the Manchester (New Hampshire) Historical Association* 1(pt. 2):177–188.

Crespieul, François de

1676   Prières en algonkin, montagnaix, abanaki, aesquimaux. (Manuscript in the Archbishopric of Quebec.)

Crockett, Walter H.

1921   *Vermont: The Green Mountain State.* 4 vols. New York: The Century History Company.

Cross, Dorothy

1941–   *Archaeology of New Jersey.* 2 vols. Trenton: Archaeological Society of New Jersey and
1956   New Jersey State Museum.

Cuoq, Jean-André

1870   *Jugement erroné de M. Ernest Renan sur les langues sauvages, par l'auteur des Études philologiques.* Montreal: Dawson Brothers.

1882   *Lexique de la langue iroquoise avec notes et appendices.* Montreal: J. Chapleau.

1886   *Lexique de la langue algonquine.* Montreal: J. Chapleau.

1894   Anotc Kekon. *Proceedings and Transactions of the Royal Society of Canada for the Year 1893,* Vol. 11(1):137–179. Toronto.

1898   Les missions de St-Sulpice. (Manuscript in the Archives of Notre-Dame de Montréal.)

Dalla Torre, Karl Wilhelm von, and Hermann Harms

1900–   *Genera Siphonogamarum ad Systema Englerianum Conscripta.* Leipzig: Gulielmo En-
1907   gelmann.

Daubenmire, Rexford F.

1947   *Plants and Environment.* New York: John Wiley.

Day, Catherine M.

1869   *History of the Eastern Townships.* Montreal: J. Lovell.

Day, Gordon M.

1956–   [Ethnographic and Linguistic Notes from Fieldwork Among the Saint Francis Abe-
1979   naki.] (Manuscript in Gordon M. Day's papers.)

1953   The Indian as an Ecological Factor in the Northeastern Forest. *Ecology* 34(2):329–346.

1961   A Bibliography of the Saint Francis Dialect. *International Journal of American Linguistics* 27(1):80–85.

1962a   Rogers' Raid in Indian Tradition. *Historical New Hampshire* 17(June):3–17.

1962b   English-Indian Contacts in New England. *Ethnohistory* 9(1):24–40.

1962c   Unpublished Saint Francis Abenaki fieldnotes. (Manuscript in Gordon M. Day's papers.)

1964   A St. Francis Abenaki Vocabulary. *International Journal of American Linguistics* 30(4): 371–392.

1965   The Indian Occupation of Vermont. *Vermont History* 33(3):365–374.

1967a   An Agawam Fragment. *International Journal of American Linguistics* 33(3):244–247.

1967b   Historical Notes on New England Languages. In *Contributions to Anthropology: Linguistics I (Algonquian),* edited by A. D. DeBlois, 107–112. Anthropological Series 78, National Museum of Canada Bulletin 214. Ottawa.

1970   Golden Lake Algonquin field notes. (Manuscript in Gordon M. Day's papers.)

1971   The Eastern Boundary of Iroquoia: Abenaki Evidence. *Man in the Northeast* 1(March): 7–13.

1973   The Problem of the Openangos. *Studies in Linguistics* 23:31–37.

1975   *The* Mots loups *of Father Mathevet.* National Museums of Canada, Publications in Ethnology 8. Ottawa.

1976   An Iroquois Raid on Saint Francis in Abenaki Tradition. Paper read at the Conference on Iroquois Studies, Albany, N.Y.

1977a   Indian Place-Names as Ethnohistoric Data. In *Actes du huitième congrès des algon-quinistes,* edited by William Cowan, 26–31. Ottawa: Carleton University.

1977b   *The Abenaki Identity Project.* National Museum of Man, Canadian Ethnology Service, Canadian Studies Report No. 2. Ottawa.

1981   *The Identity of the Saint Francis Indians.* National Museum of Man, Canadian Ethnology Service, Mercury Series Paper 71. Ottawa.

De Forest, John W.
1851   *History of the Indians of Connecticut from the Earliest Known Period to 1850.* Hartford, Conn.: W. J. Hammersley.

Delabarre, Edmund B.
1935   Chief Big Thunder: A Problematic Figure in Rhode Island Annals. *Rhode Island Historical Society Collections* 28:116–128.

De Laet, Johannes. *See* Laet, Johannes de.

Deming, Mrs. Edwin Willard
1902   Abenaki Witchcraft Story. *Journal of American Folk-Lore* 15(56):62–63.

Densmore, Frances
1928   Uses of Plants by the Chippewa Indians. In *44th Annual Report of the Bureau of American Ethnology for the Years 1926–1927,* 275–397. Washington, D.C.

Denton, Daniel
1845   *A Brief Description of New York, Formerly Called New Netherlands, with the Places Thereunto Adjoining. Likewise a Brief Relation of the Customs of the Indians There* [1670]. New York: William Gowans.

De Vries, David P. *See* Vries, David P. de.

Dixon, Roland B.
1909   The Mythology of the Central and Eastern Algonkins. *Journal of American Folk-Lore* 22(83):1–9.

Donck, Adriaen van der
1841   A Description of the New Netherlands . . . [1656]. *New York Historical Society Collections,* 2d ser., 1(5):125–242.

Douglas-Lithgow, Robert Alexander
1909   *Dictionary of American-Indian Place and Proper Names in New England; with Many Interpretations, etc.* Salem, Mass.: The Salem Press.

Driver, Harold E., John M. Cooper, Paul Kirchoff, Dorothy Ranier Libby, William C. Massey, and Leslie Spier, eds.
1953   *Indian Tribes of North America.* Indiana University Publications in Anthropology and Linguistics 9. Bloomington, Ind.

Druillettes, Father Gabriel
1857   Journal of an Embassy from Canada to the United Colonies of New England, in 1650. John G. Shea, ed. *New York Historical Society Collections,* 2d ser., 3(1):303–328.

Du Creux, François
1951–   *History of Canada, or New France* [1664]. James B. K. Conacher, ed., Percy J. Robinson,
1952   trans. 2 vols. Toronto: The Champlain Society.

Dundes, Alan
1967   North American Indian Folklore Studies. *Journal de la Société des américanistes de Paris* 56(1):53–79.

Dwight, Theodore
1821   *Travels in New England and New York.* New Haven, Conn.: Published by the author.

Eastman, Charles Alexander
1902   *Indian Boyhood.* New York: McClure, Phillips.

Eccles, William J.
1972   *France in America.* New York: Harper and Row.

Eckstorm, Fannie H.
1924   Katahdin Legends. *Appalachia* 16(1):39–52.

1932   *The Handicrafts of the Modern Indians of Maine.* Lafayette National Park Museum Bulletin 3. Bar Harbor, Maine.

1941   *Indian Place-names of the Penobscot Valley and the Maine Coast.* Maine Bulletin 44(4), University of Maine Studies, 2d ser., Vol. 55, Orono.

1945   *Old John Neptune and Other Maine Indian Shamans.* Portland, Maine: Southworth-Anthoensen Press.

Edwards, Jonathan
1788   *Observations on the Language of the Muhhekaneew Indians.* New Haven, Conn.: Printed by J. Meigs.

Eliot, John
1832   The Indian Grammar Begun [1666]. *Collections of the Massachusetts Historical Society,* 2d ser., 9:223–312.

Ellis, C. Douglas
1962   *Spoken Cree: West Coast of James Bay.* Toronto: Church of England in Canada.

Emmons, Ebenezer
1841   Fifth Annual Report of Ebenezer Emmons, M.D., of the Survey of the Second Geological District. *Geological Survey of the State of New York, 1840–41.* Albany.

Fabvre, Bonaventure, comp.
1970   *Racines montagnaises* [1695]. Gerard E. McNulty, ed. Centre d'études nordiques, travaux divers 29. Quebec.

Faillon, Étienne-Michel
n.d.   Recherches pour servir à l'histoire du Canada. Vols. 2–10. (Manuscript in the Archives of Notre-Dame de Montréal.)

Fenton, William N.
1940   Problems Arising from the Historic Northeastern Position of the Iroquois. In *Essays in Historical Anthropology of North America,* 159–252. Smithsonian Miscellaneous Collections 100. Washington, D.C.

1942   Contacts Between Iroquois Herbalism and Colonial Medicine. In *Annual Report of the Smithsonian Institution for 1941,* 503–526. Washington, D.C.: Smithsonian Institution.

Ferland, Jean Baptiste Antoine
1882   *Cours d'histoire du Canada.* 2 vols. Quebec: Hardy.

Fewkes, J. Walter
1890   A Contribution to Passamaquoddy Folk-Lore. *Journal of American Folk-Lore* 3(11): 257–280.

Fisher, Margaret W.
1946   The Mythology of the Northern and Northeastern Algonkians in Reference to Algonkian Mythology as a Whole. In *Man in Northeastern North America,* edited by Frederick Johnson, 226–262. Papers of the Robert S. Peabody Foundation for Archaeology 3. Andover, Mass.

Fitch, John
1870   The Schaghticoke Tribe of Indians. *History Magazine* (New York), 2d ser., 7:385–390.

Flannery, Regina
1939   *An Analysis of Coastal Algonquian Culture.* Catholic University of America, Anthropological Series 7. Washington, D.C.

Franquet, Louis
1889   Voyages et mémoires sur le Canada [1752]. In *Annuaire de l'Institut canadien de Québec* 13:29–240. Quebec: A. Coté.

Gahan, Lawrence K.
1941a   Letter to the editor. *Massachusetts Archaeological Society Bulletin* 2:12.

1941b   The Nipmucks and Their Territory. *Massachusetts Archaeological Society Bulletin* 2:2–6.

Galinée, René Bréhant de
1903   *Exploration of the Great Lakes, 1669–1670, Dollier de Casson and Bréhant de Galinée.*

Galinée's Narrative and Map. James H. Coyne, ed. Papers and Records of the Ontario Historical Society 4, pt. 1. Toronto.

Gallatin, Albert
1836　*A Synopsis of the Indian Tribes Within the United States East of the Rocky Mountains, and in the British and Russian Possessions in North America*. Archaeologia Americana: Transactions and Collections of the American Antiquarian Society 2. Cambridge, Mass.: American Antiquarian Society.

Gatschet, Albert S.
1886　The Beothuk Indians. *Proceedings of the American Philosophical Society* 23(123):411–432.

Geary, James A.
1941　Proto-Algonquian *çk: Further Examples. *Language* 17(4):304–310.

Gerard, William R.
n.d.　Letter. (Bureau of American Ethnology Archives, File 2842-C, Box 6, Washington, D.C.)

Gibbs, George
1867　*Instructions for Research Relative to the Ethnology and Philology of America*. Smithsonian Miscellaneous Collections 7(11). Washington, D.C.: Smithsonian Institution.

Gill, Charles I.
1886　*Notes sur de vieux manuscrits abénakis*. Montreal: Eusèbe Senéca et Fils.

Gladwin, Harold Sterling
1947　*Men Out of Asia*. New York: McGraw-Hill.

Goddard, Ives
1965　The Eastern Algonquian Intrusive Nasal. *International Journal of American Linguistics* 31(3):206–220.
1967　The Algonquian Independent Indicative. In *Contributions to Anthropology: Linguistics I (Algonquian)*, edited by A. D. DeBlois. Anthropological Series 78, National Museum of Canada Bulletin 214. Ottawa.
1970　The Eastern Algonquian Dialect Chain and Split-off from Central Algonquian. Paper read at the Algonquian-Iroquoian Conference, Peterborough, Ontario.

Gookin, Daniel
1792　Historical Collections of the Indians in New England [1674]. *Collections of the Massachusetts Historical Society*, 1st ser., 1:141–227.

Gordon, Charles H. M.
1925　How Chekapash Snared the Sun. *The Beaver* 4(12):436–437.

Gordon, Robert Benson
1940　*The Primeval Forest Types of Southwestern New York*. New York State Museum Bulletin 321. Albany, N.Y.

Gorges, Ferdinando
1837　A Briefe Narration of the Original Undertakings of the Advancement of Plantations into the Parts of America. *Collections of the Massachusetts Historical Society*, 3d ser., 6:45–93.

Gray, Asa
1884　Characteristics of the North American Flora. *American Journal of Science*, 3d ser., 28:323–340.

Haas, Mary R.
1958a　Algonkian-Ritwan: The End of a Controversy. *International Journal of American Linguistics* 24(3):159–173.
1958b　Notes on Some PCA Stems in /k-/. *International Journal of American Linguistics* 24(4):241–245.
1967　Roger Williams's Sound Shift: A Study in Algonkian. In *To Honor Roman Jakobson*, 1:816–832. The Hague: Mouton.

Hagar, Stansbury
1895　Micmac Customs and Traditions. *American Anthropologist* 8(1):31–42.

1896   Micmac Magic and Medicine. *Journal of American Folk-Lore* 9(34):170–171.
1900   The Celestial Bear. *Journal of American Folk-Lore* 13(49):92–103.

Hale, Horatio E.
1883   *The Iroquois Book of Rites.* Brinton's Library of Aboriginal American Literature 2. Philadelphia: D. G. Brinton.
1888   Indian Etymologies. *American Anthropologist* 1(3):290–291.

Hallowell, A. Irving
1918–   [Ethnographic and Linguistic Notes from Numerous Visits to the St. Francis Abenaki.]
1932   (Manuscripts in Gordon M. Day's papers.)
1928   Recent Changes in the Kinship Terminology of the St. Francis Abenaki. In *Proceedings of the 22nd International Congress of Americanists* 2:97–145. Rome: International Congress of Americanists.
1932   The Hunting Grounds and Hunting Customs of the St. Francis Abenaki. (Manuscript in Gordon M. Day's papers.)
1949   The Size of Algonkian Hunting Territories: A Function of Ecological Adjustments. *American Anthropologist* 51(1):35–45.
n.d.   (Manuscript on Abenaki vocabulary of acculturation in Gordon M. Day's papers.)

Hanzeli, Victor E.
1961   Early Descriptions by French Missionaries of Algonquian and Iroquoian Languages: A Study of Seventeenth- and Eighteenth-century Practice in Linguistics. Ph.D. dissertation, Indiana University.

Harrington, E.
1869   Notes taken at St. Francis, Quebec. (Manuscript in Gordon M. Day's papers.)

Harrington, John P.
1955   The Original Strachey Vocabulary of the Virginia Indian Language. *Bureau of American Ethnology Bulletin* 157:189–202. Washington, D.C.

Harrington, Mark R.
1901   An Abenaki 'Witch Story'. *Journal of American Folk-Lore* 14(54):160.

Harrisse, Henry
1892   *The Discovery of North America: A Critical, Documentary, and Historical Investigation, With an Essay on the Early Cartography of the New World, Including Descriptions of Two Hundred Fifty Maps or Globes Existing or Lost, Constructed Before the Year 1536; . . .* London: H. Stevens.

Hatt, Gudmund
1916   Moccasins and Their Relation to Arctic Footwear. *Memoirs of the American Anthropological Association* 3(3):149–250. Lancaster, Penn.

Haugen, Einar
1942   *Voyages to Vinland.* New York: Alfred A. Knopf.

Hawes, Austin Foster
1923   New England Forests in Retrospect. *Journal of Forestry* 21(3):209–234.

Hedrick, Ulysses Prentiss
1933   *A History of Agriculture in the State of New York.* Albany: Printed for the New York State Agriculture Society.

Hemans, Fanny
1826   *The League of the Alps, and Other Poems.* Boston: Hilliard, Grey, Little and Wilkins.

Hemenway, Abby Maria, ed.
1868–   *The Vermont Historical Gazetteer: A Magazine, Embracing a History of Each Town, Civil,*
1891   *Ecclesiastical, Biographical and Military.* 5 vols. Burlington, Vt.

Hewitt, John Napoleon Brinton
1888   Etymology of the Word Iroquois. *American Anthropologist* 1(2):188–189.
1891   Iroquoian Etymologies. *Science* 17(April):217–220.
1910   Nanabozho. In *Handbook of American Indians North of Mexico,* edited by Frederick W. Hodge, 2:19–23. Bureau of American Ethnology Bulletin 30. Washington, D.C.

1928   Iroquoian Cosmology. In *43rd Annual Report of the Bureau of American Ethnology for the Years 1925–1926,* 449–819. Washington, D.C.

Higgeson, F.
    1859   New-England's Plantation [1630]. With appended letter from Mr. Graves. *Collections of the Massachusetts Historical Society,* 1st ser., 1:117–124.

Hockett, Charles F.
    1948   Implications of Bloomfield's Algonquian Studies. *Language* 24(1):117–131.
    1957   Central Algonquian Vocabulary: Stems in /k/. *International Journal of American Linguistics* 23(4):247–268.

Hodge, Frederick W., ed.
    1907–   *Handbook of American Indians North of Mexico.* 2 vols. Bureau of American Ethnology
    1910   Bulletin 30. Washington, D.C.

Hoffman, Bernard G.
    1955a   The Souriquois, Etechemin and Kwĕdĕch: A Lost Chapter in American Ethnography. *Ethnohistory* 2(1):65–87.
    1955b   The Historical Ethnography of the Micmac of the Sixteenth and Seventeenth Centuries. Ph.D. dissertation, University of California, Berkeley.

Holden, Austin Wells
    1874   *A History of the Town of Queensbury in the State of New York.* Albany: J. Munsell.

Holland, C. G.
    1962   Review of *The Origin and Meaning of the Indian Place Names of Maryland,* by Hamill Kenny. *International Journal of American Linguistics* 28(4):296–299.
    1963   Review of *Iroquois Place-names in the Champlain Valley,* by Floyd G. Lounsbury. *International Journal of American Linguistics* 29(2):178–180.

Holmes, Abiel
    1804   Memoir of the Moheagan Indians. *Collections of the Massachusetts Historical Society,* 1st ser., 9:75–102.

Hopkins, Samuel
    1753   *Historical Memoirs Relating to the Housatunnuk Indians.* Boston: S. Kneeland.

Hough, Walter
    1926   *Fire as an Agent in Human Culture.* United States National Museum Bulletin 139. Washington, D.C.

Howley, James P.
    1915   *The Beothucks, or Red Indians: The Aboriginal Inhabitants of Newfoundland.* Cambridge: Cambridge University Press.

Hubbard, William
    1815   A General History of New England from the Discovery to MDCIXXX. *Collections of the Massachusetts Historical Society,* 2d ser., 5 and 6.
    1865   *The History of the Indian Wars in New England from the First Settlement to the Termination of the War with King Philip, in 1677.* Samuel G. Drake, ed. 2 vols. Roxbury, Mass.: W. E. Woodward.

Huden, John C.
    1957   *Indian Place Names in Vermont.* Burlington, Vt.: Published by the author.
    1962   Indian Place Names of New England. *Contributions from the Museum of the American Indian, Heye Foundation* 18.

Hunt, George T.
    1940   *The Wars of the Iroquois: A Study in Intertribal Trade Relations.* Madison: University of Wisconsin Press.

Hurd, Duane Hamilton
    1886   *History of Chesire and Sullivan Counties, New Hampshire.* Philadelphia: J. W. Lewis.

Hutchinson, Thomas
    1936   *The History of the Colony and Province of Massachusetts-Bay* [1760]. 3 vols. Cambridge, Mass.: Harvard University Press.

Irving, Washington
  1934   *Journal* [1803]. S. T. Williams, ed. New York: Oxford University Press.
Ives, Edward D., ed.
  1964   Malecite and Passamaquoddy Tales. *Northeast Folklore* 6:5–81.
Jack, Edward
  1895   Maliseet Legends. *Journal of American Folk-Lore* 8(30):193–208.
Jackson, Kenneth
  1955   The Pictish Language. In *The Problem of the Picts,* edited by F. T. Wainwright, 129–165. Edinburgh: Nelson.
[Jacobs, Sarah] "S. J. of N."
  1856   Indian Names of the Months. *New England Historical and Genealogical Register* 10:166.
Jeffrey, James
  1720   *A Draught of the Part of the Province of New Hampshire that Lies to the Eastward of the River yt Comes Out of Winnipissiokee Pond. . . .* (Manuscript in Crown Collection, British Museum, London.)
Jogues, Isaac
  1909   Novum Belgium [1646]. In *Narratives of New Netherland, 1609–1664,* edited by J. Franklin Jameson, 255–264. Original Narratives of Early American History. New York: Charles Scribner's Sons.
Johnson, Edward
  1910   *Johnson's Wonder Working Providence, 1628–1651* [1654]. J. Franklin Jameson, ed. Original Narratives of Early American History. New York: Charles Scribner's Sons.
Johnson, Frederick
  1940   The Indians of New Hampshire. *Appalachia* 6(89):3–15.
Johnson, James
  1757   Deposition of James Johnson. (Manuscript in the Massachusetts Archives 38A:329, Boston.)
  1902   *Scout Journals, 1757; Narrative of James Johnson, A Captive During the French and Indian Wars.* G. Waldo Brown, ed. Manchester, N.H.
Johnson, Sir William
  1921–   *The Papers of Sir William Johnson.* James Sullivan et al., eds. 15 vols. Albany: University
  1965   of the State of New York.
Josselyn, J.
  1672   *New-Englands Rarities Discovered.* London.
  1833   An Account of Two Voyages to New-England [1673]. *Collections of the Massachusetts Historical Society* 3d ser., 3:211–354.
Judd, Sylvester
  1857   The Fur Trade on the Connecticut River in the Seventeenth Century. *New England Historical and Genealogical Register* 11:217–219.
Juet, Robert
  1909   From "The Third Voyage of Master Henry Hudson," 1610. In *Narratives of New Netherland, 1609–1664,* edited by J. Franklin Jameson, 11–28. Original Narratives of Early American History. New York: Charles Scribner's Sons.
Jury, Elsie McLeod
  1967   Tessouat (Besouat). In *Dictionary of Canadian Biography,* edited by David M. Hayne, 1:638–639. Toronto: University of Toronto Press.
Kalm, Pehr
  1937   *Peter Kalm's Travels to North America* [1770]. Adolph B. Benson, trans. and ed. New York: Wilson-Erickson.
  1966   *The America of 1750: Peter Kalm's Travels in North America; The English Version of 1770.* Adolph B. Benson, ed. 2 vols. New York: Dover Publications.

Kellogg, Joseph
  1744   Joseph Kellogg to William Shirley. (Manuscript in the Massachusetts Archive 31:518–520, Boston.)
Kendall, Edward A.
  1809   *Travels Through the Northern Parts of the United States, in the Years 1807 and 1808.* 3 vols. New York: I. Riley.
Kidder, Frederic
  1859   The Abenaki Indians; Their Treaties of 1713 and 1717, and a Vocabulary; With Historical Introduction. *Collections of the Maine Historical Society* 6:229–263.
Kimball, James
  1878   The Exploration of the Merrimack River, 1638 by Order of the General Court of Massachusetts, with a Plan of the Same. *Historical Collections of the Essex Institute* 14(3):153–171.
Kroeber, Alfred L.
  1927   *Arrow Release Distributions.* University of California Publications in American Archaeology and Ethnology 23(4):283–296. Berkeley: University of California Press.
  1939   *Cultural and Natural Areas of Native North America.* University of California Publications in American Archaeology and Ethnology 38. Berkeley: University of California Press.
La Chasse, Pierre de
  1929   Une relation de la mort du P. Sébastien Râle, 1724. *Nova Francia* 4:342–350.
Laet, Joannes de
  1909   From the "New World," 1625, 1630, 1633, 1640. In *Narratives of New Netherland, 1609–1664,* edited by J. Franklin Jameson, 29–60. Original Narratives of Early American History. New York: Charles Scribner's Sons.
Lafitau, Joseph-François
  1724   *Moeurs des sauvages amériquains, comparées aux moeurs des premiers temps.* 2 vols. in 1. Paris: Saugrain l'aîné.
  1845   *Moeurs, coutumes et religions des sauvages américains* [1724]. Extracted from original by A. S. Paris: Périsse.
Lafontaine, Urgel
  n.d.   Histoire du Lac. 23 vols. (Manuscript in the Archives of Notre-Dame de Montréal.)
Lahontan, Louis Armand de Lom d'Arce de
  1905   *New Voyages to North America by the Baron de Lahontan* [1703]. Reuben G. Thwaites, ed. 2 vols. Chicago: A. C. McClurg.
Lapham, William B.
  1891   *History of Bethel . . . Maine, 1768–1890.* Augusta, Maine: The Maine Farmer.
Laurent, Joseph
  1884   *New Familiar Abenakis and English Dialogues, the First Ever Published on the Grammatical System, by Jos. Laurent, Abenakis Chief.* Quebec: Léger Brousseau.
Laurie, Thomas
  1885   *The Ely Volume.* Boston: American Board of Commissioners for Foreign Missions.
Laverdière, Charles-Honore, ed.
  1870   *Œuvres de Champlain, Publiées sous le patronage de l'Université Laval.* 2 vols. Quebec: G.-E. Desbarats.
Leach, Douglas E.
  1958   *Flintlock and Tomahawk: New England in King Philip's War.* New York: W. W. Norton.
Leland, Charles G.
  1884   *The Algonquin Legends of New England, or, Myths and Folk-Lore of the Micmac, Passamaquoddy, and Penobscot Tribes.* Boston: Houghton Mifflin.
Leland, Charles G., and John D. Prince, trans.
  1902   *Kuloskap the Master, and Other Algonkin Poems.* New York: Funk and Wagnalls.

Lemoine, Georges
 1901 *Dictionnaire français-montagnais avec un vocabulaire montagnais-anglais, une courte liste de noms géographiques et une grammaire montagnaise.* Boston: W. B. Cabot and P. Cabot.
Lescarbot, Marc
 1907– *The History of New France* [1618]. W. L. Grant, trans. 3 vols. Toronto: The Champlain
 1914 Society.
LeSueur, Jacques-François
 1720 Dictionnaire abnaquis-françois. (Manuscript in the Musée de la Société historique d'Odanak.)
 1952 History of the Calumet and of the Dance [1864]. *Contributions from the Museum of the American Indian, Heye Foundation* 12(5):1–22.
Lillard, Richard Gordon
 1947 *The Great Forest.* New York: Alfred A. Knopf.
Lincoln, Charles H., ed.
 1913 *Narratives of the Indian Wars, 1675–1699.* New York: Charles Scribner's Sons.
Lindeström, Peter
 1925 *Geographia Americae with an Account of the Delaware Indians Based on Surveys and Notes Made in 1654–1656* [1691]. Amandus Johnson, ed. Philadelphia: The Swedish Colonial Society.
Little, Elbert E., Jr.
 1953 *Check List of Native and Naturalized Trees of the United States (Including Alaska).* Agricultural Handbook 41. Washington, D.C.
Little, Silas, and E. B. Moore
 1945 Controlled Burning in South Jersey's Oak-Pine Stands. *Journal of Forestry* 43(7):499–505.
 1949 The Ecological Role of Prescribed Burns in the Pine-Oak Forests of Southern New Jersey. *Ecology* 30(2):223–233.
Livingston, Robert
 1956 *The Livingston Indian Records, 1666–1723.* Lawrence H. Leder, ed. Gettysburg: Pennsylvania Historical Association.
Longfellow, Henry Wadsworth
 1847 *Evangeline: A Tale of Acadie.* Boston: Houghton Mifflin.
Loskiel, George H.
 1794 *History of the Mission of the United Brethren Among Indians in North America.* Christian Ignatius La Trobe, trans. 3 pts. London: Printed for the Brethren's Society for the Furtherance of the Gospel.
Lounsbury, Floyd G.
 1960 *Iroquois Place-names in the Champlain Valley.* (Reprinted from the Report of the New York-Vermont Interstate Commission on the Lake Champlain Basin, 1960, Legislative Document 9:23–66.) Albany: University of the State of New York, State Education Department.
Lowie, Robert H.
 1909 The Hero-Trickster Discussion. *Journal of American Folk-Lore* 22(86):431–433.
Lutz, Harold John
 1934 *Ecological Relations in the Pitch Pine Plains of Southern New Jersey.* Yale University School of Forestry Bulletin 38. New Haven, Conn.
McAleer, George
 1906 *A Study of the Etymology of the Indian Place Name Missisquoi.* Worcester, Mass.: The Blanchard Press.
McClure, David
 1899 *Diary of David McClure.* New York: Published by the author.
MacLeod, William Christie
 1936 Conservation Among Primitive Hunting Peoples. *Scientific Monthly* 43(December): 562–566.

Magon de Terlaye, François-Auguste
n.d.   Dictionnaire onontagué-français. (Manuscript in the Archives of Notre-Dame de Mon-tréal.)
Margry, Pierre, ed.
1876–   *Découvertes et établissements des Français dans l'ouest et dans le sud de l'Amérique sep-*
1886   *tentrionale, 1614–1754. Mémoires et documents originaux.* 6 vols. Paris: D. Jouaust.
Marie-Victorin, Frère
1935   *Flore laurentienne.* Montreal: Imprimerie de LaSalle.
Marsh, George Perkins
1885   *The Earth as Modified by Human Action.* New York: Charles Scribner.
Marsh, T. N.
1962   An Unpublished Hakluyt Manuscript? *The New England Quarterly* 35(2):247–252.
Massachusetts (Colony)
1853–   *Records of the Governor and the Company of Massachusetts Bay in New England.* Nathan-
1854   iel B. Shurtleff, ed. 5 vols. in 6. Boston: William White.
Massé, Enemond
1870   L'Oraison dominicale, tradvite en langage des montagnars de Canada, par le R. P. Massé de la compagnie de Jésus. In *Œvres de Samuel de Champlain* 5(2):16–20. Quebec: G.-E. Desbarats.
Mason, Otis T.
1894   North American Bows, Arrows, and Quivers. In *Annual Report of the Board of Regents of the Smithsonian Institution . . . to July 1893:* 631–679. Washington, D.C.
Masta, Henry Lorne
1932   *Abenaki Indian Legends, Grammar and Place Names.* Victoriaville, Quebec: La Voix des Bois-Francs.
Mather, Cotton
1702   *Magnalia Christi Americana: Or, the Ecclesiastical History of New-England; from its First Planting, in the Year 1620, unto the Year of Our Lord 1698.* London: T. Parkhurst.
Mather, Increase
1864   *Early History of New England, Being a Relation of Hostile Passages Between the Indians and European Voyagers and First Settlers . . . With Introduction and Notes by Samuel G. Drake.* Albany: J. Munsell.
Maurault, Joseph P. A.
1866   *Histoire des Abenakis depuis 1605 jusqu'à nos jours.* Sorel, Quebec: L'Atelier Typographi-que de la "Gazette de Sorel."
Maurault, Olivier
1930   Oka: Les visissitudes d'une mission sauvage. *Revue trimestrielle canadienne* 16(June):121–149.
Maxwell, H.
1910   The Use and Abuse of Forests by the Virginia Indians. *William and Mary Quarterly* 19(2):73–103.
Mechling, William H.
1914   *Malecite Tales.* Anthropological Series 4, Memoirs of the Canadian Geological Survey 49. Ottawa.
1958–   The Malecite Indians, with Notes on the Micmacs, 1916. *Anthropologica* 7:1–160,
1959   8:161–274. Ottawa.
Michaux, François-André
1805   *Travels to the Westward of the Allegany Mountains . . . Undertaken in the Year 1802* [1803]. B. Lambert, trans. London: Printed by W. Flint for J. Mauman.
Michelson, Truman
1912   Preliminary Report on the Linguistic Classification of Algonquian Tribes. In *28th Annual Report of the Bureau of American Ethnology for the Years 1906–1907,* 221–290. Washington, D.C.

1914   Notes on the Stockbridge Language. (Manuscript No. 2734 in National Archeological Archives, Smithsonian Institution, Washington, D.C.)

1925   Micmac Tales. *Journal of American Folk-Lore* 38(147):33–54.

1935   Phonetic Shifts in Algonquian Languages. *International Journal of American Linguistics* 8(3/4):131–171.

1939   *Linguistic Classification of Cree and Montagnais-Naskapi Dialects.* Bureau of American Ethnology Bulletin 123:69–95. Washington, D.C.

Montgomery, George H.

1950   *Missisquoi Bay (Philipsburg, Quebec).* Granby, Quebec: Granby Printing and Publishing.

Mooney, James

1928   *The Aboriginal Population of America North of Mexico.* John R. Swanton, ed. Smithsonian Miscellaneous Collections 80(7). Washington, D.C.

Mooney, James, and Cyrus Thomas

1907   Algonquian Family. In *Handbook of American Indians North of Mexico,* edited by Frederick W. Hodge, 1:38–43. Bureau of American Ethnology Bulletin 30. Washington, D.C.

1910   Pennacook. In *Handbook of American Indians North of Mexico,* edited by Frederick W. Hodge, 2:225–226. Bureau of American Ethnology Bulletin 30. Washington, D.C.

Moore, Ellwood Birdsall

1939   *Forest Management in New Jersey.* Trenton: New Jersey Department of Conservation and Development.

Moorehead, Warren K.

1931   *The Merrimack Archaeological Survey: A Preliminary Paper.* Salem, Mass.: Peabody Museum.

Morgan, Lewis H.

1877   *Ancient Society or Researches in the Lines of Human Progress from Savagery through Barbarism to Civilization.* New York: Henry Holt.

1901   *League of the Ho-dé-no-sau-nee or Iroquois* [1851]. Herbert M. Lloyd, ed. 2 vols. New York: Dodd, Mead.

Morris, Richard B.

1953   *Encyclopedia of American History.* 2 vols. New York: Harper and Brothers.

Morse, Edward S.

1922   *Additional Notes on Arrow Release.* Salem, Mass.: Peabody Museum.

Morton, Thomas

1838   New English Canaan or New Canaan [1632]. In *Tracts and Other Papers Relating Principally to the Origin, Settlement, and Progress of the Colonies in North America to the Year 1776,* edited by Peter Force, 2:1–125. Washington, D.C.: Peter Force.

Munns, Edward Norfolk

1938   *The Distribution of Important Forest Trees of the United States.* United States Department of Agriculture Miscellaneous Publications 287, Map No. 62.

National Cyclopedia of American Biography

1897 [Article on Chandler E. Potter]. Clifton, N.J.: J. T. White.

Newberry Library

1941   *A Bibliographical Check List of North and Middle American Linguistics in the Edward E. Ayer Collection.* Chicago: Newberry Library.

New Hampshire Historical Society

1795– *Philip's Grant Papers.* (One Volume of Manuscripts and Facsimiles in New Hampshire
1810   Historical Library, Concord.)

1832   Penacook Papers, 1659–1668. *Collections of the New Hampshire Historical Society* 3:212–224.

Newman, Stanley

1952   American Indian Linguistics in the Southwest. *American Anthropologist* 54(4):626–634.

"New Yorker"

1835   *A Winter in the West.* New York: Harper and Brown.

Nicolar, Joseph

1893   *The Life and Traditions of the Red Man.* Bangor, Maine: Glass.

Niles, Grace Greylock

1912   *The Hoosac Valley, Its Legends and Its History.* New York: G. P. Putnam.

Notre-Dame de Montréal, Archives

n.d.   Mission du Lac des Deux-Montagnes. (Manuscript.)

Nouvel, Father Henry

1957   Journal of the Last Winter Mission of Father Henry Nouvel, Superior of the Missions of the Ottawa. Margaret Guta, trans. *Michigan Archaeologist* 3(1):13–20.

Nudénans, Jean Baptiste

1760   Index alphabeticus correspondens Sylva vocum Uanbanakaearum. Et Radicum Uaba-nakkaearum Sylva Ex Variis Veterum et Recentiorumque Manuscriptis Codicibus Collecta Ordini Alphabetico Reddita à J. B. Nudénans Anno 1760. (Manuscript in Nicolet Seminary Archives, Nicolet, Quebec.)

NYCD = O'Callaghan, Edmund B., ed. 1853–1887

O'Callaghan, Edmund B., ed.

1849–   *Documentary History of the State of New York.* 4 vols. Albany: Weed, Parsons.
1851

1853–   *Documents Relative to the Colonial History of the State of New York; Procured in Holland,*
1887   *England and France,* by John R. Brodhead. 15 vols. Albany: Weed, Parsons.

Pacifique, Père Henri

1939   *Leçons grammaticales théoriques et pratiques de la langue micmaque.* Ste-Anne de Restigouche, Quebec: Bureau du "Messager Micmac."

Palfrey, John G.

1882   *History of New England During the Stuart Dynasty.* Boston: Little, Brown.

Palmer, Peter

n.d.   *History of Lake Champlain.* New York.

Paquin, Jacques

[1833] Mémoires sur l'Eglise du Canada. (Manuscript in the Public Archives of Canada, Quebec.)

Parker, Arthur C.

1910   Iroquois Uses of Maize and Other Food Plants. *New York State Museum Bulletin* 144(482):5–113.

1922   The Archaeological History of New York. 2 pts. *New York State Museum Bulletin* 235–236.

Parkman, Francis

1867   *The Jesuits in North America in the Seventeenth Century.* Boston: Little, Brown.

1909a *France and England in North America.* Boston: Little, Brown.

1909b *The Conspiracy of Pontiac.* Boston: Little, Brown.

1910   *A Half-Century of Conflict.* 2 vols. Boston: Little, Brown.

1947   *The Journals of Francis Parkman.* Mason Wade, ed. New York: Harper.

Parsons, Elsie Clews

1925   Micmac Folklore. *Journal of American Folk-Lore* 38(147):55–133.

Peattie, Donald Culross

1950   *A Natural History of Trees.* Boston: Houghton Mifflin.

Peckham, Howard

1964   *The Colonial Wars 1689–1762.* Chicago: University of Chicago Press.

Percy, George

1906   Observations Gathered Out of a Discourse of the Plantation of the Southerne Colonie in Virginia by the English, 1606. In *Hakluytus Posthumus or Purchas, His Pilgrimes,* 18:403–419. Glasgow: J. MacLehose and Sons.

Perrot, Nicholas
  1911   Memoir on the Manners, Customs, and Religion of the Savages of North America. In *The Indian Tribes of the Upper Mississippi Valley and Region of the Great Lakes,* edited by Emma H. Blair, 1:23–272. Cleveland: Arthur H. Clark.
Perry, John B.
  1882   A Lease of Land by the Missisquoi Indians, 1785. In *The Vermont Historical Gazetteer,* edited by Abby M. Hemenway, 4:962–972. Burlington, Vt.
Philower, Charles A.
  n.d.   *Indian Lore of New Jersey.* Trenton: New Jersey Council.
Pickering, John
  1837   [Untitled]. *Missionary Herald* 32:268.
[Pierson, Abraham] "Abraham Peirson"
  1658   *Some Helps for the Indians: A Catechism.* Cambridge, Mass.: Samuel Green.
Pilling, James C.
  1888   *Bibliography of the Iroquoian Languages.* Bureau of American Ethnology Bulletin 6. Washington, D.C.
  1891   *Bibliography of the Algonquian Languages.* Bureau of American Ethnology Bulletin 13. Washington, D.C.
Pinchot, Gifford
  1899   A Study of Forest Fires and Wood Production in Southern New Jersey. *Annual Report of the State Geologist for 1898.* Trenton.
Potter, Chandler E.
  1853   Language and Religion of the Pennacooks. *The Farmer's Monthly Visitor* 13(11):321–324.
  1856a   *The History of Manchester, Formerly Derryfield, in New Hampshire.* Manchester, N.H.: Published by the author.
  1856b   Appendix to the Language of the Abenaquies, or Eastern Indians. *Collections of the Maine Historical Society* 4:185–195.
Powers, Grant
  1841   *Historical Sketches of the Discovery, Settlement, and Progress of Events in the Coos Country and Vicinity, Principally Included Between the Years 1754 and 1785.* Haverhill, N.H.: J. F. C. Hayes.
Pownall, Thomas
  1949   *A Topographical Description of the Dominions of the United States of America* [1776]. L. Mulkearn, ed. Pittsburgh: University of Pittsburgh Press.
Price, Ebenezer
  1823   *A Chronological Register of Boscawen, in the County of Merrimack, and State of New Hampshire, from the First Settlement of the Town to 1820.* Concord, N.H.: Printed by J. B. Moore.
Prince, J. Dyneley
  1899   Some Passamaquoddy Witchcraft Tales. *Proceedings of the American Philosophical Society* 38:181–189.
  1900   Some Forgotten Indian Place-names in the Adirondacks. *Journal of American Folk-Lore* 13(49):123–128.
  1901   Notes on Passamaquoddy Literature. *Annals of the New York Academy of Sciences* 13(4):381–386.
  1902   The Differentiation Between the Penobscot and the Canadian Abenaki Dialects. *American Anthropologist* 4(1):17–32.
  1905   A Tale in the Hudson River Indian Language. *American Anthropologist* 7:74–84.
  1906   A Micmac Manuscript. In *Proceedings of the 15th International Congress of Americanists,* 1:87–124. Quebec.
  1910   The Penobscot Language of Maine. *American Anthropologist* 12(2):183–208.
  1921   *Passamaquoddy Texts.* Publications of the American Ethnological Society 10. New York.

Prince, J. Dyneley, and Frank G. Speck

1903   Dying American Speech-Echoes from Connecticut. *Proceedings of the American Philosophical Society* 42(174):346–352.

1904   Glossary of the Mohegan-Pequot Language. *American Anthropologist* 6:18–45.

Pring, Martin

1906   A Voyage Set Out from the Citie of Bristoll with a Small Ship and a Barke for the Discouerie of the North Part of Virginia . . . 1603. In *Early English and French Voyages, Chiefly from Hakluyt, 1534–1608,* edited by Henry S. Burrage, 345–352. Original Narratives of Early American History. New York: Charles Scribner's Sons.

Provost, Honorius

1948   Les Abénakis sur la Chaudière. *Publications de la Société historique de la Chaudière* 1:13–27.

Public Archives of Canada

n.d.a   Quebec Series, Manuscript Group 8. Quebec and Local Records.

n.d.b   Archives des Colonies C11A. Correspondence générale.

n.d.c   Archives de la Marine B2. Ordres et dépêches du roi.

Purchas, Samuel

1905–   *Hakluytus Posthumus or Purchas, His Pilgrimes* [1625]. 4 vols. Glasgow: J. MacLehose
1907   and Sons.

Pynchon, John

1650   Account book. (Manuscript in the Sylvester Judd Papers, Forbes Library, Northampton, Mass.)

1856   Indian Names of the Months. *New England Historical Genealogical Register* 10(2):166.

Quinney, J.

1795   *Assembly Catechism.* Stockbridge, Mass.: Printed . . . by Loring Andrews.

Radin, Paul

1956   *The Trickster: A Study in American Indian Mythology.* New York: Philosophical Library.

Radisson, Pierre E.

1967   *The Explorations of Pierre Esprit Radisson.* Arthur T. Adams, ed. Minneapolis, Minn.: Ross and Haines.

[Râle, Sébastien] "Sebastian Rasles"

1833   A Dictionary of the Abnaki Language in North America, [1691–1722], edited by John Pickering. *Memoirs of the American Academy of Arts and Sciences* 1:375–565. Cambridge, Mass.

Rand, Silas Tertius

1888   *Dictionary of the Language of the Micmac Indians Who Reside in Nova Scotia, New Brunswick, Prince Edward Island, Cape Breton and Newfoundland.* Halifax, N.S.: Nova Scotia Printing Company.

1894   *Legends of the Micmacs.* Wellesley Philological Publications. New York: Longmans, Green.

1902   *Micmac Dictionary; Prepared from Phonographic Wordlists by S. T. Rand. Transcribed and Alphabetically Arranged by Jeremiah S. Clark.* Charlottetown, P.E.I.: Patriot Publishing Company.

Rasieres, Isaack de

1909   Letter of Isaack de Rasieres to Samuel Blommaert, 1628. In *Narratives of New Netherland,* edited by J. Franklin Jameson, 97–115. Original Narratives of Early American History. New York: Charles Scribner's Sons.

Rasles, Sebastian = Râle, Sébastien

Raup, Hugh Miller

1937   Recent Changes of Climate and Vegetation in Southern New England and Adjacent New York. *Journal of the Arnold Arboretum* 18(2):79–117.

Ray, L.

1843   The Aboriginal Inhabitants of Connecticut. *The New Englander* 1(July):312–326.

Renaud d'Avène des Méloizes, Nicolas
   1929   Journal militaire tenu par Nicolas Renaud d'Avène des Méloizes. In *Rapport de l'Archi-
           viste de la province de Québec, 1928–1929,* 1–86. Quebec: Imprimeur du Roi.
Robinson, Rowland E.
   1860–   Papers of Rowland E. Robinson at Rokeby, Ferrisburgh, Vt.
   1881
   1867   A Sketch of the Early History of Ferrisburgh. In *The Vermont Historical Gazetteer,* edited
           by Abby Marie Hemenway, 1:31–34. Burlington, Vt.
   1892a   *Vermont: A Study of Independence.* Boston: Houghton Mifflin.
   1892b   What's In a Name? *Atlantic Monthly* 70(October):576. [Unsigned article.]
   1896   Old-Time Sugar Making. *Atlantic Monthly* 77(4):466–471.
   1901   *Sam Lovel's Boy.* Boston: Houghton Mifflin.
   1905   *Out of Bondage and Other Stories.* Boston: Houghton Mifflin.
   1934a   *Sam Lovel's Camps and In the Green Wood.* Rutland, Vt.: The Tuttle Company.
   1934b   *Uncle Lisha's Outing, The Buttles Gals, and Along Three Rivers.* Rutland, Vt.: The Tuttle
           Company.
Rogers, Robert
   1765   *Journals of Major Robert Rogers.* London: J. Millan.
Róheim, Géza
   1952   Culture Hero and Trickster in North American Mythology. In *Indian Tribes of Aborigi-
           nal America,* edited by Sol Tax, 190–194. Selected Papers of the 29th International
           Congress of Americanists. Chicago.
Rosier, James
   1906   True Relation of Waymouth's Voyage [1605]. In *Early English and French Voyages,
           Chiefly Out of Hakluyt, 1534–1608,* edited by Henry S. Burrage, 353–394. Original
           Narratives of Early American History. New York: Charles Scribner's Sons.
Rousseau, Jacques
   1947   Ethnobotanique abénakise. *Archives de folklore* 2:145–182.
Rousseau, Pierre
   n.d.   Histoire générale de toutes les missions. (Manuscript in the Archives of Notre-Dame de
           Montréal.)
Roy, Pierre-Georges
   1927–   *Inventaire des concessions en fief et seigneurie, fois et hommages et aveux et dénombrements, con-
   1929   servées aux Archives de la province de Québec.* 6 vols. Beauceville, Quebec: L' "Éclaireur."
   1946   *Hommes et choses du Fort Saint-Frédéric.* Montreal: Éditions du Dix.
Ruttenber, Edward M.
   1872   *History of the Indian Tribes of Hudson's River; Their Origin, Manners and Customs, Tribal
           and Sub-tribal Organizations, Wars, Treaties, etc., etc.* Albany, N.Y.: J. Munsell.
Sabine, Lorenzo
   1857   Indian Tribes of New England. *Christian Examiner and Religious Miscellany* 62:27–54,
           210–237.
Sagard-Théodat, Gabriel
   1866   *Histoire du Canada et voyages que les Frères Mineurs recollects y ont faicts pour la conversion
           des infidèles depuis l'an 1615. Avec un dictionnaire de la langue huronne* [1636]. 4 vols.
           Paris: Librarie Tross.
   1939   *Father Gabriel Sagard: The Long Journey to the Country of the Hurons* [1632]. George M.
           Wrong, ed. Toronto: The Champlain Society.
Saltonstall, Nathaniel
   1913   A Continuation of the State of New England, 1676. In *Narratives of Indian Wars, 1675–
           1699,* edited by Charles H. Lincoln, 51–74. New York: Charles Scribner's Sons.
Sargent, Charles S.
   1885   *The Native Woods of Essex County, Massachusetts.* Reports of the Tenth Census of the U.S.
           Salem, Mass.

Schoolcraft, Henry R.

    1851– *Historical and Statistical Information Respecting the History, Condition, and Prospects of*
    1857   *the Indian Tribes of the United States.* 6 vols. Philadelphia: Lippincott, Grambo.

Seton, Ernest Thompson

    1912   *The Book of Woodcraft and Indian Lore.* London: Constable.

Sévigny, Pierre-André

    1976   Les Abénaquis: habitat et migrations (17e et 18e siècles). *Cahiers d'histoire des Jésuites* 3.

Shaler, Nathaniel Southgate

    1884   *Kentucky: A Pioneer Commonwealth.* New York: Houghton Mifflin.

Shantz, H. L., and R. Zon

    1924   Natural Vegetation. In *Atlas of American Agriculture,* Pt. 1, Sec. E., 1–24. Washington,
            D.C.: United States Department of Agriculture.

Shea, John D. Gilmary

    1881   *History of the Catholic Missions Among the Indian Tribes of the United States, 1592–1854.*
            2d ed. New York: P. J. Kennedy.

Sheldon, George

    1895   *A History of Deerfield, Massachusetts.* Greenfield, Mass.: E. A. Hall.

Sherwin, Reider T.

    1940   *The Viking and the Red Man.* New York: Funk and Wagnalls.

Siebert, Frank T.

    1941a Review of *Penobscot Man,* by Frank G. Speck. *American Anthropologist* 43(2):278–280.

    1941b Certain Proto-Algonquian Consonant Clusters. *Language* 17(4):298–303.

    1980   The Penobscot Dictionary Project: Preferences and Problems of Format, Presentation,
            and Entry. In *Papers of the Eleventh Algonquian Conference,* edited by William Cowan,
            113–127. Ottawa: Carleton University.

S. J. of N. *See* [Jacobs, Sarah].

Smith, John

    1836   A Description of New England [1616]. In *Tracts and Other Papers Relating Principally to*
            the Origin, Settlement, and Progress of the Colonies in North America to the Year 1776,
            edited by Peter Force, 2. Washington, D.C.: Peter Force.

    1906   Description of Virginia [1625]. In *Hakluytus Posthumus or Purchas, His Pilgrimes,* edited
            by J. MacLehose, 18:403–459. Glasgow: J. MacLehose and Sons.

Smith, Robinson V.

    1952   New Hampshire Remembers the Indians. *Historical New Hampshire,* October:32.

Smith, Samuel

    1765   *The History of the Colony of Nova-Caesaria or New-Jersey.* . . . Burlington, N.J.: James
            Parker.

Speare, Eva A.

    n.d.   *Indians of New Hampshire.* New York: Littleton.

Speck, Frank G.

    1903   A Pequot-Mohegan Witchcraft Tale. *Journal of American Folk-Lore* 16(61):104–106.

    1904   A Modern Mohegan-Pequot Text. *American Anthropologist* 6(4):469–476.

    1911   A Visit to the Penobscot Indians. *The Museum Journal* (University of Pennsylvania)
            2(1):21–27.

    1914   The Family Hunting Band as the Basis of Algonkian Social Organization. *American
            Anthropologist* 17(2):289–305.

    1915a The Eastern Algonkian Wabanaki Confederacy. *American Anthropologist* 17(3):492–
            508.

    1915b Some Micmac Tales from Cape Breton Island. *Journal of American Folk-Lore* 28(107):
            59–69.

    1917   Malecite Tales. *Journal of American Folk-Lore* 30(108):479–485.

    1918   Penobscot Transformer Tales. *International Journal of American Linguistics* 1(3):187–
            244.

1922   *Beothuk and Micmac.* Museum of the American Indian, Heye Foundation. Indian Notes and Monographs, Misc. Ser. 22. New York.

1926   Culture Problems in Northeastern North America. *Proceedings of the American Philosophical Society* 65:272–311.

1927   *The Nanticoke and Conoy Indians with a Review of Linguistic Material from Manuscript and Living Sources: An Historical Study.* Papers of the Historical Society of Delaware 1. Wilmington, Del.

1928a   Native Tribes and Dialects of Connecticut: A Mohegan-Pequot Diary. In *43rd Annual Report of the Bureau of American Ethnology for the Years 1925–1926,* 199–287. Washington, D.C.

1928b   Wawenock Myth Texts from Maine. In *43rd Annual Report of the Bureau of American Ethnology for the Years 1925–1926,* 165–197. Washington, D.C.

1931   Montagnais-Naskapi Bands and Early Eskimo Distribution in the Labrador Peninsula. *American Anthropologist* 33(4):557–600.

1935a   *Naskapi.* Norman: University of Oklahoma Press.

1935b   Penobscot Tales and Religious Beliefs. *Journal of American Folk-Lore* 48(107):1–107.

1935c   "Abenaki Clans"—Never! *American Anthropologist* 37(3):528–530.

1938   Aboriginal Conservators. *Bird Lore* 40(July–August):258–261.

1940   *Penobscot Man: The Life History of a Forest Tribe in Maine.* Philadelphia: University of Pennsylvania Press.

1945   Abenaki Text. *International Journal of American Linguistics* 11(1):45–46.

1947   Review of *Old John Neptune and Other Maine Indian Shamans,* by Fannie H. Eckstorm, *American Anthropologist* 49(2):284–287.

n.d.   Speck Papers. American Philosophical Society Library, III D 13. Philadelphia.

Speck, Frank G., and Ralph W. Dexter
1951   Utilization of Animals and Plants by the Micmac Indians of New Brunswick. *Journal of the Washington Academy of Sciences* 41(8):250–259.

Speck, Frank G., and Loren C. Eiseley
1939   Significance of Hunting Territory Systems of the Algonkian in Social Theory. *American Anthropologist* 41(2):269–280.

Speck, Frank G., and Jesse Moses
1945   *The Celestial Bear Comes Down to Earth.* Reading Public Museum and Art Gallery, Scientific Publications 7. Reading, Penn.

Speck, Frank G., and Gladys Tantaquidgeon
n.d.   Analytic and Comparative Notes on the Transformer Myths. (Manuscript cited by Fisher.)

Stamp, Harley
1915   A Malecite Tale: Adventures of Bukschinskwesk. *Journal of American Folk-Lore* 28(109):243–248.

Stewart, Omer C.
1951   Burning and Natural Vegetation in the United States. *Geographical Review* 41(2):317–320.

Stiles, Ezra
1809a   Indians on Connecticut River. *Collections of the Massachusetts Historical Society* 10:104–105.

1809b   Memoir of the Pequots. Collected from the Itineraries and Other Manuscripts of Pres. Stiles. *Collections of the Massachusetts Historical Society* 10:101–154.

Stirling, Matthew W.
1937   America's First Settlers, the Indians. *National Geographic Magazine* 72(5):535–596.

Stone, W.
1911   The Plants of Southern New Jersey. In *Annual Report, New Jersey State Museum for 1910.* Trenton.

Strachey, William
    1849   *The Historie of Travaile into Virginia Brittania* [1612]. Hakluyt Society Edition. R. H.
            Major, ed. London.
Sullivan, James
    1795   *The History of the District of Maine.* Boston: I. Thomas and E. T. Andrews.
    1804   The History of the Penobscot Indians. *Collections of the Massachusetts Historical Society,*
            1st ser., 9:207–232.
Sulte, Benjamin
    1886   *Histoire de Saint-François-du-Lac.* Montreal: Imprimerie de "L'Étendard."
    1918   *Mélanges historiques 1.* Montreal: G. Ducharme.
    1929   *Mélanges historiques 15.* Montreal: G. Ducharme.
Sutcliff, Robert
    1812   *Travels in Some Parts of North America, in the Years 1804, 1805, and 1806.* Philadelphia:
            B. and T. Kite.
Swadesh, Morris
    1955   Towards Greater Accuracy in Lexicostatistic Dating. *International Journal of American
            Linguistics* 21(2):121–137.
Swanton, John R.
    1928   Aboriginal Culture of the Southeast. In *42nd Annual Report of the Bureau of American
            Ethnology for the Years 1924–1925,* 673–726. Washington, D.C.
    1952   *The Indian Tribes of North America.* Bureau of American Ethnology Bulletin 145.
            Washington, D.C.
Teeter, Karl V.
    1973   Algonquian. In *Linguistics in North America,* edited by Thomas A. Sebeok, 1143–1163.
            Current Trends in Linguistics 10. The Hague: Mouton.
Temple, Josiah H., and George Sheldon
    1875   *History of the Town of Northfield, Massachusetts, for 150 Years, with an Account of the Prior
            Occupation of the Territory by the Squakheags, and with Family Genealogies.* Albany, N.Y.:
            J. Munsell.
Terrell, John Upton
    1968   *La Salle: The Life and Times of an Explorer.* Toronto: Clarke.
Thevet, André
    1575   *La cosmographie universelle.* Paris: Chez Guillaume Chandière.
Thomas, Peter A.
    1971   Middle Connecticut Valley Indian House Types: A Cautionary Note. *Man in the North-
            east* 1(March):48–50.
Thompson, Zadock
    1842   *History of Vermont, Natural, Civil, and Statistical in Three Parts with a Map of the State
            and 200 Engravings.* Burlington, Vt.: Goodrich.
Thoreau, Henry David
    1950   *The Maine Woods* [1864]. New York: Norton.
Thwaites, Reuben G., ed.
    1896–   *The Jesuit Relations and Allied Documents.* 73 vols. Cleveland: Burrows Brothers.
    1901
Trager, George L., and Felicia E. Harben
    1958   *North American Indian Languages: Classification and Maps.* Studies in Linguistics Occa-
            sional Papers 5. Buffalo, N.Y.
True, N. T.
    1864   Names and Locations of Tribes on the Androscoggin. *Historical Magazine,* 1st ser.,
            8:150–151.
    1868   Collation of Geographical Names in the Algonkin Language. *Historical Collections of the
            Essex Institute* 8(3):144–149.

Trumbull, Benjamin
  1818   *A Complete History of Connecticut, Civil and Ecclesiastical, from the Emigration of the First
          Planters, from England, in the Year 1630, to the Year 1764, and to the Close of the Indian
          Wars.* 2 vols. New Haven, Conn.: Malthy, Goldsmith.
Trumbull, James Hammond
  1870   The Composition of Indian Geographical Names, Illustrated from the Algonquian
          Languages. *Collections of the Connecticut Historical Society* 2:1–50.
  1872   Notes on Forty Versions of the Lord's Prayer in the Algonkin Languages. In *Transactions
          of the American Philological Association for 1872,* 113–218. Philadelphia.
  1903   *Natick Dictionary.* Bureau of American Ethnology Bulletin 25. Washington, D.C.
Tufts, Henry
  1807   *A Narrative of the Life, Adventures, Travels and Sufferings of Henry Tufts, Now Residing at
          Lemington in the District of Maine. In Substance, as Compiled from his Own Mouth.*
          Dover, N.H.: Samuel Bragg, Jr.
U.S. Geological Survey
  n.d.   Cohoes, New York, and Greenfield and Mount Toby, Massachusetts, quadrangle maps.
Van der Donck, Adriaen. *See* Donck, Adriaen van der.
Van de Water, Frederick Franklyn
  1941   *The Reluctant Republic: Vermont 1724–1791.* New York: John Day.
Vassal, Henri
  [1811– Papiers Vassal. (Papers of Several Agents of the St. Francis Abenakis in the Archives of
  1889]   the Séminaire de Nicolet, Nicolet, Quebec.)
  1885   Letter. In *Canada. Department of Indian Affairs, Annual Report for 1884,* Pt. 1, 25–31.
          Ottawa.
Vaudreuil de Cavagnal, Pierre de Rigaud
  1938   Rigaud de Vaudreuil au ministre, 2 septembre 1759. *Bulletin des recherches historiques*
          44:377.
Verarzanus, John
  1850   The Relation of John Verarzanus . . . [1524]. In *Divers Voyages Touching the Discovery
          of America and the Islands Adjacent,* edited by John Winter Jones, 55–90. London:
          Hakluyt Society.
Vermont
  1939   *State Papers of Vermont. Petitions for Grants of Land 1778–1811.* Vol. 5. Montpelier, Vt.
Vetromile, Eugene
  1866   *The Abenakis and their History, or Historical Notes on the Aborigines of Acadia.* New York:
          J. B. Kirker.
Viereck, Philip
  1967   *The New Land.* New York: John Day.
Vimont, Barthélemy
  1898   Relation de ce qui s'est passé en la Nouvvel France, en l'année 1642 et 1643. In *The
          Jesuit Relations and Allied Documents,* edited by Reuben G. Thwaites, 23:259–319;
          24:20–312; 25:18–289. Cleveland: The Burrows Brothers.
Vinay, Jean-Paul
  1953   Classification de la famille linguistique algonquin-ritwan. *Anthropologica* 1:103–118.
Voegelin, Charles F.
  1939   The Lenape and Munsee Dialects of Delaware, an Algonquian Language. *Proceedings of
          the Indiana Academy of Sciences* 49:34–37.
  1941a   Proto-Algonquian Consonant Clusters in Delaware. *Language* 17(2):143–147.
  1941b   North American Indian Languages Still Spoken and Their Genetic Relationships. In
          Language, Culture, and Personality, edited by Leslie Spier et al., 15–40. Menasha, Wisc.:
          American Anthropological Association.
  1945   Delaware Texts. *International Journal of American Linguistics* 11(2):105–119.
  1946   Delaware, an Eastern Algonquian Language. In *Linguistic Structures of Native America,*

edited by Harry Hoijer, 130–157. Viking Fund Publications in Anthropology 6. New York.

Voegelin, Charles F., and Erminie W. Voegelin

1944 *Map of North American Indian Languages.* American Ethnological Society Publication 20. New York.

1946 Linguistic Considerations of Northeastern North America. In *Man in Northeastern North America,* edited by Frederick Johnson, 178–194. Papers of the Robert S. Peabody Foundation for Archaeology 3. Andover, Mass.

Vries, David P. de

1909 From the "Korte Historiael ende Journaels Aenteyckeninge," 1633–1643 [1655]. In *Narratives of New Netherland, 1609–1664,* edited by J. Franklin Jameson, 181–234. Original Narratives of Early American History. New York: Charles Scribner's Sons.

Walcott, Robert R.

1936 Husbandry in Colonial New England. *New England Quarterly* 9:218–252.

Wallis, Wilson D., and Ruth S. Wallis

1955 *The Micmac Indians of Eastern Canada.* Minneapolis: University of Minnesota Press.

1957 *The Malecite Indians of New Brunswick.* National Museum of Canada Bulletin 148, Anthropological Series 40. Ottawa.

Wassenaer, Nicolaes van

1909 From the "Historisch Verhael," 1624–1630. In *Narratives of New Netherland, 1609–1664,* edited by J. Franklin Jameson, 61–96. Original Narratives of Early American History. New York: Charles Scribner's Sons.

Watson, Winslow C.

1852 *A General View of the Agricultural Survey of the County of Essex, Taken Under the Appointment of the New York State Agricultural Society.* New York Assembly Transaction 112. Albany, N.Y.

1863 *Pioneer History of the Champlain Valley; Being an Account of the Settlement of the Town of Willsborough by William Gilliland, Together With His Journal and Other Papers.* Albany, N.Y.: J. Munsell.

1869 *The Military and Civil History of the County of Essex, New York.* Albany, N.Y.: J. Munsell.

Waugh, Frederick W.

1916 *Iroquois Foods and Food Preparation.* Memoirs of the Canadian Geological Survey 86, Anthropological Series 12. Ottawa.

Wendall, Jacob

1866 An Estimate of the Inhabitants, English and Indian, in the North American Colonies. *New England Historical and Genealogical Register* 20(1):7–9.

Westveld, Marinus, et al.

1956 Natural Forest Vegetation Zones of New England. *Journal of Forestry* 54(5):332–338.

Wheelock, Eleazar

1775 *A Continuation of the Narrative of the Indian Charity-School, Begun in Lebanon, Connecticut; Now Incorporated with Dartmouth-College, in Hanover, in the Province of New Hampshire.* Hartford, Conn.: E. Watson.

White, John

1906 The Fifth Voyage of M. John White, 1590. In *Early English and French Voyages, Chiefly Out of Hakluyt, 1534–1608,* edited by Henry S. Burrage, 301–323. Original Narratives of Early American History. New York: Charles Scribner's Sons.

1846 The Planters Plea, Or the Grovnds of Plantations examined, and vsuall Objections answered [1630]. In *Tracts and Other Papers Relating Principally to the Origin, Settlement, and Progress of the Colonies in North America to the Year 1776,* edited by Peter Force, 2(3). Washington, D.C.: Peter Force.

Whitfield, Henry

1651 *The Light Appearing More and More Towards the Perfect Day.* London: Printed by T. R. and E. M. for John Bartlett.

Williams, Roger
  1643 *A Key Into the Language of America.* London: Gregory Dexter.
  1827 A Key Into the Language of America [1643]. *Collections of the Rhode Island Historical Society* 1:17–163.
  1866 A Key Into the Language of America [1643]. J. Hammond Trumbull, ed. *Publications of the Narragansett Club* 1(2):1–219.
  1936 *A Key Into the Language of America* [1643]. 5th ed. Providence: The Rhode Island and Providence Plantations Tercentenary Commission.
Williams, Samuel
  1794 *The Natural and Civil History of Vermont.* Walpole, N.H.: Printed by Isaiah Thomas and David Carlisle.
Williamson, William D.
  1832 *The History of the State of Maine: From its First Discovery A. D. 1602, to the Separation, A. D. 1820 Inclusive.* 2 vols. Hallowell, Maine: Glazier, Masters.
Willoughby, Charles C.
  1935 *Antiquities of the New England Indians with Notes on the Ancient Cultures of the Adjacent Territory.* Cambridge, Mass.: Harvard University, Peabody Museum of American Archaeology and Ethnology.
Winsor, Justin, ed.
  1884– *Narrative and Critical History of America.* 8 vols. Boston: Houghton Mifflin.
  1889
Winthrop, John
  1853 *The History of New England from 1630 to 1649. From His Original Manuscripts. With Notes by James Savage.* 2 vols. Boston: Little, Brown.
Wislizenus, Frederick Adolphus
  1912 *A Journal to the Rocky Mountains in the Year 1839.* Translated from the German. St. Louis, Mo.: Missouri Historical Society.
Wissler, Clark
  1926 *The Relation of Nature to Man in Aboriginal America.* New York: Oxford University Press.
Wood, William
  1634 *Nevv Englands Prospect: A True, Lively and Experimentall Description of That Part of America, Commonly Called Nevv England: Discovering the State of That Countrie, Both as it Stands to Our New-Come English Planters; and to the Old Native Inhabitants.* London: Tho. Cotes.
  1865 *Wood's New Englands Prospect* [1634]. Publications of the Prince Society 1. Boston.
Wraxall, Peter
  1915 *An Abridgement of the Indian Affairs Contained in Four Folio Volumes, Transacted in the Colony of New York, from the Year 1678 to the Year 1751.* C. H. McIlwain, ed. Harvard Historical Studies 21. Cambridge, Mass.
Wright, Harry A., ed.
  1905 *Indian Deeds of Hampden County: Being Copies of All Land Transfers from the Indians Recorded in the County of Hampden, Massachusetts, and Some Deeds from Other Sources.* Springfield, Mass.
  1949 *The Story of Western Massachusetts.* 4 vols. New York: Lewis Historical Publishing Company.
Wzôkhilain, Peter P.
  1830a *Wawasi Lagidamwoganek Mdala Chowagidamwoganal Tabtagil, Onkawodokodozwal wji Pôbatami Kidwôgan.* Boston: Crocker and Brewster.
  1830b *Wôbanaki Kimzowi Awighigan.* Boston: Crocker and Brewster.
  1832 *Kagakimzouiasis ueji Uo'banakiak adali kimo'gik aliuitzo'ki Za Plasua.* Quebec: Fréchette.
  1845 *St. Mark.* Montreal.

Young, William, ed.
    1969   *The Connecticut Valley Indian, An Introduction to Their Archaeology and History.* Springfield Science Museum Bulletin 1(1). Springfield, Mass.
Zeisberger, David
    1887   [Vocabularies.] From the Collection of Manuscripts Presented by Judge Lane to Harvard University, Nos. 1 and 2. Cambridge, Mass.: E. N. Hartford.

Bibliography of Gordon M. Day

Items preceded by an asterisk appear in the present volume in whole or in part.

1940   Topsoil Changes in Coniferous Plantations. *Journal of Forestry* 38(8):646–648.

1949   A Five-Year Professional Degree. *Journal of Forestry* 47(3):222–223.

1950a   Influence of Earthworms on Soil Microorganisms. *Soil Science* 69(3):175–184.

1950b   Observations on the Growth of Red Spruce in Sand Culture. *Journal of Forestry* 48(10): 689–692. [With W. Rei Robbins.]

1950c   *Classification of Humus on Poorly Drained Soils.* Report of Committee on Humus Classification on Poorly Drained Soils, Northeastern Forest Soils Conference. [With Svend O. Heiberg.]

1950d   The Stability of Latin Names. *Journal of Forestry* 48(9):446.

1951   Red Spruce Leaves. *Torrey Botanical Club Bulletin* 78(1):88.

*1953   The Indian as an Ecological Factor in the Northeastern Forest. *Ecology* 34(2):329–346.

1958   Review of *Indian Place Names in Vermont*, by John C. Huden. *New England Quarterly* 31(2):273–274.

1959a   Review of *Les Abénaquis sur la Chaudière*, by Honorius Provost. *Ethnohistory* 6(1):87–89.

1959b   Note on St. Francis Nomenclature. *International Journal of American Linguistics* 25(4): 272–273.

*1959c   Dartmouth and Saint Francis. *Dartmouth Alumni Magazine* 52(2):28–30. [Reprinted in *From Hanover* 9(3):12–14 (1959).]

*1961a   A Bibliography of the Saint Francis Dialect. *International Journal of American Linguistics* 27(1):80–85.

*1961b   The Name Contoocook. *International Journal of American Linguistics* 27(2):168–171. [Reprinted in *New Hampshire Archeological Society Miscellaneous Papers* 1(February):18–22 (1962).]

*1962a   English-Indian Contacts in New England. *Ethnohistory* 9(1):24–40.

1962b   The Dartmouth Algonkian Collection. *Dartmouth College Library Bulletin* 5, n.s.(2):41–43.

1962c   Rogers' Raid in Indian Tradition. *Historical New Hampshire* 17(June):3–17.

*1963a   The Tree Nomenclature of the Saint Francis Indians. *Contributions to Anthropology, 1960,* Part 2:37–48. National Museum of Canada Bulletin 190. Ottawa. [Reprinted in *New Hampshire Archaeologist* 13(September):6–10 (1964).]

1963b   Review of *Indian Place Names of New England*, by John C. Huden. *American Anthropologist* 65(5):1198–1199.

*1964   A St. Francis Abenaki Vocabulary. *International Journal of American Linguistics* 30(4): 371–392.

1965a   Review of *Indian Place-Names in New Jersey*, by Donald Wm. Becker. *American Anthropologist* 67(2):592–593.

1965b   The Indian Occupation of Vermont. *Vermont History* 33(3):365–374.

*1965c   The Identity of the Sokokis. *Ethnohistory* 12(3):237–249.

*1967a   An Agawam Fragment. *International Journal of American Linguistics* 33(3):244–247.

*1967b   Historical Notes on New England Languages. In *Contributions to Anthropology: Linguistics I (Algonquian)*, edited by A. D. DeBlois, 107–112. Anthropological Series 78, National Museum of Canada Bulletin 214. Ottawa.

1967c   Iroquois: An Etymology. In *Iroquois Culture, History, and Prehistory. Proceedings of the 1965 Conference on Iroquois Research*, edited by Elisabeth Tooker, 57–61. Albany, N.Y.: New York State Museum and Science Service. [Preprint of 1968a.]

*1968a   Iroquois: An Etymology. *Ethnohistory* 15(4):389–402.

1968b   Review of *Puritans at Bay: The War Against King Philip and the Squaw Sachems in New England, 1675–1676*, by Charles T. Burke. *Ethnohistory* 15(4):439–440.

1969a   The Indian Languages of the Upper Connecticut Valley. In *The Connecticut Valley Indians: An Introduction to Their Archaeology and History*, edited by William R. Young, 74–79. Springfield Museum of Science Publications n.s. 1(1). Springfield, Mass.

1969b   Narragansetts, Nipmucs, Wampanoags. In *Dictionary of Canadian Biography*, edited by David M. Hayne, 2:xxxv. Toronto: University of Toronto Press.

1969c   Saint-François Abenakis. In *Dictionary of Canadian Biography*, edited by David M. Hayne, 2:xxxviii–xxxix. Toronto: University of Toronto Press.

1969d   Schaghticokes. In *Dictionary of Canadian Biography*, edited by David M. Hayne, 2:xxxix. Toronto: University of Toronto Press.

1969e   Sokokis. In *Dictionary of Canadian Biography*, edited by David M. Hayne, 2:xxxix–xl. Toronto: University of Toronto Press.

1969f   Atecouando. In *Dictionary of Canadian Biography*, edited by David M. Hayne, 2:25–26. Toronto: University of Toronto Press.

*1971a   The Eastern Boundary of Iroquoia: Abenaki Evidence. *Man in the Northeast* 1(March):7–13.

1971b   Review of *The Northern Colonial Frontier, 1607–1763*, by Douglas Edward Leach. *Ethnohistory* 18(1):64–65.

1971c   Review of *The New Land: Discovery, Exploration, and the Early Settlement of Northeastern United States, from Earliest Voyages to 1621, Told in the Words of the Explorers Themselves*, edited and compiled by Philip Viereck. *Ethnohistory* 18(2):162.

*1972a   The Name 'Algonquin'. *International Journal of American Linguistics* 38(4):226–228.

*1972b   Oral Tradition as Complement. *Ethnohistory* 19(2):99–108.

*1973a   The Problem of the Openangos. *Studies in Linguistics* 23:31–37.

*1973b   Missisquoi: A New Look at an Old Village. *Man in the Northeast* 6(fall):51–57.

1974a   Henry Tufts as a Source on the Eighteenth Century Abenakis. *Ethnohistory* 21(3):189–197.

1974b   The Saint-François Abenakis. In *Dictionary of Canadian Biography*, edited by G. W. Brown, David M. Hayne, and F. G. Halpenny, 3:xl. Toronto: University of Toronto Press. [Reprint of 1969c.]

1974c   Gray Lock. In *Dictionary of Canadian Biography*, edited by G. W. Brown, David M. Hayne, and F. G. Halpenny, 3:265–267. Toronto: University of Toronto Press.

1975a   Early Merrimack Toponymy. In *Papers of the Sixth Algonquian Conference*, edited by William Cowan, 372–389. National Museum of Man, Canadian Ethnology Service, Mercury Series Paper 23. Ottawa.

*1975b   The Penobscot War Bow. In *Contributions to Canadian Ethnology, 1975*, edited by David Brez Carlisle, 1–15. National Museum of Man, Canadian Ethnology Service, Mercury Series Paper 31. Ottawa.

*1975c   The *Mots loups* of Father Mathevet. National Museums of Canada, Museum of Man, Publications in Ethnology 8. Ottawa.

*1976   The Western Abenaki Transformer. *Journal of the Folklore Institute* 13(1):75–89.

*1977a   Indian Place-Names as Ethnohistoric Data. In *Actes du huitième congrès des algonquinistes*, edited by William Cowan, 26–31. Ottawa: Carleton University.

1977b *The Abenaki Identity Project.* National Museum of Man, Canadian Ethnology Service, Canadian Studies Report 2e. Ottawa. [Reprinted in *Arch Notes of the Ontario Archaeological Society* 78(3):30–31 (1978).]

1977c *Sur les traces des Abénaquis.* Musée nationale de l'Homme. Service canadienne d'ethnologie, Rapport sur les Études canadiennes 2f. Ottawa. [Translation of 1977b.]

1978a Ethnology in the Works of Rowland E. Robinson. In *Papers of the Ninth Algonquian Conference,* edited by William Cowan, 36–39. Ottawa: Carleton University.

*1978b Western Abenaki. In *Northeast,* edited by Bruce G. Trigger, Vol. 15 of *Handbook of North American Indians,* William C. Sturtevant, gen. ed., 148–159. Washington, D.C.: Smithsonian Institution.

1978c Nipissing. In *Northeast,* edited by Bruce G. Trigger, Vol. 15 of *Handbook of North American Indians,* William C. Sturtevant, gen. ed., 787–791. Washington, D.C.: Smithsonian Institution.

1978d Algonquin. In *Northeast,* edited by Bruce G. Trigger, Vol. 15 of *Handbook of North American Indians,* William C. Sturtevant, gen. ed., 792–797. Washington, D.C.: Smithsonian Institution. [With Bruce G. Trigger.]

*1979a Arosagunticook and Androscoggin. In *Papers of the Tenth Algonquian Conference,* edited by William Cowan, 10–15. Ottawa: Carleton University.

1979b *The Indians of the Ottawa Valley.* National Museum of Man, Oracle 30. Ottawa.

1979c *Les Amérindiens de la Vallée de l'Outaouais.* Musée nationale de l'Homme, Oracle 29. Ottawa. [Translation of 1979b.]

1980 Review of *Keepers of the Game: Indian-Animal Relationships and the Fur Trade,* by Calvin Martin. *Ethnohistory* 27(2):193–194.

*1981a *The Identity of the Saint Francis Indians.* National Museum of Man, Canadian Ethnology Service, Mercury Series Paper 71. Ottawa.

*1981b Abenaki Place-names in the Champlain Valley. *International Journal of American Linguistics* 47(2):143–171.

1982 Review of *The Original Vermonters: Native Inhabitants Past and Present,* by William A. Haviland and Marjory W. Power. *Vermont History* 50(spring):114–118.

1983 Le problème des identités tribales: Les Abénaquis de Saint-François (Odanak). *Recherches amérindiennes au Québec* 13(2):101–106.

1984 The Ouragie War: A Case History in Iroquois-New England Indian Relations. In *Extending the Rafters: Interdisciplinary Approaches to Iroquoian Studies,* edited by Michael K. Foster, Jack Campisi, and Marianne Mithun, 35–50. Albany: State University of New York Press.

1985a Anomalous Abenaki Affricates. *International Journal of American Linguistics* 51(4):387–388.

1985b *Identité des indiens de St-François.* Quebec: Ministère de l'education de Québec. [Translation of 1981a.]

1986 How We Came to Be: The Algonquian Conference in Perspective. In *Actes du dix-septième congrès des algonquinistes,* edited by William Cowan, 93–100. Ottawa: Carleton University. [With Charles A. Bishop.]

1987 Abenakis in the Lake Champlain Valley. In *Lake Champlain: Reflections on Our Past,* edited by Jennie G. Versteeg, 277–288. Burlington: Center for Research on Vermont, University of Vermont and the Vermont Historical Society.

1988 Review of *Spirit of the New England Tribes: Indian History and Folklore, 1620–1984,* by William S. Simmons. *Vermont History* 56(spring):133–135.

1990 *Alnôbaôdwa: A Western Abenaki Language Guide.* Swanton, Vt.: Franklin Northwest Supervisory Union, Title V Indian Education Office. [With Jeanne A. Brink.]

1991 Review of *Western Abenakis of Vermont,* by Colin G. Calloway. *Vermont History* 59(spring):111–113.

1994a Southern Algonquian Middlemen: Algonquin, Nipissing, and Ottawa, 1550–1780. In

Aboriginal Ontario: Historical Perspectives on the First Nations, edited by Edward S. Rogers and Donald B. Smith, 65–77. Toronto: Dundern Press. [With Bruce G. Trigger.]

1994b   *Western Abenaki Dictionary.* Vol. 1, *Abenaki-English.* Canadian Museum of Civilization, Canadian Ethnology Service, Mercury Series Paper 128. Ottawa.

1994c   Oral Literature of the Northeastern Algonquians and the Northern Iroquoians. In *Dictionary of Native American Literature,* edited by Andrew Wiget, 73–82. New York: Garland Publishing. [With Michael K. Foster.]

1995   *Western Abenaki Dictionary.* Vol. 2, *English-Abenaki.* Canadian Museum of Civilization, Canadian Ethnology Service, Mercury Series Paper 129. Ottawa.

[In preparation] That's the Way It Was: The World of the Western Abenaki. [Abenaki Texts.]

Index of Names, Languages, Places, and Indian Groups